The Deputy

The Deputy

"Who are we, anyway, that we dare criticize the
highest spiritual authority of the century?
Nothing, in fact, but the simple defenders
of the spirit, who yet have a right to expect
the most from those whose mission it is to
represent the spirit."

Albert Camus

About the Author

Rolf Hochhuth was born on April 1, 1931, in Eschwege/
Werra, now West Germany, of Protestant parents. He
became an editor for a large German publishing company
in 1955 and, in the fall of 1959, went to Rome to begin
his first draft for *The Deputy*. A shortened stage version
of the play was first produced by Erwin Piscator in Berlin
on February 23, 1963, and the complete text of the book
was published on the same day. The play won the "Young
Generation Playwright Award" of the 1963 "Berliner
Kunstpreis," and shared the Gerhard Hauptmann Prize of
1962. His first published work, *The Deputy* is the result
of many years of reading and research.

Rolf Hochhuth
The Deputy

Translated by
Richard and Clara Winston
Preface by
Dr. Albert Schweitzer

Grove Press, Inc. New York

To the memory of

Father Maximilian Kolbe
Inmate No. 16670 in Auschwitz

Provost Bernhard Lichtenberg
of St. Hedwig's Cathedral, Berlin

Originally published in Reinbek bei Hamburg,
Germany, by Rowohlt Verlag GmbH, as
Der Stellvertreter, © 1963.

ISBN: 0-394-17125-G
Grove Press ISBN: 0-8021-4068-8

First Paperback Edition 1964
Twelfth Printing 1977

Manufactured in the United States of America
Distributed by Random House, Inc., New York

GROVE PRESS, INC., 196 WEST HOUSTON STREET,
NEW YORK, N.Y. 10014

Preface

Rowohlt Verlag
Reinbek near Hamburg

Dear Sir:

My cordial thanks for sending me "The Deputy." I was an active witness of the failure which took place in those days, and I believe we must concern ourselves with this great problem of the events of history. We owe this to ourselves, for our failure made us all participants in the guilt of those days. After all, the failure was not that of the Catholic Church alone, but that of the Protestant Church as well. The Catholic Church bears the greater guilt for it was an organized, supra-national power in a position to do something, whereas the Protestant Church was an unorganized, impotent, national power. But it, too, became guilty, by simply accepting the terrible, inhuman fact of the persecution of the Jews. For in those days we lived in a time of inhumanity of culture, the beginning of which dates back to Friedrich Nietzsche at the end of the preceding century. The failure was that of philosophy, of free thought, as well.

To stay on the right path of history we must become aware of the great aberration of those days, and must remain aware of it, so as not to stumble further into inhumanity. It is significant, therefore, that the drama "The Deputy" has made its appearance. Not only is it an indictment of an historical personality who placed upon himself the great responsibility of silence; it is also a solemn warning to our culture admonishing us to forego our acceptance of inhumanity which leaves us unconcerned. Thought in our time is still founded in inhumanity. The history of the world in our time is still inhuman through and through, and we accept this as a matter of course.

Hochhuth's drama is not only an indictment of history, but also a clarion call to our time which stagnates in naïve inhumanity.

With best wishes,

Sincerely yours,

ALBERT SCHWEITZER
Lambarene, Gabon

June 30, 1963

Cardinal Tardini

"Pius XII could say with the Apostle: I am nailed to the Cross with Christ. . . . He took upon himself the suffering . . . that strengthened his heroic determination to sacrifice himself for his brothers and sons. . . . This exceedingly noble . . . spirit tasted the cup of suffering drop by drop."

"O Jesus . . . Thou hast deigned to elevate Thy faithful servant Pius XII to the highest dignity of Thy Deputy and hast conferred upon him the grace fearlessly to defend the Faith, courageously to stand forth for justice and peace . . . so that one day we may see him . . . partaking of the honor of Thy altars. Amen." (*Prayer from* PIO XII, IL GRANDE)

Sören Kierkegaard

"Take an emetic. . . . You who read this, you know well the Christian meaning of a witness to the truth: a man who has been scourged, beaten, dragged from one prison to another . . . until at last he is crucified or beheaded or burned.

"We must therefore object if the deceased bishop is to be presented as a witness to the truth, and canonized. He is dead now—God be praised that his glorification could be postponed while he lived. He was indeed buried with fanfares, and a monument will be placed over his grave. But let that be enough; he must on no account be allowed to go down in history as a witness to the truth."

François Mauriac

"We have not yet had the consolation of hearing Simon Peter's successor clearly and sharply condemning, without a trace of tactful circumlocution, the crucifixion of these countless 'brothers of Christ.' One day during the occupation I asked Cardinal Suhard, who worked so hard for them behind the scenes, to 'order us to pray for the Jews'; and he threw up his arms. No doubt the occupying forces were able to bring irresistible pressure to bear, no doubt the silence of the Pope and his cardinals was a most terrible duty; the important thing being to avoid even worse misfortunes. Nevertheless a crime of such magnitude falls in no small measure to the responsibility of those witnesses who never cried out against it—whatever the reason for their silence."

Contents

Characters

Pope Pius XII
Baron Rutta, Reichs Armaments Cartel

Father Riccardo Fontana, S.J.

Kurt Gerstein, Obersturmführer SS

The Doctor

The Cardinal
Professor Hirt, Reichs University Strassburg

The Apostolic Nuncio in Berlin
Luccani Sr., a converted Jew
Servant, in Count Fontana's house

Count Fontana, counsel to the Holy See
Colonel Serge, of the Army High Command

The Abbot, Father General of a religious order
Müller-Saale, of the Krupp works in Essen

Eichmann, Obersturmbannführer
A Manufacturer, prisoner of the Gestapo

Dr. Lothar Luccani
Dr. Fritsche, Sturmbannführer

Salzer, Chief of the German Police in Rome
Officer of the Swiss Guard

Julia Luccani

A Boy of nine ⎱
A Girl of five ⎰ Julia Luccani's children

Regierungsrat Dr. Pryzilla
A Roman Cobbler
A Photographer
Brother Irenäus

Helga

Carlotta

Signora Simonetta

A Father in the Papal Legation
Witzel, SS sergeant
A Jewish Kapo

Jacobson
First Militiaman, the "correct" Italian
The Officer of the Day in Auschwitz

Lieutenant von Rutta, German Air Force
Katitzky, SS soldier
A Scribe

Dr. Littke, lieutenant in the Medical Corps
Second Militiaman, the Italian "crook"
Swiss Guard in the Papal Palace

The Speakers of the monologues

The characters grouped together here by twos, threes or fours should be played by the same actor—for recent history has taught us that in the age of universal military conscription it is not necessarily to anyone's credit or blame, or even a question of character, which uniform one wears or whether one stands on the side of the victims or the executioners.

Aside from the Pope, the Nuncio, Gerstein, Hirt, and Eichmann, all characters and names are fictitious.

Act One: The Mission

> Beware of the man whose god is in the skies.
>
> BERNARD SHAW

Scene One

Berlin, a late afternoon in August 1942. The reception room of the Papal Legation on Rauchstrasse. A few pieces of Empire furniture. The only thing tempering the austerity of the room is a large copy of Rubens' Descent from the Cross. *In these surroundings the picture seems bright, even agreeable.*

Two French doors; one, rear left, leads to the Nuncio's study; the other, at right, to waiting rooms and the stairwell.

THE NUNCIO, HIS EXCELLENCY CESARE ORSENIGO, *is sixty-nine years old. Newspaper photos show him as a man of medium height, still extremely vigorous. There are no empty spaces in his lean face; it is completely dominated by a mouth and nose which, like his chin, are abnormally large. His expression is candid and tolerant. The face stamped not so much by intellect as by will and enormous self-discipline. Baron Ernst von Weizsäcker, State Secretary in the Foreign Office until the spring of 1943 and thereafter Hitler's Ambassador to the Holy See, describes the Nuncio as a realistic Milanese who preferred to avoid "elevating the irreconcilable differences between the Curia and the Third Reich into matters of principle." He also attests that when Orsenigo presented his complaints—as he did, for instance, about the treatment of Polish priests in Hitler's concentration camps—he managed to do so "in a calm spirit and with a friendly manner."*

Let us leave that aside. The Nuncio resided in Berlin throughout the Hitler era. By November 8, 1938 at the latest he must have witnessed with his own eyes the acts of terror committed against the Jewish citizens of Germany. It is hard to say how a man with so likable a face could, in good conscience, reconcile himself to the continuance of the Concordat between the Curia and the Government of the Third Reich, even when Catholic Jews were de-

13

ported. It would seem that anyone who holds a responsible post for any length of time under an autocrat—whether it be Hitler or Pius XII—surrenders his own personality. There is no way for him to express his personal feelings; in his official conduct he is reduced to the level of a flunky. Perhaps the use of equivocal diplomatic jargon makes this easier.

In bringing historical persons to life on the stage, we need no longer seek an accurate likeness. Available photographs of Adolf Hitler and Hermann Göring, no matter how carefully we may scrutinize them, even after the event, fail to provide the slightest clue to the acts of which these two of the Nuncio's confabulators were capable. It seems to be established, therefore, that photographs are totally useless for the interpretation of character. The essential thing, then, is that the Nuncio be played by an actor of mature years, and that he wear the standard attire of a titular Archbishop: pectoral, black soutane, purple cap, collar and cape.

RICCARDO FONTANA's *solidarity with the victims of persecution, and his voluntary martyrdom for the Church, are freely drawn after the acts and aims of Provost Bernhard Lichtenberg of Berlin Cathedral, who came forth and prayed publicly for the Jews, was sentenced to jail, and asked Hitler's henchmen to let him share the fate of the Jews in the East. His petition was granted. But Lichtenberg—who, by the way, was eager to know what the Pope thought of his decision—was not taken to a ghetto in the East. Instead he was sent to Dachau. He died on the way, in 1943, presumably from natural causes. The Nazis evidently were enough in awe of Lichtenberg's reputation to deem it wise to release his body, and to allow several thousand Berliners to attend his funeral.*

The Jewish community of Paris has had the name of SS Obersturmführer (Lieutenant) KURT GERSTEIN *inscribed on the memorial for the victims of Fascism. Gerstein, as the English historian Gerald Reitlinger says, undertook perhaps the most extraordinary mission of the Second World War. So uncanny, divided and mysterious a personality seems more like a fictional creation than an historical personage. This is not the place to sketch his strange biography, a resumé of which he handed to the Allies in 1945; all trace of him was lost while he was in a Paris prison. Nor can we discuss the consistently favorable statements concerning him which have been provided by reputable members of the Protestant and Catholic clergy, and by Baron von Otter, Secretary of the Swedish Embassy. Gerstein, as a photograph dating back as far as*

*1931 shows, seems to have been a marked man from the first, so
"modern" a Christian that we can scarcely understand him without considerable background in Kierkegaard. In 1942, when he
called at the Papal Legation and was ejected, he was thirty-seven
years old.*

*He wears the field gray uniform of an officer of the Waffen-SS,
the SS Armed Forces.*

THE FATHER *who serves the tea wears a habit.*

The NUNCIO *has a map of Berlin in his hands. He speaks to*
RICCARDO.

NUNCIO: You see? Over here—St. Hedwig's Church.
    Ten years ago we had no more than forty-four
    churches in Berlin—omitting, naturally,
    the chapels in the monasteries.
    The Jews had just as many synagogues.
    The number of our churches has increased,
    in spite of everything;
    but not a single synagogue is left.
RICCARDO (*casually*): Could not Your Excellency intervene?
NUNCIO (*raises his hand in a gesture of abnegation; his calm is
    imperturbable*):
    It is not my place, as Nuncio, to speak
    of *that*. When, for example, I try to remonstrate
    about conditions in Poland,
    confining my protests to the mistreatment
    of priests, Herr von Weizsäcker politely
    shows me the door. Outside of my domain,
    he says. First we must recognize the new frontiers.
    Concerning Jews, he says, they'd fall within my scope
    only if they were baptized.
    But Herr Hitler is careful
    not to deport the baptized Jews.
    Ah, the Father himself
    is bringing us our tea, how nice, thank you.
    Might there be a bit of cake to go with it?

A FATHER *has entered, and arranges the tea table. He speaks a
Bavarian dialect.*

FATHER: In a second, Your Excellency.
    I've brought you a kettle of water
    in case you should find it too strong again.

NUNCIO (*folding the map, with smiling pedantry*):
>Thank you, that's very thoughtful . . .
>There, the map's for you.
>I always like to give my aides
>who don't know Berlin a map of the city
>before anything else.
>So that you'll not get lost here.

RICCARDO (*bows, pockets the map; the* FATHER *goes out*):
>Thank you, Your Excellency, very kind of you.

NUNCIO (*at the tea table, in a more personal tone*):
>You weren't a bit nervous about coming to Berlin?
>In Rome you were safe from bombs.
>We have a raid every night.

RICCARDO: For someone of my age, Your Excellency,
>a priest's life is much too safe.
>My cousin was killed fighting in Africa.
>I'm happy to have gotten out of Rome.

NUNCIO (*amused*): How young you are! Twenty-seven
>and Minutante already.
>You will go far, young friend.
>It was considered remarkable that His Holiness
>became a Minutante at twenty-six.

RICCARDO: Your Excellency must consider
>that I've chosen the right parent.

NUNCIO (*cordially*): You are too modest.
>If you were nothing but your father's son,
>the Cardinal would never
>have called you to the Secretariat of State.
>(*Confidentially.*) Is our Chief still
>so ill disposed to me?

RICCARDO (*embarrassed*):
>But, Your Excellency, no one is ill disp . . .

NUNCIO (*placing a hand on his arm, then rising, holding the tea-cup*):
>Come now, you too are well aware
>that I have long been persona non grata in Rome . . .

RICCARDO (*hesitantly, evasively*): Possibly at the Vatican
>it seems easier to represent the Holy See
>than here in Berlin. . . .

NUNCIO (*vehemently justifying himself; he paces the room*):
>The Pope should decide what he prefers:
>peace with Hitler at any price, or else

let me be authorized to take a stand
the way my brother Nuncio in Slovakia
did two weeks ago when he spoke up
against the wholesale killing of Jews from Bratislava
in the Lublin district.
He made a strong protest . . .
My dear friend, what does Rome expect?
I would have resigned long ago
if I were not afraid my post would fall
into the hands of some nonentity!

RICCARDO: Does that mean Your Excellency favors
abrogating the Concordat with Hitler?

NUNCIO: Oh no, on the contrary. His late Holiness Pius XI
might well have done that.
But since the death of the old Pope
Herr Hitler has put a stop to certain measures
some of his more stupid underlings
wanted to take against us. He himself
is neutral in his official policy toward the Church,
impeccable, like Marshal Göring.
In Poland, though, he *is* trying to blackmail us.
Herr Goebbels, his Propaganda Minister,
can be talked to. You might almost call him
obliging. It's strange they haven't dared
touch Bishop Galen, even though he publicly
denounced, right from his pulpit,
the murder of the mentally ill.
Hitler actually gave in on that!

RICCARDO (*enthusiastically*):
Surely the Church can issue such demands,
Your Excellency! Especially now when bishops
in half of Europe are drumming up support
for Hitler's crusade against Moscow. On the train
I was reading what an army bishop
at the Eastern Front had said to . . .

NUNCIO (*energetically, vexed*): You see, Father, that is precisely
what I oppose. We should *not*
be drumming up support for Hitler
as long as this wholesale killing
goes on behind his front lines. . . .
London speaks
of seven hundred thousand Jews in Poland alone!

Of course, we've seen that sort of thing before.
Crusades begin with killing of the Jews.
But in such numbers—horrible.
I hardly think they are exaggerated.
You know how in Poland they are killing even the priests.
Our attitude should be one of great reserve.
For instance . . . just recently, did the bishop
of Bohemia and Moravia *have* to plead with Herr Hitler
about that man Heydrich,
the Police Chief of Berlin and Prague . . .

RICCARDO: The one who was shot, assassinated?

NUNCIO: Yes, right in the street. They took reprisals
against a whole village, including the women and children.
Was it *necessary* for the Moravian bishop
to plead with Hitler hat in hand
if they might ring the bells for the deceased
and read a requiem for him?
(*With great indignation.*)
A requiem for Heydrich is in bad taste.
That's really going too far. . . .
(*The* FATHER *brings cakes.*)
So—we have something to nibble on.
Thank you, my friend, thank you.

The FATHER *leaves the door open. The fanfare preceding a special communiqué can be heard: the heroic theme, with trumpets and drum rolls, from Liszt's* Preludes.

FATHER: Here you are, Your Excellency—some nice cake.
And there's a special bulletin coming on. . . .

NUNCIO: Please, have some, Father Riccardo . . . There!
Well, let us listen to the news.
(*He smiles, and says in explanation to* RICCARDO:)
The ritual introduction. The ideas
of the Hitlerites present no problems for us,
but the Nazi rituals are strong competition,
superbly geared to mass psychology.

The FATHER *steps back toward the door, but remains in the room. The music dies and is replaced by the announcer's voice:*

"Attention! Attention! This is the radio of Greater Germany.
We bring you a special communiqué from the Führer's head-

quarters, April 25, 1942: The High Command of the Armed Forces announces that at noon today German mountain troops, overcoming bitter Soviet resistance, captured the peak of the Elbrus at an altitude of 18,500 feet and hoisted the war flag of the Reich. This puts the Caucasus firmly into German hands.

The heroic theme once more, then the melody of the song: From Finland to the Black Sea.

FATHER (*proudly*):
    More than eighteen thousand, that's higher than the Mont Blanc!
    My nephew's with the mountain troops in the East.
    He was in the fighting at Narvik—was wounded, too.
NUNCIO (*with polite disinterest*):
    Ah, your nephew. God protect him.
FATHER: Thank you kindly, Your Excellency. Yes, let's hope so.

Exits, closing the door; the music fades, ceases.

RICCARDO: Does Your Excellency think there are grounds to fear
    Herr Hitler will respect the Church
    only for the duration of the war?
NUNCIO: It did seem so a little while ago, my dear Father,
    for victors always act immorally.
    But ever since Herr Hitler, much against his will,
    was pushed by Japan, and Mr. Roosevelt, too,
    into declaring war on the U.S.A.—
    ever since that folly (or was it *dira necessitas*?),
    the Church of Christ at any rate
    no longer needs to stand in fear of him.
    He will not force England *and* America
    to their knees.
    Not even if he moves into the Kremlin.
RICCARDO (*incredulously*):
    Once he has beaten Russia, Your Excellency,
    he will be economically invulnerable.
    Who would be left to overthrow him then?
    His tanks have pushed their way into Egypt
    and almost to Stalingrad,
    and in the Atlantic his U-boats . . .

NUNCIO (*interrupts again, his tone kindly, ironic, superior*):
    Gently, young friend, not quite so fast.
    In von Ranke's book on the Popes—

He goes to a bookcase, selects a volume, leafs through it.

    one of the many excellent books which we
    place on the Index—
    I recently came across a statement
    I found immensely reassuring.
    At times, says Ranke, when *any* principle, no matter what,
    seeks to impose its rule upon the Western World,
    a firm resistance counters it infallibly.
    That opposition stems from
    the deepest sources of our life; it is the very
    spirit of old Europe. Philip the Second
    found his master in England. Napoleon
    in England *and* the Czar. May not the same
    happen to Hitler?
    Baron von Weizsäcker tells me in confidence
    that Russia is far from beaten yet.
    And then the U.S.A.! No matter how
    he comes out of it, it will be a Pyrrhic victory.
RICCARDO: You think then, Your Excellency, that Herr Hitler
    will *have to* listen to reason?
NUNCIO: Oh yes! He will even prefer to.
    We saw that at Dunkirk, after all.
    He let the British make their getaway. His policy
    was obviously moderation in victory.
    I grant you, Mr. Churchill gave him no thanks for it . . .
    Please do have some more cake . . .
    With the Spaniards and the French,
    the Balkan nations and the Italians,
    the Belgians and above all his own Catholics
    here in Germany, all of them
    willingly or not supporting his crusade
    against Moscow—with half of Europe Catholic,
    even Hitler cannot risk a schism.
    If he should brand us enemies of state,
    the Rome-Tokyo-Berlin Axis would fall apart.
    It's fortunate that at this very moment
    Japan is making every effort
    to sign a Concordat with us.

The efforts of the White House to prevent it
only serve to prove
how eagerly both sides are courting us.
On Sunday in St. Hedwig's,
during the bishop's ordination ceremonies,
I saw a lieutenant of the SS. He went to confession,
took Communion—oh no,
where the Church is concerned, Herr Hitler
remains a realist.
He wants the nations helping him in Russia
to go on backing him when he is forced
to negotiate with England and the U.S.A.
Consider how in the United States
day by day the Catholics' power grows—
Herr Hitler has to reckon with that, too.
He will discover what his friends, Franco
and Mussolini, learned long ago:
Fascism is invincible only *with* us,
when it stands with the Church and not against it.
Molotov saw that ten years ago;
in 1934 Molotov admitted
that if the Church in Germany
should strike up an accord with the Hitlerites—
and at the time there were some signs of that;
a promising beginning had been made—
then Communism in Europe would be finished . . .
What's that, what's the commotion?
What's going on out there?

The NUNCIO *rises, remains standing and listening a moment, then
goes toward the door to the waiting room, murmuring to himself.
There is an excited altercation backstage; people begin to shout.
The* FATHER *is heard, his dialect thickening as his voice grows
louder. Amid fragmentary phrases, only half intelligible, sounds
the insistent, pleading voice of a man who is obviously holding himself in check with difficulty in the effort to remain polite.*

BOTH (*backstage*): You're in uniform!
But—you *must* announce me!
The Legation is extraterritorial—be off with you
or I'll send for the police.
Please, give me five minutes with His Excellency.
The Nuncio has a visitor from Rome.

He *must* hear me.
Anything the likes of you may want to say
is no affair of ours.

RICCARDO, *intrigued, has moved back against the wall, while the*
NUNCIO *opens the door to the waiting room. The SS officer,* KURT
GERSTEIN, *bursts in, cap in hand. The* FATHER *tries to block his
way and then to push him out again.*

GERSTEIN and FATHER (*simultaneously*):
Your Excellency, isn't this the limit?
I must speak with Your Excellency, just for
two minutes—please—I beg you!
Shall I call the police?
Pushing his way in like this . . . who ever heard . . . ?
NUNCIO: What's going on? Whatever are you thinking of?
GERSTEIN: Gerstein is my name, Your Excellency—please
hear me out. I have a message
for the Vatican that . . .
NUNCIO: Sir, I am astounded
that you invade this building in this manner . . .
I suppose your headquarters
are on Prinz Albrecht Strasse . . .

The FATHER *has hurried across the room to a telephone. He lifts
the receiver.* GERSTEIN *dashes after him, saying:*

GERSTEIN: Your Excellency, please, no phone calls.
If headquarters were to hear of this visit . . .
NUNCIO (*gesturing to the* FATHER *to put down the telephone*):
You call this scene a visit?
FATHER (*quickly*): Go now, just get out of here.
GERSTEIN (*just as quickly*):
Your Excellency, a message for the Vatican.
It will not bear a single day's delay,
not one single hour. I have just come from Poland—
from Belzec and Treblinka, northeast of Warsaw.
Your Excellency, daily,
every single day in those places,
ten thousand Jews, *more
than ten thousand,*
are being murdered, put to death with gas . . .

NUNCIO: For God's sake, hold your tongue!
    Tell that to Herr Hitler, not to me.
    Leave this place.
    In the German Government's view
    I am not authorized
    to say a word about these . . .
    these conditions in Poland.
GERSTEIN (*a shout*): Your Excellency!
NUNCIO: Who are you, anyhow? I am not authorized,
    I tell you, to have any dealings
    with members of the German Armed Forces . . .
    Are you Catholic? In any case I request you
    to leave at once . . . Go, go.

*His Excellency is determined not to hear confirmation of such
monstrous crimes. For he is basically a man of deep humanity,
and official acknowledgment of this message would make it difficult for him to continue to deal with Weizsäcker as he has done in
the past, "indifferently, without much distinction, in a calm spirit
and friendly manner."*

FATHER (*has gone to the door, holds it open and says very mildly*):
    Well now, will you be off at last.
GERSTEIN (*loses his temper, shuts the door violently and strides
        up to the* NUNCIO. *He speaks jerkily, under great stress*):
    Your Excellency, every hour I see trains pull in
    bringing fresh loads from all of Europe to those death fac-
        tories. . . .
    No, I am not Catholic. But Pastor Buchholz
    who cares for the condemned in Plötzensee
    is my friend. Another reference I can give
    is Superintendent Otto Dibelius and Church Councilman
    Hermann Ehlers. Before he was arrested,
    Pastor Niemöller of Dahlem . . .
NUNCIO (*politely but very firmly*): All very well, but I regret
    I must now terminate this . . .
    I'm very sorry, but you'll have to go.
GERSTEIN: Speak to von Otter
    of the Swedish Embassy, Your Excellency.
    At this point, only the Vatican can intervene.
    You must help, sir!

NUNCIO (*indignant, since he does not know what to do*):
Why do you come to *me*? You yourself
are wearing the uniform of the murderers.
I tell you, I have no authority to interfere.

GERSTEIN (*shouting*): Authority! Here in Berlin you represent
the—the Deputy of Christ,
and you can close your eyes to the worst horror
that man has ever inflicted upon man.
You hold your peace while every hour . . .

NUNCIO: Control yourself . . . keep your voice down . . .
we don't shout here.
I am terminating this conversation now . . .

GERSTEIN (*pleading*): No, please—I beg your pardon.
I know very well, Your Excellency—you can't do anything.
But the Holy Father must take action,
must speak for the world's conscience . . .

The NUNCIO *withdraws; he does not go all the way through the
door to his study only because* RICCARDO *resists following him.*
RICCARDO *stands listening in fascination to* GERSTEIN.

GERSTEIN: Your Excellency, please, listen to me;
(*As if in a trance.*) I can't bear it any more—I've seen it—
I see it all the time—it haunts
me right to this room.
Listen . . . the . . . I must
tell you about it . . .

Covering his eyes, GERSTEIN *drops into a chair. He rises to his feet
at once, not looking at any of the others in the room; his gaze is
turned inward and his eyes have a wild, restlessly flickering expression. [Thus Frau Bälz described him in her report to the Institute
for Contemporary History. His nocturnal conversation with Frau
Bälz took place at about the same time as his ineffectual call on
the* NUNCIO. *Baron von Otter, the Secretary of the Swedish Embassy, writes that* GERSTEIN *told his tale to him in the aisle of the
train "weeping and in a broken voice."]*

*The following passage is spoken in a great variety of tones. At
times* GERSTEIN's *sentences taper off into inarticulate murmurs;
then again he speaks loudly, distraughtly, or in a series of brief
outcries, like someone crying out in his sleep. After the first few
sentences the* NUNCIO *takes several steps toward him. The* FATHER

closes the door, but stays in the room, while RICCARDO *keeps his eyes on the* NUNCIO *so probingly that his look verges on the insulting.*

GERSTEIN (*abruptly*):
    So far they've been running the gas chambers
    on carbon monoxide, common exhaust gas.
    But many times the motors will not start.
    In Belzec recently I had to watch—
    this was on August 20—
    while the victims waited two hours and forty-nine minutes
    until the gas came on.
    Seven hundred and fifty persons
    in each of four chambers—
    each room with a volume of sixty cubic yards—
    three thousand human beings.
    Some pray, some weep, some shriek.
    The majority keep silent.
    The gassing operation takes twenty-five minutes.
    Now they want to speed it up,
    and so they've brought me in for consultation.
    I am an engineer and medical man.
    (*Screams.*) I will not do it, I will not do it. . . .
    Like marble columns the naked corpses stand.
    You can tell the families, even after death
    convulsed in locked embrace—with hooks
    they're pulled apart. Jews have to do that job.
    Ukrainians lash them on with whips.

He can no longer concentrate, loses himself in details, his eyes vacant.

    There was the manager of Berlin's biggest store . . .
    There was a violinist, too, decorated in World War I . . .
    Fought at the front for Germany.
    And bodies of dead children. A young girl
    ahead of the procession, naked like the rest.
    Mothers, all stripped, babies at their breasts.
    Most of them know the worst—the smell of gas . . .
NUNCIO (*starting to leave*): Enough—I cannot listen any more.
    You Germans, why! Why . . .
    My dear man, my heart is with the victims.

GERSTEIN: Your Excellency, the Vatican
has made a pact with Hitler!
Yet you can see it in the streets, here in Berlin,
in Oslo, Paris, Kiev—for more than a year
you have seen, *every* priest has seen
how they're rounding up the Jews. The Allied radio
reports that thousands upon thousands
are being exterminated.
When, Your Excellency, when,
will you tear up the Concordat?

RICCARDO (*overwhelmed*):
Your Excellency, all this agrees completely
with the reports my Order has received,
but no one could quite credit them.

NUNCIO (*with genuine concern, deeply moved but helpless*):
My dear Father, please keep out of this . . .
Why doesn't this man go to Herr Hitler!

GERSTEIN *gives a terrible laugh.*

RICCARDO (*pleading*): But he is not an agent provocateur,
Your Excellency . . . Count Ledochowsky has received
the same sort of reports from Poland . . .

NUNCIO (*tried beyond his patience, losing composure*):
Why does he come to *me*? The Curia
is not here to aggravate strife.
God has charged it with the mission
to work for peace . . .

GERSTEIN: Peace with murderers too? Your Excellency!

He points to the painting of the Crucified Christ and exclaims:

Cursed are the peacemakers!
He felt He was authorized, Your Excellency—
but His Deputy does not?

NUNCIO (*deeply moved and paternal*):
Herr Ger—stensteiner, compose yourself!
I share your sorrow for the victims.

GERSTEIN (*screaming*): Every *hour,* Your Excellency, *every* hour
thousands more are killed—those are factories
for killing. Factories, won't you understand?

NUNCIO: Please, sir—whatever my own feelings in this matter,
I cannot simply take account of them.

I intervened, in private, as far back as
nineteen thirty-nine. But I am charged
by my position not to involve myself
in any cause of conflict between Rome
and your authorities. I should not even have
this talk with you—please,
you must go. Go now, please.
God bless you, God help you.
I shall pray for the victims.

He beckons to RICCARDO *to follow him, walks to the backstage
door and opens it.*

Father, please come—I must insist.
RICCARDO: Your name is Gerstein—I will find you.

GERSTEIN *pays no attention to these words; he sees only that he
has accomplished nothing. The* NUNCIO *has returned to* RICCARDO,
*puts his hand on his shoulder and propels him almost forcibly
through the door to the study. Before the* NUNCIO *can close the
door,* GERSTEIN *follows him once more, passionate, beside himself.*

GERSTEIN: Your Excellency, listen, you must hear
the dying words of an old Jewish woman—
as she was driven on by whips into the gas
she called down on the murderers' heads
the blood they're spilling there. That blood guilt,
Excellency, falls upon us all
if we keep silent!
NUNCIO (*turning once more, softly*): Compose yourself. Pray!

Exit. The FATHER *closes the door behind him and speaks mildly:*

FATHER: Have some sense, man, how can you
come at His Excellency like this?
Can he help it? Now please, take yourself off.
There isn't anything one of us can do.
GERSTEIN (*has realized that he has lost. One more pointless attempt; he reaches into his coat pocket, takes out a batch of
papers, and tries to interest the* FATHER *in them*):
Here is more proof—look at them!
Orders from the camp commandants
of Belzec and Treblinka
for the delivery of hydrocyanide.

They want me to supply the prussic acid—
I'm with the SS Public Health Department—look at these—

He is alone in the room. He turns in a circle, the papers in his hand. The FATHER, *who has gone out and now returns with a tray to clear away the tea things, says in a voice which mingles threat and helpfulness:*

FATHER: Don't you realize
  they have policemen watching the Legation?
  If they should catch you on the premises,
  in uniform . . . Now run along, please.
  Mary and Joseph, what a tale!
  It's true they're Jews, but still. . . .

GERSTEIN *leaves before the sentence is finished.*

CURTAIN

> Because they have feet, you do not see
> they are automatons.   OTTO FLAKE
>
> The glory of Creation, man, the swine.
>   GOTTFRIED BENN

Scene Two

Nine o'clock in the evening of the same day.
  The Jägerkeller *in Falkensee, near Berlin: a small hotel which for the past several weeks, ever since the onset of regular Allied air raids on the capital, has been requisitioned as a recreation center by the Reichführung SS (Himmler's office).*
  The spacious cellar from which the hotel takes its name. The room is divided into two halves by a broad, free-standing staircase beneath which a man can pass upright. It extends a good distance forward into the foreground of the cellar. The seats for the patrons, perhaps eight persons, are in the rear to the right of the stairs, and are not visible. To the left of the stairs, also to the rear and clearly

visible is the rack and runway for the bowler, who sends the balls to the left through a "Gothic" arch in the wings—the bowling alley. Adjacent is the large scoreboard. Muted sounds of rolling balls and falling pins can be heard. At the rear wall is the ball return.

To the right, about in the middle between the forestage and the invisible corner seats at rear, is a table with an array of cold cuts and assorted garnishes, attended to by HELGA, a very young blonde, half waitress, half hostess.

A huge portrait of Hitler, engravings of hunting scenes by Riedinger, two crossed foils with the caps of a student corps, dating from the distant past. The newest item is a large photo of the death mask, made two months before in Prague, of the assassinated Reichsprotektor Heydrich.

The bowlers usually, though of course not invariably, move in the following manner: when the scorer calls out their names—which he does not do every time—they appear out of the rear, right, pass under the stairs, bowl, step up to the scorer at the foot of the stairs while he marks down their results, cross downstage, go up to the buffet and then return to their seats at the rear. Frequently they linger to watch some of their fellows bowling, make loud comments and burst into laughter. Still more frequently they disappear, rarely alone, downstage right, through a door on which an "M" can be seen, and return to the buffet, evidently with their sense of belonging reinforced, talking loudly and making a typical gesture of checking their clothing.

The conversations take place during this circuit—some of the men chatting with the man at the scoreboard, or sitting down on the steps with others for a moment, or flirting with HELGA, or moving to the foreground while munching a ham sandwich, to discuss in allusive terms something official which is not for everyone's ears.

The host is ADOLF EICHMANN, an amiable bureaucrat who did his ghastly job with so little of the sinister glamor of a Grand Inquisitor that in 1945 no one even bothered to search for him—it took study of the documents to unmask him as the most diligent shipping agent who ever labored in the employ of Death. On our stage, too, he remains as colorless as any average man who likes to study railroad schedules and is determined to get ahead at all costs.

The other members of the party: BARON VON RUTTA, an extremely distinguished-looking civilian, scion of the Ruhr aristocracy. Cold to the point of seeming inhibited, he is here making an *effort to "be one of the boys," and as spirits rise in the course of the evening he lays the Rhineland dialect on thicker. He is the representative of the circles which Ulrich von Hassell described in a note made in 1941, after a trip to the Ruhr district: " 'Morale' not bad, great deal of 'Heil Hitler' greeting, typical industrialists . . . to the extent that they are all equally incompetent in politics and accept money-grubbing as the only thing that really counts."*

His son, AIR FORCE LIEUTENANT VON RUTTA, *just over twenty, a likable boy with good manners, has just won the Knight's Cross. Disconcerted at finding himself suddenly the center of attention, he tractably assumes the vulgar bowling alley jargon, although frontline service has not yet made him cynical. Brave as a soldier, he is shyer and more chivalrous toward a girl like* HELGA, *and her engagement ring, than she would like.*

The "life of the party" is PROFESSOR AUGUST HIRT, *sixty-five years old, a tall, fat doctor in the field gray uniform of the Waffen-SS. He is an anatomist and collector of skulls at the University of Strassburg—a gargantuan, space-filling carouser with a chest like a barrel. On drinking nights he lapses into his earthy, good-natured Swabian dialect because he is aware of its humorous effect. He was never found after the war, probably never sought, although the idiocy and cruelty he pursued in the guise of science went beyond the limits common to the practice of many SS doctors. Since he is practicing his medical skills under another name nowadays, we allow him here the use of the name he was born with. (The historical Hirt was an odious cynic, a man with a vulture's head and a jawbone shattered by a bullet.)*

His assistant, DR. LITTKE, M.D., *a young lieutenant on the medical staff of an army group, is an insipid careerist, a man whose interests have so shrunk to his particular field that he is an absolute blank where all other aspects of life and knowledge are concerned. Obviously he will rise swiftly to the position of professor.*

Another army officer, COLONEL SERGE *of the High Command of the Armed Forces, Prisoners-of-War Department. During the First World War* SERGE *was a cavalry captain in the Austrian army. Tossed by the winds of destiny into the General Staff Headquarters on Bendlerstrasse, he now helplessly tries to make some improvements in the lot of the prisoners of war, but his humanity is gradually wearing down to cynical resignation and almost suicidal impulsive actions. He has decided, against his inclinations, to come to the* Jägerkeller *because* BARON VON RUTTA *has recently formed*

*the habit of staying here on his Berlin trips, in order to be able to
sleep during the air raids.* SERGE's *surly nervousness is expressed
in a comic fumbling for words and stuttering at the beginnings of
sentences. A native of Krems, he speaks in the dialect of the
Wachau region on the Danube. The phonetics of this speech, like
the differences between Bavarian and Austrian intonation, are
difficult to render in writing, and he may speak here like a Viennese.*

REGIERUNGSRAT PRYZILLA *of the Reich Ministry for Occupied
Eastern Territories wears the yellow Party tunic with black trousers,
swastika in a white circle on a red armband. He is an "ethnic
German" with a strong Polish accent and Hitler mustache, bald
and excessively careful of his manners, and as small and compact
as a night table. This is a man who would sooner choke than contradict a superior. In this scene he only opens his mouth—though
he does so fiercely enough—to follow like a bloodhound some trail
that leads back to his own department. In 1955 he held a high
post in a Bonn ministry—by then he had learned to speak German
fluently. . . .*

The DOCTOR, *who carries the little swagger stick with which he
toys while making his selections in Auschwitz, never bowls. Precisely because he takes so little part in what is going on, he gives
the impression, even in this group of Philistines, of being the secret
stage manager. If he is like the others, he is like them in the way
the puppetmaster resembles his marionettes. He is not an uncanny
figure, like* GERSTEIN. *He is cool and cheery—when he is not invisible. He has the stature of Absolute Evil—far more unequivocally so than Hitler, whom he no longer even bothers to despise—
which is his attitude toward all members of the human race. He
himself is a being no longer interested in anything or anyone; he
no longer regards it as worthwhile even to play with homo sapiens.
For the moment he makes one exception:* HELGA. *At the same time
he is not outwardly arrogant, but extremely charming. There is
something instantly engaging about him. I have deliberately devi-
ated from historical portrayals of this mysterious "master." It is
in keeping with his character that he was never caught—presumably thanks to the pleasant way in which he promised children
"a tasty pudding" before sending them into the gas chambers (a
matter of record!), or his habit of being on the railroad platform
and asking the new arrivals whether anyone felt ill as a result of
the trip. Those who said they did—relieved by this unexpected*

show of solicitude from this amiable man—were the first to be sent to be gassed. This fact comes to us from the account of Frau Grete Salus, a doctor's widow, who was the sole member of her family to survive Auschwitz. He had asked her whether she felt ill, she wrote, with "a most persuasive kindness."

I was strangely affected when, almost a year after first drafting the dialogue between RICCARDO and the Auschwitz doctor (whom I still had never been able to imagine as human), I came upon Frau Salus' narrative and read that the prisoners would constantly refer to this "handsome and likable" man as the devil, even after they had learned his name:

"He stood before us, the handsome devil who decided life and death. . . . He stood there like a charming, dapper dancing master directing a polonaise. Left and right and right and left his hands pointed with casual movements. He radiated an air of lightness and gracefulness, a welcome contrast to the brutal ugliness of the environs; it soothed our frayed nerves and made whatever was happening devoid of all meaning. . . . A good actor? A man possessed? A cold automaton? No, a master at his profession, a devil who took pleasure in his work. . . . Nothing, nothing put you on your guard; no angel stood behind him. With utter docility the people went to the right or to the left . . . wherever the master waved them. Sometimes a daughter did not want to be parted from her mother, but the words, 'You'll see each other tomorrow, after all,' would reassure them completely. . . ."

These are surrealistic scenes. However incredible it may seem that they occurred in the world we inhabit, they are nevertheless documented and even fragmentarily photographed, as for instance in the volume Der gelbe Stern by Gerhard Schoenberner.

Because this "doctor" stands in such sharp contrast not only to his fellows of the SS, but to all human beings, and so far as I know, to anything that has been learned about human beings, it seemed permissible to me at least to suggest the possibility that, with this character, an ancient figure in the theater and in Christian mystery plays is once more appearing upon the stage. Since this uncanny visitant from another world was obviously only playing the part of a human being, I have refrained from any further effort to plumb its human features—for these could contribute nothing to our understanding of so incomprehensible a being or its deeds. Seemingly human, the phenomenon of the DOCTOR is in reality comparable to no human being, not even to Heydrich whom Carl J.

Burckhardt describes—stylizing him larger than life—as a young, evil god of death.

Loud laughter while the curtain parts. Holding their beer steins, the assembled group watches as young RUTTA *removes his Knight's Cross from his neck and hands it to* HIRT, *who triumphantly shows it around.* HIRT *has long ago found out what Hermann Göring's crack officers (who always went in for innocuous extravagances with their uniforms) hang their decorations on.*

HIRT (*in thick dialect*):
> There you are—didn't I tell you—with a woman's garter—
> it's a fact.

EICHMANN (*laughing*):
> The Knight's Cross on a garter—unbelievable!

LIEUTENANT RUTTA (*at the moment still awkward; later he compensates for his embarrassment by brash answers which surprise both himself and his proud father*):
> Everybody uses them, they've come to be standard
> because they're more practical. They hold better
> than the snap fasteners on the black, white and red ribbon.

HIRT: Now, my boy, a couple of questions for you.
> First: did you win just the Cross
> under enemy fire, or the garter too?

Laughter. Shouts of: Shame! At close quarters! Don't answer!

LIEUTENANT RUTTA: Both, Professor. And both in night skirmishes.

Shouts of glee. They drink. Toasts: Cheers! Good Hunting!

HIRT: And now the second question, the real ticklish one.
> Which took more guts—to win the medal
> or the garter?

LIEUTENANT RUTTA: Guts? I was scared stiff both times.
> Though I must say, in the fight for the garter
> it was one of those cases where blood
> couldn't possibly flow any more.

Appreciative shouts. LIEUTENANT RUTTA, *confused by his own daring, pins his medal on again.*

EICHMANN: At any rate, you threw everything you had into the breach both times, eh?

LIEUTENANT RUTTA: You might put it that way, Colonel—yes, sir.
BARON RUTTA (*tightly, trying hard to join in the jollity*):
   Leave me no little mementos of your wars, my hero!
LIEUTENANT RUTTA: I'll take precautions, Father.
HIRT: The third question: did having the medal
   make it *much* easier to get hold of the garter?
LIEUTENANT RUTTA: Permit me a question in return, Professor.
   Are you, sir, in the habit of wearing your medals
   when *you* set out to win a garter?

Laughter.

HIRT: Damn it, man, you've got me there! Your boy,
   Baron, he's smart as a whip.
   Nice of you, lieutenant, to think an old dog like me
   is still up to such tricks.
EICHMANN: Well then, let's give our guest of honor
   Lieutenant von Rutta—and his distinguished father,
   Baron Rutta—three cheers. Hur-
ALL: Rah!
EICHMANN: Hur-
ALL: Rah!
EICHMANN: Hur-
ALL: Rah!
LIEUTENANT RUTTA: Thank you, gentlemen.

He has turned toward the stairs, along with the others. HELGA *has appeared on the stairs with a tray—conscious of her effect as the only woman in the company.*

EICHMANN: Fräulein Helga—will you grant the lieutenant
   a dance in honor of his Knight's Cross?

Cries of agreement. Young RUTTA *approaches* HELGA, *bows.* FRITSCHE *hurries over to the seats and puts a record on a phonograph.* EICHMANN *takes the tray from* HELGA *and, as the waltz begins, dances with it over to the buffet, pretending that he is holding a woman.* RUTTA *and* HELGA *begin to dance rather woodenly. The circle of men spreads out and some vanish backstage. Some beat time with their hands.*

HIRT (*to* BARON RUTTA): Ah, youth . . . isn't it worth more
   than all our fame and fortune, Baron?

BARON RUTTA:
> How true—she is a charming girl. This morning when she brought me breakfast, she said . . .

HIRT: I wish I had her in my room!
> Did she serve breakfast in your bed, Baron?

BARON RUTTA (*laughing*): You really want to know too much.
> She told me, as I was saying, that she is engaged
> to an SS lieutenant in Auschwitz.
> Do you happen to know him, Doctor?

DOCTOR (*unruffled*):
> Why, of course. Her boyfriend's a pal of mine.

They go to the seats; the dance is ending; young RUTTA *stiffly offers his arm to* HELGA *to bring her over to the seats. But she draws him to the buffet.*

HELGA: I really have to work, Lieutenant.
> Thanks for the dance, all the same.

LIEUTENANT RUTTA (*timidly*):
> It would be nice if we could dance again,
> some time.

He takes leave of her at the buffet. EICHMANN, *who with* FRITSCHE *has set up the scoreboard, now takes a pack of cards from his pocket.*

EICHMANN: Helga, would you hand the cards around.
> Each gentleman draw one.

DOCTOR (*seated on the stairs in a scornful attitude, yawns*):
> The German, if he is a man, must bowl or shoot!
> Bowling—the respectable German burgher's way
> of sublimation, safe and approved by every member of the
> family.

The Lieutenant laughs, just as bored, but he promptly draws the first card. As HELGA *extends the cards to the* DOCTOR, *he amicably pushes her hand aside without taking a card.*

DOCTOR (*softly*): I'll telephone Auschwitz later.
> You can ask Günter right away.

HELGA (*tersely, anxiously, as she moves away*):
> Please, don't start that again . . .

HIRT (*loudly, calling from the seats which* HELGA *is approaching*):
> So what are we going to play now?

FRITSCHE (*at the table, calling in reply*):
>How about "Clear the Deck," Professor?

HIRT: I prefer "Coffin";—the big box, you know.
>Then all we do is make the strokes—not so much figuring.

FRITSCHE: "Clear the Deck" is even simpler, if you ask me.
>Each man has three shots at the full setup. A strike
>counts twelve, a double fifteen points.
>We play a lot of it in Auschwitz.

HIRT: Are the pins set up again after each throw?

EICHMANN (*to both*): Yes, after each throw. But I like
>the big box better, Herr Fritsche.
>Then every time, when a man is dead,
>we can sing the chorus to
>"In the cool green meadow."
>(*With wry good humor.*)
>Since we happen to have such a fine baritone with us—
>eh, Professor Hirt? How about it?

Laughter. HIRT *begins to sing without more ado; the others join in.*

>They carried a corpse to the cool green meadow.
>Going home, he's going home,
>and no longer will he roam,
>far from the cool green meadow.

EICHMANN (*calling out*): Please hold the cards up! Helga—
>didn't you draw one for yourself?
>You're supposed to bowl with us.

HELGA: Do you think I can?

DOCTOR (*still sitting on the steps, close to her; softly*):
>You'll be amazed at all the things you can do.

HELGA *turns away and goes over to the buffet, downstage, right.*
EICHMANN *has written "Helga" at the top of the scoreboard. He
now calls over to the seats.*

EICHMANN: Who has the ace? Ace begins . . .

LIEUTENANT RUTTA: Here, colonel, I have the ace.

EICHMANN: Aha, the lieutenant—Rutta junior.
>Come over here with your cards, all of you.

He writes "Rutta, Jr." on the board, while FRITSCHE *puts a new
record on the phonograph. The music is muted. Some linger by
the chairs, drinking and smoking; these hold up their cards and
call out the order they have drawn. Most of the group have formed*

a circle around EICHMANN *at the scoreboard. Everything proceeds
with Teutonic orderliness, almost with formality.* EICHMANN *writes
the names one below the other: Helga, Rutta, Jr., Hirt, Fritsche, etc.*

DOCTOR (*slowly stands up, walks over to* HELGA, *who can no longer
    dodge him*):
    Come on now, kitten, are you really afraid
    to be too close to your boyfriend?
    Let me get you transferred to Auschwitz.
HELGA (*while arranging silver and paper napkins*):
    Stop it, leave me alone; I mustn't
    have anything more to do with you, Doctor.
    You're a devil—how did you ever make
    me do it this afternoon—I feel awful . . .
    I've always been faithful to him . . .
DOCTOR (*charmingly, persuasively, his irony entirely concealed*):
    We *need* secretaries.
    You can run the teletype machine
    and your fiancé will have you nearby.
HELGA (*threatening, but without believing her own words*):
    He keeps an eye on me, I can tell you that.
    He'll protect me.
DOCTOR (*calmly*): I hope so. And if it gets too tiresome for you—
    I'll always be there. I don't lock my door at night.

*He has taken a plate. He selects a few cold cuts, pretending to
choose them very judiciously.*

HELGA:
    Not me—never again! I'm keeping my door locked from now
    on.
    I'll never go where you are, *never!*
    Why pick on me—there are so many girls.
DOCTOR (*with barbed gallantry*):
    Because you're such a darling little prude.
    The way you put your hands over your face
    when I pulled you into the saddle—very attractive.
HELGA: I hate the thought of cheating on him . . .
    He's so *straight*—he'd never cheat on me.
    Why, I never even saw you till this morning.
EICHMANN: There, all the names are down. Except yours, Doctor.
    Don't you have a card?

DOCTOR (*goes out up the stairway*):
    I have to make a phone call—be right back . . .
EICHMANN: Come, Helga, you go first.
HELGA (*after* EICHMANN *has handed her a ball*):
    Oh, this one is heavy . . .
HIRT (*hands her a lighter ball*):
    Here you are, Fräulein, this is more your caliber.
    Small and light but just as hard.
    You can make top score with this one.
FRITSCHE: All right, let 'em roll.

Silence while the ball rolls down the alley. Cheers as the ball strikes.

HIRT: Only the kingpin standing. The *last* king
    still standing in Europe.
EICHMANN: Don't forget the Danish one, Professor.
    He's been quite a nuisance.
BARON RUTTA (*truly interested*):
    Really? How can the Danes make trouble for us?
EICHMANN: Denmark won't go for the yellow star,
    and all because the King's against it.
FRITSCHE (*calling from the scoreboard*):
    Your turn, Colonel Eichmann.
EICHMANN: I'm coming. Join me, Baron.

*Those who have had their turn at bowling stroll over to the buffet
and are served by* HELGA. *Holding their filled plates, they go offstage to the seats. The bowling goes on, more or less mechanically.
The attention of the audience is focused chiefly upon the speakers
who alternate downstage. Interest in the bowlers who are not
speaking at the time is aroused now and then by a succession of
shouts and exclamations at the runway and behind the scene, such
as:*

    "Go ahead, Fritsche, take your stance."
    "You'll be boxed in a moment."
    "It's your turn. No, it isn't mine, yours."
    "Two more strokes and I'll be dead."
    "Come on, fellows, keep it moving."
    "Damn it all, missed again."
    "You've dropped one—here it goes."
    "Nothing but splits tonight."
    "Penalty."
    "Dead apple."

These and similar cries are interspersed throughout the scene. Thus there is constant movement, without too much interruption of the conversations which now and then are also conducted between the seats and the buffet or even at the runway while the speaker is preparing to bowl or weighing balls. SALZER, *a minor officer, has descended the stairs.* EICHMANN *sees him first and approaches him cordially.*

EICHMANN: Heil Hitler, Salzer. What's up?
SALZER: Heil Hitler, Colonel. Bad news.

They shake hands. EICHMANN *draws him downstage; the bowling goes on.*

EICHMANN:
　　Gentlemen, excuse me for a few minutes. Over here, Salzer.
　　Are you just in from Slovakia?
　　For a moment I thought you were Gerstein—
　　I'm expecting him here.
SALZER: Your secretary told me, drive
　　right out to Falkensee—nice setup here!
EICHMANN: It was about time we rated a recreation center.
　　There won't be any bombs out this way . . .
　　Well, what's wrong in Pressburg? Aren't things moving?
SALZER: No, they're not moving, sir.
　　The Church is kicking up a fuss.
EICHMANN: The *Church!* Why, that's impossible.
　　It was in Pressburg that the government
　　made no distinction between baptized Jews and others.
　　Mostly, I assume, because they have a priest
　　heading the government there. Monsignore Tiso
　　is quite an understanding man, you know.
SALZER: I know, sir. And of course
　　the first train to Auschwitz, in March,
　　did come from Pressburg.
EICHMANN (*animated*):
　　There you are—and it was the Hlinka Guard,
　　the Catholic People's Party, that rounded up
　　the Jews for us.
　　These are people you can count on, Salzer.
SALZER: They've lost their nerve all of a sudden.
　　It seems the Nuncio, the Papal Nuncio,
　　forbade them to support the deportations . . .

HIRT (*shouting as he takes a ball*):
  Come on, cut out the shoptalk, Eichmann.
  Bowling's a patriotic act, too.
EICHMANN: One second, Professor—I'll be right there.
SALZER: The Nuncio went to Tiso with the news
  that we incinerate the Jews at Lublin.
  Now Tiso calls for an investigation.
  That's why he sent me here to talk to you.
  What do we do?
EICHMANN (*agitated, pacing back and forth*):
  Investigation! What's there to investigate? Ashes?
  Damn it to hell—the Nuncio in Rumania
  is starting to stir up trouble too.
  The *bishops* in these countries don't much bother me.
  But a *Nuncio* as representative of the Vatican . . .
  There's nothing we can do, we'll have to
  take it easy in Slovakia for a while. Shit.
  All we need now is for our own bishops . . .
  If they begin to raise a stink
  about the Jews the way they did about the loonies . . .
  and if the Berlin *Nuncio* gives us trouble too—
  it's a bleak prospect. Well, Salzer,
  have a bite to eat. Helga!
  Where's Helga gone to? Come meet everyone.

He leads SALZER *over to the head of the bowling alley and introduces him. The introductions go very rapidly, with the standard phrases:* "Heil, Salzer," "Glad to know you," "Heil Hitler."

  Gentlemen, may I introduce
  Sturmführer Salzer—
  Professor Hirt, from the University of Strassburg;
  Baron von Rutta, Head of the Armaments Cartel;
  Lieutenant von Rutta—congratulate him on the Knight's
      Cross,
  Salzer.
SALZER: My heartiest congratulations, Lieutenant.
LIEUTENANT RUTTA: Thank you, Sturmführer.
EICHMANN: You know Doctor Fritsche from Auschwitz, don't you?
FRITSCHE: 'Evening, Salzer,
  nice to see you here.

EICHMANN: Colonel Serge of the General Staff;
Regierungsrat Pryzilla—Reich Ministry for the
Occupied Territories in the East.
That's it—and Doctor Littke—on furlough from Russia,
attached to the staff of the Central Army Group.
(*To* FRITSCHE *at the scoreboard.*)
So, Fritsche, put Salzer's name down on the list.
We haven't been playing long, Salzer.
You can catch up by taking a few extra shots
after you've had some refreshments.
Helga, find something extra good for Salzer.

HELGA: There's plenty here of everything—good evening.

SALZER: Hello—don't we know each other?

HELGA: I'm sure our paths have crossed.
I'm engaged to Lieutenant Wagner in Auschwitz.
Didn't we meet in Prague some time ago . . .

SALZER: I knew it. Sure, on the Hradschin.

They converse at the buffet. Colonel SERGE, *who has just bowled,
addresses* BARON RUTTA, *who has also just bowled and reappears
downstage.*

SERGE: I hear you're spending the night here, Baron, right?
There's something I had in mind to tell you, Herr Direktor—
that's chiefly what I came for.
The sort of thing that's going on
inside the fine old firm of Krupp—
the way they treat the prisoners of war
there—that's outrageous, sir.
Perhaps you've heard about the letters
we've been receiving at the High Command,
anonymous letters from the local population
about the stinking mess at Krupp's.

BARON RUTTA (*vexed*): But, Colonel, why tell that to *me*?
That's an affair for the Krupp management.

SERGE (*surly, nervous, his voice rising*):
You mean I ought to go with this to
Herr von Bülow? Him! That man is never in.
Must General von Schulenburg himself
go all the way to Essen to tell
Herr Krupp von Bohlen once and for all

to stop giving the prisoners the whip—
yes, the whip!—instead of potatoes . . .
(*As* BARON RUTTA *is about to remonstrate.*)
Baron—I—I've heard it from a reliable source:
For the past six weeks the prisoners at Krupp's
haven't been issued their potatoes.

RUTTA (*icy and precise*):
Whipping is administered only in the firm's
re-education camps. Otherwise only to the incorrigible—
the incorrigible kitchen thieves caught stealing food.
You wouldn't believe what gluttons those fellows are.
Herr von Bülow has seen to perfect order.

SERGE (*so angry that he can no longer listen*):
No sense beating around the bush, Baron.
W-W-When my horse's had nothing to eat
it can't pull the cart.
As for the other things we hear from Krupp:
about the Ukrainian women who surely,
didn't care too much for being shipped off to the Ruhr . . .

BARON RUTTA: I'm surprised at you, Colonel. For the most part
these people are outright Bolsheviks. The firm
is even planning—for prisoners who show effort,
to give incentive bonuses for extra work,
and is even setting up a cultural program . . .
to help them to appreciate their work.

SERGE (*with bitter sarcasm*):
Why, that's just dandy: old Krupp
giving culture to the Russians!

BARON RUTTA: Colonel, do you suggest the workers from the East
be treated even *better* than they are? There is a war on!
They multiply in Essen, even though
we've put a doctor in, a Russian, for abortions.
Those women simply can't be trusted.
All they think about is having relations . . .

SERGE (*carried away, throwing all caution to the winds*):
Aha, relations—relations, Baron—
I hadn't heard about that part of it.
If, after all, a young Russian girl
is, mind you, privileged to manufacture arms for Krupp
ten hours day for day,
she's certainly got no call to sleep

with her Russian after dark. Of course, of course,
you're guardians of morality . . .

EICHMANN (*who has come up to them and is half eavesdropping*):
Gentlemen, no arguments—let's bowl.
We're here to enjoy ourselves.

BARON RUTTA (*bitterly amused, prissily*):
Colonel Serge, you see, feels
that the Russian women at Krupp's
should be allowed to have healthy sex lives.
(*His voice takes on a steely ring.*)
Enough of them get themselves knocked up, Colonel,
to be able to shirk work for six weeks each time.
It's scandalous. Krupp sends the children to a home in Voerde
where they receive the best of care, with balanced diets,
butter, milk and fruit . . .

SERGE: Well, well, milk and fruit! You know,
I wouldn't mind sending my grandchildren there
for a vacation. If only some lousy liar
hadn't told me that out there in Voerde
out of a hundred and thirty-two kids
eighty-nine died . . .
I suppose those Russians can't stand our climate.
Or do you think the butter didn't agree with them?

*He gives an artificial laugh, for he is justly afraid that he has gone
too far.*

I noticed, though, that many of the kids are blond,
so they should . . .

EICHMANN: Krupp will be relieved of *those* worries,
Baron Rutta, once the branch in Auschwitz
is set up. In Auschwitz
nobody complains. And I've never heard
(*he laughs knowingly;* RUTTA *joins him*)
of any pregnancies in Auschwitz either.

FRITSCHE (*coming downstage*):
Please, gentlemen, take your turns.
Come along, Colonel Serge.

SERGE (*grateful, hastily*): Yes, I'm coming, I'm coming.

BARON RUTTA (*calling to his son, who is at the buffet*):
My boy, bowl for me this time.

EICHMANN: And you for me, Helga, will you, please?

HELGA: I won't be responsible for the result, Herr Eichmann.
EICHMANN: You'll bring me luck, I'm sure.

To BARON RUTTA, *with a gesture in the direction of* SERGE, *who is selecting a ball:*

> Don't let him rile you, Baron,
> with that humanitarian nonsense.
> If I may say so, his type is gradually
> dying out in the Army too . . .

HIRT (*calling to* SERGE):
> Slant it, Colonel—don't take your shots so straight
> or you'll be in the coffin before you know it.

Everyone laughs at SERGE'*s comic gesture.*

BARON RUTTA (*to* EICHMANN, *at the buffet*):
> I've been meaning to ask you, Colonel Eichmann,
> how our generals in Russia are reacting to your measures?
> My son's superior in the Balkans—though that's
> the Air Force, of course—has pitched right in . . .

EICHMANN: You see, Baron, that confirms
> what I often tell my associates:
> Don't overestimate the rivalry
> between the Army and the SS!
> Of course there are generals here and there
> with what I'd call an ostrich complex. They pretend
> they don't see anything when we
> move in to clean up their zones.
> But others pitch right in, as you say.
> After all, last year alone,
> when Auschwitz wasn't operating yet,
> in barely four months in Russia we were able to process
> three hundred and fifty thousand Russian children of Israel.
> And it was the Army made that possible—
> we must give credit where credit is due.
> Between you and me, it's ridiculous
> that Himmler talks of Marshal Manstein's
> Slavic racial ties because his real name
> is said to be Liwinsky, or something like that.

BARON RUTTA: Oh, really, there's time for that sort of thing
> after the victory.

EICHMANN: Right you are! Manstein is certainly
    no National Socialist. But I'd say
    he showed the right spirit
    when he told his troops in the East
    not only to observe the usual rules
    of war, but also to show understanding
    for the stern atonement that awaits the Jews.

BARON RUTTA (*smiling*):
    Don't be in too great a hurry, Herr Eichmann,
    for otherwise there won't be any labor
    when Krupp goes into production in Auschwitz.

They begin to move away, but linger because the DOCTOR *has appeared on the stairs, and* HIRT *calls out to him.*

HIRT: Come on, Doctor, give us a song!
    These fellows here are talking too much shop.
    Come on, let's have some entertainment.
    You're not so proud
    to be asked more than once.

EICHMANN (*producing a harmonica from his coat pocket*):
    Yes, let's have a song, Doctor.
    I have my harmonica with me.

DOCTOR (*pointing to* PRYZILLA *in his yellow tunic*):
    Let the canary bird over there sing for us!

PRYZILLA (*cravenly*): Impossible, Doctor—even in school,
    impossible—never could sing a tune. Bad people, ha, ha,
    bad people, says the poet, have no songs. . . .

DOCTOR: True enough—that's why I have a whole songbook full . . .

He addresses the larger circle which has gradually gathered around the stairs; SERGE *is not among them.*

    You'll give me claustrophobia, boys—why
    crowd me. I was recently in Paris
    (*ironically*)—in Greater Germany's Amusement Park,
    as the Führer says.
    Hardly a Christian burg. Eichmann, you know
    the tune for Poor Little Lisa?
    Pretty, isn't it! Would do for a Christmas party
    for our pisspot girls in the auxiliaries.
    I've got a song for you—unfortunately adapted

by parsons of both sexes—
of both religious faiths, I meant to say—
for the youth—the more experienced youth, of course . . .

Guffaws. The DOCTOR *hums a melody.* EICHMANN *hums along, then improvises on his harmonica. The* DOCTOR *begins with gruesome harmlessness . . .*

It is typical of him that his verses can shock even these hard-boiled men—professionals so cold-blooded that they could discuss the plans for the gas chambers during their meals at the office, as Reitlinger reports. "The horrible cynicism of these conferences exhausted Nebe so much that he had twice to go on sick-leave with a nervous breakdown." And the Herr Nebe in question was no "weakling"; as leader of an extermination group in Russia he had rendered honorable service in the cause, before he joined the conspirators of July 20, 1944. Swagger stick in hand, the DOCTOR *recites and sings in varying manners, the first lines with diabolic sanctimoniousness, the later lines cynically and offhandedly, as if he were improvising them at the spur of the moment. As he sings he slowly descends the stairs.*

She had no room and she had no tent.
The hotels were full, not a bench by the Seine.
The parks were crowded wherever we went—
Oh, where can we go, Madeleine?

For fear she might be seen by a compatriot—
For we were meaning to collaborate—
She led the way to an ideal spot.
It was in Père-Lachaise, right near the gate.

It's the swankiest graveyard in gay Paree,
Where the mighty of France all sleep serene:
Héloise and Abelard, Molière, de Vigny.
That's where I laid Madeleine.

My baby hung her panties and slip
On Thorwaldsen's noble statue of Christ.
But just to show she wasn't flip,
She wrapped her dress round the Saviour's eyes.

Some Christian pigs who are legally wed
Have a crucifix hanging right over their bed
And the things Christ sees would turn His cheeks red—
You'd think they'd be ashamed, she said.

For her delicacy I kissed her heart,
Which was halfway between her neck and toes.
Then—suddenly I gave a start—
Poor joke: Proust's ghost arose.

Chopin and Wilde stood watch while we screwed,
The Polack and the Englishman grinning,
And beating the time, as gloriously nude,
Madeleine and I went on sinning.

Spurred on by these notable pillars of art,
Our lust reached its feverish crest,
When a frightening vision gripped tightly my heart
And Madeleine sank down on my chest.

The self-assurance with which he twits the company, as he alone would dare to do, suggests that he is a mythical figure—incomprehensible, not answerable to a mortal superior. While singing he goes up to each of the men in turn and flings a few words at him like a verdict. He particularly dislikes "that crapper," BARON RUTTA. *He has conceived the blasphemy of Christ solely for* RUTTA's *benefit—otherwise he would consider blasphemy a total waste of time. His careless and insulting manner, especially in the fourth from the last line, reflects his attitude toward this band of criminals whose master he is.*

As for the vision that the three provided—
Don't ask! I'd rather end my song right there.
For the moral of the story, I've decided,
Is one you fellows might find hard to bear.
(Cassandra never saw the like, no sir!)

You still think life's a breeze. Not me.
I've had it up to here.
My tongue is hanging out, as you can see
it's thick and parched. Maybe
I need a good, cold stein of beer,
Our favorite German booze . . .
Or could it be
My neck is in the noose
Already—just like *yours*?

Nobody claps. After the last line the DOCTOR *bows jauntily and leaves.* EICHMANN *had stopped accompanying him on the harmonica fairly early in the song. Strained silence.*

EICHMANN (*embarrassed*): He likes to liven things up
    just so he can give us a jolt.
    Let's get back to our bowling.
BARON RUTTA (*extremely annoyed*):
    God knows, I didn't think that was very witty.
    In bad taste, to go dragging in
    the spirits of three enemy countries.
    I wish I knew what he was driving at . . .
HIRT (*appeasingly*): Why, Baron, don't take it so seriously.
    It was just a joke, nothing but a song—
    He didn't have anything particular in mind—ah . . .

He has just bowled; now, as FRITSCHE *sets down his score, he calls out:*

    Two strokes? Do I really get two?
    Just one more and I'm dead.

He reappears downstage, where BARON RUTTA *is standing alone.*

    That damned song still on your mind?
BARON RUTTA (*firmly, coldly*): Professor, is it safe for us to talk
    when this doctor is around? Doesn't he strike you
    as—possibly . . . an *agent provocateur*?
    A decent German conscious of his nation's honor
    would scarcely take such a tone . . .
HIRT: Now, Baron, how's anyone to figure out
    what goes on in a man's mind?
    You have to tell by actions. (*Confidentially.*) The Doctor
    does the sorting in Auschwitz,
    on the railroad platform. I mean,
    he sorts out the Jews for the ovens . . .
    Satisfied?
BARON RUTTA: What! And then sings this seditious song?
    The man's an enigma, Professor, an enigma . . .

LITTKE, SERGE, PRYZILLA *and others have bowled.*

HIRT (*to* RUTTA): Go ahead, Baron—and forget it.
    Herr Fritsche, why so quiet? Anything wrong?

He grips LITTKE's *shoulder.*

    Here, Littke, won't you relieve Fritsche
    at the scoreboard for a while?

FRITSCHE: Yes, I wouldn't mind having a bite to eat.

LITTKE: *Jawohl, Herr Professor.* Of course, Fritsche.

HIRT (*coming downstage with* FRITSCHE, *then over to the buffet*):
    What's up? I know you're a pretty quiet guy,
    but tonight—anything the matter?

FRITSCHE: Nothing definite. It's just that I have to go back—
    after a wonderful furlough with the family at
    Tegernsee. I've been wondering, too,
    whether I ought not volunteer
    for the Eastern front.
    I'm sick of Auschwitz.

HIRT (*reassuringly*): You're just having your days, Fritsche.
    Men have their days just like women.
    A lot of good it would do your family
    if you got yourself bumped off in Russia.
    No, stay where you are in Auschwitz, my friend.
    Or better yet, come to Strassburg for a week
    some time. Visit my Institute.
    That's it, we'll fix up an official trip for you.
    You'll surely have a couple of interesting skulls
    coming up one of these days.
    Bring me the critters *alive* for my collection.
    Then you'll have a reason for the trip.
    I've got to take photos and measurements;
    they can be liquidated later in Strassburg.

He points to LITTKE, *who has just bowled and is returning to the scoreboard.*

    I've commissioned Littke there
    to bring me some real commissar skulls, from Russia.

FRITSCHE: Of course I'd like very much to come
    to Strassburg some time, Professor, if you think
    an order to that effect could be drawn up . . .

HIRT: Sure it can! I'll see you have distractions.
    Why, the *Cathedral* alone!—I'd trade you all
    Berlin for that . . . Didn't I hear something
    about your being musical, Fritsche?

FRITSCHE: I might say I am. Heydrich at the cello—

He points to the death mask; they step up to the photograph together.

myself on the viola. In March, just a short while
before the assassination, we played quartets—
on the Hradschin.

HIRT (*looks at the mask for a moment in silent tribute; then,
softly*):
Yes, yes, Heydrich—between you and me, he had
the Jew's nose for artistic quality.
Purified, naturally, by the hardness
of the *Aryan* component in his blood.
An unusual man. I was once present
When he gave a reading of a Kleist story. Masterly.
(*Louder.*) Fine—just fine: you'll visit me.
Maybe there'll be a concert in the Cathedral.
You ought to hear the B-minor Mass there some time—
heavenly music. The text is rot,
of course, but rot in Latin—
doesn't get on your nerves.
But that Gloria Dei—my friend,
that's just the greatest thing there is. That's the way
I want to celebrate the final victory—
in my own quiet way.
Just the B-minor Mass—but in Strassburg.
Nowhere else—in Strassburg!
And no speeches, no speeches, after all
these sacrifices.
And then, maybe, just once, a chance
to show the Führer my skulls . . . Littke!

LITTKE (*with dutiful alacrity*): Professor?
(*To Lieutenant* RUTTA, *who has just bowled.*)
Would you mind scoring for a moment, Lieutenant?

LIEUTENANT RUTTA: Gladly—give me the chalk.

LITTKE (*to* FRITSCHE, *when he reaches* HIRT'*s side*):
Herr Fritsche, it's your turn—and yours too,
Professor—you come next.

HIRT: The next ball will be the death of me.
I don't have my eye tonight.

FRITSCHE *has gone to bowl; he reappears downstage, rejoining*
HIRT *and* LITTKE.

HIRT (*sternly*): You musical too, Littke, like Herr Fritsche?

LITTKE (*alarmed; he is anxious to make the best possible impression*):

No, Professor, I'm afraid not—hardly at all.

HIRT (*sternly*): But it's not just medicine and nothing else,
I hope. You've got some outside interests, eh?

LITTKE (*sounding not very credible*):

When I was younger I was always pretty good
at drawing, Professor. In fact I had . . .

HIRT (*placated*): Good, very important. Keep in practice.
A surgeon has to know how to draw, absolutely . . .

He opens a bottle of beer.

Or, let's say, he's got to have
a sure hand, dead sure. You can
draw my skulls and the Cathedral
and the picturesque roofs . . . Goethe
in his time made some wonderful sketches. But first
(*with the greed of a philatelist*)
you've got to bring me more skulls. This is
the chance, the *last* chance, I tell you.
Science, Littke, has hardly a single
decent commissar skull!
What's become of our whole commissar order?

He pours a beer for LITTKE *too, chews and goes on talking.*

You're getting a *direct* order from
Reichsführer Himmler—I guess that Army Group
of yours knows what that means! Everything that's picked up
from now on in the way of Jewish-Bolshevist commissars . . .

LITTKE: But they don't *have to* be Jews, do they,
Professor?

HIRT: Of course not, no, any commissars,
no matter what, Russian or Jew—though Jews
are more interesting, of course, aren't they?
The main thing is: in the future no on-the-spot
liquidations of commissars. They're to be brought
alive to the SS military police.
You'll have your armored truck and driver
and will be responsible for the safety
of all the material . . .
Above all—

(*very anxiously, with pedantic emphasis*)
above all, don't injure the head. For heaven's sake
don't injure the head! I'll give you
blanks to fill out. You'll enter on them—
as far as *possible,* of course—
origin, date of birth and other
personal data. Then go ahead with the measurements—
photographic and anthropological.
Only after you've got all that
is the Russki to be liquidated. You cut off the head
from the trunk and . . .

LITTKE (*in a cold sweat*):
Jawohl, Herr Professor. May I inquire, sir,
whether—whether I . . . personally . . .
(*He hesitates, fearful that he has again made a bad impression.*)
after I've done the measurements, must I
see to the execution myself . . .

EICHMANN: Professor, duty is duty. You must bowl.

HIRT (*to* LITTKE *as he goes to the rack*):
Of course not—the SS police take care of that.
Don't worry, Littke . . . All right, I'm coming,
I'm on my way. Though I'm afraid
this will make the last stroke on my coffin . . .

He bowls; shouts of glee, for HIRT *is "dead." Shouts from offstage.*

"Professor—order a round!"
"They carried a corpse to the cool green meadow."
"Not this war beer—you might just as well
pour it straight into the chamber pot."

HIRT: Right you are! Helga, what else d'you have?
Helga, how about a double schnapps
all around?

HELGA: Are you drinking too? You're dead, you know.

She pours; EICHMANN *has started the song; most of the others join in.*

They carried a corpse to the cool green meadow,
Going home, he's going home . . .

BARON RUTTA (*making an effort to "thaw out," recites the following doggerel*):
Be honest as the day is long
And pay for every piece of cheese.

But after dark there's nothing wrong
In grabbing anything you please . . .

They go on bowling, with increased intensity.

BARON RUTTA (*at the buffet with* HIRT):
So very glad, Professor Hirt, that we've
had the chance to meet here. I'm tired
of being nothing but the specialist.
The wider scene—basically, that's what interests me,
even nowadays, in the midst of the war.
We men in industry are far too much
caught up in material things. Before you know it
you can do nothing but read production figures.
Tell me—what is the ultimate purpose
of the skull collection you've been making
in Strassburg? What does science hope for from it . . . ?
HIRT: We're idealists, Baron, and certainly don't
ask about ultimate purposes right off.
Even today your genuine scientist can't
lose himself in utilitarian considerations alone.
But still, you know, from the photographs
and the measurements of the head and finally the skull
our team in Strassburg can carry out *exacting*
researches in comparative anatomy.
Racial stock, pathological phenomena
related to shape and size of brain—all expressed
in a *single* formula: in days to come our grandchildren
should know why the final solution of the Jewish question
was absolutely necessary and in the nature of things
from the *scientific* point of view as well as others.
BARON RUTTA: I see that quite clearly—yes, of course.
HIRT: Do I understand you get to Auschwitz often, Baron?
BARON RUTTA: Now and then I meet directors of I. G. Farben there.
The plant for Krupp is still
only in the planning stage, you know.
HIRT: Fine, fine—so glad you take an interest.
Next time you're in Auschwitz, Baron,
ask for Dr. Beger—Captain Bruno Beger—
yes, write it down—give him my regards
and ask him to show you his collection
of skeletons. Enormously interesting.
Let him show you the specimens he's still working on

as well. Seventy-nine Jews, thirty Jewesses, two Poles,
and even four absolutely authentic Central Asiatics.
He's got them in quarantine now. Aha, here comes
my dear colleague who likes to pull my leg
because I, as a pathologist . . . what's up,
Doctor?—you always see him
with that kind of supercilious smile on his mug,
as though he knew more than he was telling.
What *do* you know, you scoundrel?

DOCTOR (*very engagingly, in a "defeatist" tone*):
Don't know a thing—only that all my work
has been in vain, like every kind of heroism.

HIRT (*sensitive about his principles, now that he is good and drunk*):
What's that you say? Science is never,
never, never, never in vain!

LITTKE: Baron Rutta—please, it's your turn.

HIRT: Go along with you—I'm out of it.
Blessed are the dead—good luck, Baron.

BARON RUTTA (*going to the rack, with pretended indignation*):
Hasn't anyone bowled a single strike yet?
What a pack of heroes we are tonight!

HIRT: Your little ditty made him pretty sore . . .

DOCTOR (*amused*): That crapper! I was hoping it would.
I'd like to dissect him alive some day
with his own coupon clippers . . . What do you think
he makes on the war every day, on the average?

HIRT: Let him be, the old eunuch. You rubbed his Catholicism
the wrong way—Rhineland nobility, you know!

DOCTOR: Parchments proving venereal disease in the family
since the year one thousand and eighteen, eh?
He's the kind to write in his ledger: With God!
With God for Führer, country and profits . . .

HIRT (*laughing*): You're sure in a mood tonight. All the same,
he produced a fine, upstanding son. I'm still waiting
to hear about some progeny from you, my friend.

DOCTOR: Idealist that I am, I recently
sterilized myself. Wanted to see what it was like.

HIRT: Seriously, though, how far *have* you come with that?

DOCTOR (*matter-of-fact, but indifferent*):
As far as I'm concerned, we're ready to go.
Painless for women, takes no time at all.

It was meant for Jewesses married to Aryans.
I could sterilize them on the assembly line.

HIRT: Really—well, my congratulations.

DOCTOR: Congratulate the ladies—but for the present
nobody dares to start on them. On March 6
the Propaganda Ministry raised objections
even to forcible divorces of such marriages
because they're afraid of a protest from the Vatican.

HIRT: A protest from the Vatican? Why would they?

BARON RUTTA *has returned.*

DOCTOR: You see, those marriages in many cases
were sealed by priests of the Holy Roman Church.

HIRT: Goebbels scared of the Vatican?

DOCTOR: An old Jesuit never forgets the power of Rome . . .

All three laugh. But BARON RUTTA, *who takes this sarcasm rather ill, says sourly:*

BARON RUTTA: The Armaments Cartel has other problems.
But as a Rhinelander I can still be a good Catholic,
even today, since the Pope by his wise conduct
has spared me the necessity of being a bad German
at the same time. As far as I know, he does not
meddle in German internal affairs.

EICHMANN *joins them. The* DOCTOR *goes over to* HELGA, *who has been talking with* LIEUTENANT RUTTA, *and draws her along to the bowling alley.* HELGA *bowls.*

HIRT: Pacelli, Baron—there's a prince for you.
That Concordat he made with us
after we took over here—that was a stroke of luck.
On the other hand think of Galen, that blabbermouth.
I was fit to be tied, let me tell you, when the Führer
called off the euthanasia program just . . .
just because of the rabble-rouser of a bishop.

EICHMANN: When we came to take him to the interrogation,
the fox put on his vestments, clutched his crook
and popped the miter on his head—anyhow, you know,
he's as big as the statue of Arminius.
Then he says to the fellows: "I'll go on foot—
I won't enter your car of my own free will."

At that the Gestapo gave it up.
They were afraid of the populace in Münster.
Rightly so—think of the *fuss* the people
would have made.
To my mind, the Führer shows his stature
the way he spares religious feelings in wartime.
My father, for example, is minister
of the Protestant congregation in Linz.
He, too, couldn't grasp that we only wanted
to release the insane from their suffering.
What's the sense of angering the people
while there's a war on. We've got time.
It doesn't cost us anything to wait.

BARON RUTTA (*laughing*): Oh, but it costs the economy plenty,
Herr Eichmann, to go on feeding the insane!
If you ask me, it makes more sense
to feed the Jews as long as they can work.
I tell you, gentlemen, we see it every day,
one Jew is worth more to industry
than two Ukrainians, if only because he understands us.
He speaks our language after all, and doesn't sabotage.
And he's cheaper, too; we don't have to bring him
two thousand miles to put him to work.

EICHMANN: Are you bringing in still more Ukrainians?
I thought I'd heard, Baron,
that the opposite course was being taken now:
not Ukrainians to Krupp, but Krupp to the Ukraine.

BARON RUTTA (*slyly, half alarmed, half flattered; he indicates the
others*):
Please, gentlemen—this calls for discretion!
You can imagine that young Krupp von Bohlen,
as well as Flick, Röchling—the whole cartel,
are not, God knows, terribly keen about those
Russian plants.
That kind of sponsoring can be expensive,
let me tell you. And the amounts
that have to be invested!

HIRT (*laughing aloud; then, as* RUTTA *puts his finger to his lips,
subsiding*):
How about it, Eichmann? We two wouldn't mind
laying our mitts on a piece of that Donets Basin, hey?

Laughter. PRYZILLA, *who has bowled, comes up behind* RUTTA'*s back and eavesdrops. They are all standing at the buffet.*

HIRT (*so tipsy that he has forgotten about "discretion," now actually draws* PRYZILLA *into the conversation*):
You see, this fellow only needs to hear
that something's being handed out, and he's right there!
Eichmann, no cash comes our way . . . c'mon,
let's have another drink. . . .

PRYZILLA (*harsh, jerky, staccato speech, rolled r's*):
Baron, did you fly to the Ukraine
with Alfried von Krupp and Röchling,
the financier?

BARON RUTTA (*coldly, ironically*): Why no, my dear sir, no. Please
do not overestimate my connections
with such distinguished gentlemen.
I don't have anything to do
with Krupp directly . . .

PRYZILLA (*aggressively*): Then let me tell you that Alfried Krupp
von Bohlen personally will introduce
his men into the official German bureaus
in the Ukraine. He personally, I am certain.
And you know what that means, Baron.
The name of Krupp's enough. Quite enough!
Everybody's chasing down the best factories
so that they'll be in full possession
later on, when the official distribution begins.

BARON RUTTA (*icily, condescendingly*):
But, my dear sir, I don't know what it is
that so enrages you. Herr von Krupp . . .

PRYZILLA (*trembling with "righteousness"; he produces each syllable even more jerkily than before*):
You know what the cartel has its hands on? The
cartel is already established in Stalino.
Krupp inspecting—in Dniepropetrovsk, of course . . .
The Molotov Works!—just fine—just—fine!

BARON RUTTA (*with infinite haughtiness*):
Yes, yes, but *why* not? I do not see . . .

PRYZILLA: We in the Ministry—excuse me, but
we *also* have the good of Germany at heart!
The interest of the Reich! The *people*

are paying for this war with their blood.
The people ought to profit—not just private companies!
If they're divvying up already, what's there left
for the Göring National Trust, say?
What's left for the Volkswagen Works, say?
What's left, say, for . . .

EICHMANN (*loudly*): One moment, quiet, gentlemen—
please be quiet for a moment. Air raid!

The distant sound of sirens is heard. Everyone listens. Then several of the men hastily rush out. Now the sirens begin howling loudly in Falkensee itself. EICHMANN has come downstage.

SERGE (*goes up to him*): Colonel, I'll thank you now
for your hospitality—enjoyed very much
having—having a chance to talk to the Baron.
But now . . . my family is in town.
May I—I'd like to say goodbye now . . .

EICHMANN (*shaking hands with him*):
It was a pleasure—but, Colonel, do you
really want to drive out in the middle of the raid?

PRYZILLA (*quickly to* SERGE):
Will you take me along, Colonel? I live
in Charlottenburg and really must . . . Heil Hitler,
Herr Eichmann! Baron, I suppose
you'll be staying here in Falkensee overnight?
May I telephone you tomorrow, around nine?

BARON RUTTA (*icily*):
Why certainly, Herr Regierungsrat. But as I say,
I have no information whatsoever. Heil Hitler.
Heil Hitler, Colonel Serge—see you in Essen.

PRYZILLA (*turns twice around his own axis—he looks like a corkscrew—and blurts out repeatedly*):
Heil Hitler, Heil Hitler, Heil Hitler . . .

SERGE: Good night, all . . .

Both leave. LITTKE *and* SALZER *have not reappeared. The* DOCTOR *and* HELGA *vanished as soon as the sirens started.*

LIEUTENANT RUTTA:
Those planes arrived right on schedule tonight.
Papa—the air's stale with smoke in here. I'm going
outside with Herr Fritsche for a few minutes.

Want to see how they approach Berlin.
Would you care to come?

BARON RUTTA: Yes, I'll just fetch my coat.

All three go out.

HIRT (*very drunk, calls after them*):
Keep your eyes peeled for where the Doctor
and Helga have gone off to. Wouldn't want the two
to be catchin' the sniffles.

He gives a nasty laugh and then claps EICHMANN *on the shoulder.*

I'll have another turn at bowling—
we can't shoot any of the bombers down.
No sense getting excited—I'm bowling.

EICHMANN: Yes, go ahead, Professor, I'll join you.

He has turned to GERSTEIN, *who has entered the room with a cautious step while* HIRT *was speaking about* HELGA, *and who now reports:*

GERSTEIN: Colonel—back from special assignment,
Treblinka, Belzec, Maidanek.
I was told
you wanted to see me immediately . . .

EICHMANN: Why, Gerstein—at last, at last!
I'm on pins and needles to hear. Did it work all right?

To HIRT, *who has come over to them, a ball in his hand:*

Lieutenant Gerstein—Professor Hirt
of the University of Strassburg.
Herr Gerstein's background is both in medicine and engineering,
he's head of the technical disinfection service.
Last year he stopped the epidemics of spotted fever
in our barracks.

HIRT: Heard about it, heard about it, my friend.
A technical genius, that's what you are.
Glad to meet you—Heil, Herr Gerstein!

GERSTEIN (*ambiguously*): Heil Hitler, Herr Professor—when
will you get around to publishing a paper—
for professionals only, of course—
on your collection of skulls?

HIRT: What an idea—it would be nice, though—
  my lifelong dream! But for the present,
  unfortunately, it has to be kept secret.
GERSTEIN: Oh, people exaggerate. There wouldn't be any harm
  in having a pamphlet printed
  for use in the medical schools.
HIRT: Delighted to hear your interest. I'll try . . .
EICHMANN: Let's get down to business, gentlemen.
  Gerstein was in Belzec to find out
  whether we can't handle the final solution
  more efficiently, and above all more quickly
  with Cyclon B.
HIRT: I thought you were working with carbon monoxide?
GERSTEIN: Yes, so far. But Diesel exhaust gas
  is useless; the generators are always breaking down.
  (*Sharply, with undisguised outrage.*)
  Why, Colonel Eichmann, I myself have seen
  the people waiting in the chambers
  for almost three full hours
  before the Diesel motors got started.
  And then—it's inconceivable—it took
  another half hour for them to die!

EICHMANN *is horrified, speechless.*

HIRT (*in a booming voice*):
  Why, boys, that's grisly. Do it humanely!
  Why don't you simply shoot 'em down
  the way they do in Russia?
EICHMANN (*agitated, no longer in the least pedantic*):
  Shoot them! Easier said than done, Professor.
  You try shooting at forty railroad cars
  full of a naked, screaming horde!
  Although, in fact, they seldom scream.
  Most of them stand fatalistically
  before the pits, only their eyes show shock
  that this is actually done to them . . .
  That's even worse. Say what you will,
  en masse their bearing is, well, simply Aryan.
  But still, just picture it: the grandmother, her grandson
  in her arms; the teenage girl
  calling to mind the first date you undressed.

And then the pregnant ones!
The toughest rifleman can't stand
that sort of thing for long, not even
when he's doused himself with schnapps so that
his blood is ninety per cent alcohol. No—*shooting* is impos-
    sible.
Why, it would give the men insomnia
and leave them impotent, Professor.
Just bear in mind, we have a good eight million
to process in Europe, and we must finish it
before the war is over.

HIRT (*plaintively*):
Well then, a more efficient method *must* be found.
We certainly can't bungle through the way
Gerstein describes it. Impossible!
You ought to leave the whole thing
to us doctors, Eichmann.

EICHMANN: That's exactly why Gerstein
has just made this experiment with prussic acid.
How did *that* work, Gerstein?

GERSTEIN: It didn't, sir; I couldn't get
the testing off the ground.

EICHMANN: But, man, you had your orders!
You mean you didn't even *try*?

GERSTEIN: I couldn't, Colonel. First of all,
I was opposed at every turn by Captain Wirth
of Belzec. He urged me many times not to propose
to Berlin any changes in his installations.

EICHMANN: Why, that's ridiculous!
As far back as a year ago—yes,
in September—I proposed to Höss
in Auschwitz that we try
Cyclon B on six hundred Russians.
We sealed the windows of the penal block
hermetically with mud, and tossed the crystals through the
    door.

GERSTEIN (*pulling himself together with a violent effort*):
But then . . . on that occasion, sir,
as Captain Wirth told me just yesterday,
some of the Russians were still very much alive
the following afternoon.

EICHMANN: But after all, Gerstein, that was a *first* experiment!
>   You don't get speed by magic. After all,
>   the room was jammed as full
>   as a pail of herrings.

He falls silent, indicating the loudspeaker at the back of the room, from which the following announcement comes:

> "Attention, attention, here is the air raid report: The British light bomber formation is approaching Hanover on a course to the southeast. The heavy bomber formation approaching Berlin from the southwest has reached the belt of anti-aircraft defenses surrounding the capital."

EICHMANN: Going to be some nasty fireworks!
>   How could the others have driven into town—
>   preposterous! Where in the world is Helga?
HIRT (*cheerful*): Ask the Doctor where she is.
>   He said he was going to help her
>   carry her bags down to the cellar . . .
>   I guess they've got to sort out her underthings first.

He yawns cavernously, unbuttons his jacket and stretches out in an armchair, feet on another chair. Sleepily, rather to himself, he says:

> Things starting to pop already?
> When are those others going to come down?
EICHMANN (*to* GERSTEIN, *reproachfully*):
>   Then your whole trip was for nothing?
GERSTEIN (*firmly*): Not at all, sir. Although the prussic acid
>   was already beginning to disintegrate.
>   I couldn't have carried out the experiment anyhow.
>   I made sure it was buried carefully.
>   But in my own specialty,
>   disinfection, I was able to . . .

The rumble of the bomber squadrons attacking Berlin now swells to a roar; if it can be done, the audience should hear the anti-aircraft guns raising a barrier around Berlin. The light flickers, goes out once, but comes on again immediately. EICHMANN *points tensely to the ceiling; no one speaks for a moment.*

EICHMANN (*suspiciously, with even a touch of sarcasm*):
>   Prussic acid received
>   fresh from the factory just the week before—

disintegrates so fast, you say?
Strange, Gerstein!

GERSTEIN (*meeting his eyes, begins an elaborate explanation*):
You see, sir, once the acid starts—
with all the heat and all that jogging—
the ride over those dreadful Polish roads . . .

EICHMANN (*lays a hand on his shoulder*):
Oh yes, I don't doubt it happened.
You're the chemist, not me. But it didn't exactly
make you *mad,* did it, Gerstein, old jailbird.
Don't take it amiss (*laughing*), but you really weren't *mad*
that . . . well, that you couldn't try out the stuff!

GERSTEIN (*with convincing indignation, in an extremely official
tone*):
Sir! If your allusion to my spell
in concentration camp is meant as a new
expression of distrust, then I request
a formal disciplinary hearing.

Very rapidly, with a pretense of being deeply offended, as EICH-
MANN *waves this aside in alarm:*

I thought that on the basis of my achievements
in the disinfection service, my probation . . .

EICHMANN (*without suspicion*):
Why, Gerstein, can't you take a joke!
I trust you one-hundred per cent . . . Helga!
Come, enough shoptalk!
Have something to eat, Gerstein. Helga,
will you be so good . . .

HELGA *has appeared on the stairs, dressed in a light summer coat,
carrying a suitcase which* EICHMANN *promptly takes from her.*

HELGA: Were you looking for me? I telephoned
my fiancé in Auschwitz. The Doctor had a call
to make there anyhow, so that gave me
a chance to talk to Günter.

She smiles, indicating HIRT, *who is snoring voluptuously.*

EICHMANN: Enviable—he can sleep like Napoleon.
GERSTEIN: Good evening, Fräulein, how are you?
HELGA: Oh, Herr Gerstein—all right, if only the bombers

She gestures toward the ceiling, then rapidly fixes a plate of cold cuts for GERSTEIN.

> didn't upset me so. . . .
> What a dreadful racket there is tonight!
> Herr Eichmann, my fiancé says I ought
> to come to Auschwitz as operator in the Signal Corps.
> He says I should get out of Berlin,
> on account of the raids . . .

EICHMANN: What!—Oh well, a fiancé's wish is a command.
> But we'll be sorry to lose you here . . . Where are . . .
> (*turns nervously*) . . . where the devil are . . .

GERSTEIN (*to* HELGA):
> Stay in Berlin! Auschwitz is . . . not a place for you.
> There won't be any bombs in Falkensee.

The conversation halts; the roar is terrible.

EICHMANN (*beginning again*):
> Where are the Ruttas and all the others?
> They'd do better . . . Good Lord,
> there must be several *wings* of them. Hundreds . . .

The light flickers briefly and flares very brightly; the others now come rushing down the stairs precipitously, without the DOCTOR. *An aerial mine descends, not very far away. The characteristic whistling noise is heard, mounting to a tornado-like howl.*

EICHMANN (*shouts*): Look out!

As it strikes, the light goes out completely.

CURTAIN

Scene Three

The following morning. GERSTEIN's *apartment in Berlin W35.* GERSTEIN, *in an old SS uniform, stands on a stepladder, a trowel in hand, mending a long crack in the wall. He scoops the plaster from a used marmalade tub. He is smoking as he works. Newspapers are spread out at the foot of the ladder.*

The room bears many marks of the severe air raid the night before. A fallen lamp is still lying on the floor. A picture, badly torn, is leaning with its face to the wall. Cardboard has been tacked over the window at the back of the stage, which looks out on the street, but is open at the moment, revealing a ruin across the street, evidently left by a raid some time ago. The room's other window, at the right of the door, is undamaged, as are its curtains. A large carpet lies rolled up diagonally across the room. The simple furnishings of a man's room have been pushed together in one place so that the splinters of glass, dirt, bits of plaster and tatters of wallpaper can be swept up. The sweeping is done by a man of about thirty, in civilian dress, who looks older than he is. He is a Jew named JACOBSON *whom* GERSTEIN *is hiding. He speaks cautiously, timidly; his movements are somewhat awkward. It is evident from his manner that he misses freedom; he also looks as if he has not been in the fresh air for a long time. Both men work in silence.* JACOBSON, *too, smokes a cigarette. The noise of a big city can be heard, although not very intrusively; after a while, from far away, come the fanfares of an approaching parade of Hitler Youth.*

GERSTEIN: Can we close the window now?
JACOBSON: The air is still so dusty; a minute more.

He goes into the next room and brings back two pails filled with trash, and a dust pan.

There, now, the place is fairly clean again.
Herr Gerstein, why don't you let *me*
plaster the wall, there's nothing else to keep me busy.
With the window covered over
nobody can see me on the ladder.
GERSTEIN: All right—if you would like to, by all means.
I'll take the pails down to the yard.

He steps down from the ladder and closes the window, hands the trowel to JACOBSON, *who climbs the ladder and sets to work.*

I must say, Jacobson, I felt concern for you last night,
a raid as bad as that, and you can't
even go down to the cellar.
JACOBSON (*smiling*): Lucky my parents
can still go to the cellar in their house.
Would you drive by a little later
and see whether their house came through the raid?

GERSTEIN (*his back to* JACOBSON): Gladly, Herr Jacobson.
JACOBSON: Thanks. It wasn't any fun, I must admit,
    when window glass began to fly last night.
    But I'd sooner catch it here than—
    than in Auschwitz.
    Forgive me, please, I know that's very selfish.
    But how much longer can I stay with you?

GERSTEIN *hands him another cigarette. They cannot go on talking because of the blare of the band. But now, as the column of marchers passes directly by the house, it begins singing. In spite of the closed windows, the song penetrates into the room.*

> Es zittern die morschen Knochen
> der Welt vor dem grossen Krieg.
> Wir haben die Ketten zerbrochen,
> für uns war's ein grosser Sieg.
> Wir werden weiter marschieren,
> wenn alles in Scherben fällt,
> denn heute gehört uns Deutschland
> und morgen die ganze Welt.

GERSTEIN (*glancing briefly into the street, with intense disgust*):
    They have to have their music all the time. Even in Auschwitz
    they've organized a band of Jewish women
    who must play Viennese waltzes
    while victims for the gas are picked.

Both fall silent. After a while GERSTEIN *says reassuringly*:

    I'll have a passport for you
    before the house is bombed to smithereens.
    They won't come looking for you here, unless
    they get suspicious about me, my own
    past record of imprisonment
    in a concentration camp.
    (*Smiling.*) Too bad you're just a shade too dark
    to pass for a typical Swede.
    I haven't yet been able to make contact
    with any Spaniards or Italians.
JACOBSON (*as he plasters the wall*): Next time you see the Swede,
    the one here at the Embassy,
    you'd better have a passport issued
    for yourself. Go off to Sweden.

Only your wife would know you've gotten out.
Officially, you'll just go down as missing.

GERSTEIN (*pauses in his sweeping*):
Go into exile just like that? My God,
I see men dying in the chambers every hour.
As long as there is still the slightest hope
that I can save a single one of you
I have to face the chance that later on
I may seem the spit and image of the murderers.

JACOBSON: Your visit to the Nuncio was the last
risk you should take. It's time for you to go
to England by way of Sweden. Here, by now,
it's very likely they found out about you.

GERSTEIN (*with a sphinxlike smile*):
Found out about me? Not a chance.
No one has found out about me yet.
It may be that they have their eye on me—
that worries me, sometimes, especially
for my family's sake and yours.

JACOBSON: You'd better telephone your wife
before the daily communiqué reports
that Berlin's had another raid.
No need to let her know about the wrecked apartment.
She's got enough to worry her.

GERSTEIN: I'll have the call to Tübingen placed
at the office; they'll put it through without delay.
I hope I'll have a chance to drive back home
over the weekend . . . Have you enough to eat?

JACOBSON: Yes, quite enough, thank you.

GERSTEIN: You really must tell me if you're hungry.
You're not depriving me at all, you know.
I get enough to eat at headquarters.

JACOBSON: Thank you again, Herr Gerstein.
But I would appreciate a few more books . . .
Let me give you some money . . .

He takes out his wallet.

And maybe you could try once more
to find a Russian grammar for me . . .

GERSTEIN: Oh yes. Hold on to your money
until I know what the books will cost.

As for the grammar, I'm sure I can locate one secondhand.
Well—let's go on.

JACOBSON *picks up the trowel,* GERSTEIN *the pail, intending to carry it down. Just as* GERSTEIN *is about to leave the room, the doorbell rings. Both show their nervousness. Without a word,* JACOBSON *jumps down from the ladder and flees into the adjoining room.* GERSTEIN *closes the door behind him. The bell rings again.* GERSTEIN *goes out. He can be heard opening the hall door and saying:*

Heil Hitler—oh, it's *you,* Doctor.
DOCTOR: How are you, Gerstein. Have you heard? It's frightful. . . .
GERSTEIN: What's happened?

During this exchange he has admitted the DOCTOR *and closed the door behind him. Rapid footsteps in the hall. The* DOCTOR, *in a smart long black cape with silver clasps and chain, has preceded* GERSTEIN *into the room and now says breathlessly:*

DOCTOR: I suppose the bombs knocked out your radio.
Then you don't know . . .
GERSTEIN: Speak up, Doctor, I have no idea.
DOCTOR: Assassination of Hitler?—Göring and Himmler
were also on board—a plane crash.
GERSTEIN (*stunned by this turn of affairs, shaken*):
Good God—all three of them?
That can't be true, Doctor!
No one was saved?
DOCTOR (*diabolically grinning*): Saved? Why yes! Guess who.
GERSTEIN: Who . . . ?
DOCTOR: GERMANY!

His infernal laughter clatters like sheets of metal roofing being loaded on a truck. GERSTEIN *has sat down, partly because he is frightened at this sudden descent by the* DOCTOR, *partly because he is unnerved by his disappointment.*

GERSTEIN (*slowly*): Not very funny, Doctor, I fail to see the joke.
DOCTOR: Maybe you think it funny your apartment
has undergone such stylish renovations?
My girl friend's house is wiped out down to the cellar.

GERSTEIN (*carrying a second chair over from the table*):
    Sit down, Doctor. Nice of you to drop by.

DOCTOR (*both arms still hidden under the cape*):
    No, thanks, I'm rushed. I won't sit down.
    I tried to call you but your telephone,
    it seems, has also been knocked out.
    I'm driving down to Tübingen tomorrow morning,
    so I can offer you a ride to see your family.
    Also we'll have a chance for a good talk.
    You're the only one worth talking to.

GERSTEIN (*smiling to conceal his fear*):
    I'm complimented—but how do you mean,
    the only one?

DOCTOR: Just that. The rest of our colleagues are,
    without exception cold-blooded, heavy-footed
    German blockheads. What brains
    they have is all used on technology . . .
    I plan to leave at seven—does that suit you?

GERSTEIN: Fine. I'll be waiting by the front door,
    if it's still standing, the front door, I mean.
    What's taking you to Tübingen? Don't tell me
    you're going to be a professor after all?

DOCTOR (*has been seated, but is again on his feet*):
    Not so fast. I still have to get my degree.

GERSTEIN: Will you be allowed
    to use the experiments you've done in Auschwitz?
    I ask because of the matter of secrecy.

DOCTOR (*lost in thought; he has been looking at the ripped
    painting*): Oh, that—no, I don't plan to go to Tübingen
    as a *medical* man. No, no, to teach philosophy.
    Medicine is only my profession, not my chief interest.
    Aside from that: the human experiments on prisoners
    aren't so secret as all that. We did some right here in Berlin
    only last May—everybody who counted
    was present, including the Army and Air Force.
    Even Professor Sauerbruch put in his two cents.
    Incidentally, instead of flowers, might I
    leave this with you for a while?

*He abruptly draws his left hand from under his cape. He is holding
a glass jar shaped like a melon mold, which he has been clasping*

under his arm. He shows its contents, a mass of grayish-white
organic matter, the brains of two Jewish children, to the horrified
GERSTEIN, *who does not conceal his repugnance. Casually*:

> Brain tissue from a pair of Jewish twins,
> two kids from Calais, preserved in formaldehyde.
> Rather interesting comparative sections.
> I brought the specimen with me for a girl
> who's taking her first course in histology.
> But her house has been bombed out and I've no idea
> where my little student has moved to.
> I gave her a skull a while back.
> I suppose that's buried in the rubble now.

GERSTEIN: Nice little gift . . . Twins' brains . . .

DOCTOR: As soon as I find out if she is still alive
> she can come here to pick it up, all right?

GERSTEIN (*hesitantly takes the glass jar, again hesitates as he is*
> *about to set it down on the table and finally deposits it on a*
> *chair*): Easier had in Auschwitz than flowers, eh?

DOCTOR (*seemingly only concerned with teasing* GERSTEIN):
> For you, as Christ's disciple, this must be upsetting.

GERSTEIN (*anguished*): I know what you are doing . . . horrible.

DOCTOR: Tell me this, it interests me.
> How can these two things be reconciled
> in our day and age:
> To have a good mind—and still remain a Christian?

GERSTEIN (*he expresses himself slowly, with deep awareness of the*
> *need for caution*):
> You may recall how Bismarck answered that,
> who also, in his youth, was wild and Byronesque
> and later had to make the same detour
> common to so many intellectuals:
> the way to God through nothingness.
> He said—and for my part I know no better answer;
> I think it is the ultimate wisdom for us—
> he said: I have, *with full awareness,* stopped
> at a specific stage of my development.

DOCTOR: And you suppose that helped him
> plot three wars without compunction?
> Come, now—
> he knew he was pretending to himself.

All those old fellows knew quite well
their systems had a factor of illusion, even Hegel.
And so do you—today—you know it too:
the man who says what he thinks is finished
and the man who thinks what he says is an idiot.

GERSTEIN (*laughing*): Then so am I. I thought
what I just said to you, and always say what I think.

DOCTOR (*close to him, diabolically*):
Sometimes, Gerstein, sometimes . . . you're a sly dog!
You don't fool me.
Whom are you swindling anyway—
the church and yourself,
or us—the SS?

GERSTEIN (*senses that he won't be able to stand up to this interrogation; therefore he makes a great show of putting all his
cards on the table and revealing himself as an unworldly
idealist*): What do you mean, swindling! I do say what I think.
Forget about the Christian, Doctor—of course
I'm a Christian—and with Himmler's blessing, if you want
to know.
But—is it necessary for a man to be a Christian
to—to have his doubts? (*Deliberately wandering.*)
You know, day before yesterday the news came
that my cousin had been slaughtered by partisans.
When we first marched into Russia
there weren't any partisans.
A man who's truly loyal to the Führer . . .

DOCTOR (*attempting to trip him up*):
As you are—as loyal as you are, Gerstein!

GERSTEIN (*hardly daunted*):
What's that? . . . Yes, but who am I to tell him:
race policy excludes a policy of conquest.
That much I learned in high school.
It's either one way or the other; you never could have both.
Alexander the Great married his Macedonians off
to daughters of the conquered peoples.
But we exterminate the conquered.
Do *you* believe this bodes well for the future?

DOCTOR (*laughing, his hand already on the door knob*):
Believe! Who still believes in belief?
Or in the future for that matter!

Why look at me that way? I know,
to you I am the principle of evil in the flesh.
GERSTEIN (*laughing, tries to sidestep the trap*):
The principle of evil! Whose phrase is that?
DOCTOR (*amused, quotes*): Otto Weininger's.
"The principle of evil is despair
at giving life some meaning."
GERSTEIN (*laughing*): I shall have to report that to Eichmann.
You read Viennese Jews.
DOCTOR (*not without vanity*):
Oh well, I *roast* them too.
On Tuesday I piped the sister of Sigmund Freud
up the chimney.

He gives his characteristic laugh. Already outside, he calls back:

Seven in the morning, then. Looking forward to our trip . . .
GERSTEIN (*outside*):
It will be nice to have a chance
to spend some time together. See you, Doctor.

*Slowly returns to the room. Leans for a moment, exhaling heavily,
against the door, then starts to go in to* JACOBSON *in the other room,
sees the glass jar, picks it up, does not know what to do with it,
and repeats:*

Instead of flowers. . . .

The doorbell rings again. GERSTEIN *starts violently; for the moment
unable to move he says:*

What does he want *now*.

*He makes a motion to open the door, cannot complete it, and only
forces himself to it when the bell rings for the third time. He is
heard saying outside:*

Heil Hitler—what can I do for you?
RICCARDO: Good morning, Herr Gerstein . . .

GERSTEIN *has evidently admitted him. The closing of the door is
heard, then footsteps in the hall.* RICCARDO *precedes* GERSTEIN *into
the room and says with some embarrassment, since* GERSTEIN *is
extremely reserved in manner toward him:*

Oh, the raid certainly hit you hard.

GERSTEIN (*coldly*):
>   What brings you here? Who are you?

RICCARDO (*even more constrained*):
>   We met yesterday at the Papal Legation,
>   Herr Gerstein.

GERSTEIN (*interrupts him with sharp reproof*):
>   Where? Where did you say!
>   I don't know you, I've never seen you.
>   What do you want?

RICCARDO (*with animation*):
>   I told you yesterday, at the Nuncio's,
>   that I would look you up.
>   I wished I could have gone right out with you.
>   My name is Father Fontana, I am attached
>   to the Secretariat of State of the Holy See.

GERSTEIN (*still cautious, without looking straight at* RICCARDO):
>   What do you have to say to me?

RICCARDO: That the Vatican will help you.
>   You and Hitler's victims.
>   Believe me, I was ashamed
>   to watch the conduct of the Nuncio.
>   But I suppose his situation forced him
>   to speak in such a neutral tone.

GERSTEIN (*impersonally*):
>   How can I possibly go on believing that
>   the Vatican will summon up concern
>   for the suffering of the Jews.
>   A good two months have passed
>   since the reports from London, and the Pope
>   has not yet intervened. (*Abruptly.*)
>   Whom did you just meet on the stairs?
>   Did you see an army officer in a cape?

RICCARDO: Oh yes, I noticed him. But in front of the house.
>   He was getting into his car.

GERSTEIN (*agitated*):
>   Good. I'm glad he did not see you on the stairs.
>   Do you know *who* it was you met?

RICCARDO: I had the feeling he looked back at me.

GERSTEIN (*forcing himself to remain calm*):
>   Oh well, this is a large apartment house.
>   You might have come to any one of twenty families.

Let's come right to the point, Father Fontana.
Undoubtedly the Polish government in exile
already notified the Pope himself as well.
The Father General of the Jesuits in Rome
has now for many years received exhaustive and precise
reports from Polish agents—as I said, *for many years.*

RICCARDO (*embarrassed*):
Before the day is out a courier will be taking
a letter to my father. My father
is a layman at the Holy See, most highly placed.
I give my *guarantee,* Herr Gerstein,
His Holiness will make a protest.
I have the honor to know the Pope well,
personally.

GERSTEIN (*close to cynicism*): Be careful with your guarantees!
They may come back to haunt you.
Why didn't he do something for old Lichtenberg,
Cathedral Provost of St. Hedwig's?
The scum threw him in jail merely because
he included the Jews in his prayers.
Your priests pray for the Führer too, you know—
how can the Pope look idly on
when priests are thrown in jail because they pray for Jews?
Since 1938 he's done no more
than that—merely looked on.
Lichtenberg, whose sentence is completed,
petitioned the Gestapo for permission
to let him share the fate the Jews
of Eastern Europe must endure—are you aware of that?

RICCARDO: I've heard of Lichtenberg,
Herr Gerstein. I ask you, please, to understand
that all these painful problems are still new to me.
Believe me, though,
the Pope will help. The commandment
"Love Thy neighbor" . . .

GERSTEIN (*now cordial; he grasps* RICCARDO's *shoulder*):
I've come to be so terribly despairing
of hope, as far as all the churches are concerned.
As for myself, I am a member of the Confessing Church;
I am a friend of Pastor Niemöller
who's been in concentration camp

for nearly five years by now . . . He used to call me
an inveterate saboteur,
and I suppose he understands
the reasons why I sneaked my way into the SS . . .
You cannot fight the Nazis
with pamphlets, as I used to do.

RICCARDO: You *voluntarily* put on this uniform?

GERSTEIN: Yes—I had to—but, please, do have a seat,
if you can find one in this mess . . .
Here.

He brings two chairs from the cluster around the table, dusts them off; they sit down. But after a moment GERSTEIN *gets up again, restless as a wolf in a cage.*

Yes, last year they finally found out
that I'd been locked up twice before
because of Christian leaflets I distributed.
I drew a prison sentence first, and then the camp.
Of course, I had not told them when I entered
the SS. They made a lot of trouble,
but then, on orders from the highest quarters
nothing was done to me. I was forgiven.
You see, in 1940 I suppressed
a typhus epidemic in the barracks and prison camps—
engineering and medicine are my specialities.
That saved my life. They think I'm mad.
In the eyes of those gangsters I am a cross
between technical genius and unwordly idealist.
Unwordly because I'm Christian!
They laugh at that and let me go
to church without much fuss.
They also know that many of my friends
are highly placed among the Protestants.
All the same! (*Suddenly extremely uneasy, jerkily.*)
But why, Father—what did you say your name was?

RICCARDO: Father Fontana.

GERSTEIN: Fontana—why have you come to see me, Father?
We must prepare an explanation
if one of my associates—these splendid men,
each one a murderer with academic honors—
should happen by just now.

(*He considers, then grasps* RICCARDO'S *arm.*)
Listen—how come you speak such perfect German?
RICCARDO: As a child I lived in Königsberg a while.
My mother, dead now, was a German and a Protestant.
GERSTEIN (*coldly, almost rude, but reassured*):
I have it: we'll say
you're an SS spy,
Foreign Intelligence Department 2, Italy.
RICCARDO (*swallows, offended; then speaks with cool aloofness*):
Well—that seems far-fetched, to say the least.
I am a Jesuit priest—do you believe
they would credit such a story?
GERSTEIN (*impassively, perhaps glad to have an occasion for saying
this for once*):
More plausible than any other story, Father.
You would not be the first priest, after all,
to serve these hangmen as a spy.
There's a spy right in the Vatican itself.
The right-hand man of Heydrich told me once
he was recruited into the Gestapo
by a Jesuit—yes, a Jesuit priest,
when he was at the university in Bonn.
Himmler is a great admirer of your organization;
he fashioned the Order of the SS
according to the rules of St. Loyola.
Pedantically, as he does everything,
he read his way through a whole Jesuit library.
RICCARDO (*offended*): And is there no way of finding out just who
the SS agent is in the Vatican?
GERSTEIN: Impossible, since I don't belong to the Gestapo.
In any case, they use no names, just numbers.
(*Abruptly, once more very uneasy.*)
No, there wouldn't be any point to it
if *he* comes back, the man you just ran into.
RICCARDO: The officer in the black cape?
GERSTEIN: Yes—I won't even try a bluff.
It wouldn't work with him.
RICCARDO: Who was that man?
GERSTEIN (*frazzled with nervousness*):
Man? Not a man at all, not human.
You've just met the Auschwitz angel of death.

He comes here just to sound me out
and hopes to hand me over to the hangman.
But let's not talk of that. Please, I must ask you,
if the doorbell rings,
hide quickly in the other room.
And don't say anything. There's someone else in there.
(*Only outwardly composed.*)
Now we have taken care of that . . . Why
do you look at me that way? You're horrified
at all the tricks that I have up my sleeve?
But if a man plays poker with assassins
he has to wear a poker face like theirs.

RICCARDO: But why, Herr Gerstein,
do you choose to play with them at all?

GERSTEIN: You cannot drive unless you're at the wheel.
Dictatorships can be demolished only from within.
But let us come straight to the point: my visit
to the Nuncio and your bishop's secretary
was high treason . . . (*Smiling.*)
You're shocked.

RICCARDO (*uncomprehendingly, with reserve*):
I don't presume to judge you.
No doubt you underwent some terrible ordeal
before embarking on this treasonable course.
You swore an oath to Hitler, did you not?

GERSTEIN: I must disillusion you, Father.
There was no terrible ordeal,
no pangs of conscience, none at all.
Hitler himself has written: the rights of men
invalidate the rights of states. *Therefore:*
oath or not, a man who sets up factories
which serve no other purpose but
to kill his fellowman with gas—
this man must be betrayed,
must be destroyed, no matter what the cost!
His murderer would only be his judge.

RICCARDO: But if we overlook what Hitler
is doing to the Jews and to the Russian prisoners . . .

GERSTEIN (*outraged*): Overlook it! How could you as a priest . . .

RICCARDO: I beg your pardon—I did not mean it that way.
But, Herr Gerstein, what troubles me

as much as does the awful fate of all these victims
is this: How can it be that this is done
by the *one* man who, without doubt,
is now the last of Europe's men, with Europe at his side,
to follow in Napoleon's path?
Who can deny this man who fought at Kiev
the greatest battle in world history—
six hundred thousand prisoners of war—
who overran France in six weeks—
who can deny him greatness?

GERSTEIN: Father, you speak like the historians of the future.
 Perhaps they also will dispose
 of Hitler's victims in two sentences.
 I cannot tell you *how* that horrifies me,
 how it disgusts me . . .

RICCARDO: Of course, my father looks on Hitler's victories
 also with grave misgivings;
 but recently we entertained at home
 the Spanish Foreign Minister
 (who had just come from Hitler.)
 All evening long he told us of
 his meeting in the German Chancellery.
 Our friend is using every trick he knows
 to keep his country out of conflict—he's a patriot.
 In short, he has no love for Hitler.
 But *how* he talked about him!
 I was impressed. A man, he said, who with
 the invincibility of the chosen
 follows his destiny, a Messiah—
 and if he were to fail, he said, he
 would pull all of Europe down with him.
 He's come a long way, a legend in his lifetime . . .

GERSTEIN (*can no longer listen*):
 For God's sake, Father, do not talk that way!
 Believe me, no legend will attach to that
  man's name.
 (*Very uncertainly.*) Be on your guard against attributing
 the qualities of diabolic genius to
 a man who's nothing but a master criminal,
 only because—because his
 foolish and irresolute contemporaries,

cabinet ministers, parliamentarians, generals, priests,
surrendered all of Europe for a time
to such a scoundrel.
(*Gradually becoming more firm and forceful.*)
Let's not get off on this. Remember,
every hour costs a thousand—please,
just think of what this means—
every hour costs a thousand victims,
whole families pushed into the ovens,
after a ghastly death.
Act. If you cannot sway the Nuncio,
go to Rome.

RICCARDO: Of course . . . Only, please understand:
How shall I identify my source?
Who my informant is?

GERSTEIN: I understand: in the eyes of Rome
a traitor is too questionable to . . .

RICCARDO: I beg your pardon—no, I meant . . .

GERSTEIN: I don't mind—I'm altogether insensitive
on that score, God knows!
The traitors, they alone, today
are saving Germany's honor.
For Hitler is not Germany,
he's Germany's destroyer—the verdict
of history will acquit *us*.
I will not survive the work that I must do.
A Christian in these days *cannot*
survive if he is truly Christian.
I don't mean Sunday Christians—
beware the steady churchgoers—
I am thinking of the Christians Kierkegaard
had in mind: the spies of God. I am
a spy in the SS.
And spies are executed—
I am aware of that.

RICCARDO: No, you must think of your safety.
I shall not speak of you by name.

GERSTEIN: No need to shield me. But aside from that,
it would be better anyhow for you
to quote reports from London and from Poland.
No need for you to tell Rome anything that's *new*.

Only arouse a sense of outrage.
Those who keep silent are accessories to murder,
and they imperil their immortal souls.

RICCARDO: You can rely on me.
I'll go now, to endanger you no further.

GERSTEIN: No, please stay.
I have a question for you . . .

RICCARDO (*with animation*): So do I, Herr Gerstein, so do I.
One question that leaves me no peace.

GERSTEIN: Yes?

RICCARDO: Why the German people,
the nation of Goethe, Mozart, Menzel—
how the Germans could become so barbarous.

GERSTEIN: We Germans are no worse
than other Europeans. First of all
the great majority have no specific knowledge
about the killings, though, of course,
a lot of soldiers in the East have watched
the massacres, and the whole nation looks on
while Jews are shipped out of the cities
like cattle. But anyone willing to help—what can he do?
Are we to castigate a man
who does not want to die for others?
Not long ago the Jews employed in Berlin factories
were to be sent to Auschwitz. The police
did not descend at once, but first informed
the factories. And the result was that
four thousand Jews managed to disappear.
They were hidden by Berliners, fed by them—
four thousand—and every Berliner
involved is risking his own life!
The lives of his whole family as well.
You see, not every German has forgotten
the debt he owes to Germany's name.
And there are scoundrels everywhere. In Holland
the Dutch police are working hard
to round up every Jew; in France they don't cooperate
with so much zeal, but still they do their part.
In Hungary too, but worst of all in the Ukraine . . .
The Ukrainians shoot their Jews themselves.
Some time ago, when seventeen thousand Jews
were shot in Maidanek, a lot of Poles

got drunk to celebrate this festive day. Only
on rare occasions can a Jew in Poland find a place to hide
outside the towns. His kindly neighbors
turn him over to the German murderers
for a small bounty. *We* have no right to speak,
Father. The Germans
bear the greatest guilt. Their leader
has conceived the program. As for the *people*—
the other peoples hardly are much better.

RICCARDO: What you tell me is shattering,
Herr Gerstein—and nevertheless,
as an Italian and as a priest
I have to disagree. At home in Rome
(*with pride, slightly declamatory*)
such things would be impossible. From the Holy Father
down to the chestnut peddler in the piazza,
the entire nation would rise up
against such cruelties, if Jewish fellow citizens
were arrested. Or at any rate, arrested
by policemen of a foreign government.

GERSTEIN: It's touching, Father, it is enviable,
to be so sure of one's own countrymen.
I believe you! (*Now cynically.*) All the more bitter, then,
if in its attitude the Church should be
equivocal. Not long ago Dr. Edith Stein,
Europe's most celebrated nun, I believe,
was gassed in Auschwitz. A convert
for many, many years, a famous
Catholic writer. I ask you:
How could the Gestapo have discovered
that this one nun had Jewish blood?
They came and got her, right out of her Dutch convent.
I simply cannot understand why in a convent
of her own order a nun can't be concealed.
Poor woman!
I suppose she could not understand it herself.

RICCARDO: The raid must have come too suddenly.

GERSTEIN (*sarcastically*):
It's clear, then, how much protection
the Church will offer the converted Jew.
A dozen members of various orders
were actually *handed over* from Dutch religious houses.

RICCARDO: But only under duress.
>   The bishops protested, Dutch labor groups protested,
>   But that just made the situation worse.

GERSTEIN (*angered, violently*):
>   Worse? There was no consistent policy.
>   *Rome* left the bishops in the lurch!
>   It's not the Dutch I blame.
>   But how can Rome be silent
>   when monks and nuns are carted off?
>   With the result that no one even knew
>   of these outrages.

Silence.

>   There is another question preying on my mind,
>   it's one I'd like to place before a priest.
>   The facts are these: by the end
>   of the coming month I am ordered to store
>   more than two tons of poison gas—
>   Cyclon B, the very gas with which the Jews
>   are being killed—in a warehouse in Berlin.
>   I don't know what they mean to do with it;
>   I rather feel they don't know yet themselves.
>   It's just to have the poison gas available.
>   Maybe they mean to kill some foreign workers
>   or prisoners, as the occasion offers.

Pause. RICCARDO *is speechless.*

>   This, Father, is the question I must face:
>   should I instruct the firms to send the bills
>   to this address, and in my name?

RICCARDO: Of course not. What would be the point of that?

GERSTEIN: Because only that way am I in a position
>   to keep my eye on the poison after delivery.
>   Then, some time in the near future, I might—
>   *might* get rid of it, by using it for
>   disinfection, say, in various places.
>   I can also say that part of it
>   has decomposed.
>   I have already worked things so that
>   this poison gas will *not* be stored here in Berlin—
>   I gave the air raids as a reason.

RICCARDO: Bills for such materials in your name!
  Is there no other way?
GERSTEIN: Of course, I could easily get out to Sweden.
  I have some business in Helsinki soon.
  Only—who would get my job,
  and what could a fanatic do with it?
RICCARDO: It's difficult, yes, Herr Gerstein.
  What does your conscience say?
GERSTEIN: Conscience? Who could trust that!
  Conscience or God:
  men never have wreaked such havoc
  as when invoking God—or an idea.
  Conscience is a treacherous guide. I am convinced
  that Hitler acts according to his conscience.
  No, I need an answer from outside myself.
  We Protestants depend too much
  upon ourselves. One cannot always bear it.
  Don't we, indeed, have every ground to doubt . . . ?
  But answer me with the objectivity
  only a priest can have: what must I do?
RICCARDO (*after a pause*):
  To lend your name to something monstrous . . .
GERSTEIN (*alarmed and therefore indignant*):
  My name! What is a name?
  Is it my *name* that matters? Only the lukewarm,
  who are scarcely better than the murderers,
  only they find it easy to survive
  in times like these with a good name and
  a reputation as immaculate as—
  forgive me, Father—
  the Pope's white vestments.
RICCARDO (*trying to conceal the fact that he is offended*):
  You asked me my opinion, Herr Gerstein.
  You have another choice: to flee to England.
  (*He gathers animation.*)
  Broadcast from London. You, Sturmführer Gerstein
  of the SS Public Health Department, speaking
  ex officio and offering as your affidavit,
  figures, dates, bills for poison,
  reporting all the details
  of what is happening here.

(*Enthusiastically, naïvely.*)
Make a full confession,
what you have done, what you have managed to prevent . . .
and what you could not prevent.

GERSTEIN (*passionately*):

Good Lord, are you aware of what you are asking.
I'm willing to do anything—but this I cannot do.
One speech by me on Radio London
and my entire family in Germany would be wiped out.

RICCARDO: Oh, I'm sorry, I didn't realize!

GERSTEIN (*more calmly*): They would not only kill my wife,
my children—they would also
torture my brothers to death in a camp.

RICCARDO: Forgive me . . .

GERSTEIN (*his tone colder*): Nor is there any need for it,
no need at all!
Reports on Radio London long ago told all
about what's going on in Poland. People already know!
They must at least suspect, if they have sense.
And Thomas Mann as well has recently repeated all the
figures.
Did he not also broadcast news
about the gassing of the Jews from Paris and from Holland?
All I could do is tell it all again, along with details
no one would believe.
And who am I? Nobody heard of *me*.
I'd only be a questionable renegade, and nothing more.
Why is there not a single word
heard from the only man in Europe
still free today from any taint of propaganda:
the Pope.
(*Laughing hysterically.*) Oh God—my God! Here I contend
with Him as I did in my student days. Did He,
I wonder, not become a Christian
only to ease His conscience with the thought that—
just like His Deputy today—
Jews do not fall within His competence.

RICCARDO (*kindly, but firm*):

No more, Herr Gerstein—you don't want
to give up God as well, not now.

GERSTEIN: He must forgive me for it, since He
taught me that object lesson in Poland and . . .

since the Nuncio in Berlin
has thrown me out.

RICCARDO (*solemnly, very sure of himself*):
The Vatican will act—God knows,
it will be done, I promise you.

GERSTEIN (*unmoved*): How can I still believe you now?

RICCARDO (*indignant*):
Herr Gerstein, please—what did I do to merit that!

GERSTEIN: I beg your pardon—I thought of you
only as representing your superiors.
It's not your personal sincerity I doubt.
My candor should assure you that . . .
(*Without transition.*)
Would you, right now, put in my hands
your cassock and your passport?

RICCARDO (*shocked*):
What do you want with them—my passport,
my cassock?

GERSTEIN (*mysteriously*): A proof of your good will.

RICCARDO (*with mounting distaste, indignantly*):
Proof—no, Herr Gerstein.
I vowed when I was consecrated
never again to lay aside the cassock.
What are you asking of me?

GERSTEIN: It's not that I mistrust you—the truth,
then. Your passport and your clothing
can help a Jew to cross the Brenner Pass.
You, as a diplomat, should have no trouble
getting a new passport from Rome.

RICCARDO (*reluctantly, hesitantly*):
Oh, I see. Need it be right away?

GERSTEIN (*has opened the door to the adjoining room*):
Herr Jacobson?

JACOBSON: Yes, Herr Gerstein?

He appears quickly, instinctively starts back, composes himself and enters the room.

Good day.

RICCARDO: Good day.

GERSTEIN (*adroitly, rapidly*):
Father Fontana—Herr Jacobson.
Gentlemen, let's not deceive ourselves.

Black hair and similarity of age
are poor prerequisites for an exchange of passports.
But, on the other hand, Herr Jacobson—I hardly think
I'll have another chance to offer you
a cassock and a diplomatic passport from
the Holy See. Are you prepared
to try to cross the Brenner Pass with them?

JACOBSON (*no longer as quick to apprehend as he has been in
the past*): What's that—do I hear right—is there a chance . . .
(*Now addresses* RICCARDO *cordially.*)
You are offering me escape?

RICCARDO (*struggling not to show his reluctance*):
Oh yes, of course—indeed. When would you want . . .

GERSTEIN (*quickly*): I propose tonight—if there's
a sleeping car available, Herr Jacobson.
I'll buy your ticket when I drive the Father
back to the vicinity of the Papal Legation.
Without a passport and in Herr Jacobson's attire
it will be better for you not to walk
through town. (*Smiling.*) I wonder, Jacobson, if you could
do without your glasses altogether.
Or maybe only when the border check comes up?
I hope the collar fits.
Can we change right away—Herr Jacobson,
good Lord, man, what's the matter?
You're finally through with living like a prisoner!

JACOBSON *has dropped into a chair; he is done in. He takes out
a handkerchief, smiles, cleans his glasses with an embarrassed air.*

JACOBSON (*with frequent pauses*):
Forgive me, it was only the surprise.
Just now, back in the room there,
when I heard your voices—and also,
last night's air raid . . . the excitement,
I kept thinking if the place caught fire
and people came to put it out
and found me here with you—an officer of the SS—
you would be—they'd tear you to pieces . . .

GERSTEIN: That's all over now, Herr Jacobson.

JACOBSON: Yes—over. How easy it is to say.
Five minutes ago the thought passed through my mind
that next time there's an air raid

I'd better leave
in order not to put you . . . in . . .
GERSTEIN (*to* RICCARDO):
You see—a nasty case of cabin fever—it's high time . . .
JACOBSON: How can I ever thank you—and you . . .
(*To* RICCARDO.) Now you are the one I am endangering.
Do you know that?
RICCARDO (*has come round completely; warmly*):
I thank God for the opportunity to help.
It's little enough. I live at the Papal Legation.
Not even Hitler personally could harm me there.
Be sure to send a card from Rome, won't you?
GERSTEIN (*friendly but anxious, looks at the clock*):
You must brief Jacobson about your father,
your own and his position in the Vatican . . .
You have to know enough to answer
any questions from the German border guards.
The rest remains a gamble. Change your clothes.

He gestures toward the door to the adjoining room.

JACOBSON (*has composed himself*):
Sleeping car—really—is that essential?
GERSTEIN (*smiling, impatient*):
If possible, yes—you're a diplomat, remember?
RICCARDO: There is only one inspection at the border
and that's done very courteously, I think.
JACOBSON: Oh, fine. But if I go by sleeping car, of course,
I cannot leave before tomorrow night, Herr Gerstein.
When it gets dark tonight I'm going home
to see my parents and to say goodbye.
(*Almost happily, not noticing* GERSTEIN's *embarrassment;
resolutely.*)
And once in Rome I'll leave no stone unturned
to have the two placed under the protection
of some neutral power.
An emigration visa—perhaps that can be . . .
GERSTEIN (*quite convincingly*):
Don't put your parents into danger—
depart tonight, at any cost.
I'll drive you to the station in the car.
(*Rather uncertainly.*) No visits home.

JACOBSON (*disturbed, mistrustful*):
> You mean I am not to say goodbye?
> Herr Gerstein, it's not like you to be so nervous . . .
> (*Sees through him, horrified.*)
> Or—tell me—have they—please, the truth!
> Have they already shipped my parents off?
> Please—now you must . . .

GERSTEIN (*softly*): Yes. I couldn't deliver your letter
> on Tuesday.

He takes a letter from his jacket, relieved that he can report something factual. He speaks rapidly, but jerkily.

> But I could not tell you either. The door is sealed.
> I almost didn't notice, almost dropped
> the letter in their box.
> If I had left it there, they would be looking for you now.
> The people who now run the store
> saw me go off. They wanted to give me
> a message—the woman beckoned to me
> through the store window . . .

JACOBSON (*fighting back his tears*):
> Frau Schulze—yes, she was always decent.
> Without her help my parents would have starved to death
> > by now.
> Did she—have a chance to speak to them?

GERSTEIN (*at first cannot answer; then*):
> I left. I suddenly felt scared.
> I looked away—I had to force myself to walk, and not to run.
> (*He grasps* JACOBSON'S *arm, emotionally ravaged.*)
> I'm sorry—I—I—I thought
> I'd go to see the woman in the store
> some time during the next few days . . . and ask what . . .
> I'll go there afterwards, at once.

JACOBSON turns the letter in his hand back and forth. RICCARDO speaks to break the silence.

RICCARDO: Should I try to ascertain where
> they were taken? The Nuncio surely could find out.

JACOBSON: Don't bother. They're sure to get to Auschwitz now.
> Tuesday . . . three days . . . Do you think, Herr Gerstein,
> it was on Tuesday? Or could it have been earlier?

How long do those transports take?—Ah, questions!
(*To* RICCARDO, *making an extreme effort to control his voice.*)
No point in asking questions. The old—
it's true, isn't it, Gerstein—are—gassed immediately.

GERSTEIN: N-not always, no. Some are—
your father, as a badly wounded veteran
of the first war, would surely have been sent
to Theresienstadt.

JACOBSON (*changed, composed*):
Germany, your gratitude! Gerstein,
you saved my life. But there's no need
for you to lie to me. I—don't you understand—
I don't want consolation now.
I've known that it would have to happen—
known it long. (*Violently, tormented, but firmly.*)
It will not kill me—I won't do the murderers
that favor. I will . . . now . . .
now I must . . . get out of here . . . get away.

*He crushes the letter in his hand; then he tears it twice. His
movements are tightly, spasmodically resolute. He is wholly trans-
formed, unnaturally composed, and now speaks with something
of the harshness of the Old Testament, while his pallid, kindly
librarian's face takes on a streak of cruelty.*

Gerstein, reconsider
whether you want to help me cross the Brenner.
For now—after this news—
I am no longer German. Now,
whether or not you understand,
each German—every one—becomes my enemy.
This is no longer flight—I want to leave
in order to come back, as an avenger. An avenger.
Once I reach Italy I'm practically in England.
(*Wildly, alarmingly.*)
No one shall say we Jews let ourselves
be driven to the slaughterhouse like cattle.
I shall come back—as murderer,
as bomber pilot. Killing for killing.
Phosphorus bombs for gas, fire for fire.
Gerstein, I warn you. This is my thanks to you
for hiding me. I tell you honestly,

the man you're helping to escape is now your enemy.
Drive me out on the street as I stand here.
For I shall never—never forgive the Germans,
all Germans, for this murder of my parents—
good Germans themselves.

He has dropped the scraps of the letter into one of the trash pails. GERSTEIN *goes over to it without a word and takes the scraps out again. With his lighter he ignites the pieces one after the other and lets them fall flaming into the pail.*

RICCARDO (*to* JACOBSON; *he sounds theoretical but sincere*):
Do not harden your heart—you simplify.
(*He points to* GERSTEIN.)
How many Germans help your brothers!
Is it their children that you want to bomb?
Hatred can never be the final word.
JACOBSON (*aloofly, objectively*):
Hate strengthens. I must now stand firm.
GERSTEIN (*morosely, hoarsely, without looking at* JACOBSON):
Each to his post. Neither of us
is going to survive this war.
Change your clothes—it's getting late.

He takes the two pails and carries them out to the hall. As he returns, JACOBSON *is holding out to* RICCARDO *his passport [a large boldface J is visible on the inner pages] and the yellow star, a scrap of cloth as big as a man's palm.*

JACOBSON (*smiling*): You are making a poor trade, Father.
You give me your cassock, and I—
here—this—this is all I have to offer:
only the stigma of the outlaw.

All three fall silent. RICCARDO *takes the yellow star and examines it. He looks at the star, then looks up at* GERSTEIN *and* JACOBSON. *Shakes his head. Holding the star against his cassock over his heart for a moment, he asks, as the curtain swiftly falls—*

RICCARDO: Here?

CURTAIN

Act Two: The Bells of St. Peter's

Rome, February 2, 1943. Palazzo Fontana on the Monte Gianicolo. Grand salon. Under a conventional painting of the Madonna stands a narrow Renaissance prayer bench. To the left and right family portraits. Women of various eras, soldiers, a cardinal. In the foreground, surrounded by flowers, a large photograph of a middle-aged woman: RICCARDO's *recently deceased mother.*

The backstage wall of the room is almost entirely taken up by tall windows, and by the veranda door; through these we see a steeply sloping garden with stone pines and cypresses. Above the wall of this garden, chalky gray, very large and sharply silhouetted against the cold blue sky, is the nearby dome of St. Peter's.

The veranda door stands open. The bells of St. Peter's are clanging loudly.

COUNT FONTANA, *sixty years old, rimless glasses, heavy mustache, belongs—along with a tiny, select group of European aristocrats, such as, for instance, Herr von Papen, Hitler's Vice-Chancellor—to the Apostolic Privy Chamberlains* di spada e cappa. *His is the high honor of being permitted to stand, on ceremonial occasions, in Spanish court dress directly beside His Holiness.*

But FONTANA, *as one of the highest-ranking laymen in the service of the Holy See, regards the costume as something of an affliction, for he has nothing in common with the many picturesque trappings and museum pieces which contribute so much to the general atmosphere of the Vatican.* FONTANA *is a "manager." He is overworked, intelligent, cultivated, capable of kindliness and suffering, even graced with some fair understanding of the social necessities of the twentieth century. His discomfort at being photographed now in the rich and somber court dress of Henry II is quite genuine. He is a sober, self-assured financier who knows very well that he has performed unique services for the Curia and for that very*

*reason does not like being uniformed like the other chamberlains,
who for the most part are entitled to wear their buckle shoes, silk
stockings, knee breeches, ruffs, slashed sleeves, lace cuffs, cardinal's
hats, swords and medallion chains only because they are descended
from families formerly important in Rome. The Fontanas still have
fresh, vigorous blood. Like the Pacellis, they were first ennobled
in the middle of the nineteenth century, still do serious work, and
hence are not taken quite seriously in their circles.*

*Nevertheless, His Holiness Pius XI had early nominated the
"exemplary Catholic employer" Fontana a Knight of the Order
of the Holy Sepulchre, and at the Pope's request His Majesty,
Victor Emmanuel III, in 1939 made Fontana a count, with the
title to pass to his descendants.*

As the curtain parts, an old-fashioned PHOTOGRAPHER *with mustache and velvet jacket, crouched behind the black cloth, is directing
his cumbersome photographic apparatus at the open veranda door.
Then he himself steps to the threshold of the veranda, where his
subject is to pose, and looks directly into the lens in a posture of
"importance." As he stands there, trying to look like Garibaldi,
he is caught in the act by the old* SERVANT, *who has noiselessly
entered the room. The* SERVANT *looks at him, shaking his head
contemptuously, until the* PHOTOGRAPHER *again busies himself with
his camera.*

SERVANT (*watering flowers*):
    Don't keep His Honor the Count long
    or he'll send you packing.
    He hasn't even been told that the young master
    is back from Germany.
    When he knows, I can tell you right now,
    he'll have no time for you.
PHOTOGRAPHER (*flamboyantly emotional*):
    Who could forbid me to congratulate
    my old patron, His Honor the Count,
    on his receiving the Order of Christ!
    Moreover—his portrait is supposed to go
    on the front page! Moreover . . .
SERVANT: All right, all right, but now I'm closing the door.
    I'm not heating the garden, and the noise . . .

*He closes the veranda door; the clang of the bells is considerably
muted.*

PHOTOGRAPHER: You'll have to open the door again in a minute.
    His Honor the Count is to stand outside,
    so that he'll have the dome of St. Peter's
    behind him.
SERVANT: I don't have to do anything. Here he comes.

Exit swiftly. The PHOTOGRAPHER *wipes his mustache and mouth as footsteps are heard in the next room. He nervously fingers his tie and retires behind his camera, where he assumes an "at ready" posture.*

FONTANA (*entering swiftly, nervously pleased*):
    Wonderful, what a surprise! When did he arrive,
    Vittorio? Let him sleep.
SERVANT (*following*): Barely an hour ago, sir. But he said
    I was to wake him straight off when you returned.
    He's so pleased too, our young master,
    he won't want to go on sleeping . . .
FONTANA (*has noticed the* PHOTOGRAPHER, *distractedly*):
    Ah yes, well, tell him that I'm here.

Exit SERVANT. *To* PHOTOGRAPHER:

    Oh, do you have to? Good morning.
    Don't you have enough pictures of me?
PHOTOGRAPHER: But not a single portrait yet that shows Your
                    Honor
    Wearing the Order of Christ. Permit me, Your Honor,
    to extend my most respectful congratulations!
    Besides, tomorrow's front page is supposed to . . .
    absolutely has to . . .
FONTANA (*who has greedily lit a cigarette, quite accommodating*):
    Well, all right. Where? Here? Go ahead.
PHOTOGRAPHER (*who has quickly opened the veranda door; the
    sound of the bells becomes very loud again*):
    Here, if you don't mind, Your Honor, here on the threshold,
    so that besides the costume Your Honor
    will have St. Peter's dome at your back.
    The most effective . . .

He stands with a helpless air.

FONTANA: You've already set the camera, haven't you?
    What are you waiting for?

PHOTOGRAPHER: Permit me, Your Honor, if you don't mind . . .
　　Do you think the cigarette and the court costume . . . ?
FONTANA: What's that—you want my hands
　　to show as well? The whole paraphernalia?
　　I thought, only a bust . . . ?

He lays the cigarette aside.

　　Very well, very well, get it over with.
PHOTOGRAPHER: Perhaps your hand on the sword and
　　head a little higher—a little more to the left.

He squeezes the rubber ball.

　　Many, many thanks. Perhaps one more shot
　　at the desk, preserving for posterity
　　Your Honor in full exercise of business . . .
FONTANA (*trying not to laugh*):
　　Ah yes, preserved for posterity. Posterity
　　might even fancy that I opened letters
　　in this costume I'm wearing, with my sword.

He points to the SERVANT, *who has re-entered, picks up his cigarette
and says merrily*:

　　Here, take a picture of our Signor Luigi.
　　He will be seventy soon.
　　The picture will make a nice gift to his wife
　　on his birthday. Go on, over there!
SERVANT: But Your Honor, that doesn't do!

Angrily to the PHOTOGRAPHER, *as he closes the door*:

　　Am I heating the garden? Keep the door closed.
FONTANA: Go on, Vittorio, your wife will be pleased.
　　Over there! Don't make such a face . . .

RICCARDO *enters.*

　　My boy, what a surprise!
RICCARDO (*embraces his father, who kisses him*):
　　Congratulations, Father! My, how grand!
　　(*Nervously.*) Why do the bells keep going on and on?
FONTANA: So good to have your company a while.
　　How long can you stay?

RICCARDO (*now, like his father, distracted by the scene between the* PHOTOGRAPHER *and the* SERVANT *in the background*):
That's fine, Vittorio.

SERVANT: It's a waste. And my teeth
are being fixed . . .

PHOTOGRAPHER: One, two, three . . . One more picture
of Signor Riccardo, Count Fontana? I would suggest . . .

RICCARDO (*pleasantly*): Better not, I need a shave.
Some other time.

FONTANA: Thank you, thank you, do please pack up your things.

PHOTOGRAPHER (*while* SERVANT *is helping him fold his equipment*): The thanks are all mine, Your Honor.

FONTANA: Are you ill, my boy? You look so worn.
Really, you do need looking after.

RICCARDO: I could not catch a wink of sleep while on the train.
It's only that the trip has tired me, Father.
There's really nothing wrong with me . . .
Why (*nervously and irritably*) do they go on ringing that
way?

FONTANA: Because the Pope this morning consecrated
the world to the Immaculate Heart of the Blessed Virgin.
A very tiring ceremony. Right after came
my audience—and then the decoration
suddenly came my way—I had no idea.

RICCARDO: Mama would have been happy—how we miss her
in the house and everywhere . . .

Both look up at the portrait. The PHOTOGRAPHER *has by now
packed up and speaks.*

PHOTOGRAPHER: Much obliged, Your Honor.
(*To* RICCARDO.) Your Honor!
Good day—good day!

FONTANA: Thank you. Goodbye.

RICCARDO: Goodbye.

PHOTOGRAPHER *leaves.*

SERVANT: God reward you, Your Honor.

FONTANA: Keep it a secret from your wife.

SERVANT *leaves.*

FONTANA (*as he prepares a cocktail, skeptically, ironically*):
    Ah yes, my boy—the dogma of Mary's Ascension
    may now, quite seriously, await us
    when the war is over.
    As a result, he'll merit an important chapter
    in every history of the Popes . . .

RICCARDO (*bitterly amused, takes a glass from his father*):
    The things they think about in Rome!
    Take poverty, for instance, which, in practice, means
    that as a nation's churches grow in number,
    so do its prostitutes. Naples and Sicily—
    centers of vice beneath the windows of the Vatican.
    Instead of helping, we debate
    how frequently a married couple may cohabitate.
    Or if a widow may remarry.
    And now, to top it off, the dogma of the Virgin.
    Does he have nothing else to do?

FONTANA: Don't be too hard on him, my boy! An hour ago
    the Pope, who almost always asks about you,
    told me that nowhere in the world today
    can you acquire the experiences
    available at the Legation in Berlin . . .
    Have you brought more bad news from the Nuncio?

RICCARDO: None at all. I left without assignment.
    I could not stand it any longer. (*Reproachfully.*)
    You must know that for months the Jews all over Europe
    are being wiped out systematically.
    Each day—Father, just think of it:
    each day, six thousand!

FONTANA: I read that too, but it
    must be enormously exaggerated.

RICCARDO: Suppose it is exaggerated!
    (*Despairingly.*) I gave my word
    the Pope would protest,
    would raise a hue and cry
    to stir the world to pity,
    to outrage and to action!

FONTANA (*agitated*):
    You had no right to do that, Riccardo.
    Temerity—to dare to speak for him!

RICCARDO: Temerity, you say? Why, could I have thought
  he would do otherwise?
  The children of an entire people in all Europe,
  from Narvik to the Don, from Crete to the Pyrenees,
  are being born today only
  to be murdered in Poland.
  Hitler is systematically reducing
  life itself to an absurdity. Just read
  the ghastly details from Poland and Rumania
  published two weeks ago.
  How shall we ever find apologies
  for our silence. And those bells!
  (*He almost shouts, hands clapped to his ears.*)
  They ring and ring as though the world
  were Paradise. What sheer unfeeling idiocy
  to offer *this* earth to the Blessed Virgin's heart.
  Does not the Pope who holds
  within his hand five-hundred million Catholics—
  twenty per cent subjects of Hitler now—
  does he not share responsibility
  for the moral climate of this world?
  How can he have the audacity . . .
FONTANA (*loudly, checking him*):
  Riccardo, I will not have you use such language!
  Is this the way you thank the Pope
  for always—always favoring you?
RICCARDO: Father, please, what do personal affairs
  matter here?
FONTANA (*warningly*): You are very ambitious. Lucifer,
  the favorite of his Lord,
  also fell from ambition.
RICCARDO (*smiling sadly*): Not ambition but disappointment
  will make me an antagonist. Father:
  (*imploringly, as urgently as possible*)
  the greatest manhunt which the world has ever seen.
  Divine creation—shipwrecked. Faith
  locked in battle with the new ideologies,
  with insights gained by science. And human wreckage
  strewn upon the oceans, upon
  the countries of the earth. Men sacrificed

on every front, slain in the fire,
on the gallows, in the gas—and God's ambassador
thinks he can *win,* yet venture nothing?
Suppose God has elected, in these days
unprecedented in all history,
to let *him* perish too.
Would *that* not be ordained as well?
Does no one in the Vatican grasp
this? They still cling
to the hope that *everything*
is preordained; the greatest pyres
ever reared, however, are made out to be
the whims of a dictator who is soon to pass.
Let us admit at last:
these flames are also *our* trial by fire!
Who will, in times to come, respect us still
as moral arbiters if, in *this* time,
we fail so miserably?

Both fall silent, worn out by contention; the ringing of the great bells of St. Peter's can still be heard, more muted. FONTANA *struggles to master his agitation; he tosses the ridiculous sword aside, lights cigarettes for himself and* RICCARDO, *and says appeasingly—*

FONTANA: Let's look at this realistically. I ask you
    as a member of the Secretariat of State
    how can the Pope, without surrendering
    his policy of neutrality,
    force Hitler not to deport the Jews.
RICCARDO: Let him exploit the fact
    that Hitler fears his influence.
    It wasn't out of piety
    that Hitler has refrained from all infringements
    upon the Church for the duration of the war.
FONTANA: That policy may change tomorrow. How many
    priests has he not killed already!
RICCARDO (*passionately*):
    That's right—and Rome, despite that fact, has not
    called off her friendship. Why?
    Because Rome feels there is no cause to?
    The facts are there: the Pope

chooses to look the other way when his own brother
is slain in Germany. Priests there
who sacrifice themselves do not do so
on orders from the Vatican—rather, they violate
its principle of non-intervention.
And since Rome has abandoned them,
their deaths cannot be counted as atonement
for Rome's own guilt.
As long as Rome permits her priests to go on
praying for Hitler—praying for that man!—
just so long . . .

FONTANA: Please, stick to the point. Why do you ignore
the protests of the Bishop of Münster?

RICCARDO: Oh, Father, Galen's example proves my point.
In the very heart of Germany he raised his voice
against the murderers—in summer, '41.
Hitler's prestige was at its height, but lo and behold
they let the bishop speak out with impunity.
He did not spend a single hour in jail!
And his protest stopped the extermination of the sick.
Only one bishop had to stand up
and Hitler retreated. Why?
Because he fears the Pope—the Pope
who did not even back up Galen's speeches!
There is no one Hitler fears now but the Pope, Father.
In Potsdam I met Herr von Hassell—
he sends his greetings to you. Almost
his first question was: Why did Rome
let Galen fight alone?
And my question was: Why had Galen
not also come forth to defend the Jews?
Because the mentally ill were baptized?
That is an ugly question, Father—
let us admit it.

FONTANA: Riccardo, do not judge!
You dare reproach a bishop for not
risking his life for Jews as much as Christians?
Do you know, Riccardo, what it's like
to risk your life? I found out in the war.

RICCARDO: I admire Galen, I honor him.
But, Father, we in Rome, here in the Vatican,

which cannot be assailed—we must not
be content with Galen's risk
while in Poland . . .

FONTANA (*remonstrating*): My boy, your arrogance disturbs me.
The Pope, daily contending
with the world, with God, knows what he is doing.
He knows why he must be silent.
He will not always be. The tides of war
are shifting. Time is on Great Britain's side.
Once reasons of state permit
the Pope to rise up against Hitler without
imperiling the Church, then . . .

RICCARDO: Then not a single Jew will be alive
in Poland, Germany, or France, or Holland!
It's time you understood—every day counts!
I gave my word. I guaranteed this officer . . .

FONTANA (*beside himself*): Whatever made you do that?

RICCARDO (*flaring up, throwing moderation to the winds*):
Because—because I lacked the cynicism
to cite reasons of state when
things like these come to my ears.

FONTANA: How you simplify! Good God,
do you believe the Pope could suffer to see
even a single man hungry and in pain?
His heart is with the victims.

RICCARDO: But his voice? Where is his voice?
His heart, Father, is of no interest.
Even Himmler, Hitler's police chief,
could not tolerate the sight of his victims,
so I have been assured.
The orders sift down from bureau to bureau.
The Pope does not see the victims;
Hitler does not see them. . . .

FONTANA (*approaches* RICCARDO *threateningly*):
Enough—I'll cut this conversation short
if you mention Pius XII and Hitler in the same breath.

RICCARDO (*scornfully*):
Confederates have to put up with that, Father.
Have they not made a pact with one another?
Pius the Eleventh would long ago
have abrogated the Concordat.

FONTANA: That's not for you to say.

RICCARDO (*after a pause, softly, with a note almost of spite*):
Father, do you believe the Pope—
are you quite *sure* the Pope
is actually tormented by a conflict
between reasons of state and Christian charity?

FONTANA: How do you mean that, Riccardo?

RICCARDO (*controlling himself with effort*):
I mean—he stands so very high above
the destinies of the world, of men. For forty years
he's been immersed in canon law, diplomacy.
He's never been—or only for two years—and that
in the last century—a priest, working with people,
entrusted with the care of souls.
He never condescends to say a word
to one of the Swiss guards at his door.
Neither in his garden nor at table
can he tolerate the face of a fellow man.
His gardener, remember, has strict orders
always to keep his back turned to the Pope!
Oh, Father—is there anything he loves
except his dictionaries and
the cult of the Madonna?
(*Suddenly full of hatred, with flashing Roman mockery.*)
I see the way he cleans his pen with utmost care—
and, worse yet, expatiating on that ritual—
and I ask myself whether—
or rather I no longer ask
if he was ever able to regard
a single one of Hitler's victims
as his brother, a being in *his* image.

FONTANA: Riccardo, please—that's hardly fair,
that verges on demagogy. Granted his coldness,
granted his egocentricity,
he still attempts to help, to understand. The victims . . .

RICCARDO: The victims—does he truly bring them to his mind?
Do you believe he does? The world press,
the ambassadors, our agents—all come
with gruesome details. Do you think
that he not only studies the statistics,
the abstract figures,

seven hundred thousand dead—starvation,
gassing, deportation . . .
Do you think he is *there,*
that he has ever watched
with his mind's eye—has ever seen
the way they are deported from Paris:
three hundred suicides—before the journey even starts.
Children under five snatched from their parents.
And then Konin, near Warsaw:
eleven thousand Poles in mobile gas chambers—
their cries, their prayers—and the laughing SS thugs.
Eleven thousand—but imagine
you and I—that we were in it.

FONTANA: Riccardo, please—I know you tear at your own heart.

RICCARDO (*as if delivering an ultimatum*):
My question! Father, please, answer
that question. Does the Pope—does he
bring *such* scenes to his mind?

FONTANA (*uncertain*): Of course, of course. But what of that?
You know he cannot act according to his feelings!

RICCARDO (*beside himself*):
Father! What you are saying cannot be—
how can you say it!
Does nobody here realize—you, Father,
surely you must realize . . .

The ringing of the bells stops. It is very quiet. Neither speaks. Then
RICCARDO, *extremely agitated but stressing every word, continues
very softly at first, with slowly mounting intensity:*

A deputy of Christ
who sees these things and nonetheless
permits reasons of state to seal his lips—
who wastes even one day in thought,
hesitates even for an hour
to lift his anguished voice
in one anathema to chill the blood
of every last man on earth—
that Pope is . . . a criminal.

RICCARDO *collapses into a chair and is overcome by a fit of weeping. After some hesitation* FONTANA *approaches him. His indigna-*

*tion, which had at first left him speechless, is softened by the sight
of his "prodigal" son.*

FONTANA: You see what talk like this
   can lead to. My boy, how can you . . .

The old SERVANT *enters quickly, but quietly, holds out a file folder
and says:*

SERVANT: At last, Your Honor, here is . . .
FONTANA (*shouting, more intemperately than anyone would have
   thought him capable of*): Let us be!

As the SERVANT, *shocked, slowly retreats toward the door,* FON-
TANA *manages to say:*

   Vittorio, not now—excuse me.
   I can see no one just now . . .

SERVANT *leaves.* FONTANA, *after a long look at* RICCARDO, *with
forced calm:*

   Your monstrous insult to the Pope
   as well as all who serve him . . .
RICCARDO (*still distraught*):
   My own share in the guilt—I, too,
   am guilty—this gives me the right . . .
FONTANA: You are not guilty.
RICCARDO: Yes, guilty as is any bystander.
   And as a priest . . .
FONTANA: Contrition can be pride as well.
   Your duty is *obedience*.
   You are far too—too insignificant
   to bear this guilt . . . aren't you aware
   that hard as you take all this,
   your point of view is superficial,
   humanely biased, distorted by the lenses
   of pity and contemporaneity.
   Proceeding as you do, you cannot grasp
   the meaning of this visitation.
RICCARDO: The meaning! It would take
   the sensibility of a meatgrinder
   to see a meaning in it.
   (*Springing to his feet.*)

Would you have me look down,
supercilious and serene,
with the notorious glazed eyes
of the philosopher,
and dialectilize a meaning
into this murdering?

FONTANA: No sacrifice is wasted, although history
may fail to register the sacrifices. God does.
How can you, a priest, doubt that?
The Pope draws strength from that belief as well.
And he *can* act only when animated by
this confidence. And thus he also can refuse to
blindly grant the promptings of his heart.
He *cannot risk*
endangering the Holy See!
(*After a pause.*) Do not forget one thing, Riccardo:
Whatever Hitler may be doing to the Jews,
only he has the power
to save all Europe from the Russians.

RICCARDO (*wildly*):
A murderer is not a savior! What nonsense, all this talk
about the West, about Christianity!
Let the devil take us
if a murderer of millions
can be accepted by the Pope as a Crusader.
The Russians were defeated long ago.
Hitler stands at the Volga.

FONTANA (*firmly*):
History is not yet over,
a Russia occupied not yet a victory.
The Pope no doubt knows that his protest
would be without effect, or place
the Church in Germany in grave jeopardy.

RICCARDO (*violently*): He does not know that, cannot know!
Galen's success holds promise that a protest
from the *Pope* would certainly
stop Hitler in his tracks.
No doubt he would continue to oppress the Jews,
as slaves working in industry—but *kill* them?
That is highly questionable. And aside from mere
pragmatic grounds . . .

FONTANA (*quickly*) : One cannot disregard these when one
    is responsible for five-hundred million believers
    on this globe.

RICCARDO: It is nowhere written that St. Peter's successor,
    when he appears on Judgment Day,
    will be the world's outstanding stockholder.
    Suppose the Vatican forfeits its power
    over banks, industries, and ministries
    by fighting against Hitler—
    surely the mission God has charged it with
    would be fulfilled with greater honesty.
    Don't you believe the suffering
    and defenselessness of the Fisherman
    who first held the key
    are more becoming to the Pope?
    In time, Father, it must come:
    the Deputy of Christ's return to martyrdom.

FONTANA: Riccardo, you are a visionary!
    You scoff at power, yet you ask us to
    take measures against Hitler. The Pope as a
    poor fisherman—think what Napoleon
    would have done with him, let alone Hitler.
    No, the Pope can only carry out his mission
    as long as he stands at the victor's side.

RICCARDO (*passionately*) : On the side of truth!

FONTANA (*smiling, waving that aside, then dryly*) :
    Truth *is* with the victor—who, as you know,
    also controls the historians.
    And since the history of the world—it's an old saw—
    comes to have meaning only when
    historians have assigned it one,
    you can easily conceive for yourself
    how many footnotes Hitler as the victor
    would concede the Jews . . .
    All of this, Riccardo, can only be endured
    if we never lose our belief
    that God some day will recompense the victims.

RICCARDO: These consolations!
    Would Christ have turned away?

FONTANA: I am no priest—but I know
    that the Pope is not, like you and me, an individual

permitted simply to obey his conscience
and his feelings.
He, in his own person, must preserve the Church.

RICCARDO: And yet it is this very Pope as an individual,
this twelfth Pius, whom Hitler fears.
Pacelli's prestige in Germany is greater
than anywhere else. Perhaps for centuries
no Pope has enjoyed such a reputation
in Germany. He is . . .

The SERVANT *has entered, still obviously cowed. He announces:*

SERVANT: His Eminence, the Most Reverend Cardinal . . .

The name is not heard, for FONTANA *swiftly, slightly alarmed,
replies.*

FONTANA: Oh—yes, please show him in.
   (*To* RICCARDO.) Is it all right for him to see you here?
RICCARDO (*quickly*): He is bound to find out anyhow
that I came here without official orders.
Ask him to lunch.

*Behind the stage, the sonorous, attractive laughter of a fat man is
heard. Evidently His Eminence has condescended to jest mildly
with the servants. The prelate, rotund, florid, but nervous, in fact
irritable at work and in conversation, is a noted flower fancier. In
addition he takes a lively interest in all the illnesses in his wide
circle of acquaintance.*

*At first sight, but only at first sight, he looks like a clubwoman:
with advancing age (although he is little older than* FONTANA*) he
has become visibly more female. But that is deceptive. The* CARDINAL
*is a suave, even ruthless diplomat, and his blue eyes can suddenly
assume the coldness of Göring's or Churchill's eyes, belying the
grandmotherly amiability of his plump face. At such times his
fondness for flowers seems as improbable as Göring's delight in
toy railroads. He has another trick and that is to fall silent and by
his engaging manner seduce his interlocutors into talking until they
have said more than they can justify.*

The CARDINAL *is a man who has risen out of poverty. When he
was still slim and straight, and his black curly hair formed a
troubling contrast to his light, large, laughing eyes, he must have
found it rather difficult to avoid women. He was reputed to have*

had affairs; these rumors were no doubt prompted by envy and were possibly an injustice to him. As long as the power of Eros disturbed him, he was feared for his biting wit. Now malicious sarcasm has given way to an effervescent gaiety.

But the CARDINAL'*s bent for sarcasm was always held in check by his remarkable intelligence, and his mind is still far too alert to reveal anything like its full brilliance in the presence of His Holiness. This prince of the Church always lags perceptibly behind the Pope, whom he refers to as "Chief" and of whom he is not especially fond. He would rather appear stupid than ever show himself superior. He knows why.*

His intellect, however, has never overcome one weakness—and like all such distinctive traits, it has grown stronger with the passing years: the CARDINAL *adores being the bearer of news. News as such fires him, no matter whether it is good or bad. And today a piece of news is burning on the tip of his tongue, a matchless news item, although unfortunately by evening the whole world will know it.*

Like many fat men, the CARDINAL *is extremely deft in his movements. He enters with characteristic vivacity, laughing infectiously.*

His huge head tilted to the right, hat still covering his zucchetto and wearing a light silk cape, the CARDINAL *spreads his arms wide to embrace Count* FONTANA, *who has come forward to meet him. In celebration of the day he is wearing his red hat. In his right hand he holds a choice orchid. He continues to laugh and goes on laughing as he says a few half-finished sentences during the casual embrace. He even laughs in between words as he becomes aware of* RICCARDO'*s presence. This does not actually displease him, but is an annoying surprise. His noisy joviality instantly arouses liking, for it is altogether genuine. Here and now His Eminence is a very good man. Today, on this festival of the Blessed Virgin and the occasion of Count* FONTANA'*s honor, he is quite uncomplicatedly delighted that his high blood pressure is not troubling him.*

CARDINAL: My dear Count—well, well, God
   bless you! We *should,* indeed, don't you think?
   Yes, this time it's gone to the right man! Well, well,
   I mean, I myself must—the Cross of Christ—indeed.
   No! It really—most cordially—indeed.
   I had no idea, really not, you know.
   Yes, straight from the heart. Here—this,
   my *Bletia verecunda,* you know.

FONTANA: Why, thank you, Eminence—how thoughtful.
　　　　What an amazing flower!
　　　　An orchid—what variety, did you say?
CARDINAL: Riccardo! Why, what a joy! Well, well,
　　　　such a surprise. Punctually in Rome
　　　　to congratulate your Papa, aren't you?
RICCARDO (*bending over the* CARDINAL's *ring*):
　　　　Good morning, Your Eminence. Right after dinner
　　　　I intended to call upon Your Eminence
　　　　and ask for an audience.
FONTANA: You will stay for lunch, Eminence?
CARDINAL: What's that? Yes, oh yes, gladly. Look, Count,
　　　　the boy has his high blood pressure again—
　　　　well, well, Riccardo, such a flushed face.
　　　　Aren't there any doctors left in Berlin?

He talks on, as he gives the SERVANT *his hat and cape, alternately addressing father and son, without waiting for answers to any of his questions.*

　　　　Well, well, how splendid, what a surprise.
　　　　And today of all days—any time, for that matter,
　　　　now that your father is so much alone.
　　　　The Nuncio has not advised us of your arrival?
　　　　—Ah yes, the orchid interests you, Count.
　　　　Yes, you know, that is my belovèd
　　　　Bletia verecunda—oh, don't place it in the draft.
　　　　Plenty of light, you know, but no wind!
　　　　Yes, it rarely blooms for me—the only times,
　　　　so to speak, when the Order of Christ is conferred.
　　　　It's old in Europe—we first raised them
　　　　in England back in 1732.
FONTANA (*who obviously does not know quite what to do with
　　　　the noble blossom, very courteously*):
　　　　So very thoughtful, so kind of you,
　　　　Eminence. And fascinating.
　　　　Did it not cost you a pang to cut it for me?
　　　　But please—let us sit down—please,
　　　　Eminence—here.

They continue to stand. FONTANA *hands the orchid to the* SERVANT *and gives him a word of instruction. His Eminence handles the cigar cutter with pleasurable fussiness.* RICCARDO *offers him a light —all this while the conversation continues.*

CARDINAL: Riccardo looks very worn, you know!
  Yet Berlin has such marvelously clear air.
  Here, in September, when no one can step outside,
  why then, you know, I always wish
  I were the Nuncio in Berlin.
  What does your blood pressure read?

RICCARDO (*with extremely cautious irony*):
  Why, Your Eminence, my health is good, very good.
  I have not seen a doctor for more than a year.

FONTANA: But you should! He becomes
  too agitated in Berlin, Your Eminence.

CARDINAL: He's too young for that! No other complaints,
  heart, stomach—you're sure?

RICCARDO: Sound as a bell, Your Eminence.

CARDINAL: Then it must simply be the change of climate,
  the difference in altitude. You felt congestion on the train?

RICCARDO (*politely*): Why yes, a little. But probably only
  because I was lying down throughout the trip.

CARDINAL (*reassured*): Of course, I saw that, you know.
  Well—you must restore the balance.
  And how is your gall trouble, Count?

FONTANA: Oh, not worth mentioning—but please,
  Your Eminence, lunch will be a while yet,
  let us sit down.

CARDINAL (*holding big cigar, takes the Count's arm*):
  Yes, let us sit, let us sit—that reminds me
  of a soirée in Paris—I was then
  as young as Riccardo, and no one looked at me.
  I stood in a corner. Have you nothing to sit on,
  the hostess called at last.
  Indeed, Madame, I have something to sit on,
  I called back across the room,
  something to sit on, yes, but not a chair—well, well . . .

His Eminence enjoys his mot *for some time, while the Fontanas
laugh respectfully.* RICCARDO's *restiveness increases. While the old
gentlemen are taking seats, the* SERVANT *brings champagne and a
precious Venetian glass vase for the orchid.*

CARDINAL: Your restlessness, Riccardo, also indicates
  high blood pressure, you know. Sit down
  over here beside us . . . Ah, yes,
  a glass of *this* will go down well even before noon,

indeed. Well, then, Count,
    once again: may you wear the Order for a long, long time!
FONTANA (*as they touch glasses*): It is really so kind of you
    to have come at once, Your Eminence . . .
RICCARDO (*after a bow*): Your Eminence! Your health, Father!
FONTANA: Thank you, my boy.
CARDINAL: To you, Riccardo!

The CARDINAL *finishes his glass of champagne before he replaces it
on the table. The* SERVANT *refills it immediately. Holding the glass
again, the* CARDINAL *now produces his piece of news, underplaying
it for dramatic effect*:

London has just confirmed the claim
    that Moscow made last night, you know. In *Stalingrad*
    the fighting is over. A German field marshal now
    Stalin's prisoner! The Volga will not be crossed . . .
    Well, that is . . .
RICCARDO (*vehemently, surprised and overjoyed*):
    Capitulated? It's true! And in Berlin
    the Propaganda Ministry was saying,
    and everyone believed it,
    that not a German would surrender!
FONTANA: What else could they have done!
CARDINAL: Moscow says that ninety thousand Germans
    have surrendered—Hitler's field marshal,
    his twenty-two divisions, or rather all that's left of them.
    That is a nasty stroke, and not only for Hitler.
FONTANA: For Hitler militarily no catastrophe,
    Your Eminence, but psychologically . . .
RICCARDO: Psychologically wonderful for us!
CARDINAL (*vexed*): Riccardo, you are very frivolous, indeed.
    This victory at Stalingrad may be the very thing
    to pose a fearful threat to us as Christians!
    (*With emphasis.*) The West, you know, indeed . . .
    Hitler's entire southern front is shaken now.
    He needs the oil in the Caucasus.
    Ah well, perhaps he will become the master
    of the situation once again.
RICCARDO (*cautiously, aware of the need to tread with utmost
    care*): But Your Eminence, you must also wish
    to see Hitler humbled.

CARDINAL (*jovially, trying not to show his impatience*):
>But hardly by the Russians, dear Riccardo.
>Let England beat him, and the USA, indeed,
>until he gets it through his head that he
>can't rule the whole world by himself, you know.
>*Defeats*—why, by all means! But let him stop
>oppressing and killing Poles and Jews,
>Czechs and priests. Oh yes, indeed, . . .
>Otherwise, peace is not conceivable, you know.

FONTANA *signs to the* SERVANT *to leave.*

RICCARDO: Peace with Hitler, Your Eminence, can never be conceivable.

CARDINAL (*first laughs, amused at* RICCARDO's *rash statement; then, as if he were on the point of weeping from sheer vexation*):
>*Never?*—Never say never in politics!
>Count, just listen to your son—such a bright boy,
>but he too, now, has caught this Casablanca nonsense.
>Well, well. Holy Madonna, who will *ever*
>persuade Hitler to surrender unconditionally!
>But, you know, must we go over all this
>today—here, on this beautiful morning, you know!
>I wanted to *congratulate* your father, Riccardo!

It must not be thought that the CARDINAL *is evading the argument out of indolence. He simply feels it unseemly for his youngest assistant to be trying to lecture him.* FONTANA, *himself an old man, feels that better than does* RICCARDO.

FONTANA (*mediating*):
>Yes, Your Eminence, let us have one more toast—
>to what—let's say, that Stalingrad
>will be a lesson to Herr Hitler.

CARDINAL: Well, well, yes. Cheers and good health.

RICCARDO: Your health.

CARDINAL (*more amiably*):
>The Chief—the Chief let Mr. Roosevelt know
>in no uncertain terms
>that he regards America's demand
>for Hitler's unconditional surrender,
>as absolutely un-Christian, you know.

FONTANA: And above all *ludicrous,* Your Eminence.
America is almost being bled to death against Japan.
And here in Europe? Why, there's no sign of them!
While Hitler can, at any rate, set
half a dozen victories like Cannae
against the drubbing he received in Stalingrad.
They will have to negotiate with him, certainly.

CARDINAL: I should hope so, although
Cannae clearly demonstrates, you know,
that victories in battle do not
necessarily decide the wars.
This time, again, the Germans might
conquer themselves to death because
they carry the fire everywhere instead
of concentrating on a single front.
Their megalomania, which was once our fear
today is our strongest hope, you know.
Already it has cost them so much blood
that even Hitler will grow temperate again.
Trouble is good for dictators, you know;
also the Kremlin, Heaven help us, last November,
just when the fight began for Stalingrad,
settled its conflict with the Church, you know.
Hitler, as soon as war began,
knew that when soldiers start to die
he could not do without the Church.

FONTANA (*who sees opportunity here*):
May we hope, Your Eminence, that the Pope
will take advantage of Hitler's predicament
to threaten him with breaking off the Concordat
if he continues murdering the Jews?
I heard ghastly reports from New York yesterday
concerning Poland and Rumania . . .

CARDINAL (*smiling, suddenly nervous, rising*):
Has Riccardo been besieging you as well, dear Count?
Lo and behold: Fontana *père et fils*
forming a single front!

FONTANA: Not quite, Your Eminence. Only Hitler's fiasco
on the Volga gives me the courage to request
that we denounce his infamy.

CARDINAL: Well . . . You know, Riccardo, I told you once before,
last summer, when you and then the Nuncio
in Pressburg and in Bucharest—and then the Poles
in London reported, you know,
the dreadful things occurring there: I told you
the Concordat is intended to protect
our fellow Catholics—the Chief will not
expose himself to danger for the Jews.

FONTANA: Not even now, Your Eminence, when Hitler
would have to be amenable?

CARDINAL (*with mounting earnestness and deep emotion; the huge
cigar smokes heavily*):
Of course we do a lot, but on the quiet, you know.
The Raphael Club has raised the money
to help thousands escape abroad, you know.
But three events in recent weeks
must alarm every Christian, you know.
First, the recklessness of the United States
in leaving Europe to Stalin's divisions;
second, the defeat of Hitler on the Volga;
and third, Stalin's reconciliation with
the Orthodox Church. That proves to me, you know,
proves unequivocally to me, that Stalin's
Communism is only a deceptive
redemptionist ideal. Communist or not, you know,
he *is* the Tsar, the Orthodox heart
of all the Russians, the Slav,
true to his nationality, who nurses
the dreams of absolute sovereignty
once cherished by Peter and by Catherine.
Naturally he had first to make a reconciliation
with those apostates from the Church of Rome,
schismatics, anti-Latins, Pan-Slavists, you know.
The soul of the East is alien to the Latin spirit.
And if this war, you know,
does not bring the old Continent closer
to realization of the ancient dream
of a Holy Roman Empire, why then,
you know, the last Christians may as well
take to the catacombs again.

RICCARDO: Your Eminence, an incendiary like Hitler
    who only squanders the power of Europe,
    who lets Mussolini lure him into
    futile adventures in Africa and Greece—
    such a man cannot unite the West.

CARDINAL: Do you imagine then that the conceited
    parliaments and debating clubs à la Geneva
    would have the force to do it? Did not
    the League of Nations perish from insincerity?
    Ah, those representatives of narrow interests
    from Warsaw to Paris, from Rome to London—
    they *talked* Europe to her death.
    Your father will tell you all about that, you know!
    No, this continent is much too old,
    too torn asunder, ravaged by prejudice,
    for its inhabitants to unify in peace.
    Did the cities of ancient Greece, for instance,
    after all their quarrels, still have the strength
    for unification?
    What if God now were using Hitler
    to chasten Europe's nations
    deluded in their grandeur—
    think of France, for instance—
    so that after all this the old frontiers
    which Hitler has overrun can never be restored again—
    what of that?
    Wars always bring about results
    different from those that people fight for.
    One need not be a general, you know,
    to sense that any idea so formidable
    as Europe's unification can only be
    accomplished amid blood and agony,
    on the battlefield—but not
    by discussions among liberal democrats
    who always merely serve as representatives
    of special selfish interests, you know.
    The fact that Scandinavians, Italians, Croats,
    Rumanians, Flemings, Basques and Bretons,
    Spaniards, Finns and Magyars, have formed
    a single front with the Germans against Stalin—
    (*indignantly*) that should have deterred Mr. Roosevelt

from giving the Kremlin leave to conquer Berlin . . .
Besides, you know, it is a vain and empty boast,
sheer megalomania, you know . . .

RICCARDO: Permit me, Your Eminence—the moral right,
surely, is on the Russian side, without a doubt.
They are waging a just war!
They were attacked, their country devastated,
their people carried off, slaughtered.
If they are threatening Europe now,
the blame is only Hitler's.

CARDINAL (*coldly, impatiently*):
That may be—but when the house is burning,
the fire must be put out—the question
of who kindled it can be investigated
later on, you know.
(*He laughs.*) Be careful, Count. Your Riccardo
is an idealist, which is to say,
a fanatic, you know. In the end
the idealist always spills blood in the delusion
that he is doing good—*more* blood than any realist.

★

*He gives a lordly laugh; he wants both to conciliate and to change
the subject. Then, with ironic hauteur, which is designed to make*
RICCARDO *seem a figure of fun:*

Riccardo—you idealists are *inhuman.*
We realists are more humane, because
we take men as they are.
We laugh at their faults, for we know we share them.
An idealist does not laugh—can Herr Hitler
laugh? Has he personally any faults?
No, he cannot laugh at this world;
he wants to improve it.
Anyone who differs with his ideals is exterminated.
This rules out compromise, I fear.
He must first smash a world so that he can
confer *his* peace upon it. No, thanks.
We realists are compromisers, conformists—
very well, we make concessions.
But why not? It's a case of staying alive
or being consistent, you know.
Let us never forget that both the devil

and the saints were placed in this world by God.
Between them stands man, whose only choice
is always between two sins, you know, Riccardo.
(*Casually.*) Your fanaticism is no service to the Church.
Hitler exists, after all—we *must*
live with him, you know.
And be on your guard—an old man
may be allowed to say this, you know—
be on your guard against judgments that will
only damn us all in the eyes of history.
Hitler, you say, *attacked* Russia!
Your father and I—don't you agree, Count . . .

FONTANA: You are quite right, Your Eminence.

CARDINAL: We content ourselves with saying: Hitler marched in.
Marched in, you know. Let us not enter
into controversy. Do you imagine
that cunning chessmaster entered Russia *gladly?*
He could not help himself—not in thirty-nine
when he concluded the pact with Stalin
(before the English could make one)
and not in forty-one, when he broke the pact.
You really have no idea, you know,
to what extent a ruler is the slave
of the events that he has brought about.
When Hitler made an agreement with Stalin,
in order to be free to go at England,
he roused the tiger at his back. He *could*
not know how long Russia would play the part
of his grain supplier; and the prices—
the Baltic, the Straits and Besserabia—
were reaching the extortion point, you know.
But Mr. Churchill, you know, was sure
of his supplies from the United States.
I grant you Stalin did not directly threaten Hitler,
no more than Alexander let Napoleon
provoke him into taking the offensive.
But let us admit that scarcely anyone
could have foreseen that Stalin would be able
to resist the Wehrmacht nearly so long.
Hitler was not alone in his mistake, you know.
A *rapid* victory in the East would actually

have made him invincible, you know. A blessing
that he did not have it—but a blessing too
that he will not be overthrown, you know.

RICCARDO (*terribly concerned, speaking as pleasantly as he can
manage*): But Your Eminence, the Holy Father really must
protest that hundreds of thousands of persons
are being literally slaughtered—killings
which have no bearing on the outcome of the war.

CARDINAL: Must, you say! Now, now, my boy,
calmness alone disarms the fanatic, nothing else.
The Chief, you know, would be risking a great deal
if he took up cudgels for the Jews.
Minorities are always unpopular,
in every country. The Jews
have long provoked the Germans, you know.
They overdrew on the credit they'd been given
there in Germany.
Pogroms do not fall from Heaven . . .

FONTANA (*cautiously; he feels that* RICCARDO's *arguments are only
having a negative effect*):
I quite agree, Your Eminence—only,
one really can scarcely speak of pogroms
in Germany. Hitler's legal experts
have drawn up whole collections of new laws
to strip the Jews of civil rights, and now
even physically to annihilate them.

RICCARDO (*with a quietness which makes its impression*):
In times gone by we Christians
were also in the minority, and perhaps
we will be soon again. I believe that God
has indissolubly linked us Christians to
the people to whom Jesus belonged . . .

CARDINAL (*with a long laugh, adroitly*):
But, but—my dear Fontanas,
to *whom* are you saying all this.
Count, do you think me an enemy of the Jews?

FONTANA (*quickly*): Certainly not, Your Eminence.

CARDINAL: I'm only saying, you know, that the share
the Jews had of the leading professions in Germany
before Hitler came to power, was certainly
unhealthy. They provided too many

doctors, lawyers, bankers and manufacturers.
Newspapermen, too, you know—naturally
because they were more capable. Members of a minority
are always more capable; right from the start, in school,
they take the whippings for the others, you know.
That makes people unpleasantly capable, you know . . .

FONTANA (*determined to save the situation*):
Too capable, at any rate, in a nation
that has more than six million unemployed.

CARDINAL (*spontaneously, gratefully*):
There you are— I meant no more than that.
The chief problem, Riccardo, is, you know,
the dreadful popularity of Hitler.

RICCARDO: Your Eminence must consider this: that since
his entry into Paris two full years—
war years—have passed. The people are tired
and afraid. Then the Allied bombers . . .
Berlin society has a wicked tongue.

CARDINAL (*animated, glad to digress, paces back and forth*):
The people love rulers whom they can fear.
Nero—I am not joking, you know—Nero
was also highly popular with the mob.
"But the people of Rome *adored* him!" Frightful, you know.
He too was an "architect"! The Circus, the Party Days . . .
The Reichstag Fire—and then the manhunts,
not of Christians this time, but of Jews,
of Communists—parallels, frightful, aren't they?
(*Half cynical, half downcast.*)
Society, Riccardo, it may be,
sees Hitler as the parvenu—although they still rejoice
when their sons receive his decorations.
But the people—I would really like to see
a people who did *not* adore a ruler
who offers it so many scapegoats, you know.
And where would the Church be, my friends,
if it had not ignited faggots for the mob
during the Middle Ages. Panem et circenses,
confiscations, indulgences and deaths by fire:
the people always must be *offered* something!
And Hitler, you know, also gave them bread.
Let us not forget that. Bread,
and a uniform and daggers.

Most of the rowdies who fought his beerhall battles
had long been running after the red flag
before the swastika was sewed on it . . .
Let us not ignore the fact, you know,
that the people gave him half of all their votes.
Or almost half—that was in thirty-three
during the last relatively fair election.
Granted, the noble Krupps and others like them
even then gave Hitler's unofficial cabinet
three million marks, you know.
He used them as bait for the rabble.
And then the bishops, you know, the bishops in Germany!
Of course we mustn't say this sort of thing—
but between ourselves, dear Fontanas, between ourselves
(*with gustatory satisfaction, savoring the words like
oysters on his tongue*)
that touches on the Chief's *point d'honneur.*
The great diplomat Pacelli, you know!
Hitler looked like a hairdresser—the Concordat
made him socially acceptable urbi et orbi.
And now you want the Chief to curse him ex cathedra?

He laughs; FONTANA *joins in.*

RICCARDO (*attempting to stand up for the Pope*):
    Your Eminence—did not the Concordat
    have to be concluded to protect our brethren?
CARDINAL (*laughs heartily, pats* RICCARDO *on the shoulder*):
    That's how history is made, you know, Riccardo.
    Let us hope it will seem so later on.
    No, ask your Papa—in those happy not-so-far-off days
    no one here believed Hitler would undertake
    those dreadful things he'd trumpeted in his book . . .
    It was there for anyone to read, you know,
    that some time somebody ought to poison—
    he's a rough one, you know—
    a few tens of thousands of the Hebrews, as he put it.
    I would have taken a look at the man first, you know.
FONTANA: The late eleventh Pius, Your Eminence,
    told me the Concordat with Hitler would be
    a platform from which to make protests
    if necessary . . . Now it *is* necessary.

CARDINAL (*digressing again*):
 The old Chief was a fighter, I grant you that.
 But above all Pacelli wanted to
 top his Concordats with the biggest one of all.
 And so, you know, the See went so far
 as to advise the poor democrats in Germany
 to give themselves up, you know.
 Hitler was seen as a second Mussolini
 with whom it would be so easy to do business . . .
 (*He laughs.*) Ah yes, the democrats . . . some years ago,
  you know,
 I met in Paris one of Hitler's predecessors . . .
 Oh yes, a very famous man, now exiled and embittered.
 "We had the same intentions!" he said. He meant
 the elimination of unemployment, the building
 of the autobahns. The plans were his, he said . . .
FONTANA: Why didn't he carry them out?
 I think, Your Eminence, I know who told you that.
CARDINAL (*laughs*):
 Yes, *why* not! That was my private thought as well.
 You know, our singers in the old days, Count . . .
 they also knew exactly how it's done,
 only *they* couldn't, you know.
 (*Serious again, with steely opportunism.*)
 As long as Hitler is winning and has the people behind him—
 Stalingrad alone will not topple his throne—
 the Chief would only make himself unpopular
 if he openly made an issue of the Jews.
 Brother Innitzer has already tried that, you know.
 The Cardinal was Hitler's mortal foe—until the day
 the amazing scoundrel marched into Vienna.
 Then the people roared a welcome—a
 quantité négligeable, sixty thousand, I think,
 were put behind bars—but the man in the street rejoiced.
 Then the Cardinal did the only clever thing:
 after the parade to the Hofburg he was
 the first to congratulate Hitler, you know.
 The Chief would lose a great deal of prestige
 if he endangered his position for the Jews, Riccardo.
RICCARDO: Among the Germans—perhaps.
 But what about the United States, Your Eminence?

CARDINAL (*firmly, conclusively*):
  Not only among the Germans, you know!
  Among the Poles, the Dutch, the French,
  the Ukrainians as well—among all those
  who are actively participating in the manhunt, you know.
  In the United States as well there are extremely militant
  foes of the Jews, you know.
  Men love butchery, alas, God knows.
  And once they start, reason will not sway them.
  No, Riccardo, I cannot advise the Chief
  to challenge Herr Hitler at this juncture.
  The defeat on the Volga is troublesome enough
  for him at this time, you know.
  How would it be if our Nuncio in Berlin
  were to speak to Herr von Weizsäcker about the matter?

RICCARDO (*bitterly*):
  All that would come of that, Your Eminence,
  would be a courteous exchange of words.
  The undersecretary undoubtedly knows nothing
  about the extermination of the Jews.
  In the streets of the German capital
  he manages to overlook completely
  the fact that Jews are being sent away
  like dangerous criminals.
  And since nobody dares to suggest
  to Herr von Weizsäcker that he might be lying
  in the name of his Führer,
  and since he so readily assures everyone
  that threats will only aggravate the situation . . .

CARDINAL (*sharply, because he feels* RICCARDO's *irony is arrogant*):
  Can *you* guarantee that threats
  will *really not* aggravate the situation?

RICCARDO (*making his last attempt; his control is slipping and he
  speaks much too loudly*):
  Your Eminence, a hundred thousand Jewish families in
      Europe
  face certain murder!
  It could not, could not, possibly be *worse!*
  (*More quietly, fervently.*)
  No, Your Eminence, please do not try
  to do anything through Weizsäcker, or through the Nuncio.

It must be: the Pope to Hitler—
directly and at once!

FONTANA (*agitated because he feels that* RICCARDO *is spoiling all
chance by the tone he takes*):
Please, my boy—are you attempting
to give orders here? I beg you . . .

CARDINAL (*places a hand on* RICCARDO's *shoulder; but the gesture
means nothing*):
He's tired from lack of sleep, you know . . .
Riccardo—I do not care to hear
such deprecating talk of Weizsäcker, you know.
He is a man of honor, the tried and true
familiar link between the Nuncio
and the Foreign Office.
In thirty-nine he was the *only* one
you possibly could go on talking to.
Though even he could not save the peace.

FONTANA (*making a feeble effort to appease*):
Yes, Your Eminence, that remains to his credit.
But many a virtue, when employed by Hitler,
is easily converted into vice.

CARDINAL (*smiling*):
It is always a virtue to speak of peace, Count.

FONTANA: While the freight cars crammed with deportees
roll on toward the crematoria? I am,
Your Eminence knows, no cynic . . .

CARDINAL: Yes, the problem is a difficult, an insoluble . . .

The SERVANT *has entered and reports to* FONTANA.

SERVANT: His Eminence is urgently wanted. An officer . . .

CARDINAL: Please!
(*To* FONTANA.) Permit me? Naturally I want
to go over the whole thing with the Chief once more.

*An officer of the Swiss Guard enters and gives a highly military
salute.*

SWISS: Your Eminence, His Holiness urgently requests
Your Eminence's presence in the Papal Palace.
I have orders to drive Your Eminence at once . . .

CARDINAL (*extremely annoyed*):
Now—before lunch? Very well,
my hat, Vittorio . . . What a pity.

I fail to see how anything we may discuss
will change the course of things in Stalingrad . . . Well.

As he dons his hat and RICCARDO *takes his cape from the* SERVANT *to help His Eminence into it,* FONTANA *speaks.*

FONTANA: A fearful pity—can't we wait with lunch?
CARDINAL: Out of the question, Count. Too bad.

Laughing intimately, as if the quarrel had been made up.

I may as well confess I asked the servants,
even before you mentioned lunch,
what the menu was for today—ah yes,
I'm without shame, you know.
And now instead of specialità della casa Fontana—
a conference on Stalingrad—it's sad, you know.
Riccardo!

He goes up to him. RICCARDO *again kisses his ring.*

Take lemons to keep down that blood pressure.
And if that doesn't work, foot baths, as hot
as you can stand . . . This afternoon?
RICCARDO: Yes, Your Eminence, many thanks. When shall it be?
CARDINAL (*casually*): Let's say, five. I think
you'd better go to Lisbon for six months.
(*Quickly, without transition.*)
My dear Count, enough politics for today.
This is your day to celebrate. God bless you.
Arrivederla.
RICCARO (*downcast*): Arrivederla, Your Eminence.
FONTANA (*bowing him out*):
It was so good of you to come, Your Eminence.
May I say, above all . . .

The SERVANT *closes the door behind them. All leave except* RICCARDO.

RICCARDO (*alone, crushed, to himself*): *Lisbon!* Sidetracked!

He nervously lights a cigarette, opens the veranda door. His father returns and says rapidly, before the SERVANT *has completely closed the door behind him—*

FONTANA: He's getting rid of you! He did not even ask
why you returned from Berlin!

       Lisbon: that's your payment
       for having gone too far.

RICCARDO: But, Father, I kept back the very worst,
       hoping he might at least *try* to persuade the Pope
       to take a position.

FONTANA: What else?

RICCARDO: Weizsäcker is coming to *Rome*.
       He will soon ask for his *agrément!*

FONTANA (*incredulously*):
       Hitler is making his undersecretary of state
       ambassador to the Vatican?

RICCARDO: No doubt entrusted with a special mission!
       In the first place, he's to keep an eye
       on Mussolini. They're afraid that Italy
       will soon be liquidating Fascism.
       Secondly—and above all—Weizsäcker,
       as Hitler's pure and stainless front,
       is now supposed to keep the Pope in person
       carefully soothed. All the old stuff:
       mutual non-intervention;
       no discussions of principles, no intrigues.
       For Hitler knows what it would mean
       if the Pope should join the protests of the Allies
       against his crimes.
       It would scotch his last hope of the West's
       agreeing on a separate peace
       and giving him a free hand in the East . . .

Silence.

RICCARDO (*heartily*): I'm so grateful that you're backing me.

FONTANA: Stalingrad marks the turning point permitting us to act.
       You are right, my boy—but you have no say!

RICCARDO: Father, I implore you:
       We must act before
       Weizsäcker arrives in Rome—immediately, Father.

*The bells begin to ring loudly again. Both look up and then ex-
change glances.* FONTANA *makes a resigned gesture.*

SERVANT: Luncheon is served.

CURTAIN

Act Three: The Visitation

The world is silent. The world knows
what is going on here—it cannot help
but know, and it is silent. And in the
Vatican, the deputy of God is silent,
too. . . .   FROM AN UNDERGROUND
POLISH PAMPHLET, AUGUST, 1943

Scene One

Early evening in Rome, October 16, 1943.

The apartment of a young teacher, DR. LOTHAR LUCCANI, *located on the lively Via di Porta Angelica, which begins at the Bernini colonnades on St. Peter's Square. The left side of the street, as far as the Piazza del Risorgimento, is enclosed by the high wall of the Vatican, the right side by tall business buildings, cafés, and tenement houses.*

LUCCANI's *apartment on the street side affords a reassuring view of the Papal Palace opposite, with His Holiness's living quarters on the fourth floor. Thus this scene bears out what Herr von Weizsäcker, by then Ambassador of the German Reich to the Papal See, reported to Berlin on October 17: that "the incident took place, as it were, under the Pope's windows."*

If possible, the view through the living room window and through the high, narrow door, which opens out on the flat roof of the building, should show the upper stories of the Renaissance Papal Palace; but the dome of St. Peter's, as in the second act, will serve the same purpose: to illustrate the fact noted by Gerald Reitlinger in The Final Solution—*Jews were "herded to their death from the very shadow of St. Peter's."*

The stage is subdivided into three areas: to the left, the narrow hallway, with the door to the outside hall in the rear and a door right, leading to the living room which takes up most of the center of the stage. The living room contains little furniture and is marked as belonging to a scholar by a fragment of an antique relief mounted on the wall and by two walls of books. On the right is the bright, colorful children's room, which is as narrow as the hall. Two small beds stand lined against the walls; a wicker doll carriage is in the middle of the room. This children's room has no door to the living room; to reach it the actors must go out through

125

*the living room door into the hall and cross the entire stage, close
to the footlights.*

*In the living room stand an open wicker trunk and four suitcases
already packed, also a cardboard carton and a schoolbag. Hats
and coats are piled on the couch. A girl of about five carries one
doll after the other out of the nursery and places them on the
suitcases. Her brother, about eight years old, is sprawled on the
floor in the children's room. He is leafing through a stamp album.*
DR. LOTHAR LUCCANI *stands at the living room window. His wife
is putting an infant to bed. The baby, lying on the table, cries at
first, then whimpers, and falls quiet after the mother has comforted
it. Her father-in-law is sitting by a floor lamp, reading the* Osservatore Romano *with the aid of a magnifying glass.*

LOTHAR: I have nothing more to do.
    Half past four and still broad daylight.
    Darkness is late in coming. My patience
    is beginning to give out.
JULIA: Why are you so nervous?
    Everything is packed.
    The priest expressly asked me
    not to get there until after dark.
    Be glad that they will hide us at all.
LOTHAR (*nervously*): You think we ought to walk? Yes, you're
      right;
    we'll all go on foot. Once we're safe
    Signora Simonetta can bring the suitcases.
    She can get a cab at St. Peter's Square.
JULIA (*trying to calm him*): But Lothar, that was all arranged
    long ago. I've given her money;
    she has the keys too—all that remains
    is to leave her money for the rent.
LUCCANI SR.: I've already taken care of that.
    The rent is paid until April.
THE GIRL: Daddy, can I take them all?
LOTHAR: That's most kind of you, Father.
    (*To his daughter.*) You may take two dolls.
    And the bear or the dog. Not both.
LUCCANI SR.: You don't need Signora Simonetta.
    I can wait for the cab here
    and give the driver the baggage.

Then we will be sure
that the apartment is securely locked.
Why have the woman sniffing around
in the rooms after we are gone . . .

JULIA (*annoyed*): But Grandfather! We're giving Pippa
into her care, and you distrust her.

LOTHAR (*leafing distractedly through a book, unable to decide whether or not to pack it*):
And don't you linger behind here either!
Why wait any longer than absolutely necessary.
I don't like . . .

JULIA (*still busy with the baby*): Lothar, don't be so nervous.
It affects the children.

LOTHAR (*very nervously, irritably, raising his voice*):
I'm not in the least!
After all, we have been warned.
I reproach myself for not having left
yesterday, when the priest came to see us.
All this damned packing.

JULIA: The Germans have been in Rome for weeks.
No Jew has been arrested yet.
Why should it be today?

LOTHAR (*vehemently*): Why! Why! Because the orders
have just been given *now*. The gold
was not enough for them. They've already
looted the synagogues. Now it's our turn.
Do you still not believe (*after a pause*) the reports from
London?
Whenever the Russians recapture their territory,
they come across mass graves
filled with murdered civilians, Jews.

LUCCANI SR. (*irritably lays down the newspaper and says very firmly*): I know the Germans better than you.
I don't believe these fables. Who was it
shot the five thousand officers in Katyn Forest—
the Germans or the Russians?

LOTHAR: I don't know. They're both capable of it.
At any rate, German ammunition
was found in the bodies.

LUCCANI SR.: That proves nothing. The Germans
exhumed the Polish victims—a sign

that they were in the clear. Stalin
killed them—just as six years ago
he killed his own General Staff.

JULIA: Please, Grandfather, have you two
nothing else to talk about?
We're not in Poland here.
The Pope is right beside us; with him there,
no one is going to come and take us away.

She points to the window, and smilingly gives her husband a kiss.

The Holy Father doesn't have to quail before Hitler.
And the Americans are already in Naples.

LOTHAR: My dear, we are not Catholic.

LUCCANI SR.: But *I* am Catholic—that's enough.
Besides, we've already made arrangements with the monastery.

LOTHAR (*ironically*):
That will make a great impression on the Germans.
How naïve you both are. All right, let's
change the subject. It's getting darker.

THE BOY *has carried the album into the living room. He speaks
to his father.*

THE BOY: Papa, can I take the stamps with me?

LOTHAR: I suppose so. Sit down at the table
and carefully remove them from the album.
The album takes up too much room.
You can put them in the box
with the unsorted ones.

THE BOY (*outraged*): Then they'll all be mixed up.
(*To his sister.*) Don't touch my stamps.

THE GIRL: They're mine, too.

JULIA: You two be good, hush up
so Pippa can get to sleep.
Then we'll carry her up to Signora Simonetta.
Lothar, would you be so good and take
all this stuff up to her now.

*She lays two bath towels on her husband's arm, and a heap of
diapers; then she puts bottles, powder, toys and baby clothes
into a bag.*

We'll leave the carriage down here.
(*Abruptly.*) Shouldn't we take Pippa with us after all?

LOTHAR (*laden, impatient, unjust, takes the bag from her hand*):
　　You always have to upset all arrangements!
　　A baby's crying doesn't belong in a monastery.
　　You wouldn't even be able to bathe her there,
　　not to speak of the communal meals.
JULIA: You're right, Lothar—only
　　it's hard for me to leave Pippa behind.
LOTHAR: Anything else? I'll be right back.
　　(*Kindly.*) It's hard for me too, Julia.

He kisses her on the forehead, then kisses the baby and goes out.

JULIA (*calling after him*):
　　Tell Signora Simonetta, in half an hour
　　I'll be bringing Pippa up.

The hall door remains open; LOTHAR's *footsteps can be heard on the stairs.* LUCCANI SR. *caresses the baby; then* JULIA *carries it into the nursery and deposits it in its basket. The grandfather goes out, saying to himself—*

LUCCANI SR.: I'll read the light meter once more
　　and turn off the gas.
　　(*To his grandchildren.*) You behave yourselves.
THE GIRL: Grandpa, the stamps do belong to me too.

But she is paying no attention to the stamps, which her brother is busy with; following her mother's example, she is diapering one of her dolls on a trunk.

LUCCANI SR.: I'll give you a doll that can really talk;
　　or a book of fairy tales—which would you like?
THE BOY: And stamps from America for me!
LUCCANI SR.: You must be very good when you're with the monks.
　　Then you'll both get something. I hope
　　(*to himself*) we'll be able to send for the rugs.
　　Those bare stone floors in winter . . .

He goes out, crossing the hall to the left. While he is talking with the children, LOTHAR *returns and goes to the nursery.* JULIA *is standing over the baby in the basket. They look at the child, then step back from the basket, downstage.* LOTHAR *embraces his wife.*

LOTHAR: Forgive me for being so irritable.

He presses his face against the back of her neck and kisses her passionately.

JULIA (*tenderly*): It will pass—it cannot last much longer.
The Allies are already at the Volturno.

LOTHAR (*again vehement*):
Good Lord, why don't they land at Ostia!
My dear, my dear, you place your hopes in the Americans,
Grandfather in the Pope—and I, I
hope for nothing at all. If only
the monastery gate were closed behind us now . . .

JULIA: Admit, Lothar, that you're always
expecting the worst—aren't you?
Is it nothing that at least
we're able to stay together?

She kisses him and caresses his arm.

LOTHAR (*gloomily*):
To have to do without my work, my books,
it's going to be hard. Then, all those people . . .

JULIA (*resignedly*): You misanthrope. The books are still
more important to you than I am, aren't they?
Sometimes I'm a bother to you.

LOTHAR: Why Julia, how can you . . .

JULIA: I am, I know. Before we had the children,
who need me, I would often be unhappy
because of that. You never even noticed, you selfish man.

She embraces him.

We quarrel so much; it's horrible.

LOTHAR (*thunderstruck*): But Julia—you know how much I need
you!

JULIA (*smiling*): A little—sometimes.

LOTHAR: We're still young; we'll make up for everything
once this damned war is over.

JULIA: One cannot make up for anything. Oh,
but I know you've done without a great deal
on my account. For a man,
you tied yourself down much too soon.

LOTHAR: Yes, but to *you,* Julia. You are
the one woman who includes all the others
I didn't have.

He has turned again, is again very restive.

Which trunk are the papers in?
And where are the bankbooks? We should
have drawn out all the balance.
JULIA: With your manuscript. But . . .
(*she frees herself from his arms*)
I almost forgot my ring in the bathroom.

She goes out to the right; LOTHAR *goes to the left, down the hall
to the living room.* LUCCANI SR. *has meanwhile also returned to the
living room and has begun some wholly pointless "work": he is
sorting out the newspapers in their basket, pedantically checking the
dates with his magnifying glass. He speaks to his granddaughter—*

LUCCANI SR.: Why have you brought all your children
in here? Let them sleep.
THE GIRL: I have to give them their baths.
Then I'm going to take them with us.
THE BOY: Take all of them? Daddy said only two.
Daddy, can she take all the dolls?
If she does, I want to take my gun too.
LOTHAR (*carrying two suitcases out to the hall, making a feeble
attempt to joke*): To the monastery?
Do you hear, Julia?
He wants to storm the monastery with his gun.
Not even the Nazis do that.

JULIA *enters the living room; both laugh.*

JULIA: You can't take guns to the monastery, darling.
Grandfather—for whom are you sorting out
those old newspapers? I suppose
you're having nerves too?
LUCCANI SR.: Not a bit. It's just
that I have nothing else to do.
(*He looks at his watch.*) But you're right. I'd better see
if all the windows are shut tight.
JULIA: They all are.

The old man goes out nevertheless.

JULIA (*to her husband*):
I'll give Signora Simonetta the key to the cellar, too.
So she can come, every few days, and bring
a jar of our preserves for the monks.

That way we'll also have a chance
(*sadly*) to see little Pippa. Otherwise, in two or three months
she won't know me any more.

There is a loud ring.

There she is now.

The bell rings again, longer this time. LOTHAR *goes out; in the
doorway he meets his father, who enters the room with a distraught
look.* JULIA *looks questioningly at him. He shrugs, cannot say a
word.* LOTHAR *closes the living room door, then, while the ringing
persists, opens the hall door. The four in the room cower together.*

*A German staff sergeant of the Waffen-SS and two Italians of
the Fascist Militia swarm into the room. The sergeant's name is*
WITZEL; *in 1943 he resembled the typical thirty-five-year-old German, just as in 1960, when he held the post of Chief Inspector
of the Municipal Government in D., he looked like most fifty-year-
old Germans. Perhaps it should be mentioned that he is very
"correct"—the rude, obscene, blustering tone he uses toward
Jews and other defenseless persons, because that is the custom,
doesn't really belong to him. Quite instinctively,* WITZEL *has picked
up this brutal loquacity from his superiors; he even parrots their
turns of speech. As soon as his superiors change after the war,
he will just as quickly unlearn these habits. By 1959 he has become
a dependable citizen. His love of order makes him dislike neo-Nazi
agitation as much as strikes or a burst water main. He is so typically
a person of his time that his clothes define him, not his face.
Consequently he can play the* FATHER *in the first scene and the
Jewish* KAPO *in the last; when he changes roles, he should not
even be disguised by a mustache or a pair of glasses.*

*The two Italians are likewise of the kind which served as raw
material for contemporary history—two ordinary louts who would
just as unconcernedly have piled the faggots for Joan of Arc. One
of them carries a rifle at the ready, but holds it tucked under his
arm so carelessly that one has the feeling if it is ever fired, it will
be by mistake. More important to him is the wicker-covered bottle
which he holds in his other hand and from which he drinks at
regular intervals. His comrade has a thin, stern face and piercing
eyes. He is "correct," dashing, and vain as a drum major on the
piazza. He holds the list of names and superfluously wields pencils
of various colors. He wears pistols and a cartridge belt. His cap is*

exactly centered, he is meticulously shaven; his uniform, with colored cord on the tunic, is clean and pressed. He wears boots, while the other man has on dirty trousers which, for all we know, he does not shed at night except in special circumstances. WITZEL has no power over him—and is irritated even by the frivolous mustache of this "crook."

FIRST MILITIAMAN (*with the list*): Doctor Lothar Luccani? Wife Julia,
    children, two: one boy, one girl.
    You are going to a labor camp.
    Pack up, quick!

WITZEL *and the* SECOND MILITIAMAN *with the bottle have pressed past them into the living room, the door to which has just been opened by* JULIA.

WITZEL (*amiably*): Pack up! Here's the whole bunch
    all together in one room.

His speech is not marked by any particular dialect, merely sloppy to the extreme. His enunciation becomes even slacker as his voice grows louder.

LOTHAR (*softly to* JULIA): Too late.

Completely resigned, he leans against the door jamb until WITZEL, *who has closed the hall door again, gives him so brutal a push that he lurches far back into the room.*

WITZEL: Get busy—pack up your stuff.
LUCCANI SR. (*is the first to compose himself*):
    What charge have you against my son?
WITZEL (*louder, paying no attention to the old man*):
    You've got ten minutes,
    or at least five. Pack, get moving, avanti!
LUCCANI SR. (*goes up to him with great resolution*):
    We are Catholics, are all baptized.
    You have no right to arrest us. Where is your order?
WITZEL (*amiably*): Where is your Jew star?
    Catholic, eh! I used to be Catholic too.
    You'll get over it.
    Ten minutes time, because you're Catholic.

He looks around, points to the packed suitcases.

All ready to leave? How did you know
we were coming for you?
The whole family all together here?

JULIA (*with composure*): Yes, the whole family.
We didn't know—we were only going on a trip.

WITZEL: I see, on a trip—to some monastery, eh?

*He laughs to his companions, who are lolling lazily about the
room, smoking, the drinker perched on the table. The* FIRST MI-
LITIAMAN *dutifully laughs, while the* SECOND MILITIAMAN *shrewdly
assesses the walls and furniture.*

WITZEL (*amiably to the little* BOY):
What monastery were you taking a trip to
all of a sudden?

THE BOY, *intimidated, does not reply. He clings to his grandfather.*
LOTHAR *has still not composed himself; nevertheless he manages
to say—*

LOTHAR: My father is on a visit here.
He has been a Catholic for decades.
And you do not have him on your list, either.
Leave him here, otherwise you
will have a great deal of trouble with the Vatican.

*The light is very dim in the room. Outside, on the third floor
of the Papal Palace, the lights go on.*

WITZEL: He don't have to complain to the Pope,
he can make his complaint direct to God Almighty—
the old man will see him soon enough.

Whatever LUCCANI SR. *might wish to say is silenced by a look from*
WITZEL. *Abruptly* WITZEL *turns to* JULIA *and* LOTHAR *and bellows*:

Do you think I got a whole moving van
for the bunch of you?

*He goes violently up to the suitcases, which are still in the room,
and tosses the hats one by one off the couch.*

Fifty pounds of baggage per Yid—
and nothing but clothes and eats.
Everything else left behind—and
hurry up about it—get moving—avanti!

JULIA (*choked with fear*): Where are you taking us?

WITZEL (*pleasantly*): You got to build roads
up in the Apennines.

LOTHAR (*his passivity suddenly gone—significantly to* JULIA *and
his father*): Our *two* children are on the list also.

LUCCANI SR. (*instantly understanding*):
Both the children, yes.
(*To* WITZEL.) Couldn't you please leave the children here.
They will only be in your way.

WITZEL (*taking the list, very amiably*):
We don't like to break up families, see?
The two kids are coming along.
And you—you aren't even on the list.
But you'll come too.
Those who can't work are given extra—
given special treatment.

LOTHAR *and* JULIA *hurriedly repack suitcases. The little* GIRL *has
crept on to her grandfather's lap.* THE BOY *too has gone to him
for protection.*

WITZEL (*matter-of-factly, to* LUCCANI SR.):
You haven't been in Rome long,
or else why hasn't the Duce
seen to you when he had the Jews
all registered?

LUCCANI SR. (*contemptuously*):
In the first place I'm only on a visit here.
In the second place I am a Catholic.

JULIA (*straightening up*): Please leave my father-in-law
and my two children here . . .

WITZEL (*whirls around, brutally*):
Get on with your packing. We don't give a damn
about religion, we Germans.

He goes up to the relief. LOTHAR *and* JULIA *pack. The room is
very quiet.* WITZEL *nudges* LOTHAR, *who is kneeling in front of a
suitcase, cautiously with his foot.*

Art collector, eh? Valuable, huh?

He indicates the relief with a jerk of his head. LOTHAR, *in the
foolish hope of striking up a conversation and so perhaps being
able to do something for the children, says—*

LOTHAR: Yes, I am an archaeologist. This sculpture comes . . .
WITZEL: I don't care where it comes from.

    Let Göring's men worry about that.

    Finish the damn packing. We've got to get going.

    (*To the* FIRST MILITIAMAN.)

    Let me have that other list . . .

The Italian takes it from his wallet. WITZEL *makes a note and asks the* FIRST MILITIAMAN:

    What's the name of the street?
FIRST MILITIAMAN: Via Porta Angelica 22, fourth floor.

WITZEL *returns the list to him, steps between* LOTHAR *and* JULIA, *who are on the floor repacking, stoops and takes from one of the suitcases a small sculpture and a pouch. He holds both out in front of him. The* SECOND MILITIAMAN *with the bottle pays close attention, but says nothing.*

WITZEL (*laughs maliciously, sets the antique bronze on the table
    and rummages in the pouch; scornfully*):

    The things you folks take on trips!

    All old coins, huh? Valuable, huh?

    We'll make a note of that.

He takes the other list again, makes a note, and then sees that the SECOND MILITIAMAN, *perched on the table, cannot take his eyes off the coins as he rolls a cigarette. He sends him out. Harshly:*

    Hey, you, make yourself useful,

    and stop wearing out your eyesight

    peeking at works of art!

    You'd better take a look around the other ratholes—

    there—and over there—

    maybe another rabbit

    like this Grandpa here

    will fall into our net.

The Italian, with provocative slowness, reluctantly, leaving his rifle behind, pushing his cap forward over his forehead and scratching the back of his head, slides off the table. JULIA, *still kneeling and packing, looks up anxiously. She bites her lower lip to keep herself from screaming, and digs her fingers into* LOTHAR'*s arm. Her husband draws his arm away from her and makes a great show of working over the suitcase.* JULIA *can so little conceal her dread that she straightens up as the Italian leaves the room. At once* WITZEL, *who is standing behind her, grips her roughly by the back of the neck and presses her back to the floor, while at the same time saying in a stupidly placating manner:*

> You don't have to worry
> about your countryman getting
> at your silver spoons. Get on with this . . .

JULIA *begins crying silently. The grandfather in the background has been signaling to the children, by placing his finger to his lips several times, that they must be quiet. He whispers to them. Then, at this moment of extreme tension, he forces himself to speak to* WITZEL, *in order to distract him.*

LUCCANI SR.: May the boy take his box of stamps along?
    This . . .

He takes the box from his grandson's hand and shows it to WITZEL, *who answers pleasantly.*

WITZEL: Of course he can, for all I care.
LUCCANI SR.: Claudia, now you ask whether
    you may take your bear and the dolls . . .
WITZEL (*impatiently*): For God's sake, yes. But come on now.
    Well? Anyone in the other rooms?

He looks up questioningly at the returning Fascist, who has also been in the nursery, has looked into the baby's basket, and then, after a moment's reflection and a glance down the hall to make sure no one has followed him, has quietly gone out again, a grin on his face which may express satisfaction at saving the child or at deceiving WITZEL—*not even he himself would be sure which.*

SECOND MILITIAMAN: Nobody there, not a soul.

He looks first at JULIA, *then stares fixedly at the pouch of coins.*

JULIA (*downstage, softly*): Will Pippa even now . . . here . . .
LOTHAR (*takes* JULIA's *arm soothingly, then stands up at once; he
    is suddenly in a hurry*): We're ready.

He slips his coat over his shoulders, takes two suitcases and leads the way. JULIA, *more composed, starts to put on the children's coats.*

WITZEL: Stop—one more little thing.
    Let's see your hands—not the kids.
    You—there, the ring, take your rings off.
    Jewelry is to be confiscated. Off with them!

LOTHAR (*begins to draw his wedding ring off his finger with some difficulty; his father and* JULIA *have not yet reacted. With bitter irony*): The wedding rings might hamper us at "work."

With a flash of fury because WITZEL *has grabbed at* JULIA, *who in her nervousness cannot get the rings off her fingers:*

    Do you happen to have a warrant to rob us?

The children press close to their mother.

WITZEL: Rob? Don't get fresh, you there.
    Time's run out for you anyhow,
    so hand over your watches—come on, your watch.
JULIA: You were right, Lothar.

WITZEL *has passed along her and* LOTHAR's *watches and their rings to the* FIRST MILITIAMAN, *who enters these objects on his list and puts them into the large leather pouch he wears at his belt. Now* WITZEL *turns to* LUCCANI SR. *who is sitting as if he were witnessing some incomprehensible happening on another planet, motionless, his stunned eyes wide open, his hands resting on his slightly spread knees. He seems almost unconscious as he lets his pocket watch with its golden chain and his two wedding rings be taken from him. The rings are pulled violently from his fingers rather than eased off.*

WITZEL: You asleep, huh?—Come on,
    time to go. Get the kids dressed.

He says this to JULIA; *now he briefly, not brutally, grasps her by the hair to look at one ear:*

    No earrings, eh. Good. Ready. Come on.

JULIA *hands* LUCCANI SR. *a small suitcase, equips herself with a knapsack, and holding a child with each hand, goes out.*

THE GIRL: I want to go with Grandpa.
LUCCANI SR.: Yes, you'll stay with me.
    (*To* THE BOY.) You too. Come, both of you.
THE BOY: And Pippa? Where is . . . Isn't Pippa coming?

LUCCANI SR. (*places a hand on his mouth*):
    Be good and quiet now.

He hastily draws the children along. The Fascist who had the list has already opened the hall door. In the throng in the little hall THE BOY *anxiously asks* WITZEL—

THE BOY: Are we going to the monastery now?
WITZEL: We're going straight to Heaven,
    right straight to God Almighty.

He pushes them out. Outside SIGNORA SIMONETTA *is standing, weeping. She comes into the hall.*

SIGNORA SIMONETTA: Oh, Signora Luccani, Oh God!
JULIA: Goodbye—will you please look into the nursery
    to see whether I closed the window there.

She begins to cry and goes out quickly.

WITZEL (*last in the apartment*): Out of here!

He pushes SIGNORA SIMONETTA *away and slams the hall door so loudly that the baby begins to cry. It is now almost dark in the apartment, for* LUCCANI SR. *has not omitted to switch out the floor lamp. Some light streams into the room from the Papal Palace. Tramping of footsteps on the stairs, then silence in the hallway. The motor of a truck can be heard starting.*
SIGNORA SIMONETTA *closes the hall door and then scurries cautiously but swiftly into the nursery. She stoops over the basket.*

SIGNORA SIMONETTA:
    Ah, poor thing—they've taken your mamma away from you.
    Come, my poor darling, come.
    Those devils!

She takes the child out of the basket, rocks it until it is quiet, then places it on a cushion, looks nervously around the room, then goes to the closed window and peers down. She cries. The SECOND MILITIAMAN *who has earlier "overlooked" the baby has reappeared and sneaked very rapidly through the open hall door into the living room, where in great haste he tries to stow the contents of the pouch of coins into various pockets. This process takes a moment. Then he takes the small sculpture, tries to hide it in his trouser pocket, realizes that it will not fit, finally opens several buttons of his blouse and tucks it in. As he does so he looks anxiously at the door—and at that moment* SIGNORA SIMONETTA *comes from the nursery and crosses the hall. Both are equally startled and alarmed, and for a moment cannot speak. The Fascist looks at her conspiratorially in great embarrassment; he has not yet completely hidden the sculpture inside his blouse. He points to the baby, then pats his pocket, laughs, pulls the sculpture from his blouse, shows it, since he has been caught stealing anyhow, then tucks it away slowly once more and comes grinning out into the hall.* SIGNORA SIMONETTA *has been able to bring out no more than a muffled "Oh!" With a grand gesture and evident delight in his own histrionics, the Fascist sways his hips and holds his arms as she is doing, as though he too has a baby in his arms—simultaneously patting the sculpture under his blouse.*

SECOND MILITIAMAN: Oh Madonna mia—*io*
  I saved it.

He hurries out.

SIGNORA SIMONETTA (*leans against the wall, exhausted and relieved, unable to take another step*): Pigs!

CURTAIN

Scene Two

Office of the Father General of a religious order. A few pieces of standard office furniture, a crucifix, not far from it and somewhat larger hangs a photograph of Pius XII praying, in profile. Four Renaissance chairs, reproductions, such as the Swiss Guardsmen use in their guardrooms. A prie-dieu. A large map of the world lit by a fluorescent light and punctuated with red dots to show the not very numerous sites of the order's missions. The longest wall of the room is dominated by an extremely ponderous baroque wardrobe with two large doors.

Downstage, near the telephone, an aged MONK *is reading his breviary. Hanging prominently near the door is a black cardinal's*

*hat and red cape. The simple office clock strikes ten times; it is
10 P.M. Footsteps are heard, reverberating loudly as if someone
were walking across the thin board floor of an empty storeroom.
The* MONK *looks up; then he rises to his feet. Now the sonorous,
likable laughter of a fat man is heard, muffled, as though it were
sounding inside a barrel. But it comes from the wardrobe, whose
doors are opened from within, heavily, with a creaking noise. His
Eminence, amused, worldly, emerges with considerable fuss. His
left hand tucks up his cassock—he is wearing red stockings and
high, black, laced shoes—and with his right arm he supports himself on the* MONK, *who has hastened to the wardrobe door to help
His Eminence out. The* CARDINAL *laughs, talks and coughs all at
once to the* ABBOT, *who is still standing in the deep recesses of the
wardrobe and sliding shut the panel of its false back. Soon the*
ABBOT *also emerges and closes the doors. He is an elderly, white-
haired man, slender, dry, obedient, rather like an officer on an
army general staff.*

CARDINAL (*with one foot still in the wardrobe, with the gaiety of
    royalty*): Jonah, you know—Jonah
    in the belly of the whale.
    Thank you, my friend, thank you.

He emerges completely. The MONK *pats some dust from his cassock, then fetches a clothes brush from the desk drawer and dusts
him more thoroughly, afterwards going on to the* ABBOT.

    A truly wonderful hiding place, you know!
    And right beside this wardrobe, my dear
    Father General, you negotiate with Hitler's henchmen?
    (*He laughs again.*) Priceless, you know. But just suppose
    one of your flock—up there (*he points to the ceiling*)
    should become deranged . . . as prisoners do . . .
    Suppose he could no longer stand captivity and ran off, you
        know—
    screaming and carrying on, you know,
    and came banging through the wardrobe and here, into your
        room,
    perhaps when you are sitting with the Gestapo chief,
    drinking Frascati. Might be somewhat ticklish, you know.

*The idea amuses him just as much as it horrifies him; he gives a
rather anxious, questioning laugh.*

ABBOT (*smiling*): No fear of that, Your Eminence.
Besides, the Germans know quite well that I
have the place full of deserters,
full of Communists, Jews, royalists.
They respect the peace of the cloister.
(*To the* MONK *who is brushing him off.*)
Thank you, Brother, thank you—no telephone calls?
MONK (*bows*):
None, Reverend Father General.
(*Genuflects.*) Your Eminence!
CARDINAL (*without interest*): Bless you, my friend . . .
ABBOT: Bring us a drop of wine.
Red, Your Eminence? New wine?
CARDINAL: No thank you—I have
the coachman and horse waiting in the piazza.
I mustn't linger, you know.
Oh well, a drop, red, you know.
(*To the* MONK.) But please, my friend, not new wine.

MONK *bows, leaves.*

And how is your rheumatism, Father General?
ABBOT: Thank you for asking, Your Eminence.
I fear it will come with the November fogs,
as it does every year. No sooner, but
no later either. I don't suppose
it will spare me this year.
CARDINAL: You know, tomorrow morning I'll send you
my cat pelt. Start to wear it right away,
don't wait until the pains come.

The CARDINAL *has taken a seat at the desk; the* ABBOT *has moved
up a chair for himself.*

ABBOT: Very kind of you, Your Eminence.
But don't you need the pelt yourself?
CARDINAL (*putting that suggestion far from him, with
austere gravity*): Why no, I take the water cure— and then,
the warm air in my greenhouse
keeps ailments away, you know.

*He points to the ceiling again and coughs—coughs himself into a
tremendous coughing fit.*

But up there—the storeroom is very dusty.
Where do *they* get fresh air,
the poor fugitives? This dust—ah.

He gradually stops coughing.

Yes, that dust up there, you know.
ABBOT: Very simple, Your Eminence, at night
they can go out on the roof, all night long
if they feel inclined.
By day they go into the garden
one by one. They help in the kitchen
and in the library also—why not?
Our secret entrance through the wardrobe, Your Eminence,
just gives a touch of color, for the present.
If, however, the Germans cease to respect
the extraterritorial buildings of Rome,
as they have done thus far so splendidly,
we will wall up the doors to the hiding place,
and then the wardrobe will be the only entrance.

The MONK *has silently returned with glasses and a bottle. He goes
out again.*

ABBOT (*pouring*): Thank you, Brother.
CARDINAL: Well then, Father General, to your protegés.
ABBOT: Many thanks! May God protect them.
With your visit and with your cordial talk
Your Eminence has brought a wonderful serenity,
a new and beneficent atmosphere,
into our refuge. Please, Your Eminence,
come often to see the fugitives.
CARDINAL (*touched*): Ah yes, I mean to visit also
the fugitives in the Campo Santo and the Anima . . .
The wine feels good, you know—it was
too dusty in the storeroom. I suppose,
Father General, that a good many of the Jews
(*he points to the ceiling*)
will be converted to the faith, you know.
ABBOT: A happy outcome, Your Eminence.
CARDINAL: And you know—you needn't tremble
for your guests. Herr Hitler will no more dare
to touch the monasteries of Rome

than touch our Chief. He is much too shrewd
to offer the world any such spectacle.
Although the Germans know that many a monastery
harbors a secret radio station . . .
they understand what lines they may not cross, you know.
Herr von Weizsäcker has even asked me
to confirm in the *Osservatore*
that the Germans are so handsomely
respecting the Curia and all its houses.
And yes, you know, we'll do it—
they've deserved it. But all the same,
we won't do it quite for nothing, eh?

ABBOT (*smiling*): Good, Your Eminence. Tomorrow morning
I'll offer the Gestapo chief a trade.
We'll publish the communiqué—
if he hands out to me a Communist,
the son of a noted Milanese scholar,
who has appealed to us for help . . .
The Pope is much concerned.
I think I can put that across.

CARDINAL: Splendid, that's fine.

The telephone rings. The CARDINAL *hands the receiver to the*
ABBOT, *then stands up, puts his hat on over his zucchetto and*
drapes his cape over his shoulder while the ABBOT *is speaking on*
the telephone.

ABBOT: Yes, speaking—who? Hm, one moment.
Your Eminence, Father Riccardo asks
to be received at once, accompanied
by an officer of the SS. May I . . .

CARDINAL (*both curious and vexed*):
Riccardo Fontana? Oh, certainly, by all means.
Don't let me be in your way.

ABBOT (*on the telephone*): Bring them up, Brother.

He hangs up and says to the CARDINAL, *who is striding rather*
angrily back and forth but cannot quite make up his mind to
leave:

Father Riccardo, Your Eminence, has urged me
several times to speak to His Holiness concerning . . .

CARDINAL (*offended, irritated*):
>Yes, yes, you know, that is Riccardo's
>everlasting subject. That seems clear by now.
>Six months ago, at the fall of Stalingrad,
>I had to remove him from Berlin
>because he was taking too much into his own hands.
>What is he doing back here in Rome?
>His place of work is Lisbon.
>He's spoiled because of his father's position, you know,
>and the Chief makes a pet of him,
>caresses him as if he were a nephew.
>He is too ambitious. Obedience
>is not at all his forte, you know.

Knocking at the door. The CARDINAL *has posted himself so that he will not be seen at once by the persons entering. The* ABBOT *opens the door.* RICCARDO, GERSTEIN *and the old* MONK *appear; the latter instantly withdraws.* RICCARDO *almost leaps down the two steps into the room.* GERSTEIN *hesitates in the doorway. Even before he introduces* GERSTEIN, RICCARDO *cries out—*

RICCARDO: *This* is how far we've let things drift.
>As of this evening Jews are being arrested
>right here in Rome! What a disgrace . . .

He sees the CARDINAL, *gives a start of great alarm, goes up to him and bends over the ring.*

ABBOT: What is that you say? Frightful!

CARDINAL: Well, well, Riccardo. Has
>the Nuncio sent you here from Lisbon? And who is . . .

He goes up to GERSTEIN, *who makes a low bow, is very constrained, and also extremely suspicious.*

RICCARDO (*quickly*): This, Your Eminence, is our liaison man
>in the SS leadership. Best for us
>not to bother with his name.
>It was he who first asked the secretary
>of Bishop Preysing to describe
>the gassings in Belzec and Treblinka
>to the Holy See.
>(*Angrily.*) That is now more than a year ago . . .

CARDINAL (*quite cordially, extends his hand to Gerstein*):
>Oh, indeed, we thank you, sir.

We were terribly shocked to hear it.
God will reward you for your having
done such a service to the victims, you know.
But, Riccardo, what did you just say?
Arrests in Rome?
(*Uncertain, irritated, indignant.*)
Why, you know, we thought—those henchmen—
my dear Father General, we felt certain they would not
arrest the Jews right here in Rome!
Let's hope that most by now
have managed to get over to the Allies!
They do hold Naples now, you know.
(*Self-justifyingly, to* GERSTEIN.)
And hundreds are concealed in monasteries . . .

In their excitement all four talk at once. The ABBOT *greets* GER-
STEIN, *the* CARDINAL *goes on speaking to* RICCARDO *as well as to the
others; the* ABBOT *addresses* GERSTEIN *alone, reassuringly.*

GERSTEIN (*nervously*): May I ask you, Monsignore,
to make sure that—that no other German
beside myself comes in here now . . .
ABBOT: No need to be concerned. If only you
attracted no attention as you entered from the street—
no one will see you here. At this time of night
none of your associates ever visit me.
GERSTEIN: Associates . . . Monsignore,
I only wear the same uniform.
ABBOT (*with sympathy*): I know, I've already heard about you—
although, you needn't fear, I wasn't told
your name . . .

The two now listen to the CARDINAL *and* RICCARDO.

RICCARDO (*while the* ABBOT *is speaking with* GERSTEIN):
Your Eminence, we now have come to this!
Citizens of Rome—outlaws!
A manhunt for civilians underneath
the windows of His Holiness! Will
no action be taken even now, Your Eminence?
CARDINAL (*guilty and therefore highly offended*):
Action *has been* taken, Riccardo.
(*With emphasis.*) We have given asylum
to unbaptized Jews as well.

Father General, show your storeroom to Riccardo, please.
(*Threateningly to* GERSTEIN.)
You Germans! Yes, you frightful Germans.
I'm so fond of you, you know, and the Chief
is too—but why won't you stop
that business with the Jews! You everlasting
peacebreakers and Protestants! Now
you've carried things so far that even the Pope
must condemn you before the whole world!
Here, under his very window,
you drag away women and children, and
everyone knows that none of them ever comes back!
You're absolutely forcing us, you know,
you're forcing the Pope publicly
to take note of those crimes, you know.

RICCARDO: God be thanked! At last he must . . .

CARDINAL (*speaks sharply to* RICCARDO, *who receives the
    rebuke with a sardonic air*):
    I will not have that, Father Fontana!
    Are you so limited as not to see
    that any anathema against Hitler by the Curia
    will become a fanfare of victory
    for the Bolsheviks?
    Mr. Stalin is marching upon Kiev. Hitler's
    summer offensive has been a total failure . . .
    (*To* GERSTEIN, *plaintively.*)
    Whatever are you doing, you Germans!

ABBOT (*to* RICCARDO): I'll take you upstairs to my protégés.
    I'd like you to see that we are taking measures . . .

RICCARDO: I am aware you are, Father General.

CARDINAL (*imperiously*):
    Nevertheless, go upstairs with the Father General.

He then turns to GERSTEIN, *while* RICCARDO *is led through the
wardrobe by the* ABBOT. *The wardrobe doors remain open until
the* CARDINAL *leans against them.*

GERSTEIN: Your Eminence, perhaps Hitler will
    draw back even if His Holiness
    for the present merely threatens,
    secretly and in writing,
    to abrogate the Concordat.

CARDINAL (*evasively, reserved*):

It's possible, you know, it's possible.
I'll speak to the Chief this very night.
Tell me, sir—how could the Germans have forgotten
the mission God assigned them
as the fulcrum of the West?

GERSTEIN (*softly*): Your Eminence, that could not be. God
would not be God if He made use of a Hitler . . .

CARDINAL: Oh yes, oh yes, most certainly, my friend!
Was not even Cain, who killed his brother,
the instrument of God? Cain said to the Lord:
my sin is too great ever to be forgiven.
And still, you know, God set a mark on Cain
so that no one who came upon him would ever kill him.
What is it your Luther says:
secular rule derives from Cain, you know.
Cain had his mission in the world, as Noah did.
What can we know
of the terrible detours of the Lord!
(*Enthusiastically.*) But one thing we know, don't we—
surely God has no wish to let
the *West*, Christian civilization, perish, you know!

GERSTEIN (*repelled*): Why not, Your Eminence? If God
did not desire us to perish, why would He
strike us Christians with such fearful blindness?
The Church, Your Eminence—may I speak frankly?

CARDINAL: Of course, certainly, have your say.

GERSTEIN: For sixteen months now Rome has known
of Hitler's savage butcheries in Poland.
Why not a word about it from the Pope—
that where the steeples of his churches rise,
Hitler's chimneys pour forth their ghastly smoke!
That where on Sundays the church bells ring,
on weekdays the flesh of men is burned.
That is the Christian West today!
Why, Your Eminence, should not God
send us a new Deluge?
Only Stalin's tanks can liberate
Auschwitz, Treblinka, Maidanek . . .

CARDINAL (*deeply horrified*):
What is that you are saying! Surely
you love your country, do you not, sir?

GERSTEIN: Permit me not to answer, Your Eminence.
In my fatherland Hitler is
a very popular man. I love many Germans
who will die when the Red Army marches in.
Presumably I too will be killed—and nevertheless . . .

CARDINAL: And nevertheless! Surely you are not a communist—
do you really want the Red Army to come?
Can't you imagine what will happen:
altars pillaged, priests murdered,
women ravished?

GERSTEIN (*brutally*):
Yes, Your Eminence, there will be grim scenes.
Like an apocalypse. And yet—the wildest band of soldiers
cannot wreak more outrages in a convent's dormitory
than the atrocities that Hitler's lawyers, doctors and SS men
have been practicing—wearing this uniform—
for years against the Jews, the Poles, and Russian prisoners.
Your Eminence, surely you can confirm these facts:
Tens of thousands from Western Europe—
tens of thousands of Jewish families
are being deported. Where to, Your Eminence, where to?
What do people imagine here in Rome?

CARDINAL (*haplessly, because he has been "caught out"*):
Naturally, yes, of course—and *nevertheless,*
dear sir, the smoke of the crematoria
has blinded you to the fact that there must be
an alternative to conquest of the territories
by the Red Army—*must* be, for the sake
of the West, you know . . .
Perhaps a landing in Normandy may . . .
But Stalin's entry into Berlin, why, dear God,
that is a price that Europe *cannot,*
that Europe *dare not* pay!

GERSTEIN: Your Eminence, after Napoleon
had senselessly led the Grand Army to its ruin,
he fabricated—in conversation with Caulaincourt
who did not believe a word of it—the legend
of the Russian colossus which, he would have it,
was aiming to annihilate Europe.
Hitler exploited this legend, which Bismarck
and Frederick and William the Second as well
had only treated as a joke. Hitler resurrected this legend

when he invaded Russia
and every criminal in Europe who greedily
looks to the East will always in the future
claim he is saving civilization.
The Vatican should never support such lies, Your Eminence!

CARDINAL (*happy to be able to go off on this tangent*):
We hope for no profit from aggression, you know.
But you simplify, sir. Frederick of Prussia
truly feared the Russian colossus, and so did Bismarck.
And because the king—like Napoleon, like Hitler—
saw no other recourse, he himself
incited Russian ambitions to expand
westward. Like Napoleon, you know, and Hitler:
an offer to collaborate, you know,
over the despoiled countries.
It is always the same, as long as it goes well.
It *never* goes well long, you know.

GERSTEIN: But Russia has never threatened the West,
Your Eminence, as gravely
as Hitler and Napoleon threatened it.
Both would have subjugated all of Europe
had not their march to Moscow
brought Russia into the fight.
Europe has been saved by *Russia* and
can fend off this dangerous rescuer
only if it agrees to live with him.

CARDINAL: With the Bolshevists too?

GERSTEIN: With any master of the Kremlin—
whether his name is Alexander or Stalin . . .

CARDINAL: Easy to say, but hard to do, you know . . .

RICCARDO *and the* ABBOT *return through the wardrobe. The* ABBOT
closes the doors again.

GERSTEIN: It was always hard, Your Eminence.
Even for Bismarck, it was a feat of balancing,
yet he did not permit himself even the *thought*
of a preventive war against St. Petersburg.

CARDINAL: The Chief himself, as well, has never
called for a crusade against Russia.
Riccardo, I understand your deep distress, you know.
But now you've seen, up there,
that the Holy See is doing what it can.

RICCARDO: Your Eminence, those are the lucky few,
a handful among millions, who reach the gate
of a monastery. And if the Pope
grants them a hiding place, he only does
what many private persons in Berlin and Amsterdam,
in Paris and in Brussels, are doing for
the persecuted. But, Your Eminence,
the doctor or the businessman,
the workingman who gives asylum to a Jew,
risks beheading. What does the Pope risk?

CARDINAL (*striving to repress his irritation, which is rising again*):
Riccardo—here, today, you know,
arrests in *Rome,* that changes everything, indeed.
The Chief will now speak as a bishop,
as other bishops did, you know.
But we are losing time, while outside
the reign of terror rages . . .
Would you not prefer, for your protection
(*he lays his hand on* GERSTEIN's *shoulder*)
to stay here in this house—
don't you agree, Father General?

ABBOT: I can guarantee you our protection as long
as no bombs fall upon the monastery.

GERSTEIN: Your Eminence—Monsignore—I'm deeply touched.
But I have a family I cannot
leave alone in Germany.

CARDINAL: God protect you, and your family as well!
I thank you. Let us pray
for the persecuted, you know . . . My
dear friend, I'll find my way out alone
with Brother Irenäeus. Please stay
here with your guests . . . Till we meet again!

ABBOT, RICCARDO, GERSTEIN (*simultaneously*): Your Eminence.

CARDINAL: Goodbye.

Starts off with the MONK, *but turns around to say to* GERSTEIN
impulsively:

One more question in haste, dear sir.
I ask not out of curiosity but despair, you know:
London, Madrid and Stockholm,
and a good many visitors who come here
are prone to talk of a German

rebellion against Hitler . . .
What is there to it? Anything at all?

ABBOT *signs to the* MONK *to withdraw.* MONK *goes out.*

GERSTEIN: Alas, Your Eminence, a few defenseless people—
pastors, socialists, communists,
Jehovah's Witnesses—yes. In September
they hanged one hundred-eighty on a single day
in Plötzensee. The women were beheaded . . .
It is a hopeless struggle.

CARDINAL (*agitated, very sympathetic; this is the first time
he has heard about it*): *Women,* you say? Women too!
Oh Blessed Virgin aid them!
What about the military? London speaks of
generals, you know. Could these officers
carry the people with them—the people
who after all love their Herr Hitler?

GERSTEIN: Only if they proclaim that *Himmler*
has assassinated the Führer! Then they could.
The rage of the people must be turned
against the SS and the police.

CARDINAL: Satanic, isn't it? Satanic, you know!

GERSTEIN: That is the only way, Your Eminence,
that revolutionaries might conceivably
seize the rudder. Conceivably.
But I do not believe that army officers
are ready to sacrifice themselves.
Not the German but the *Russian* army
will dispose of Hitler.

CARDINAL: Unless Hitler does it himself, you know.
But what a frightful situation . . . I
thank you. Good night, gentlemen,
good night.

The ABBOT *accompanies the* CARDINAL *to the door, on the other
side of which the* MONK *reappears.* CARDINAL *goes out with him.*
ABBOT *returns and says to* RICCARDO, *who is leaning against the
wall with an air of hopelessness—*

ABBOT: I am of your opinion. This evil
had to fall upon Rome too. Hitler

> will now discover what it costs
> to provoke the Holy Father.

RICCARDO *does not reply at once.*

GERSTEIN: Monsignore, are you certain
> that he will now intervene?

ABBOT: Absolutely. Aren't you, Riccardo?

RICCARDO: I am not so certain.
> Suppose the Pope does what he always does—
> I mean, does nothing. (*Passionately.*)
> Father General, what will we do then?

ABBOT (*curtly*): Obey. As we must. You know that!

RICCARDO (*defiantly*):
> That would be only too easy! Look at him—
> a German officer. If he were not disobedient,
> breaking his oath,
> he would be a murderer. And what about us?
> (*Urgently, trying to persuade.*)
> You have saved the lives of hundreds, Father General.

ABBOT: The *Pope* gave me the means to do so.
> Don't forget that, Riccardo!

RICCARDO: I do not forget it. But consider,
> this rescue work has not imposed
> the slightest sacrifice upon the Pope,
> aside from the financial one,
> nor even the merest shadow of a risk . . .
> And you, as I know you,
> cannot stand idly by when
> tomorrow—right here—
> they load the victims into cattle cars . . .

ABBOT: Good God—a priest cannot use firearms!

RICCARDO (*softly, almost to himself*):
> No, but he can go along. He can go with them.

GERSTEIN (*does not suspect how long this idea has preoccupied
> RICCARDO*): That would be utterly senseless!

ABBOT: And would not save a single Jew, not one.

RICCARDO (*still to himself*): No, not a Jew. But one's own
> superiors. When I saw Provost Lichtenberg
> in prison hospital he was tormented
> by the fact that none of us is with the Jews.
> I shall go with them, he said; the Nazis had

already given their permission. Then
they broke their word, as always,
and shipped him off to Dachau.
Now none of us is with the Jews.

GERSTEIN (*firmly*):
The SS would never permit an Italian priest
to accompany the deportees.
That would be far too interesting a matter
for Allied propaganda.

RICCARDO: What if the priest himself is Jewish,
like the monks transported to the East
from Holland?

He looks at the clock, then says with a smile:

By now he's sure to be in Naples,
safe among Eisenhower's soldiers—
I mean the Jew with whom I switched
passports this morning. (*To* GERSTEIN.) And I still have
the star of David that your lodger gave me.
I'd need only to let myself be seen with that,
and I would be arrested.

GERSTEIN (*aghast*): Riccardo—you would not be treated
as a priest. You would be gassed like any Jew!

ABBOT (*frightened and also vexed*):
Burn the star and the passport.
You are simply courting disaster!

RICCARDO (*to change the subject*):
How do you explain the fact, Herr Gerstein,
that your protegé Jacobson has never been heard from?

GERSTEIN: He was so embittered, after the death of his parents.

RICCARDO: But not against me, after all.

GERSTEIN (*shrugging*): Perhaps they caught him anyhow,
and killed him on the spot.

RICCARDO (*after glancing once more at the clock, firmly*):
Father General, please tell me—
you *must* have some idea: What are we to do
if the Pope does not protest?

Silence. Helpless gesture on the ABBOT's *part. Silence.*

RICCARDO (*while* GERSTEIN *looks at the map of missionary posts, in
a tone close to scorn*): Nothing? Nothing at all?

ABBOT (*hesitantly; he feels that he must suggest something*):
    In individual cases, offer help—as we are doing now.
RICCARDO: And look on? No, Reverend Father, that is—
    that cannot be your final word. To look on
    idly when tomorrow morning
    our fellow citizens—do not forget,
    the ranks of Jews hold many Catholics too—
    are loaded aboard cattle cars.
    Are *we* to stand by and
    (*he gives a sudden laugh*) wave our handkerchiefs to them?
    That is, if the kind Germans permit.
    (*He laughs again; then, with rhetorical shifts of tone as his
    irony and his arguments rise to their climax.*)
    And then—then we go home?
    Confess—what should we confess?
    That we have used the name of God in vain!
    And sit down to some journal, to read about
    the excavations in St. Peter's?
    And then on Sunday we ring the bells
    and celebrate our Mass—so filled with sacred thoughts,
    that nothing, surely, tempts us to consider
    those who at that very moment in Auschwitz
    are being driven naked into the gas.
ABBOT (*wearily, desperately*):
    God in Heaven—what remains for us to do!

Silence. Then—

RICCARDO: Doing nothing is as bad as taking part.
    It is—I don't know—perhaps it is
    still less forgiveable.
    (*Screams.*) We are *priests*! God can forgive
    a hangman for such work, but not a priest,
    not the Pope!

Silence. Then he speaks more calmly, calculatingly, objectively.

    Please, Father General, tell me this:
    If God once promised Abraham that he
    would not destroy Sodom if only
    ten righteous souls lived there—
    do you think, Reverend Father,
    that God might still forgive the Church

    if even a very few of her servants—
    like Lichtenberg—
    stand by the persecuted?
ABBOT (*surprised and disturbed, but sympathetic*):
    Many of us are doing all in our power.
    But I do not see what this question . . .
RICCARDO: You see as well as I, Father General.
    You must see that the silence of the Pope
    in favor of the murderers imposes
    a guilt upon the Church for which we must atone.
    And since the Pope, although only a man,
    can actually represent God on earth,
    I . . . a poor priest . . . if need be

GERSTEIN *understands and attempts to still him.* RICCARDO *goes on undeterred.*

    can also represent the Pope—*there*
    where the Pope ought to be standing today.
ABBOT (*more shocked than outraged*):
    Riccardo, I shall keep your—your accusation,
    which is monstrous, like a secret of the confessional.
    (*To* GERSTEIN, *who makes a gesture of assent.*)
    Sir, may I ask you to do the same . . .
    But I am frightened for you, Riccardo.
    What justifies your words, which ought to plunge
    each one of us into the depth of shame . . .
RICCARDO (*alarmed*): No! For God's sake, no, Father General.
    You and so many other priests—so many
    have already died on the scaffold—you have
    fulfilled your duty. You have . . .
ABBOT (*sharply*): And the *Pope* has not?
RICCARDO (*firmly*): Not to the limit of his power! Perhaps
    this very night, maybe tomorrow, he will
    at last fulfill the obligation he
    has long since had as spokesman of Christendom.
    Otherwise—otherwise one of our number
    must go along from Rome.
    And if in doing so he dies . . .
GERSTEIN: Yes, he will die!
    He will be gassed and burned . . .

RICCARDO (*undeterred*):
>   Perhaps this flame which will extinguish him,
>   if only God looks on this penance with His grace,
>   perhaps . . .

ABBOT: Riccardo!

RICCARDO (*with intense emotion*):
>   . . . perhaps it will annihilate as well
>   the guilt of our superior. The concept of the Papacy . . .

ABBOT (*vehemently*): . . . will outlive Auschwitz! Why do you
>   doubt?
>   Why lacerate yourself so, Riccardo. It is arrogance.

RICCARDO: Auschwitz is not in question now. The concept
>   of the Papacy must be preserved pure
>   for all eternity, even if temporarily
>   it is embodied by an Alexander VI,
>   or by a . . .

ABBOT (*grips him almost brutally by the shoulder*):
>   Not another syllable. Why, that is—
>   Do you know Pius XII so ill?

RICCARDO (*shaken*): Father General, the portrait
>   of Cardinal Pacelli has hung
>   above my bed since I was twelve years old.
>   On his account I entered the priesthood,
>   much as my . . . my mother begged me not to.
>   I will spend the rest of the night praying
>   that I misjudged the Pope,
>   that by tomorrow evening he will have
>   had the arrested families released—I'll pray for that.
>   I am afraid (*very softly, almost inaudibly*)—
>   I have such horror of the camp.

The ABBOT *walks up to him in a paternal gesture, while* GERSTEIN *steps between them with determination.*

GERSTEIN (*vigorously*):
>   Forsaking us will only make you guilty.
>   Forget the salvation of the Church.
>   You would no longer have it in your power
>   to aid a single human being. Riccardo,
>   you'd only take on greater guilt yourself!

RICCARDO (*with disgust*): I would only be keeping my word.

Here I cannot do a thing.
I have been trying—for more than a year.
It's all been empty talk.

ABBOT (*it is impossible to say whether he believes his own words*):
Tomorrow morning, Father, you will see
it has not been in vain. The Pope will intercede.

RICCARDO (*points to the clock*):
He *knows* what has been happening in Rome!
And *you* are his liaison with the Gestapo.
Why has he not talked with you hours ago?

ABBOT (*uncertainly*):
He will not want to deal with the Gestapo here in Rome,
but negotiate with Hitler himself.
I'm confident he will present him with an ultimatum.

Silence. Pacing. GERSTEIN *gives* RICCARDO *a long look. Then he says, hesitantly, cunningly—*

GERSTEIN: I still see one last chance, but—
no, no, I do not dare to say it.

RICCARDO: Please, speak out!

GERSTEIN: Who am I to tempt two priests
into disobedience . . . ? No, I do not dare . . .

ABBOT: What do you mean by that?

GERSTEIN: Monsignore, if you and Father Riccardo
could only take over the Vatican radio
for half an hour . . .

ABBOT (*suspiciously*): What is the meaning of "take over"?
I have free access to our radio station.

GERSTEIN (*quickly; but it can be sensed that this is no sudden inspiration on his part*):
Then, Monsignore, instruct all the priests
of Europe to follow the example of
the prelate Lichtenberg—and rally
their parishes from Narvik to Sicily
to act for the rescue of the Jews.

ABBOT (*vexed*): Do you suggest a priest take it upon himself
to speak in the Pope's name?

RICCARDO: Yes, when the Pope forgets
to speak out in the name of Christ!

ABBOT: But that is monstrous wickedness!
Is a priest in the guise of Pontifex Maximus

to command his brother priests in Europe
ex cathedra to submit to martyrdom?

GERSTEIN: Monsignore, it would never come to that.

RICCARDO: Certainly not. All Hitler's fronts are crumbling.
He will take care not to challenge
all Europe's Catholics over the Jewish issue.
There are millions, millions upon millions of us
in his army and his industries . . .

GERSTEIN: Yes, Monsignore, Hitler would draw back.

ABBOT: But, gentlemen, not for a day, not for a single day
could you maintain the fiction
that the Holy Father himself had imposed
the duty of resistance upon Catholics.
The Pope himself would deny it!
(*To* GERSTEIN, *now more vexed than agitated.*)
Sir, be realistic. Suppose some shock troops
were today to seize the Berlin radio station,
and offer peace to England and the USA,
allegedly in Hitler's name. How long
would Hitler put up with such a sham?
Thirty minutes? A full hour?

GERSTEIN: Monsignore,
I am thinking of the Pope; you talk of Hitler.
Surely there is no parallel between them.

ABBOT (*offended*): Certainly not. But naturally
both would at once issue denials.

GERSTEIN: Oh, I see. No, Hitler would have to be
prevented from doing that. First eliminate him,
then the radio broadcast saying: the SS
has killed your Führer—so that
the fury of the people . . .

ABBOT (*self-righteously, repelled—he is incapable of lies—and
firmly*): You have proposed this once before,
this diabolic plan. But we ecclesiastics
have no way of preventing the Pope
from issuing denials. A priest, sir,
this is a point you might know,
does not "prevent" the Pope from doing anything.
Absurd!

GERSTEIN (*as casually as possible*):
Of course not, Monsignore, even though

any "preventing" of the Pope, of course,
in this case too, would automatically
be blamed on the SS by all the world,
as long as the SS in Rome continues
arresting victims for Auschwitz . . .

ABBOT (*rises, clearly signalizing the end of the conversation*):
Please, sir, let's put an end to this discussion
here and now! Surely you do not wish—here
in this religious house—you do not wish
to discuss acts of . . . of violence against
His Holiness. That would be monstrous!

GERSTEIN (*seemingly offended*):
Monsignore, what are you attributing to me?

ABBOT: I attribute nothing. Your remark suffices:
that anything done to the Pope right now—
I dare not press you to be more specific—
would automatically be blamed on the SS.

GERSTEIN (*hastily*): But it never occurred to me
to suggest the use of violence against the *person*
of His Holiness . . . Monsignore!

ABBOT (*ironically*): I see—you did not mean that?

GERSTEIN (*has regained his composure*):
But, after all, in order to prevent denials,
a priest would only have to
temporarily put out of action
the Vatican broadcasting equipment.
For that, I meant, Monsignore,
the whole world would naturally
place the blame upon the SS—
especially if such destruction
comes after a radio protest
supposedly by the Pope against the SS.

RICCARDO (*fascinated by* GERSTEIN's *plan, speaks as if he has
just awakened*): Father General, at this moment
such an act could mean salvation for thousands,
for hundreds of thousands.
Their last chance for rescue.

ABBOT (*coldly*): You, Father Riccardo,
would have no access to the broadcasting equipment.
That reassures me. You are tired, nervous;
please, let us get some rest now.
I must also have some words with you alone.

GERSTEIN: Monsignore, let me thank you
    and take my leave.

ABBOT (*conciliatorily*): Live with more caution . . . Do not take
    offense at this advice from an old man
    who means to pray for you although
    he cannot follow you. God be with you.

GERSTEIN: Monsignore, I thank you most sincerely.
    Father—good night.

RICCARDO: Come to our house early, before
    my father goes to see the Pope at nine!

The MONK *is at the door waiting for* GERSTEIN

GERSTEIN: Good night—I'll come around eight.
RICCARDO: Good night.

GERSTEIN *goes out with the* MONK.

ABBOT (*after looking in silence for a moment at* RICCARDO):
    I was simply terrified, Riccardo,
    to send you out into the night
    with that strange person. His eyes! He virtually
    hypnotizes you. He is marked, this man—he wears
    the mark of Cain. What is his name?

RICCARDO: His name does not concern us, Father General.

ABBOT (*not offended*):
    You are right, forgive me. You did not
    want to leave with him, did you?

RICCARDO: No, because I have one more request of you.
    And then I still must make confession.

ABBOT: First a request from me: I am shocked
    to see that you are wax in the hands
    of this strange envoy, Father.
    Be on your guard with him, I beg you.

RICCARDO: No need—don't be concerned.

ABBOT: Riccardo, this is a man who would be capable . . .
    (*Extremely agitated.*) Why, I ask you, *why* did he twice,
    needlessly, altogether without cause,
    propose that diabolic treachery:
    assassinating Hitler—and blaming the SS.

RICCARDO: A highly moral plan.

ABBOT (*with violent indignation*):
    A plan to lead to civil war! "Moral"—come now.

You are exhausted, Riccardo.
But that is not the issue for me, my boy,
nor is it for *him* either. The man is sinister,
believe me. I watched him closely and I tell you,
he had his reasons for voicing that idea to us.
(*His repugnance grows the more he thinks the matter
    through.*)
Riccardo, that man has the power
to doom you, along with him, to hell
by suggesting to you—
more with his eyes than with his words—
that—I—I cannot say it outright,
it is so horrible . . . so . . .

RICCARDO (*still inhibited about uttering the truth*):
He suggests nothing to me, Father General.

ABBOT: He does, he does!
He sowed in you the thought that the whole world,
all of mankind, could be lashed
to a ferocity of rage against Hitler
if Hitler's personal troops, the SS
could be accused of—of killing,
(*He repeats almost in a whisper.*)
of killing the *deputy of Christ.*

RICCARDO (*groans, and in his agitation mentions* GERSTEIN's *name,
    although the* ABBOT *does not notice*):
You are reading thoughts, Reverend Father—but . . .
they are *not* Gerstein's thoughts.

ABBOT (*so repelled that he cannot control his voice; he whispers
    as he turns away abruptly*): Riccardo—what—I can think
of nothing more to say to you. Go.
(*Silence. Then, with fervor.*)
You do not know, you do not *know*
what you are saying . . . Come to the chapel.
You wanted to confess. You *must.*

*With trembling hands he lights a three-armed candelabra, then
puts out the desk lamp, takes the candelabra and starts to lead the
way, until he realizes that* RICCARDO *is not following him. The
room is now illuminated only by the candles.*

ABBOT: Why aren't you coming, Riccardo?
RICCARDO: I cannot. I cannot confess now.

You would have to refuse me absolution,
for I cannot *repent*.
Please understand me, Father General.
For the past three months, ever since Rome
has been occupied by the Germans, I have hoped
that at last the SS and the Vatican
would come together in a bloody clash.
Instead the most ghastly thing of all
is happening—they are not even
jarring one another.
They live together, harmoniously,
in the Eternal City—because the Pope
does not forbid the murderers of Auschwitz
to herd their victims into trucks
beneath his very windows.
(*With madness in his eyes.*)
How do we know if God has not
sent an assassin to the Pope only because He wants to
save him from—complete perdition?

ABBOT (*utterly uncomprehending, no longer capable of reaction*):
Riccardo—there is no limit to the sin
you have assumed.

RICCARDO (*as if obsessed*): He who said, I bring not
peace but the sword
(*firmly*) must have known there would be a time
when the sword would strike the First of His own.
The Church must know that, too,
since she has always used the sword.
(*Tormentedly.*) Am I to stand back from the struggle,
Reverend Father? Do not resist the evil one—
suppose we have been given this command
because he is destroying us?
No soldier is permitted to preserve his life—
why then a priest?
Could Judas have refused to play his role? He *knew*
(*with intense fear of his own conclusions*)
he would be damned for all eternity.
His sacrifice was greater than the Lord's.

ABBOT (*crushingly*): Riccardo—you had better not compare
yourself with Judas.
For you want to commit your crime
and shift the blame to others.

RICCARDO (*with wild passion*):
>   Not *I!* Everyone, the whole earth
>   would accuse Hitler and the SS.
>   And it must be so. It must be.
>   I myself would still atone
>   on earth and before God.

ABBOT: Though you stumble, God still sustains you.
>   Would you otherwise have opened your heart to me?

RICCARDO (*is matter-of-fact and nevertheless fanatical. The* ABBOT
>   *listens only because he is incapable of saying anything more*):
>   Because I cannot do the thing alone!
>   Because I need you. You must announce over the radio
>   that the SS took action
>   because the Pope wanted to save the Jews.
>   Once our radio has announced this news,
>   once it has spread from Iceland to Australia,
>   then for the remainder of his days
>   Hitler would stand before the world
>   as the adversary of the Creation
>   which he is, as the greatest abomination.
>   No one, no Goebbels and no Cardinal,
>   could credibly repudiate the charge,
>   before the fires were extinguished
>   in all the crematoria of Auschwitz.

He falls to his knees before the ABBOT.

>   Help me, Reverend Father.
>   You must help me.

ABBOT (*with icy horror*): Let me be—go.
>   You said the word—abomination,
>   the word applies to *you.*
>   Repent—begone—out of my sight—
>   or come to confession.

RICCARRDO (*screams*): I cannot do it without you!
>   (*Rising, making a last frenzied effort.*)
>   If you won't help me, Father General,
>   then I must pray for you as well . . .

ABBOT: Go, go now,
>   if you persist in this criminal madness.
>   Go, this instant!

(*He has turned his back on* RICCARDO. *He gasps.*)
Go—get out—murderer!

RICCARDO *goes out. The door remains open. The candles flicker wildly; then the draft blows them out. The* ABBOT *falls to his knees on the prie-dieu.*

CURTAIN

Scene Three

Dawn, October 17. The headquarters of the Gestapo in Rome, located in the former Cultural Section of the German Embassy on the Via Tasso. The vestibule is furnished as a large office which leads on one side to the cellars—where the cells are—and on the other side is open to a gloomy courtyard with an invisible gate.

Heavy trucks can be heard driving into the courtyard. People are unloaded and led into the cellar behind the stage. Shouted commands such as:

Get down! Out of there! Come on, move!

Dogs bark. A command:

Get out! Shut your trap!

Then WITZEL *is heard counting amiably:*

Forty-six, forty-nine, fifty,
fifty-two—all right, with them there and
the two snotnoses we've got sixty head in the lot.
Throw them in with the others.

Before the sergeant appears on the stairs which connect the yard with the building, SALZER (*the SS officer of Act One*), *rises; he has been sleeping in an armchair, boots beside him, feet resting on a chair, covered with a light coat. He yawns as dogs do, with his whole body, stretches voluptuously, runs his hand through his hair and over his cheeks, drinks from a bottle of soda, walks in his*

socks over to the glass door and looks down into the courtyard until
WITZEL *appears and reports.*

SALZER *is an officer like a thousand others, tall, broad and insignificant, bursting with vigor, in his mid thirties, even more devoted
to his Führer Adolf Hitler than most others since this devotion
allows him the privilege of hunting defenseless civilians in the occupied territories instead of risking his life on the Russian front like
the great majority of men his age.*

*Just as the Father General in this play is not intended as a
representation of the historical Salvatorian Abbot, so* SALZER *is
not patterned after the historical Obersturmführer (Lieutenant) Kappler, one of those SS officers who did not succeed in remaining
anonymous; in 1945 he had the bad luck to be convicted of specific
acts. For his work as a German police chief during the years
1943-44 Kappler had to pay with a life sentence in the peniten-
tiary; of his own accord he had 335 hostages executed, instead of
the 330 ordered by Berlin. We shall, however, confer upon our
police chief one remarkable trait of Kappler's which Consul Moellhausen reports. We do so because it affected the course of the
historical events and, moreover, is typical of most people perform-
ing similar functions in the past, today, or tomorrow: this intelligent, unconditionally obedient officer did not even have a distaste
for his victims. On orders, he would just as conscientiously have
arrested the prostitutes or nuns of Rome. He was no racist fanatic
and worked with as little passion as a guillotine.*

*Nevertheless, history records that terror reigned in the cellar
of his prison.*

WITZEL (*appears on the stairs, enters the room and reports*):
    Lieutenant—I can report the operation completed,
    eleven hundred and twenty-seven arrests.
SALZER (*beginning to pull on his boots*):
    Thank you. Pretty scanty.
    Rome used to have eight thousand Jews.
    All skipped out to the South,
    to join the Yanks—well, let *them* feed them.
    I said right off it wasn't worth the trouble.
WITZEL: And hundreds more are holing up in monasteries.
    We grabbed thirty of them just as they tried
    to slip away.

Our Italians from the mobile battalion
Wouldn't mind taking a look inside these monasteries.
We know for sure that out of every hundred
monks, twenty at least are fakes,
communists, Jews and Badoglio traitors . . .

SALZER (*with rising impatience; he is fiercely self-righteous, and all the more autocratic toward subordinates, the more uncertain he is of his position*):
Crazy, Witzel, you're crazy as a loon.
Why not liquidate the Pope too, while you
are about it. Can't you get it through your head:
(*shouting*) we aren't in the Ukraine here.
(*Threatening.*) Witzel, you're responsible to me!
You'll be aboard the next train to the Eastern front
if you don't see to it that these
idiotic Fascisti behave themselves.
These *avanti* satellites of ours
who're always such brave boys when
the enemy are civilians. Raiding a monastery,
—I wouldn't put it past them—
or preferably a convent, the lewd bastards.
(*He claps his hand to his brow.*)
You're crazy as a loon!
(*Firmly.*) No Catholics are to be offended, get it?

WITZEL: Sure, I know that, but we have to . . .

SALZER (*screaming*): Did you or didn't you hear what I just said?

WITZEL (*cowed*): Yes sir, very well, sir.

SALZER (*calmly*): All right. What else did you want to say?

WITZEL (*confused*): That we've stuck straight to the lists,
the lists from Mussolini, I mean.
Of course lots of the young fry weren't on them.
And so on, I mean, for instance,
if somebody happened to be visiting . . .
naturally he wouldn't be on the list.
But they're all Jews, guaranteed.
Only some of them got fresh
and started threatening us with the church
because they're Catholic—so they say,
some say by birth and all that,
I mean . . .

SALZER (*has put on his tunic; desists buttoning it, extremely disturbed*): What's that you're yammering, idiot!
You should've told me that *last night*.
Then I would have had a reason
to call off the whole stupid mess.
Arresting Catholics in Rome—man, I . . .
(*perplexed, in a lower voice*)
maybe some of them really aren't Jews!

WITZEL (*cautiously*):
But, Lieutenant, you couldn't have checked on that.
How can you tell which of them is lying!
(*With more assurance.*)
Lieutenant, my orders were the same as usual.
And if you don't mind my saying so,
we could always blame the excesses,
I mean, if he makes a fuss,
the Pope, I mean, we can blame
the excesses on the militia, on the Italians.
They jump right in and there's no way
we can help it if they steal.

SALZER (*resigned*): All right, Witzel, it's my mistake.
I shouldn't have trusted
your intelligence. Go to the photographer
and pose for a hero's picture—you dummox!
Witzel, for weeks you've seen me negotiating
here—did you ever see me negotiating
with priests in Poland?

WITZEL (*abashed*): No, sir.

SALZER: Never thought of it, did you—
why, here in Rome, I have to put up with
that black crow, that Jesuit priest,
coming to see me every goddamn minute
about setting some louse we were lucky to catch
at liberty again? Never gave it a thought, did you?

WITZEL: Yes, sir, I did, certainly.
Only—he doesn't come about the *Jews*.
The Pope only sends him because . . .

SALZER: Jews! You blockhead,
we hadn't locked up any of them till now!
The hell with it. Beat it. In five minutes
I want you to bring up to me

all of those bastards in Cell One
who claim that they are Catholics. Get it?

WITZEL: Yessir.

SALZER: One more thing. Double the rations
for that bunch today. Once we have them
safely across the Brenner, we'll cut
the rations down again.
And no beatings, and enough fresh air
in the cellars, understand?

WITZEL: Yessir.

He hurries away. SALZER *opens the glass door to the courtyard,
which is gradually growing lighter. He whistles loudly through
four fingers and beckons to the two Italian soldiers who had
helped* WITZEL *arrest the* LUCCANIS. *They appear. The* FIRST MILI-
TIAMAN *enters rapidly, salutes smartly; the* SECOND MILITIAMAN
*ambles up the stairs and into the room, grins and chews noisily at
a very large quarter of melon which he holds in both hands,
balancing it like a crescent moon in front of his handsome, ill-
shaven face. Once in the room, he coquettishly and ironically clicks
his heels—making fun of German "discipline."*

SALZER (*indifferently*): Morning. At ease. What are you grinning
at?

SECOND MILITIAMAN (*complains emotionally*):
No fun, Commander. Duty hard.
No sleep, very hungry,
inherit nothing.
Night work very bad.

SALZER (*amused*): You're impossible. "Inherit!"
You better watch it!
(*To the* FIRST MILITIAMAN.)
I suppose his girl friend waited up all night for him?

FIRST MILITIAMAN (*offended because* SALZER *as always takes more
interest in the other man*):
Don't know his girl friend. Mine's waiting anyhow.
I request dismissal, Commander.

SECOND MILITIAMAN: Nice girls with those Jews, Commander!

SALZER: I'll let you go in a minute.
Don't you dare touch any of them!
Just one more thing: You two are good Catholics, right?

FIRST MILITIAMAN: No, I am no longer a Catholic.

SECOND MILITIAMAN: Not good, just ordinary Catholic.

SALZER: No matter, you're to examine the wise guys
    downstairs who say they're Catholics. We'll see
    whether they know anything at all
    about the dear old practices of your Church.
    Can you handle that?

FIRST MILITIAMAN (*laughs spitefully*):
    They'll have to pray. Shall we make them pray?

SECOND MILITIAMAN (*pleased*): Sing! Singing is more fun!
    Or else we'll baptize them in the Tiber.

SALZER (*seriously*): You are not to torture anybody, understand?
    No one's to be beaten!

FIRST MILITIAMAN: Suppose they won't pray?

SALZER: They'll be glad to if they can.
    Have coffee and rolls sent in, will you.

FIRST MILITIAMAN: Yes, Commander, yessir.

He goes out.

SECOND MILITIAMAN: Can we make physical examination,
    Commander?
    Very pretty, very young girls with the Jews.

SALZER: Don't you dare touch any of them!
    Another hour and you can go home
    and screw your girl friend. You're not
    one of those old monks
    who caught themselves a pretty woman as a witch
    whenever they were hard up.

SECOND MILITIAMAN: Me—a monk—oh no!
    I couldn't make it as a monk.
    (*Now sincerely sad, with a gesture of cutting the throat.*)
    Commander, the girls among the Jews—
    they go to Poland too?

SALZER (*finishes washing up, brushes his hair*): None of this batch
    are going to Poland. They'll be sent to work
    in Austria . . . We have a summer resort there
    in Mauthausen. Aha, here's Witzel
    with the religious bunch.

WITZEL *appears at the door to the cellar, with* CARLOTTA, *a girl
of about twenty, a man of forty, and old* LUCCANI. *None of them is
wearing the yellow star. All are exhausted; the men unshaven,
without shoelaces, belts or ties. The beautiful girl is pale, disheveled.*

WITZEL (*shouting at the Jews*):
>Faces to the wall! About-face! These are
>the three from Cell One, sir. Some more
>claim they're Catholic,
>but it doesn't say so in their papers.
>It doesn't say so in his either—the big fellow there.
>He only says he's an arms manufacturer.

SALZER (*downstage, low-voiced*):
>I see, I see—fine goods you've packed for me!
>Man alive, Witzel, it's incredible—
>I'm sending you to the Eastern Front.
>You numbskull, you!
>(*Louder, intemperately.*)
>I don't want to see them before breakfast!

The SECOND MILITIAMAN *looks at the girl, then quietly and quickly slips over to her. He draws her away from the men, talks assiduously to her, tries to thrust a cigarette into her mouth, etc.*

WITZEL (*extremely abashed, points to the man of forty whom he has just mentioned—a man who was evidently, before being roughed up, singularly well dressed*):
>That one . . . he even claimed . . .

SALZER: I don't want to know what he claimed right now.
>Damn it to hell, I want to have my coffee.
>(*Quietly.*) Didn't you round up any tailors—
>a good tailor for uniforms?

WITZEL: No, sir, no tailors.
>But we've got a shoe salesman;
>picked up one in a shoe shop. And a barber . . .

SALZER: Rubbish, barbers! But you remind me, I do need a shave.
>A man can go completely to the dogs
>because of this filthy trash,
>they make you lose a whole night's sleep.
>After the coffee send our acquired Nordic in
>to shave me.

WITZEL: Yessir. Here comes the coffee now.

He hastens to spread a tablecloth. The FIRST MILITIAMAN *has brought in a large tray laden with coffee and rolls.* WITZEL *takes it from him zealously and sets the table.* SALZER *promptly takes a roll, still standing. Now he sees the* SECOND MILITIAMAN *upstage, who has been trying to kiss the girl. The girl is fending him off;*

he has seized her around the shoulders and waist. She breaks away and slaps him in the face so hard that his cap goes flying into the room. SALZER, *who was about to interfere, laughs loudly; he laughs until tears fill his eyes. The* FIRST MILITIAMAN *is also pleased, while* WITZEL, *with the orderliness of the weakminded and with Nazi sense of honor, grips the* SECOND MILITIAMAN *by the collar.*

WITZEL: You swine, don't you have a sense of honor!
　　Get out! Fuck Jews, would you?

He forces him out into the yard, propelling him finally with a kick. It takes him some time to simmer down. His sense of order is so keen that he picks up the SECOND MILITIAMAN's *cap, actually dusts it off with one hand, then opens the door and throws the cap out after him. He shouts:*

　　Ten lira worth of honor.
　　The bastard—I'd teach him a lesson.
SALZER (*still laughing*): They don't understand that, Witzel.
　　The Italians look like Jews themselves.

Holding a roll and cup, he goes up to the girl. Friendly, impressed:

　　Well I'll be damned! Are you always so standoffish
　　when a man comes near you?

The girl does not answer.

　　You don't look the kind. I'll bet
　　you have a boy friend! He wouldn't be
　　down there in the cellar too?
CARLOTTA (*coldly*): My fiancé was killed in Africa.
SALZER (*touched, speaks quickly*):
　　What's that? When? Killed? Where?
　　On the British side? Or what?
CARLOTTA: On the German side, of course.
　　He came from here, from Rome.
SALZER (*to change the subject*): Since when is a Jewess here
　　allowed to marry an Italian?
CARLOTTA: That's why I became a Catholic.
SALZER: I see. I'm sorry, but then we must
　　take you to Austria for munitions work.
　　Since you were not yet married to this Aryan,
　　by law you are still a full-blooded Jewess.

Your religion does not matter here. We Germans
are tolerant—everybody can pray as he likes.

CARLOTTA (*tearfully*):
But I would have been married long ago,
and so been half-Aryan by law
if my fiancé had not fought and died
for . . . for Germany! Please let me go.
It's already arranged with the nuns—
on November first I am to enter
the convent as a novice.

SALZER (*embarrassed, very gravely*):
Your case is complicated. I can't
decide that right now . . . Here . . .
(*He beckons to the* FIRST MILITIAMAN.)
Don't touch her, understand?

FIRST MILITIAMAN: Yes sir, Commander!

SALZER: Take her back to the cell.

CARLOTTA (*terrified*): Oh no—please not!

SALZER: By November first
it will all be straightened out.

FIRST MILITIAMAN *goes out with the girl. It can be sensed that*
SALZER *feels better as soon as he no longer has the girl in sight.*
Downstage, WITZEL *is drinking coffee. He stands up as* SALZER
comes over to him.

SALZER: Don't get up. Listen, Witzel,
if that shoe salesman you mentioned before
knows how to make boots himself, good custom work,
then he—and his whole family too, for all I care—
is temporarily an Aryan, get me? Then he stays here.

WITZEL: Yes, a good shoemaker is worth something.

SALZER: It's time I had some boots
that I can make a decent showing in.
And you could use a pair yourself.
Pliant and stiff at the same time,
made of leather that can take a shine.
This (*he points to his boots*) shitty stuff belongs in the
garbage.
Every time you take a step you feel
this is the fourth year of the war.
The leather won't polish up at all.

WITZEL: Yessir.

WITZEL *is done with his breakfast. He goes out.* SALZER, *changing his voice as suddenly as a jukebox, immediately after speaking with* WITZEL *shouts roughly at the two men who are still standing with their faces to the wall. What follows by no means runs counter to* SALZER's *policy of treating the Jews well as long as they are in Rome. The "treatment" of the Jews who were arrested in other countries, aside from some exceptions, could not be represented on any stage.*

SALZER: You baptized Hebrews there—squad, about-face!
   Come on, about-face, I say, shake a leg.

Only now does old LUCCANI *also turn to face the audience.*

   Now show me that you're Catholics.
   Hand me your passport.

The man of forty shows his passport.

   What are you doing here in this office? You
   aren't a Catholic at all! Witzel!

He turns around. WITZEL *is not there. The* FIRST MILITIAMAN *returns, gathers up the dishes, and removes them without saying a word. Meanwhile the interrogation continues.*

MANUFACTURER (*eagerly, as if rehearsed*):
   I work for your war industry. I own
   large textile factories. My family is Catholic.
   Catholic nobility. I was in town just by chance,
   picked up in this round-up by sheer chance.
   They pulled me right out of my car.
   I tell you, my arrest will have
   the greatest repercussions.
SALZER (*angered*): You've got to work like all your brothers!
   After all, you're a Jew—I can't do more
   than let your family know . . .
MANUFACTURER (*eagerly reaches into his wallet and takes out a notebook*): Please do so. Here, this is
   the address, my telephone number, please . . .
SALZER (*gives an ugly laugh, snatches the notebook from his hand and throws it across the room. Then, scornfully*):
   How are your relatives going to complain
   if they don't even know
   that you have been arrested by us?

MANUFACTURER (*frightened*): What's that? But . . . ! Word gets
      around
    that you have arrested us.
    All Rome and all of Italy knows by now!

SALZER (*violating his policy of discretion, as malicious as he
    ordinarily is*): If you threaten me, Mr. Manufacturer,
    Mr. Owner of a textile factory, why then,
    you'll simply disappear for good and all.
    Reported missing—how do I know where—
    maybe fell down a manhole,
    or in the cunt of some Via Appia whore,
    how should I know . . .

MANUFACTURER (*loquacious out of fear*):
    I beg your pardon, but—since forty-one
    I have been working for the German army.
    My factories . . .

SALZER: They'll go on working for us.
    You're going with your fellow Jews . . .

MANUFACTURER (*ostentatiously takes a step away from* LUCCANI):
    They are not my fellow Jews, have
    never been. I had a Catholic wedding.
    A cardinal performed the ceremony
    in St. Peter's.
    That was more than sixteen years ago.
    I've nothing in common with the Jews.
    My arrest is a mistake which will lead
    to the gravest consequences for you!

SALZER, *extremely angered since he does fear these very consequences, knows that no matter whether and when the Pope protests,
this particular Jew, witness of the events in the Gestapo cellar, must
never again be allowed to open his mouth.* WITZEL *has entered,
smartly followed by SS Private* KATITZKY, *a tall, fair-haired Latvian,
who carries a shaving mug.*

SALZER: So you're threatening again . . . Oh,
    I'm scared stiff . . . of your consequences.
    All right, Katitzky, you can lather me.

KATITZKY: Very well, sir.

WITZEL *has pushed the chair in which* SALZER *was sleeping into
the middle of the room. He puts a chair in front of it, on which*
SALZER *places his feet.*

SALZER: If your factories work for the German army,
    then I suppose you ought to sympathize
    with our measures as regards the Jews.
    Do you have sympathy for them or don't you?

He settles in the chair, but pushes KATITZKY *aside for the moment.*
WITZEL *sits down at a table and begins carefully stamping a heap
of forms, breathing on the rubber stamp each time, as if he intended
to swallow it. Then he thoroughly picks his teeth and cleans out
his ears while he watches the interrogation.*

MANUFACTURER: Sympathy, yes. But as for myself,
    at least since my marriage more than sixteen
    years ago, I must . . .
SALZER: Your marriage doesn't interest us at all.
MANUFACTURER: I'm only saying that both in my heart
    and in my actions I have long been alienated
    from Judaism. For ages. After issuance
    of Mussolini's anti-Jewish laws,
    I promptly—the fact can easily be verified—
    dismissed all the Jews in my factories
    who held positions of authority.
    I have personal ties with Count Ciano . . .
SALZER (*amiably*): Who is awaiting execution in Verona.
MANUFACTURER: And the Duce himself has always treated me
    as an exception.
SALZER: As a good taxpayer?
MANUFACTURER: No, as a good Fascist. I could have
    left the country ten times over . . .
SALZER: Once would have been enough.
MANUFACTURER: But I wanted to make my contribution
    to the victory of the West over Bolshevism.
    I thought . . .
SALZER (*stands up*): Well, well, you do talk like a book. So you
    regard our fight as good and just, I take it?
    And also agree with our policy
    of making the Jews responsible
    for instigating the war?
MANUFACTURER: Disturbers of peace should always be punished.
SALZER: You put things in very general terms.
    But I want to hear a clear declaration:
    Do you declare yourself against your people

  and for Adolf Hitler, who will
  liberate the world from that people?
MANUFACTURER: My conduct in this war has all along
  represented a clear declaration.
SALZER: When a man makes as much money as you
  are making out of the war, his work
  is no declaration of principles. Stop jawing:
  Do you favor the extermination of the Jews,
  yes or no?
MANUFACTURER: The Führer must know what he is doing.
SALZER: Yes or no, damn it—don't waste my time.
MANUFACTURER: Yes.
SALZER: That sounded very feeble. Here—
  spit in this Jew's mug!
MANUFACTURER: Really now, the old man
  is Catholic. And he's done me personally
  no harm. No!
SALZER: Has he done anything to me personally?
  Come on, spit at him.
MANUFACTURER: No, I won't do it.
SALZER: All right. Witzel! Take this
  industrialist to his fellow Jews.
WITZEL (*standing up*): C'mon, get going, into the cellar.
MANUFACTURER (*almost relieved that he is being taken away*):
  Lieutenant, you'll be called to account
  for this by the Duce and the Pope.
  Don't you dare . . .
SALZER (*convinced now he must destroy the man*):
  Threatening again, fellow!
  You're not even a Catholic—
  so you owe me every possible proof
  that in your heart at least you've overcome
  the Yid boy that you were.
  What else would give me a justification
  (*with extreme cynicism*)
  for letting you go. Don't imagine
  that anyone will look for you here.
  If your widow misses you, where would
  she look? Naturally she'd search
  in the brothels of the Via Veneto. That is,
  she'd search a while, a little while.

But people forget other people quickly.
We are all like matches, supplied in quantity,
one like the other—you too.
We're taken out of the box,
we flicker a little, set fire to something—
and are tossed away. Nobody looks to see.
Nor will your widow look for long.
If you want to get out of this fix—good.
But by *threats!* Ridiculous
to threaten me. Come on, spit at
the old man, and then you won't
have to return to the cellar—on my word of honor.
Come on, spit—that will be a declaration!

*The man is finished. He has realized that he, too, despite all his
advantages, can actually go out "like a match" in this place. What
happens to him now is not pleasant, but it is human. Only after
this deepest abasement does he regain his full dignity—later, on
the platform at Auschwitz, we will see him supporting old* LUC-
CANI. *Now, after* SALZER's *last words, he demurs no longer; he
rapidly brings his hand to his eyes, his face painfully contorted,
and spits at the old man's coat.* SALZER, WITZEL *and the Italian
laugh, each one differently.* WITZEL's *laugh is longest and ugliest.*

SALZER: Too bad, that would have been a snapshot
    for the *Stürmer.* All right, take him away.
    Not to the cellar—we keep our word.
    We'll put this gentleman
    in our dog kennel.

The others laugh again; SALZER *does not.*

MANUFACTURER (*cries out*): No! You swine!
WITZEL: Get going, to the dogs. Take
    your pants off right now. Get going, move!
MANUFACTURER (*has suddenly regained his self-control*):
    To the dogs—yes.
    (*Imploringly, to* LUCCANI.) Forgive me—please forgive
    me . . .

LUCCANI *looks silently at him.*

    (*Desperately.*) Please, don't despise me.
    The fear—this frightful fear—
    I am ashamed.

LUCCANI: It no longer touches me. Pray.

WITZEL *brutally drags the* MANUFACTURER *away, pushing him out of the room.* SALZER *is now in full swing and he temporarily forgets his scruples about such actions in Rome. He promptly turns upon* LUCCANI.

SALZER: Pray yourself, go on, pray, pray,
    prove that you're Catholic.
    Sing away, get on with it, sing an Ave Maria!
    Come on, hurry up, sing.
LUCCANI: No, I will not take God's name in vain.
SALZER: In vain! My good man, if you don't sing now,
    you will soon in heaven with the angels.
    Or with the men in the fiery furnace.

He draws the FIRST MILITIAMAN *over to confront* LUCCANI.

    Your last chance. One of your brothers
    will see whether you can sing an Ave Maria
    properly. Come on, you substitute priest,
    test him.
LUCCANI (*intensely, with boundless contempt*):
    I will not have dealings with
    this traitor to his country.
FIRST MILITIAMAN (*shouts*): Traitor, you say?

He gives LUCCANI *a badly aimed blow on the chest. The old man staggers, stumbles, quickly regains his balance.* SALZER *grasps the* FIRST MILITIAMAN*'s arm and holds him back.*

SALZER: Hey there! You're not to hit him.
FIRST MILITIAMAN: Commander—insult. Traitor!
    I won't stand for that!
SALZER (*dangerously interested, to* LUCCANI):
    What exactly did you mean by that?
LUCCANI (*articulate and incisive*):
    That an Italian who betrays
    an old Italian officer to the Germans
    is a traitor to his country. Who knows,
    I may have stood beside the father of this traitor
    on the Isonzo—see . . .

He reaches into his pocket and produces two medals. SALZER, *affected and embarrassed, says quickly—*

SALZER: Why didn't you say right off
    that you're an officer?

LUCCANI (*to the* MILITIAMAN): Aren't you ashamed, you coward?
    We fought at the front against
    Austrian alpine troops—marksmen all,
    and where are you fighting?
    Against defenseless fellow citizens. Traitor!

SALZER *remains silent; he is glad to see the* MILITIAMAN, *whom he despises as he does all Italian soldiers, put to shame—and does not realize that* LUCCANI'S *words also apply to his own role in the war. The old man has turned his back on the* MILITIAMAN *and speaks to* SALZER *with great composure*:

    As consul-general in Innsbruck
    and as a soldier in the First World War
    I learned to respect the Germans—
    and I still cannot believe, sir—
    please, permit me a question, a request . . .

SALZER (*is psychologically imperiled; the old officer who has seen front-line service has struck his sentimental vein, chiefly because* SALZER *himself has always shirked the front lines*):
    All right, of course I respect you as an officer.
    Naturally you won't be sent to Auschwitz but to
    Theresienstadt where you will be kept
    in honorable internment until the war ends.

LUCCANI: Thank you for—for this proof
    of your fairness. But my request—you see,
    I am seventy-two. Don't give preferential
    treatment to me—leave me with my son
    and daughter-in-law—down there in the cellar.
    I know you are only doing your duty. But, sir,
    you no doubt have children of your own—my
    grandchildren, a boy of nine, a girl of six.
    Let the children go. I know some nuns
    who could come for them and raise them
    as Catholics. Please . . . I . . .
    (*He gradually loses his composure.*)
    I have never in all my life begged any man
    for anything, but now I beg you—
    think of your own children—I, I . . .
    (*He stammers, weeping.*)

SALZER (*hoarsely*):
> Not a hair of the children's heads will be touched.
> What do you think of us Germans!
> They will be sent to Theresienstadt.
> The younger Jews are to build roads,
> up in the Apennines.

LUCCANI: But certainly not the children. Last night
> they were violently taken from their parents.
> Are we really to believe the stories
> we hear about your camps in Poland . . .

SALZER: All lies, Churchill's propaganda lies.
> Don't listen to what the English radio says.
> If those stories the hate-propagandists tell
> were true, do you imagine that the Pope
> would give such friendly audiences to
> thousands of members of the German army?
> Go along now. We won't touch a hair of your head.

LUCCANI (*more composed, but deeply apprehensive, for which
reason he uses such inflated language*):
> As an officer you are a man of honor.
> How could you ever again look your
> wife in the face, your children!
> I ask you in the name of your mother . . .

SALZER *has turned his back to him, struck to the heart, and repelled.
While* LUCCANI *talks,* WITZEL *enters with the shoe salesman, who
carries a briefcase; he is a rotund Jew, middle-aged. He stands
shyly at the door until* WITZEL *with a gesture indicates that he is
to turn his face to the wall.*

At LUCCANI's *last words* SALZER *suddenly begins screaming like a
madman at the* MILITIAMAN *and* KATITZKY, *then at* WITZEL *also.
His own ranting intensifies his inner stress. Finally he snatches his
pistol from its holster, as though this ridiculous reaching for a
weapon can protect him from humane emotion.*

SALZER: What're you three gaping like idiots for!
> Take him away—take him away, I ordered.
> And don't touch him. Get out of here,
> all of you—take him away too. (*He points to the shoe
> salesman.*)
> Get moving, what are you standing around for!

Get them out, hurry. Witzel,
do you ever come when you're really needed?

WITZEL: This is the bootmaker, Lieutenant.
He's brought his tools, too.

SALZER (*still screaming*):
I don't give a damn, right now.
I don't want to see anybody. You either.
Beat it, get out of here, all of you!

WITZEL: Lieutenant?

SALZER: If any more of the bunch protest,
pull off their pants and see
whether they're circumcized.
Catholic or not—no matter.
Are they circumcized—that's what I want to know.

WITZEL: Yessir. But what about the women?
How do you check that in women?

SALZER (*screaming again*):
Don't drive me out of my mind—idiot!
Get the hell out of here—I don't want to see you!

WITZEL: *Jawohl, Obersturmführer.*

As all go out, GERSTEIN, *behind* SALZER's *back, comes through
the courtyard door, almost stealing into the room. He is just in
time to see* WITZEL *and the* MILITIAMAN *leading the two Jews
away. Then he places a hand on* SALZER's *shoulder, and as he
does so his expression, which has revealed extreme exhaustion,
changes completely. His face is now charged with energy and alert-
ness, which he attempts to conceal behind a smile that seems false.*

GERSTEIN: You haven't had much sleep, eh?
Heil, Salzer! How pale you are.

SALZER (*upset*): Why, Gerstein—you startled me.
You always come in so secretive and quiet.
Where were you all night?

GERSTEIN: What was the matter with you just now?

SALZER (*still embarrassed*):
How can a man's nerves stand it—this idiot,
my sergeant, picked up a whole sackful of Catholics
during the round-up—out of sheer stupidity.

GERSTEIN (*who can scarcely conceal his satisfaction, deliberately
exaggerating*):
What! You've arrested Catholics as well!

You've really botched things up this time.
If there's one thing that the Führer doesn't need right now
it's trouble with the Pope.

SALZER: I'm afraid so. And I'm going soft, Gerstein.
Here's an old army officer, shows his medals
and begs for the lives of his grandchildren.
I'll never let it happen again, never.
We always wind up as the fools
each time we let one of that scum
we're supposed to send into the gas
come close to us on a human basis.
I'm not hardboiled enough. Anyhow I
am sick to death of it. You weren't there
in Posen, on October 4, when Himmler said
our welfare work for Israel's children
would be—how did the old man put it—
would be a *never written* and *never to be written*
page of glory in the annals of Germany . . .
There you are, Gerstein, that's the thanks we get—
inglorious and dreadful.

GERSTEIN (*instantly sees a chance, pretends to be simultaneously
    indignant and scared*):
Aha, so even Himmler thinks that way!
This confirms my impression, Salzer, that
there will soon be a complete change of course.
Hm, a never to be written page of glory.
Imagine that—the Reichsführer
frankly admitting that the final solution—
the mightiest effort of will of the century,
of the millennium, perhaps—can never
be acknowledged before the bar of history . . . Ah yes,
(*darkly, with an air of being well informed*)
they aren't only rumors. I begin to see
a light, a floodlight, in fact.
(*Pretending to change the subject, as if he has already said
far too much.*)
Would you have a roll for me, a cup of coffee?

SALZER: What! What are you referring to?
Sure, you can have coffee here.
Come on, Gerstein, *talk!* You know
what's going on, you're always in Berlin.
I don't hear a thing. What's happening?

GERSTEIN (*mysteriously, significantly*):
    Salzer, I'm not allowed to say—but
    here's a bit of advice, between friends:
    Every so often these days a diplomat
    has been traveling to Stockholm—to see the oddest
    people. It would be outright fatal
    if just at this particular time the Pope
    were to open that big mouth of his.
    Don't antagonize him. The Führer knows
    why he hasn't cleaned out the Vatican,
    that lousy espionage center, why he
    treats it with kid gloves instead.

SALZER (*excitedly*): To Stockholm? But with *whom*
    are they negotiating? With the Russians or . . . ?
    Word of honor, I'll keep my mouth shut.

GERSTEIN (*who has no idea; he has merely been hearing the wild
    rumors put out by foreign radio stations during these
    months*): Not another word, Salzer, not a syllable.
    You've always been a good comrade, so take
    my warning: don't do anything in Rome
    that might stir up an international outcry
    against Germany. The handful of Hebrews
    aren't worth it!

SALZER (*irritably*): Then why does Berlin send me *orders*
    to ship the goddamn lot of them!

GERSTEIN: What do you mean, Berlin? Eichmann orders!
    He likes to make himself important, he's always
    going on about the Führer's decree—because
    on his own hook he wouldn't risk a thing.
    He'll drop you like a hot potato if
    the Führer throws a fit because a protest
    from the Pope breaks all our wires to the . . .
    all the wires in Stockholm.

SALZER (*furious, uncertain*): Can I dope out high policy?
    How could I? I just get my orders.

GERSTEIN (*shrugging*):
    They'll say you should have seen the dangers
    threatening us from the Vatican.

SALZER (*extremely agitated*):
    That's just what I've done, Gerstein. Don't
    get me all confused. I've tried,

twice I tried to get off the hook,
avoid this idiotic operation. End of September
the order came to start arrests on the tenth.
Consul Moellhausen declared that it would be
politically unwise, and dragged me off
to Kesselring. Thank God, the Marshal claimed
he had no troops to spare for all the raids.
So I had a chance to weasel out of it.
Berlin gave way, but sent new orders
that we were to demand a ransom from the Jews
of a hundred pounds of gold. I did,
that was three weeks ago. The Pope
knows all about it. He was even willing
to contribute gold if it turned out
the Jews could not raise the full sum.
That reasonableness on the Pope's part—
we'd been expecting him to raise a howl!—
gave us the courage to deport the Jews.
Probably it will work out alright. If the Pope
kept his mouth shut then, after such
a fantastic demand—why not now?
You know he is very friendly to us Germans—
really, not a bad fellow at all.
You ought to see, Gerstein, how nice he is
about granting audiences to our Wehrmacht boys.
He's seen thousands of them already.
Berlin doesn't like it—but you ought
to go to one some time; it's an experience!

GERSTEIN (*taken aback, for a long time cannot reply. Then*):
Your conclusion seems to me too optimistic.
The fact that the Pope would contribute
gold for the Jews, Salzer, clearly shows
that he is on their side. If he kept
his trap shut then, three weeks ago, he did that
because he thought the Jews could buy their freedom
with the gold. But now you've cheated him.
Watch out, he'll go on the air tomorrow
and broadcast what you were doing all night.

WITZEL (*has entered, to* GERSTEIN): Heil Hitler, Lieutenant.

GERSTEIN (*wearily*): *Heil und Sieg!*

SALZER: Let's have some more of that coffee and rolls, Witzel.

WITZEL (*going out*): Yessir.

SALZER: It's quite possible that the Pope
will make a fuss today. The main thing is,
nobody can put the blame on me. Not me.
Besides, Gerstein, Berlin won't take a chance
and roast the Jews from Rome immediately.
The first batch are to go to Auschwitz
via Mauthausen. If the Pope starts kicking up a fuss,
they can always be sent back home. They won't
be *roasted* until it's certain
that he isn't worrying any more about them.

He offers GERSTEIN *cigarettes.* GERSTEIN *tries once more to frighten* SALZER.

GERSTEIN: Thanks. That was an odd speech
that Himmler gave in Posen.
So that's the reason why ever since August
Blobel has been exhuming our mass graves in Russia
and burning the cadavers around the clock.
Nice work! Compared to that, you have it easy! So far.

SALZER: Really. I don't quite understand
why we go to all that trouble. Do you see it?

GERSTEIN: Why, take a good look at the map: in August
Blobel was cleaning up the graves at Kiev—
low-flying Russian planes unfortunately watched.
Yes, Salzer, I do understand it: the Führer,
damn it all, does not seem to be counting
on Kiev as the future capital
of a *German* Ukraine. It's a bitter pill to swallow . . .
The tables have been turned . . . Don't quote me.

He stops talking because WITZEL *reappears with coffee and rolls. To* WITZEL:

Thank you very much—thanks.

WITZEL: You're welcome, Lieutenant.

SALZER (*concerned*):
Is that the reason for the trips to Stockholm?
Pretty depressing, this news of yours.

GERSTEIN *puts his finger to his lips behind* WITZEL's *back.*

SALZER (*to* WITZEL, *in an effort to find a harmless subject*):
　　What about our shoemaker, Witzel?
　　(*To* GERSTEIN.) We've caught us a shoemaker
　　who'll make some boots for us.
GERSTEIN: Really! I could use a new pair myself.
WITZEL: He's got his tools with him—I asked him.
　　Only no material—we'll have to pick that up
　　from his shop. But he's got tools all right,
　　a whole bag full. What made you bring them,
　　I says to him. He says, I've got to provide
　　for my kids in Poland, you know.

WITZEL *is amused, laughs knowingly. The numbing bestiality of
the whole "operation" is expressed most frankly in these few
sentences, spoken with the ugliest kind of vulgar jocularity.*

　　Sooo, I say, you want to provide for your kids.
　　Then provide for them. You're a hard worker.
　　We'll set up a shop for you in Auschwitz—first class,
　　with show windows, or maybe even, I say,
　　a big business for you in Warsaw.
　　Just because it's you.
　　You can provide for your family there.
　　What a dumbbell!

He laughs with glee. GERSTEIN *is unable to go on with his breakfast; he gets up, making a great effort not to show his disgust. But
even* SALZER *is repelled by* WITZEL'S *stolid, moronic cynicism.
He says irritably—*

SALZER: All right, Witzel—here, have a cigarette
　　and beat it. We have things to discuss.
WITZEL (*taking the cigarette*): Thanks, Lieutenant.

He leaves.

SALZER: You aren't eating a thing, Gerstein.
　　You were pretty keen on breakfast when you came in.
GERSTEIN (*turning*):
　　That speech of Himmler's keeps preying on my mind.
　　They'll be changing course completely pretty soon.
　　Then we'll be the inquisitors they're ashamed of,
　　the way the Church is nowadays ashamed
　　of those who burned the witches.

SALZER (*intimidated*): Yes, if Blobel was ordered to exhume,
that certainly makes it seem the Führer thinks
we're going to lose the Ukraine again. Hell!

GERSTEIN (*again takes a roll; he tries to put this suggestion across
as casually as possible*):
That's why you absolutely must not bring
the Pope down on the Führer's head!
Put off the deportations until
the day after tomorrow. He's certain to protest,
and then *you'll* be in trouble.

SALZER (*weary, sentimental and quite concerned*):
It's easy enough for you to talk, Gerstein.
I wish I were here in Rome
to look at churches and museums;
I'd like to take my kids to swim at Ostia,
or buy my wife something pretty on Via Veneto . . .
And instead—but good Lord,
am I to be more popish than the Pope?
If he keeps his mouth shut till this evening,
I've got to load those trains during the night.

The telephone rings. SALZER *points significantly at it, and comments, as he goes to it*:

Speak of the devil—
this is the time of day—you'll see,
here comes the Pope already . . .
(*At the telephone.*) Yes, put him on.
(*To* GERSTEIN.) The City Commandant!
Jawohl, Salzer. Heil Hitler, Herr General.
Aha—we were just discussing that.
Really! By God, a protest after all!

He beckons to GERSTEIN, *who comes over in extreme suspense
and stands beside* SALZER, *so that he can listen in.*

I was expecting something of the sort.
Yes—what's that? Thank you, yes . . . yes.
Have you received the full text yet, sir?
Ah yes, already on the way to me—good.
Many thanks, sir. Aha—I see.
Well, that's not quite as drastic as it might be.

So it's *not* the Pope himself who issued it.
But is expressly threatened. I see.
My opinion? As you are well aware, sir,
I carried out the operation against my better judgment.
But unfortunately this letter from the bishop
to you, sir, does not relieve us
of the duty to deport . . . Very well, sir.
That *won't* be all? I'm afraid so, too.
Of course, sir, very well, sir.
As long as I have them in the cellar
the Jews will be given specially good treatment.
We'll have to wait and see, yes, sir,
most grateful to you sir, yes, sir.
Heil Hitler, Herr General.

He hangs up and looks at GERSTEIN.

GERSTEIN: You'd best report that to Berlin at once.
    If there's a fuss, they'll blame it on you.
SALZER: Damn it all, *what* should I do!
    (*Very loudly.*) If only this damn Pope
    would tell us bluntly where he stands!
    (*Lowering his voice again.*)
    If he gives us a free hand the way he's done,
    and thinks this letter from the bishop is enough
    to square things with his dear old Christian conscience—
    then I've got to start deporting tonight.
GERSTEIN: Good Lord, Salzer—this *is* his protest!
SALZER (*almost suspiciously*):
    How can you say a thing like that, Gerstein?
    This is just a representation from a bishop,
    nothing like a protest. In Berlin
    they'd laugh their heads off at me
    if I let the scum go on that account.
    Not a word about releasing until . . .
GERSTEIN (*somewhat more cautiously*):
    I don't want to confuse you, Salzer.
    But I don't think the Pope will ever
    give you a free hand here in Rome.
SALZER (*again vexed*):
    Of course I don't think so either, Gerstein!
    This letter from the bishop seems to prove

Pius is getting ready
to raise a hue and cry about his lambs.
And the Führer will give way, naturally.
Who cares about eleven hundred Jews!
But, Gerstein, that's not my affair.
I don't feel like dodging orders once again.
As long as the Church merely tosses off
a lot of empty generalities . . .

During SALZER's *last few sentences* GERSTEIN *has begun to show signs of extreme restiveness; he looks constantly at the clock and paces back and forth. He is anxious to keep his appointment with* RICCARDO. *Now he takes his leave with rather startling abruptness. It has turned full daylight outside.*

GERSTEIN: Well, Salzer—time for me to go.
So long—go easy with the blackcoat.

SALZER (*without suspicion, smiling, more and more amused*):
I don't know anybody as nervous as you are!
Like a wolf in the zoo—always pacing
back and forth. As if you were locked up.
Now too, Gerstein, and you don't even notice it.
What's all this Jewish haste all of a sudden!

GERSTEIN (*at first mistrustful, then assuming a calm manner*):
What do you mean? Am I really so nervous?
I still want to see a bit of Rome—
(*An allusion.*) Who knows whether I shall ever again
be able to stand beside the Tiber as a German.
You've made me feel terribly low . . .

He pretends that SALZER *has been the one who indulged in "defeatist" talk.*

You know, the things you told me, Salzer . . . and then,
the American army now in Naples,
the Russians already in Kiev—
I guess your lousy mood's infected me.

SALZER: Good Lord, I was just a little bit off balance
because of that interrogation.

GERSTEIN (*shaking hands with him*):
And thanks for the coffee and rolls.

SALZER: A pity you're going, Gerstein.
I'm the one to thank you for the visit.

You know the way to the airport, don't you?
Say hello to Finland for me—Heil!

WITZEL (*enters and reports*): Lieutenant, the Abbot is outside,
he wants urgently to see you.

SALZER (*while* GERSTEIN *gives a visible start of alarm*):
That's all I need right now—all right,
there's nothing else to do but wish him a friendly
good morning. Send him in.

WITZEL *goes out*.

SALZER (*to* GERSTEIN): You were right. Here comes that protest.
The man drops by here every third day.
A tough scoundrel who always wheedles something out of me.

WITZEL (*reports in an official tone*):
Lieutenant—His Reverence, Monsignore . . .

SALZER *has quickly buckled on his shoulder straps and donned his
cap. Now he turns toward the door to face the* ABBOT, *who enters
with swift, self-assured steps.* GERSTEIN, *behind* SALZER's *back,
shakes his head in a gesture of denial and puts his finger to his
lips as soon as* WITZEL *has closed the door behind the visitor.*

ABBOT (*giving no sign that he has seen* GERSTEIN *only a few hours
ago*): How do you do, Herr Salzer—I'm sorry
I must disturb you so early.
But you have a visitor . . .

SALZER (*smiling pleasantly*):
Good morning, Father General—yes, a visitor
from Berlin—an old associate of mine.
This is the Father General of the Salvatorians.
Every week he comes from His Holiness
to pry a Communist loose from us wicked Nazis.

All three laugh, GERSTEIN *with relief.*

GERSTEIN: Pleased to meet you, Monsignore.
My friend Salzer here was just
complaining about you. He says you are
a very tenacious man to deal with . . .

ABBOT (*flattered*): Well, well—so he complained. Why yes,
I take that as a compliment. Today I've come
again about a Communist—what you
call Communist, that is. I mean

eighteen-year-old Tagliaferro,
whom you arrested in Milan. Dear God,
if he's a Communist, why then
I'm a Mohammedan.
(*He laughs.*) His father is the leading lawyer
in Milan. Yesterday he appealed to the Pope.
Let the rascal go. He'll get a beating
from his father if ever again he
tries to hand out leaflets, the stupid boy . . .

GERSTEIN (*as disappointed as* SALZER *is relieved that the* ABBOT *has not come because of the Jews, says swiftly*):
Please excuse me now, Monsignore—
I really must go, Salzer.
Be seeing you, goodbye!

ABBOT (*slyly, holding* GERSTEIN's *hand firmly and irresistibly asking*): Goodbye! What was your name again?

GERSTEIN: My name is Gerstein. I'm flying back to Germany today.

ABBOT: Aha, Herr Gerstein, well—a common fault of mine,
I didn't quite catch your name a moment ago.
Well then, a good flight, fine weather!

GERSTEIN: Thank you, Monsignore. Goodbye.

SALZER *accompanies* GERSTEIN *to the door.*

SALZER: Now don't you think your jitters
(*with a nod in the* ABBOT's *direction*)
are a bit exaggerated?
(*Calls to the* ABBOT.) Please sit down, Father General!

GERSTEIN (*softly, likewise with a gesture toward the* ABBOT):
I hope so for your sake, Salzer. But
no—the news, I guess, has not yet
got around to him. Well, I must be going.
Good morning, gentlemen . . .

SALZER and ABBOT (*simultaneously*):
Heil Gerstein, goodbye, bon voyage . . .

CURTAIN

Act Four: Il Gran Rifiuto

> And I, who was gazing, saw a banner, that whirling ran so swiftly that it seemed to me to scorn all repose, and behind it came so long a train of folk, that I could never have believed death had undone so many. After I had distinguished some among them, I saw and knew the shade of him who made, through cowardice, the great refusal.
>
> DANTE, *Inferno, Canto 3*,
> TRANS. NORTON

In the Papal Palace. A small, almost empty throne room which is often used as an intimate audience hall and as a place for discussions of business matters. It is draped in scarlet, the color of cardinals' robes, which, as is well known, are meant to symbolize readiness to suffer for the faith "even to the shedding of one's own blood." The POPE *wears white, of course. His cassock is as white as the dove with the olive branch in his coat-of-arms. This coat-of-arms, with tiara and the two crossed keys, is woven into the tapestry above the golden throne.*

The tapestry extends to the canopy, which hangs too high above the throne to be visible on the set. To both sides of the slightly elevated throne are tall, narrow doors, likewise hung with red and gold. On the wall at left is a baroque console table with astronomical clock and writing materials. Above hangs a large crucifix bound in brass. Several gold hassocks along the walls. No guards.

The CARDINAL *is conversing with* FONTANA SR.

Count FONTANA, *a briefcase under his arm, is wearing the Order of Christ on the lapel of his tailcoat. His Eminence, although he is at home here, is more impersonal than he was on the occasion of his visits to* FONTANA's *house and to the monastery; he is quieter and more sparing of word and gesture.*

CARDINAL (*plaintively*): At any rate, you know, it was not until September that Herr Hitler after all . . .

FONTANA: Ah yes, just recently . . .

CARDINAL: Exactly!
>He informed the Chief in confidence
>that he regarded bombers as the same
>as any other weapon, you know. He said
>the government of the German Reich
>had first applied this weapon, and hoped
>soon to retaliate with utmost force
>against the present Allied counterblow.
>Well, we will see, you know.

FONTANA: Naturally his pride prevented Hitler
>from asking the Pope to plead for him at the White House.

CARDINAL (*with some malice*):
>But the Chief is so miffed, you know—
>he always is whenever his services
>as mediator are rejected.
>He is so fond of writing letters to
>Mr. Roosevelt with nothing in them, you know.

FONTANA (*impetuously*):
>He should write to *Hitler,* Your Eminence!
>Outrageous—what that scoundrel dares to do
>to the Jews—even here in Rome.

CARDINAL: Do you think Herr Hitler has any idea
>how that rabble of his are behaving here?
>We shall also be discussing that today.
>I have prayed for the Jews . . .

FONTANA (*coldly*): At least it saves our honor that the Pope
>has protested at last. I heard about it
>early this morning from the confidant
>my son has in the SS.

CARDINAL (*extremely surprised, in fact alarmed*):
>Protested? Out of the question.
>The Chief most certainly did not protest, Count!
>Here he comes. No, I know nothing about it.

FONTANA (*surprised and disturbed*):
>But he did! This morning he . . .

The CARDINAL *and* FONTANA *have spoken these last words in a whisper, for the right-hand wing of the double door has just been noiselessly opened by a Swiss Guard. The* POPE *enters swiftly and without speaking, and the door is closed again. At first His Holiness appears only as an intense white gleam. He stands before the two*

men, who bend their right knees and kiss the ring. The CARDINAL
rises first; the POPE *graciously raises the Count to his feet and
draws him close and still closer to his cold, smiling face. After
the Holy Father's first words—he begins discussing affairs without preamble—*FONTANA *gradually withdraws a few steps. His
Holiness more and more turns to the Count, finally speaking
almost exclusively to him. After a while he seats himself on the
throne, and cleans his glasses while sitting there. When the* POPE
is seated, the CARDINAL *steps over to his left side. The actor who
plays Pacelli should consider that His Holiness is much less a
person than an institution: grand gestures, lively movements of
his extraordinarily beautiful hands, and smiling, aristocratic coldness, together with the icy glint of his eyes behind the gold-rimmed
glasses—these should suffice. The rest should be largely conveyed
by the uncommon, elevated language of the Pontiff. Pacelli is at
this point sixty-eight, by no means an old man, and at the peak
of his powers.*

POPE: Dear Fontana! We are pleased to receive you, to hear your
    advice and that of Our venerable brother as well—for
    We are filled with burning concern for Italy's factories.
    Power plants, railroad terminals, dams, indeed every
        enterprise
    stands in imperative need of protection.
    Naturally We assess the chances of Our pleas being heard
    most realistically, where factories and mines are concerned.
    How different the situation of Our Eternal City:
    no one will dare to sin against Rome once more!
    Herr Weizsäcker has been so obliging and has requested
    Marshal Kesselring to reduce the German garrison
    down to some thousand men. Indeed, the Germans, one must
        concede,
    have on this point shown far more friendliness
    than the destroyers of San Lorenzo.
    But even the White House will now be chary
    of provoking Us once more. We have declared
    with utmost firmness that We, as bishop of this city,
    as spokesman for five hundred million Catholics
    who look toward Saint Peter
    will protest vigorously—and without delay.
    (*Plaintively.*)

Yet the bombing of armaments plants
is legitimate by the laws of war!
You have recommended to Us, Count Fontana,
that We invite the men around Roosevelt,
industrialists and generals in the U.S. . . .

FONTANA: And also in London, Your Holiness.

POPE: Yes, very well—to purchase securities.
But how will you persuade influential financiers, Count,
to take shares in Italy's industries
which are in such peril?

FONTANA: Good securities, the best we have,
are as desirable as ever, Your Holiness.
I am thinking principally of securities held
by the Society of Jesus, which . . . :

POPE (*as if fending off a physical danger*):
No, my dear Count, oh no—no!
We do not wish to court
any new conflict with the Jesuits. No, how fruitless.

CARDINAL: Heaven forbid, the Order of Jesus—you know!
Why does it conceal its books from us!
Eight thousand *patres* in America are refractory, you know.

POPE (*instantly placatory*):
Only as far as money is concerned.
Otherwise they are devoted servants of our cause.
The Lord preserve us from overlooking that, Your Eminence.

CARDINAL (*respectfully*): Yes, otherwise, of course, certainly.
And they are not stingy, you know.
The diocese in New York alone—that one diocese
contributes more to the Holy See than all
the remainder of the West taken together, you know.
But that they still refuse to show their books!

POPE (*astringently*): We'll see those books yet, Eminence.

FONTANA (*smiling as he takes two checks from his briefcase*):
Your Holiness, there is no need to be ungrateful
to the Jesuits, the Order my son belongs to.
One of these two checks
I have the pleasure of presenting to your Holiness
in fact comes the Order of Jesus—a sum

He hands the two checks to the POPE *who removes his glasses to
read the figures.*

which may well allay His Eminence's anger
at the independent manner of those *patres*.

CARDINAL (*laughing, extremely curious to see the checks*):
Do I seem so implacable?

POPE (*expressionlessly returns the checks to* FONTANA. FONTANA
hands him a pen and holds out the briefcase, on which the
POPE *signs the checks, then passes them on to the* CARDINAL):
Dear Count—Eminence, will you both give the donors
in Our name Our thanks for this Peter's pence.

CARDINAL (*who has added up the sums at a glance, looks at the*
POPE *and then at* FONTANA):
Oh yes! Why, that comes to . . . really, you know!
I shall thank Brother Spellman.

He returns the checks to FONTANA, *who replaces them in his
briefcase.*

FONTANA (*insisting*): Something *must* be done, Your Holiness.
Otherwise the Order's mines
in Tuscany will be bombed.
I must be permitted to ask the Jesuits
to sell securities of Idria and Monte Amiata . . .

POPE: At a loss?

FONTANA: Not at a loss. The *patres*, after all,
acquired the securities mostly at face value;
they will still realize a profit.

POPE: Try it! You may try, Fontana.
For Our feelings go out toward
the families of the proletarians
whom the destruction of the factories,
and, above all, of the mines,
would reduce to even greater poverty
and still worse, radicalism—
they would become anarchists—dreadful to conceive.

CARDINAL (*sincerely bothered*):
Ah yes, you know—now, after the fall
of Mussolini, who after all acted as a check
to Communism and a guarantor
of social order, a vacuum
has certainly arisen, one that
fills me with great anxiety, you know.

Thank God the Germans are still in the country;
they won't permit a strike or indolence, you know.
But what will happen when their troops withdraw?

POPE: Then we shall have Americans here, Eminence.
We intend to receive the President's envoy
this afternoon. But unfortunately
Mr. Taylor in his interviews with Us
keeps reverting to Mr. Roosevelt's plea
that we condemn Hitler's atrocities.
It was not the Germans who bombed San Lorenzo!
The Germans saved every book and every parchment
from Monte Cassino and brought them
safely to the Castle of St. Angelo.
(*Fretfully.*) Then Mr. Roosevelt's bombers came along
and reduced that place of peace to dust and rubble.
All the more *tactless* of the Germans now
to carry off the Jews of Rome as well.
(*With great indignation.*)
Have you heard about that, Count . . . Eminence?
It is extremely bad behavior!

FONTANA: Rome is shocked, Your Holiness.

CARDINAL: Yes, a wicked outrage, you know!

FONTANA: Permit me, Your Holiness—on behalf also
of those Israelites who have sought refuge
in my house, to express
most heartfelt gratitude for . . .

POPE (*full of kindliness, with spontaneous cordiality*):
Why, my dear Fontana, it is only natural
that We will do
all in the power
that God has given Us to aid, as always,
the unfortunates.

FONTANA: It is a veritable *salvation* that
Your Holiness has now so vigorously
threatened to take a public stand.
May I ask in all humility
whether the German City Commandant
has in any way reacted yet?

The POPE *looks at the* CARDINAL *with suspicion and incomprehension, then at* FONTANA.

CARDINAL: The German commandant? Reacted to what?

POPE (*suspiciously*): Reacted? But to what, Count?

FONTANA (*rather uncertainly; he already suspects what is to follow*): Why, I heard from my son, you see,
that early this morning Bishop Hudal
warned the German commandant
that Your Holiness would make a *protest,*
for the first time since the beginning of the war.

POPE (*sharply*): The Bishop warned? In Our name!
Your Eminence, did you empower Hudal
to speak in the name of the Holy See
or even in Our name?

CARDINAL: God is my witness, Your Holiness!
I have just this moment heard about the protest
for the first time from the Count here.
I will not, cannot believe, you know . . .

FONTANA (*nervously*):
I do not know the wording! Perhaps the Bishop
did not make a protest *in the name*
of His Holiness, but only announced
that a statement from the Holy Father
was to be expected. My son says. . .

POPE (*very angrily*): Your son, Count Fontana—where
is your son? Does he not belong in Lisbon?

CARDINAL (*alarmed, dutifully*):
The Minutante is expecting me downstairs,
in the Secretariat of State, Your Holiness.

POPE (*extremely annoyed*):
Have him come up! We wish to be informed
how it is he ventures,
as a member of our Foreign Office,
constantly to interfere in these affairs.
The Jews and the Germans
are matters for the two Jesuit fathers
whom We have specially appointed for that purpose.

The CARDINAL *instantly goes to the door and whispers a command to one of the Swiss Guards. Confronted with the* POPE's *rage, his obedience goes so far that he now puts on a stony face toward* FONTANA.

FONTANA: Your Holiness, I ask forgiveness for my son.
His zeal is desperation. He was
an eyewitness in Berlin when the Nazis
threw Jewish children on to trucks . . .

POPE (*angrily waves that aside; he now speaks naturally and
impulsively*): Eyewitness! Count, a diplomat
must see many things and hold his peace.
Your son has no discipline.
As long ago as July of last year
the Nuncio in Pressburg learned
that Jews from Slovakia were being gassed
in the district of Lublin. Has he
run away from Pressburg for that reason?
No, he goes on doing his duty, and behold:
he managed to arrange that no more Jews
are being sent away to Poland.
Whoever wants to help must not
provoke Hitler.
Secretly, as our two Jesuit fathers,
silently, cunning as serpents—
that is how the SS must be met.
We have hidden hundreds of Jews in Rome.
Have issued thousands of passports!
Herr Hitler is no longer dangerous.
In Portugal and Sweden they are saying
that he is talking peace with Stalin. We are glad
to hear such rumors because We know
that there is nothing to them, but they may,
We hope, persuade the White House and Downing Street
to be somewhat readier for compromise.
They ought to negotiate, ought not
to play vabanque with all of Europe
and make Stalin into the heir of Hitler.
We leave it to the local parish priest
to use his own discretion on the spot
and to decide what measures of reprisal
to expect in the event there is a pastoral protest.
Even if We keep silent, dear Count,
We do so *also*
ad maioram mala vitanda.

FONTANA (*in agitation*): But after all, the Nuncio of His Holiness
    in Pressburg did succeed in saving, by his protest,
    the lives of countless victims,
    without incurring the reprisals of the murderers.

POPE: Remember Our last Christmas message:
    one single plea for brotherly love.
    What was the end result? The murderers ignored it.

FONTANA: Your Holiness, I too was sadly disappointed
    that it remained without effect.
    However, in that message Your Holiness
    did not, unfortunately, mention the Jews
    expressis verbis—nor, I might add,
    the terror bombing of open cities.
    It seems to me that anything addressed
    to Hitler and to Churchill requires
    words so blunt as not to be misunderstood.

The POPE *impatiently turns from* FONTANA *to* RICCARDO *who has entered.*

POPE (*more friendly, smiling*): Your son! There he is, the hothead.

RICCARDO *is constrained because he assumes that the* POPE *has issued his protest after all, and therefore feels that he gravely misunderstood him last night. He kisses the ring. The* POPE *smiles.*

RICCARDO: Holy Father . . .

He bows to the CARDINAL, *who coldly refers him to the* POPE.

POPE: We are delighted with you, Riccardo.
    and contemplate your zeal with affection. He who
    defends the persecuted, always speaks as We would wish.
    But—We have just heard with dismay
    that you or Bishop Hudal in Our name
    has protested the arrest of the Jews. Is that so?
    Eminence—please send for the Father General.

CARDINAL, *at the door, gives a command to the Swiss Guard.*

RICCARDO (*still not understanding, very politely*):
    I? No, Your Holiness, I heard
    from my liaison man in the SS
    that Your Holiness through Bishop Hudal
    has threatened to protest.

POPE (*angered*): What have you arrogated to yourself—
   to conspire with the SS?

CARDINAL (*malignantly*):
   The Holy Father, you know, has just heard
   the first word of his alleged statement.

POPE: I am speaking to him, Eminence!

RICCARDO (*crushed, turns to his father, but does not lower his
   voice*): So—after all—nothing whatsoever has been done!
   (*He still cannot believe it.*)
   But Your Holiness did threaten a protest.
   I do not understand . . .
   (*However, he has understood; he says passionately, almost
   crying out.*)
   Your Holiness, the Jews are being shipped out, murdered.

CARDINAL: Be still!

POPE (*smiling*): Why, no, Your Eminence . . . God bless you,
   Riccardo. Speak, your heart is good.
   Only you must not negotiate with the SS.
   The Father General will tell us what has happened.
   Hold yourself back!
   At your age modesty alone
   honors one.

RICCARDO: I am not concerned about my honor,
   Your Holiness.
   I am concerned for the honor of the Holy See,
   for that is dear to me . . .

FONTANA: Riccardo!

The POPE *remains silent; the* CARDINAL *answers swiftly for him.*

CARDINAL: Aha, he is concerned for the honor of the Curia!
   And have you never heard that we
   have set up whole bureaus,
   offices and committees,
   solely in order to help, to rescue—why, you know,
   it seems to me that we have several times
   discussed that very matter, haven't we?

RICCARDO (*more and more losing his self-control*):
   Such assistance reaches only some Jews in Italy,
   Your Eminence. That too has been discussed
   often enough. (*He now turns to the* POPE.)
   But the terror rages in the other countries!

In Poland alone
one million eight hundred thousand Jews
have already been slaughtered! Since that figure,
Your Holiness, was confirmed last July,
and officially communicated
by the Polish ambassador in Washington
to the Papal Legate there—God cannot wish
Your Holiness to ignore it!

CARDINAL (*indignantly*): Leave at once!
What language in the Holy Father's presence!
Count, say something to your son . . .

During RICCARDO's *last words the* POPE *had risen, but he sits down again. A moment passes before he is able to speak, with utmost effort.*

POPE: "Ignore!" We do not intend to account for Our actions
to Riccardo Fontana—does his father make no comment?
Nevertheless, We would be pleased if We might also
be permitted to speak a word on the matter.
(*With mounting bitterness, attempting to change the subject.*)
Do you know, for example, my young man,
that weeks ago we were already prepared
to help the Jews of Rome, who were threatened with arrest,
out of their predicament with gold, considerable gold.
Hitler's bandits offered the Jews freedom
for a ransom.
They attempted to extort from Us a sum
that was no longer realistic.
Nevertheless we would have paid it!

RICCARDO (*has turned, aghast, to his father; now speaks softly
to the* POPE): Then Your Holiness has already known—
for weeks—
what the SS here intended to do to the Jews?

POPE (*agitated, evasively*): What are you saying!
Father General can bear witness to
all that has already been accomplished.
The monasteries stand open . . .

The Father General has entered. The POPE *turns quickly toward him. Monsignore kneels, kisses the ring, bows to the* CARDINAL, *and is promptly drawn into the conversation. The* CARDINAL *avoids*

looking at RICCARDO, *who has gone over to stand beside his father.
Before the Swiss Guard withdraws, the* CARDINAL *claps his hands
and has four hassocks brought from their places along the walls
and grouped around the* POPE. *The* CARDINAL *sits down, and his
example is followed by old* FONTANA, *who is intensely nervous and
worn out.*

POPE (*coldly to the* ABBOT):
　　Father General, please inform Us
　　what Bishop Hudal has done in Our name
　　about the arrest of the Jews.
　　Did he conceive this praiseworthy idea himself?
ABBOT: Herr von Kessel at the German Embassy
　　called on me secretly at dawn and asked
　　that His Excellency, the Bishop, threaten
　　the German commandant with
　　a forthcoming protest from Your Holiness.
POPE (*pleased, relieved*):
　　Well, well! A German does that—how gratifying.
　　What times these are, when high treason is
　　the last weapon of the righteous! A German
　　is ashamed of the SS! Well—Kessel is the man's name.
　　We will remember it. Now, then, this letter
　　from the Bishop will do its work and save
　　whatever there is left to be saved.
RICCARDO (*with the bluntness of one who has already lost
　　everything*): That letter will save nothing at all,
　　Your Holiness. Only you yourself . . .
FONTANA (*steps between* RICCARDO *and the* POPE):
　　May I speak in my son's stead, Your Holiness?
POPE: What is it, Count?
FONTANA: Your Holiness, may I ask in all humility:
　　Warn Hitler that you will *compel*
　　five hundred million Catholics to
　　make Christian protest
　　if he goes on with these mass killings!
POPE (*senses that he must answer this seasoned adviser to the point.
　　He is embarrassed, vexed; he speaks as if he has frequently
　　explained the matter, and nevertheless he overcomes his
　　irritation to the point of going up to* FONTANA *and placing a
　　hand on his shoulder*):

Fontana! An adviser of your insight! How bitter
that you too misunderstand Us. Do you not see
that disaster looms for Christian Europe
unless God makes Us, the Holy See,
the *mediator?*
The hour is dark. To be sure We know
they will not touch the Vatican.
(Hitler has only recently renewed his guarantee.)
But what of Our ships out in the world, which We must steer?
Poland, all of the Balkans, even Austria and Bavaria?
Into whose harbors will they sail?
They may easily be shattered by the storms,
or else drift helplessly to land on Stalin's shores.
Germany today *is* Hitler. They are visionaries
who maintain that overthrow of the present regime
in Germany
would not result in the collapse of the front.
We expect less than nothing from
Hitler's generals who want to dispose of him.
They wanted to act as far back as the spring
of nineteen-forty.
And how did they act?
They let Hitler pin decorations on them
and smashed all of Europe into kindling wood.
We know that manner of men from Our own days in Berlin.
The generals themselves have no opinions.
When Hitler falls, they will all go home . . .

CARDINAL: And Stalin would then have an open road
to Warsaw, Prague, Vienna—even to the Rhine, you know.

POPE (*has sat down again*):
Do you think the President realizes that?
Stalin will not even talk about him.
Since Casablanca reason alone
no longer wields the scepter in the White House.
And Mr. Churchill is too weak. Moreover,
he too seems unwilling to establish
a second front in the West. He is pleased
if the Russians thoroughly exhaust themselves
against the Germans,
and the Germans against the Russians.

CARDINAL: We too would not be averse to that, you know.

POPE (*at every word pounding the arm of the throne*):
    Hitler alone, dear Count, is now defending Europe.
    And he will fight until he dies
    because no pardon awaits the murderer.
    Nevertheless, the West *should* grant him pardon
    as long as he is useful in the East.
    In March We publicly declared that We
    have nothing, nothing at all, to do with the aims
    of Great Britain and the United States.
    Let them first come to an accommodation with Germany.
    Unfortunately the Spanish Foreign Minister
    proclaimed that view for all the world to hear.
    However that may be: reasons of state forbid
    our pillorying Herr Hitler as a bandit.
    We have no choice.
    Hitler's secret service here in Rome
    has told the Father General of the Jesuit Order—
    a pity, Signor Minutante, that you
    know nothing of the efforts of your Chief . . .
RICCARDO: I know of that, Your Holiness.
    But I cannot understand
    how we so much as consider
    using Hitler as a tool.
POPE: A tool that we will drop
    as soon as possible . . .
CARDINAL: God be praised, Signor Minutante,
    that you have no authority at all.
RICCARDO (*with hostility*):
    The Holy Father was addressing me, Your Eminence!
    May I reply, Your Holiness?
POPE (*coldly*): To the point, yes, to the point. To the point.
RICCARDO (*rushing ahead, with the sole result that nothing he says makes any real impression*):
    Your Holiness, let me remind you that
    for years we Jesuits have had in training
    specialists for Russia whose mission is
    to follow after Hitler, that is, the German army,
    and preach the Faith among the Russians.
CARDINAL (*indignantly*): Well—what of it? Would you, Signor Minutante,
    have known before Hitler attacked
    that Stalin could hold out so long?

RICCARDO (*continuing to address the* POPE):
>Moreover, the remarks of many bishops
>about this so-called crusade of Hitler
>are—sheer blasphemies.
>The Vatican must also share the guilt,
>Your Holiness, if now the red storm
>approaches Europe. Who sows the wind . . .
>Russia was after all attacked!

The POPE *makes two uneasy gestures. He remains silent, either because he is so agitated that, as before, he cannot speak, or because he considers it beneath his dignity to reply.*

CARDINAL (*immediately after* RICCARDO *has spoken*):
>Your Holiness, please break off this conversation!
>Outrageous what the Minutante . . .
>(*To* RICCARDO.) I always thought you talented, you know.
>But we have precious little use
>for argumentative debaters in the Secretariat.
>You talk like—like a London newspaper, you know.

POPE (*his voice sounds as if it were coated with rust; then with caustic irony*): Count Fontana, it seems to Us your son
>is badly in need of a vacation.

FONTANA: Your Holiness, what Riccardo
>learned in Berlin from the arrested provost,
>Lichtenberg, and what he saw for himself . . .

POPE (*sarcastically, but still quivering with outrage*):
>Ah yes, we are concerned for him—Riccardo,
>you go to Castelgandolfo for three months,
>and catalogue our library—if your nerves
>are up to such a task. Above all take walks,
>go tramping for hours, and contemplate
>the Campagna and the water.
>A morning at Lake Albano soothes the spirit.
>The cool clarity of October days
>and the broad prospect out to sea provide
>many an insight into one's soul . . .
>Go right out there this very day.
>We gladly give you leave.

CARDINAL: Yes, you know, and very little reading,
>so that you spare your nerves. But read,
>I'd suggest, Ferrero's new masterpiece
>on the Congress of Vienna—disturbingly topical!

(*Seriously, to the* POPE; *he becomes rather loquacious in his effort to save the situation.*)
Those gentlemen in the Foreign Office and Washington
should be set to reading it like schoolboys,
you know. For *that* is what they must preserve
in Germany, after all—a person
like Talleyrand. He, too, like everyone
who served Napoleon, had blood on his hands.
But nevertheless he was accepted as
a partner in negotiation. The way in which he, in Vienna,
split France's enemies, the Allies of those days,
and secretly ranged Austria and England
against Tsar Alexander:
this surely is his wisest counsel to our time.
Moreover—allow me, dear Minutante,
to enlighten you a bit, since
you are so concerned about the welfare of the Kremlin—
Russia also benefited by
restraint upon her craving to expand!
The peace of Europe lasted for decades.
The balance of power lasted for a century.

RICCARDO (*bows to the* CARDINAL *with barely perceptible irony.*)

POPE (*as though the Fontanas were no longer in the room; he speaks with spontaneous ease, delighted to have another subject*): Yes, Eminence, those were indeed true diplomats, there, at the Congress of Vienna! When we compare
their wisdom with the Casablanca formula,
that primitive unconditional surrender!
All that the Allies gain by that
is to force the poor Germans to identify
even more intensely than before
with that wretched Hitler of theirs.
Why don't the Allies proclaim they will make peace
as soon as Herr Hitler is eliminated?
That would be a basis permitting Us as well
to denounce Herr Hitler without necessarily
directing Our protest against Germany.
The Germans, if not Herr Hitler, must remain
acceptable partners in negotiations!

CARDINAL: Yes, Your Holiness, I have no doubt
that even a German Talleyrand might be found.
For example, Herr von Hassell, or . . .

ABBOT: The Allies will not deal even with *him,* Your Eminence.
    The Germans have incurred far too much hatred.
POPE: Quite right, Father General—yet all the same
    in Europe there can be no peace without the Reich
    as central bulwark of the Continent,
    holding East and West sufficiently far apart.
    Great lords remain good friends
    only when their lands do not adjoin.
CARDINAL: Yes, if the Reich is simply divided up,
    as so much booty, you know,
    the consequences would be the same
    as the partition of Poland between Hitler and Stalin,
    or as the Peace of Tilsit in 1807.
    The seeds of a new war would be sown.
POPE: Exactly what We always tell the President's
    Envoy, Eminence!
    Herr Hitler must not be disposed of
    unless the Reich survives his downfall
    as a buffer state between the East and West,
    a *small* but independent military power,
    not strong but strong enough so that
    it cannot be completely occupied
    and torn to pieces.
CARDINAL: But the way the Germans are behaving now—
    carrying off Catholics too, you know—
    such impertinence should teach a lesson:
    the Germans must be kept upon their knees!
FONTANA (*bitterly*): For decades, Your Eminence—forever.
    The Germans must be kept on their knees forever.
CARDINAL (*coolly to* FONTANA. *His first sentence is addressed to*
    RICCARDO, *whose mother was German, as all those present*
    know. As he talks, he works himself up):
    Why, you know, Protestantism—I mean,
    megalomania—and good music:
    these are their gifts to the world;
    they must be taken in small doses,
    or else we'll have them on our necks again, you know.
    If the sole outcome of their war against Moscow
    should be that the Russians march all the way
    to . . . to Silesia and Stettin—
    and now it very nearly looks that way—
    the Germans will have lost the right

ever again to carry arms.
If that turns out to be the case, we should,
you know, do what was done during the days
before Bismarck, their barbare de génie:
allow them no more guns than they would need
to let each others' blood
while they indulge their passion
for war and slaughter.
For several thousand years, you know, that's been
their chief amusement, and Europe has
come off pretty well, you know . . .

POPE (*impatiently*):
Tempi passati, Eminence. Very long past.
Certainly the terror against Jews is loathsome,
but we must not allow it to incense Us so
that We forget the duties that devolve
upon the Germans for the immediate future
as the present protectors and rulers of Rome.
Moreover, Germany must remain viable
not only to hold the frontiers against the East,
but also to hold the balance of power.
The balance of the Continent is more important
than its unity which hardly corresponds
to Europe's ancient national traditions.
Very seldom indeed has God guided the rivers of Europe
into a single bed or in a single direction.
When He did, the stream swelled to a raging torrent
flooding and washing away the older orders.
So it has been under Philip, under Napoleon, under Hitler.
No, let each land have its own river,
its own direction, to confine it and keep it within its confines.
That is the sounder pattern, more easily controllable.
Alliances, yes, but no unity.
We wonder indeed what God may have intended
when in the winter of nineteen thirty-nine
He prevented England and France, as they had planned,
from coming to Finland's aid in the war against Russia.
The plans were made but came to nothing.
Those days, so little noticed, settled the fortunes of the world.
France and England allied against Stalin—
that would have brought Hitler—who even then knew
he would break with Russia—to Britain's side.

The Continent, under Hitler's leadership,
would have emerged united from the struggle.
Great Britain would have kept her empire.
Why did God not wish it so?
Why did He permit it to come to this:
the West now rending itself asunder?
For a long time We failed to perceive its meaning—
however, now we know:
had Hitler triumphed, he would have crushed
everything, everything including Ourselves. It will be
just barely tolerable if he merely survives.
So that this hour too was God's hour.
The Lord had made his decision for Our salvation.
God be praised . . . We must now end this audience.
Our beloved congregation is awaiting Us.
We wish to further the canonization
of Innocent the Eleventh. It is indeed
a matter of great concern to Us to bring
that noble predecessor once more within
the range of vision of thinking Europeans.
Under his guidance Christianity concluded
an Alliance to resist the Turks.
God grant that this new assault from the East
will once more come to naught because Europe
has recognized in good time
that she must bury her internecine feuds
before *this* menace from without.

He starts to leave, but after a few steps, as if sensing that the Fontanas wish to block his way, he says:

And pray, all of you dear ones in the Lord,
pray for the Jews also, of whom so many
will soon be standing before the face of God.
FONTANA: Your Holiness, with all due respect
for the considerations that impose this silence on you,
I beg you in all humility, implore you . . .
POPE (*after a moment's embarrassment instantly recovering his composure*): Why, did you indeed believe, Fontana,
We would permit this sacrilege beneath Our very windows
to pass completely without comment? Of course not!
It goes without saying,
a proclamation shall attest it—the Pope,

in deepest sympathy, stands on the victims' side . . .
Eminence—we have time for *that*. Let us do it at once.
Send for the Scribe, please. No one shall say
We sacrificed the law of Christian love
to political calculations—no! Today,
as always, Our spirit dwells upon the unfortunates.

As though he had never intended to follow any other course, the POPE *now acts as if he were going to protest publicly against the arrest of the Jews. The* CARDINAL *has called in the* SCRIBE, *a tall, spidery monk with the gauntness of a Gothic painting, who seems as marvelously servile as a fourth-generation bureaucrat, and whose exquisite politeness would shame any normal man. He took his doctorate in Germany with a thesis on the symbol of the lily in the late Pre-Raphaelite painters. While this aesthetic Benedictine transforms the prescribed three genuflections into a ritual all his own, and then sits down at the console table and takes his pen in hand, the Deputy of Christ composes his thoughts. The coldness and hardness of his face, which Church publicists are fond of describing as "unearthly spiritualization," has virtually reached the freezing point. He strikes the pose in which he likes to be photographed, gazing over the heads of all around him, far into the distance and high up in the air.*

It is inevitable that the scene suddenly takes on an unreal, in fact a phantasmagoric atmosphere. Words, words, a rhetoric totally corrupted into a classic device for sounding well and saying nothing. It is a blessing that in this scene it is technically impossible to show some of the victims in the background: families in tatters, from infants to old men—several hundreds of thousands of European families, including Catholics, including a number of nuns and monks—on their way to the gas chambers, abandoned by everyone, abandoned even by the Deputy of Christ. So it was in Europe from 1941 to 1944.

POPE (*dictating*): Even more insistently . . . and awakening
ever greater compassion, there has come
to the Holy Father's ears the echo of
those misfortunes which protraction of
the present conflict . . . constantly increases.

CARDINAL: That will certainly be a blow to the Germans, you know.

The Fontanas silently look at one another. The ABBOT's *face is impassive.*

POPE (*begins pacing back and forth as he dictates*):
    The Pope, as is well known, in vain endeavored
    to prevent the outbreak of the war
    by . . . by warning the heads of all nations
    against resorting to arms, which today are
    so frightful in their power. Ever since he has not ceased
    to use all means within his power
    to alleviate the sufferings which . . . which are . . .
    in any form *whatsoever*
    consequences of the worldwide conflagration.
    With the augmentation of so much suffering,
    the Pope's universal and fatherly work of mercy
    has still more increased—semicolon. Increased; it knows
    —this is to be printed in italics—
SCRIBE (*in thin voice*):
    Very good, Your Holiness: to be printed in italics.
POPE (*with a grand gesture, raising his voice*):
    . . . knows no limits, comma, neither of
    nationality, comma, nor of religion
    nor of *race*.
    (*To the Fontanas.*) Content, you beloved in the Lord?
CARDINAL (*pretending to be impressed*):
    Race, too, Holy Father—ah yes,
    that is burningly relevant, you know.
    But ought we not also add, if I
    may suggest in all humility and gratitude,
    to add, you know (*Turning to the* SCRIBE, *in a
    declamatory vein*:)
    This varied and unresting activity
    of Pius XII
    (*he bows, as does the* ABBOT) has in recent days
    become still further intensified
    as a result of the arrests just undertaken
    in the Eternal city itself
    of Israelites who . . .
POPE (*vehemently checking him with a wave of his hand*):
    No, Eminence, absolutely not!
    Not so direct and not so detailed.
    That would amount to taking a position
    on military events. The Holy See must
    continue to shelter the spirit of *neutrality*.

(*Impatiently.*) Not so direct . . . Now then, Scribe:
what came before Rome and the Jews
were spoken of so directly?
SCRIBE (*rising, bowing, thin voice*):
This varied and unresting activity
of Pius XII (*genuflects, then continues to stand*)
has in recent days become still further intensified
as a result of . . .
of was the last word, Your Holiness.
POPE: Then let us say: of the aggravated . . . yes:
of the *aggravated* sufferings of so . . .
so *many* unfortunates.
Eminence, We think that is more comprehensive
than if We mention only the Jews.
CARDINAL: No doubt about that, Your Holiness.
More comprehensive, certainly.
POPE (*appeased*): Since you, dear Cardinal and brother,
have seen fit to speak of Our humble self,
it is only fitting to speak with gladness
of the prayers of all believers. Now, then, Scribe:
(*He now dictates very rapidly.*)
May this beneficent activity, comma,
supported above all else by the prayers of believers
throughout the world . . . my dear Count!
FONTANA (*goes to the* POPE, *who stands in the foreground, and
says coldly*): Your Holiness?
POPE (*friendly and intimate*): One of those checks, Fontana,
which you delivered to Us today, reminds Us
of the securities of the Hungarian Railroads.
Will you see to it, dear Count, that We
suffer no losses even if
the Red Army should occupy Hungary?
FONTANA: I am offering the shares in Zurich, Your Holiness,
through intermediaries. Some have
been sold already, and on terms
not as bad as might have been expected.
Only it must not be bruited about
who is unloading them.
POPE: Of course, We understand. Dispose of them quickly.
No need to make a profit; just dispose of them.
Who knows if Hitler can protect Hungary . . .

RICCARDO *has meanwhile turned to the* ABBOT *and attempts to draw him away from the* CARDINAL, *downstage right. He succeeds in doing so while Pius continues to dictate and* FONTANA *steps back.*

POPE: Where were We?
SCRIBE (*bows, then repeats in a thin voice, almost singing*):
    Prayers of believers throughout the world.
    I thought, if I might humbly suggest a
    phrase to Your Holiness . . .

The POPE *gestures assent.*

    . . . believers throughout the world who
    with hearts in one accord and with burning
    fervor unceasingly raise their voices to Heaven.

The CARDINAL *and the* POPE *glance at each other.*

POPE: Yes, very much what We wish to say. Good.
    How did you put it: raise their voices to Heaven—yes.
    Comma, accomplish still *greater* results
    in the future, and soon bring about the day
    (*With great emphasis, in an almost liturgical chant.*)
    when the *light of peace* will once more shine
    over the earth, when men will lay down their arms,
    all discords and resentments shall fade away
    and men shall meet as brothers once again
    to work righteously together at long last
    for the common welfare. Period.

During this long last sentence the POPE *has approached close to the* SCRIBE. *After the phrase "lay down their arms" he goes up to the* CARDINAL *and* FONTANA, *almost singing the last words of his dictation. Meanwhile* RICCARDO *has been passionately urging his arguments upon the* ABBOT.

RICCARDO: These empty phrases! Father General,
    you know as well as I, he does not mean
    Hitler even to notice them.
    Please help! Today I must—
    we *both* must make a broadcast . . .
ABBOT (*already turning away from* RICCARDO, *in a low, harried voice*): You are insane! Be quiet!

CARDINAL (*while* RICCARDO *is still speaking with the*
　　　ABBOT): This proclamation, Your Holiness,
　　　justifies, you know, the hope that . . .

The POPE *has heard the* ABBOT *talking insistently to* RICCARDO. *He
turns away from the* CARDINAL *and says, smilingly, but without
friendliness—*

POPE: Well, Signor Minutante, still not satisfied with Us?

The CARDINAL *also turns to* RICCARDO. *Before* RICCARDO, *who is
extremely perturbed, can reply, his father speaks.*

FONTANA: Your Holiness, this message,
　　　in which not one word mentions the arrests,
　　　cannot be construed as a reference
　　　to the Jewish problem.
POPE (*his patience exhausted*):
　　　Have we not spoken expressis verbis
　　　of men *of all races,* Count Fontana?
CARDINAL: The proclamation will go down in history.
ABBOT: We do what we can.
FONTANA: Father General, as you well know,
　　　the Holy See has other means
　　　to command a hearing.
　　　Your Holiness, send Hitler an ultimatum,
　　　or even just a letter that Weizsäcker can deliver.

The POPE, *agitated, glances at the* SCRIBE *and signs to him to leave.*

SCRIBE (*bows*): If I may humbly remind Your Holiness,
　　　Your Holiness has not yet signed.

The POPE *goes up to him and in extreme vexation reaches for the
writing case which the* SCRIBE *holds out. Meanwhile* RICCARDO *takes
out the yellow Star of David and pins it to his cassock. At this
moment the* POPE *sees it. He is struck dumb. He reaches or rather
gropes for the golden pen which the* SCRIBE *holds out to him, his
gaze fixed on* RICCARDO, *intending to dip the pen into the inkwell.
It should be a goose quill like the one with which, on November 1,
1950, the* POPE *signed the Dogma of the Assumption of the Virgin.
Absently, he dips the pen into the ink, and as he starts to sign the*
CARDINAL *speaks.*

CARDINAL (*breathless, furious*):
>   Minutante, now you forget yourself!
>   Remove—this—this thing.
>   How dare you, in the presence of the Holy Father.
>   Blasphemy—on a priest's robe—blasphemy!

FONTANA (*pleadingly*): Riccardo—please don't . . .

RICCARDO (*undeterred, passionately*):
>   Your Holiness, what you have set your name to
>   grants Hitler unrestricted license to go on
>   treating the Jews as he has always done . . .

While the POPE, *intensely agitated, swiftly traces his signature,
the pen slips from his fingers; he smears ink over his hand and
holds it out reproachfully so that the others can see.*

CARDINAL (*exclaims immediately after* RICCARDO *has spoken*):
>   Be still! Holy Father, I humbly request
>   that we end this discussion.

The POPE *has recovered sufficiently to find his voice again. He
speaks haltingly, but without the stammer which frequently afflicted
Pacelli as Cardinal, rarely as Pope.*

POPE: In the name of the victims . . . this . . . *this*
>   arrogance as well! And this impertinence—
>   the Star of David on the habit of Christ's servants!

*He again looks at his inkstained hand, normally so painstakingly
groomed, and deeply offended, shows it to the others like a wound.
The* CARDINAL *gives the* SCRIBE *an order and bustles him out. Then,
turning to* RICCARDO, *he points with horror at his own chest, at
the spot to which* RICCARDO *has pinned the Star of David.*

RICCARDO (*readily answering the* POPE's *reproach*):
>   This star which every Jew must wear
>   as soon as he is six years old,
>   to show he is an outlaw—I shall wear it too
>   until . . .

POPE (*quivering with rage*): He will *not!* We forbid him—
>   forbid—on a cassock—this . . .

He stops, his voice failing him.

RICCARDO (*almost quietly, soberly*): I shall wear this star until
>   Your Holiness proclaims before the world

a curse upon the man who slaughters
Europe's Jews like cattle.

The POPE *is silenced by his obvious inability to check* RICCARDO
or to find his voice.

CARDINAL: Criminal folly! Get out!
RICCARDO (*his voice rising*):
    Folly? No, Your Holiness. The King
    of Denmark, a defenseless man,
    threatened Hitler that he would wear this star,
    along with *every member* of his house,
    if the Jews in Denmark were forced to wear it.
    They were not forced. When will the Vatican
    at last act so that we priests
    can once again own without shame that we are
    servants of that Church which holds
    brotherly love as its first commandment!
CARDINAL: Obedience, unconditional obedience
    is the Jesuit's first commandment, Minutante!
RICCARDO: Yes, obedience to God.
CARDINAL: Who speaks through the voice and will of
    His Holiness, you know. Obey!

The POPE *remains ostentatiously silent.*

CARDINAL: What vow did you take as a member
    of the Society of Jesus?
RICCARDO: Your Eminence, forgive me. Does not every Cardinal,
    true to the color of his scarlet robe,
    vow to stand by his faith even unto
    the spilling of his own blood?
    But our faith, Your Eminence, rests
    upon brotherly love—remember the deportees
    before you judge me.
CARDINAL: I do not judge you, I pray for you, you know.
    But this sacrilege—on your cassock . . .
    But now go—leave the presence
    of His Holiness.
POPE (*makes an effort to leave; he is sincerely shaken, extremely
    agitated*): Rebellion in *these* rooms!
    Disobedience and arrogance—Protestantism.

Ugh! This is our recompense
for all the benefits we have conferred
upon the Minutante!

FONTANA: I ask permission to take my leave, Your Holiness.

POPE: Remain, Count. This son of yours
is trial enough for you. You need not pay for his folly.

FONTANA: Please, Your Holiness, permit me to go.

POPE (*with cold imperiousness*):
You stay, and that is that. You, Father General

He turns to the Father General. The SCRIBE *has entered noise-lessly carrying a large brass or copper basin of water and a towel.*

will be responsible to Us: make sure that this—
this scandalous behavior stops.
Accompany the Minutante to his home.
God watch over him, he knows not what he speaks.
We have forgiven him.
Of course he cannot return to his post,
nor to Lisbon . . .

RICCARDO *stands by as though all this has ceased to concern him; it is impossible even to tell whether he is listening. The* SCRIBE *approaches the* POPE, *carrying the basin.* FONTANA, *crushed, falls to his knees before the* POPE. *The* SCRIBE *looks as if he were dying of sheer horror.*

FONTANA: Your Holiness, please . . . I beg you, Holy Father . . .

POPE (*embarrassed*): Fontana, do stand up, you're not to blame.
Your son's behavior cannot make a breach
between the two of us.
(*At last, with crystal clarity and hardness.*)
Non possumus.
We cannot—will not—write to Hitler.
He would—and in his accursed self
the Germans in corpore—
only be antagonized and outraged.
But we desire them, and also Roosevelt,
to see in us impartial go-betweens.
Now, that is enough. Ad acta.

As he speaks the last sentence he returns to the throne and is about to begin washing his hands in the proffered basin. RICCARDO, *already at the door, says firmly and quietly—*

RICCARDO: God shall not destroy His Church
only because a Pope shrinks from His summons.

Speechless, the POPE *rises. He is unable to conceal the effect of these words which have struck him to the heart. All stare at the open door, through which* RICCARDO *has made an abrupt exit. All are stunned, but not a word, only gestures and expressions betray the shock.* FONTANA, *like the rest of course unaware of* RICCARDO's *intentions, feels that more is at stake here than an unforgivable "offence." Completely helpless, he takes three steps toward the door, in great anxiety, as though he intended to follow* RICCARDO, *then turns around and stands shattered. He looks down at the floor and supports himself by leaning against the console table. A Swiss Guard with a halberd appears at the door. The* CARDINAL *signs to him in extreme agitation; the door is closed again from outside. The* POPE *sits down once more and begins to wash his hands. He is incapable of speech; fortunately he can conceal the shaking of his hands in the basin. The* CARDINAL *watches him, taken aback; then he goes up to him and says in an intimate tone which he seldom uses—*

CARDINAL: Holy Father, you must not be . . .
so offended by such stupidities.
It is simply outright rudeness, you know!

The POPE *smiles painfully and gratefully at him. He has recovered his voice, and speaks to the* ABBOT, *somewhat appeasing his troubled conscience—*

POPE: Dear Father General, are the monasteries
supplied with enough food for the fugitives?
ABBOT (*in the pacifying tone of one addressing a gravely ill person*): For the first few weeks, Your Holiness, there are
undoubtedly ample provisions in all the monasteries.
POPE (*pained at having been so misunderstood*): Summa iniuria!
As though We did not wish to give succor to all, *all!*
Whatever *has been granted Us to do was done.*
We are—God knows it—blameless of the blood
now being spilled. As the flowers
(*He raises his voice, declaims.*)
in the countryside wait beneath winter's mantle of snow
for the warm breezes of spring,

so the *Jews* must wait, praying and trusting
that the hour of heavenly comfort will come.
(*He has dried his hands; now he rises.*)
We who are here assembled in Christ's Name
will pray in conclusion . . . Fontana, please,
you too come into our circle . . .

FONTANA *reluctantly moves forward between the* ABBOT *on the
left and the* CARDINAL *on the right, who have knelt at the steps
of the throne. The* SCRIBE *has placed the basin and towel on the
table and is kneeling there, almost prostrate. The* POPE *descends
the two steps and leans toward* FONTANA, *saying mildly—*

POPE: Fontana—who should know it better than We,
to be a father is to wear a crown of thorns.

FONTANA *must kiss the proffered ring. Then the* POPE, *once more
completely stage manager of the situation, steps back to the throne.
"The gaunt, tall figure straightened up . . . and turned his eyes to
Heaven . . . With arms outstretched the Pope seemed to wish to
close all mankind in a fatherly embrace."*

POPE (*while the curtain falls*):
Exsurge, Domine, adiuva nos, et libera nos
propter nomen tuum—
sit super nos semper benedictio tua—

CURTAIN

Act Five: Auschwitz, or Where Are You, God?

When the weather was bad or the wind strong, the smell of burning was carried for many miles. The result was that the entire population of the vicinity talked about the burning of the Jews, in spite of the counter-propaganda of the Party and the government authorities. Furthermore, Air Raid Defense objected to the nocturnal fires, which were visible for a great distance from the air. However, the cremations had to continue at night, rather than stop the incoming transports. A timetable conference of the Reich Ministry of Transportation had drawn up a precise schedule of the various operations, and this schedule had to be maintained in order to avoid clogging and confusion on the railroad lines involved. This was especially important for military reasons.

I particularly noticed one young woman who was extremely busy helping to undress the younger children and the older women. She was constantly running back and forth . . . She did not at all look like a Jewess. She lingered behind to the last to help the women with several children who had not yet finished undressing; she talked encouragingly to them and soothed the children. Then she went into the gas chamber with the last group. In the doorway she paused and said: "I have known from the beginning that we were coming to Auschwitz to be gassed. By taking care of the children, I avoided being selected as one of those fit for work. I wanted to experience the whole procedure consciously and exactly. I hope it is over quickly. Goodbye."

STATEMENT BY HÖSS, COMMANDANT OF AUSCHWITZ

The most momentous events and discoveries of our time all have one element in common: they place too great a strain upon the human imagination. We lack the imaginative faculties to be able to envision Auschwitz, or the destruction of Dresden and Hiroshima, or exploratory flights into space, or even more mundane matters such as industrial capacity and speed records. Man can no longer grasp his own accomplishments.

For that reason the question of whether and how Auschwitz might be visualized in this play occupied me for a long time. Documentary naturalism no longer serves as a stylistic principle. So charged a figure as the anonymous Doctor, the monologues,

*and a number of other features, should make it evident that no
attempt was made to strive for an imitation of reality—nor should
the stage set strive for it. On the other hand, it seemed perilous,
in the drama, to employ an approach such as was so effectively used
by Paul Celan in his masterly poem* Todesfuge, *in which the gassing of the Jews is entirely translated into metaphors, such as:*

> Black milk of the dawn we drink it at evening
> we drink it at noons and mornings, we drink it at night.

*For despite the tremendous force of suggestion emanating from
sound and sense, metaphors still screen the infernal cynicism of
what really took place—a reality so enormous and grotesque that
even today, fifteen years after the events, the impression of unreality
it produces conspires with our natural strong tendency to treat the
matter as a legend, as an incredible apocalyptic fable. Alienation
effects would only add to this danger. No matter how closely we
adhere to historical facts, the speech, scene and events on the stage
will be altogether surrealistic. For even the fact that today we can
go sightseeing in Auschwitz as we do in the Colosseum scarcely
serves to convince us that seventeen years ago in our actual world
this gigantic plant with scheduled railroad connections was built
especially in order that normal people, who today may be earning
their livings as letter carriers, magistrates, youth counselors, sales-
men, pensioners, government officials or gynecologists, might kill
other people.*

Scene One

*The stage is as dark as possible. It would be well if the guardroom
downstage, left, were not yet visible.*

*The speakers themselves are scarcely distinguishable. The mono-
logues are spoken or thought in the interior of a freight car. The
sound effects make that apparent: a freight train moving and then
being switched back and forth is heard. Pallid morning light dimly
illuminates the set, so that only the outlines of the deportees are*

visible. They crouch on the floor to the right and far upstage, jammed in tightly among suitcases and bundles.

Aside from the monotonous pounding of the train's wheels, which continues to be audible during the monologue, there are at first no realistic effects, such as the murmur of voices, the crying of children, and so on.

THE MONOLOGUES

THE OLD MAN:

> Not to die in the car, with my grandchildren watching.
> Fear has long since rubbed out the shape of their faces,
> Quelled their questions. They sense what I know:
> The journey's end will be our end as well.
> Wherever that may be, You terrible God,
> Your Heaven is above us, and the hangmen
> Are men like us, authorized by You.
> Are You watching now? Yes, You will watch. Faithfully
> I have always served you among the many who
> Despised you, for I believed in Your omnipotence.
> How can I doubt, Inscrutable One, that
> This too is the operation of Your power!
> From youth to age has not my comfort been
> The certainty that no one, no one, can wrest the rudder from
>   You?
> This faith in You is my destruction now.
> Yet let me warn You for Your glory's sake:
> Vaunt not Your greatness by throwing children to the flames
> Before their mothers' eyes so that
> In their terrible screams You may hear Your name repeated.
> Who can trace your bidding to turn away from sin
> Within the smoke of crematoria?
> Untrammeled God—is man most like you
> At his most untrammeled? Is he
> Such a pit of depravity, because You
> Have created him in Your own image?
> I can no longer contend with You, Terrible God,
> No longer pray, only beseech You:
> Do not let me die in the car,
> Not where my grandchildren can see.

THE WOMAN: They smirked when they found the little shirts
   And diapers in my suitcase. They listened
   Courteously when I explained I was in my eighth month,
   And put me questions about my husband
   As though they had not, two days earlier,
   Dragged you from your workshop and down the stairs.
   The blood ran from your mouth.
   How you looked around—your face. Oh,
   If only I knew what you meant to say!
   Did you mean our baby? What did you mean?
   And how they guffawed
   When you called to me that you would be coming back.

   How close to each other we were in our daily round.
   We were at odds with no one, could bask
   Out on our kitchen balcony, or take the sun
   In the piazza. We sat in the park for shade.
   Once a week we went to see a movie.
   And now our family is broken—never to be three!
   Never to sit round our table, eating and talking,
   Never to have a room that shelters us,
   Walks in safety and dreams without terror,
   Milk every morning, and in the evening light and a bed,
   And a husband who loves his work and gives me
   Comfort and warmth in the night. And protection.
   We had forgotten the menace of the world.

   How menaced the child is even in the womb,
   How menaced even the old man who wanted only to die
   In his room like a wounded beast in the woods
   After the hunt of life. We always spoke of you,
   We chose names for you and happily,
   Month after month, we bought your first clothes, your crib.
   How can it be? You live!
   I feel your hands, your heart.
   Another month and you'd be born.
   But who will look after you?
   Madonna, Mother of God, don't let it happen!
   Let me have my child—let us live!

THE GIRL: No hope, beloved, that you will ever find me.
   Cold, God is cold as the pomp of San Giovanni's.

It's nothing to Him that this woman next to me
Will never bear her child, that I will never be yours.
Cold, God is cold; my hands grow numb
When I try to fold them to pray with.
And the gods of the ancients are dead as their legends,
Dead as the antique rubble in the Vatican museum,
The morgue of art. Or else I would hope you would find me
As Orpheus found Eurydice.

But this car is no boat going down to Hades,
This railroad track to Poland is not the Styx.
Even the nether world has been wrested from the gods,
Now held by prisonguards no song can move.

You'll never find me, however long you look.
Don't waste time looking. Take a girl
Who'll give you more than I could. Forget things. Be happy
    with each other.
And don't put off love! Lovers are always hunted and in
    danger.
Don't miss your day, as we missed ours in the Campagna.
Seize the evening by the sea, when the beach,
The black sand of Ostia, is still a warm bed for you.

But don't forget everything, keep the memory
Of the sound of the waves, the warm sand,
The surf flooding our hearts,
Carrying out to sea your words and our murmurings,
Where no man could hear them. Against your body I shrank,
Sheltered as never again, sheltered and cherished,
And your mouth broke me open.
Why didn't we take the night that was given us?
Why—forgive me, darling—did I resist
Your hands. If only you were beside me now.
I am so terribly alone. But we missed our hour.
If I were with you on the beach, and a monstrous wave
Came and drowned us and carried us out to sea—
But together. I am so alone. Take, take once more
The sand of Ostia into your hands
And throw a handful to the waves,
As though it were my ashes,

And call my name,
As you did, that time, in Ostia.

*After the last monologue the loud noise of shunting can be heard.
The train stops and now, as the sliding doors open, begins what
has been noted in various chronicles—the "yelling" with which
the Kapos had to unload the trains. It is a series of often-repeated
commands to be reproduced with great realism:*

    "Get out, on the double!"
    "The baggage stays here."
    "Faster! Faster!"
    "The sick stay behind."
    "Stay behind."
    "Get out, move, man!"

Children crying. A woman shouts: "Rachele—Rachele—where are
you, Rachele!"

*The sounds merge with other noises—dogs barking, shrill whistling,
the steam escaping from the engine. Very quickly and brutally,
the startled people are dragged from the imaginary car. They
disappear in the darkness of the stage. Silence.*

Scene Two

*Throughout the entire scene the light is never bright; it remains
dusky. The "cloud," present in almost all the existing drawings
made by prisoners, hung continually above Auschwitz, as did the
pestilential stench of burning flesh and the swarms of flies. Pas-
sengers on the rail line from Cracow to Kattowitz would crowd
to the windows when the train passed by the camp.*
    *The pall of smoke and the glow of fires visible to a distance of
thirty kilometers, the showers of sparks from the crematoria and
from the ten vast pyres on which a thousand corpses could be
burned at once in the open air—all this created the infernal atmosphere which surrounded even the railroad yards and outer reaches*

of this death factory. What took place in the interior of this under-world, at the crematorium itself, exceeds imagination. There is no way of conveying it.

The set is dreamlike and ghostly even if the actuality could be "realistically" communicated. It is enough to provide some bare hints:

On the forestage, at far left, is the guardroom. Flanking it on the right several flower beds, inhumanly neat, and a bench. The stage is raised at the rear and slopes down slightly to the right, so that the deportees remain visible as long as possible on their way to the gas chamber, which is out of sight. At the rear of the stage stands the much-photographed gate house, preserved un-changed today (1959), through which the trainloads of prisoners entered Auschwitz. It is a gloomy, barnlike, oblong building with few windows and a low watchtower like a silo in the center.

The guardroom is elevated two steps and is open to the audience. A large window in the back wall is blacked out at the beginning of the scene. In front of this stands a table with typewriter and telephone, and a few office chairs. At the far left of the room is a narrow army cot. Beside it, a low table with coffee pot and cups, rolls, and numerous bottles of schnapps—liquor was always ready to hand where people were being killed under the aegis of that teetotaler Adolf Hitler.

It is, however, that constant pall of smoke and fire which makes the stage setting characteristic of Auschwitz. The audience must sense that the dreary hut with its little garden represents a com-paratively human façade—but a façade that rather exposes than conceals what goes on behind it.

Unfortunately we cannot reassure ourselves with the thought that a camp like Auschwitz was run by madmen or pathological criminals. Ordinary human beings regarded this as their "place of work." To remind ourselves of that, let us begin with a detailed picture of HELGA.

An old-fashioned alarm clock rings loudly. HELGA, *an SS tele-graphic aide (called* Blitzmädel *in the slang of the time) turns it off at once, throws back her blanket, and sits up on the army cot; she had fallen asleep with the desk lamp on. She is young, ex-tremely good-looking, is wearing only a gym outfit. A sports badge is sewed to her blouse over her well-formed left breast, and the white shorts are ornamented in black with the jagged, runic letter-ing of the SS. For the time being, however, these are not seen, for she still has her back to the audience. Slowly the right and then the left leg appear—very pretty bare legs. At last she rises to her feet beside her bed and immediately begins humming Hans Leip's* Lili Marlene. *She skips barefoot over to the electric immersion heater, places it in a pot and then gets her stockings from the revolving chair by the typewriter. She pulls them on with voluptuous care, for stockings are a rarity in the fourth year of the war. By now she is wide awake and moves with agility. She puts on a blouse and black tie, then her rather mannish gray suit, which emphasizes the lines of her fashion-magazine figure. She opens the door, sniffs briefly at the fog and smoke, and claps her fatigue cap on her blond hair. Her night shift is over at seven o'clock—that is, very soon. She folds up the blanket, pours hot water into a filter coffee pot, and picks up the fat book which lies beside her bed, in order to read while she breakfasts. At this moment Lieutenant Colonel* FRITSCHE *appears, accompanied by two industrialists.*

A few more comments on HELGA. *She is well-endowed with the specifically feminine abilities to adopt the opinions of those who impress her, and to see nothing that might disturb her. Like all distinctly feminine traits, those qualities are so innate in her that she would find even Auschwitz "all right," if she ever gave it any thought. Of course she never does. Hence, she is a particularly tempting opiate for the men here, who sometimes see ghosts at night. She has nothing in common with the witches who serve as female guards in the camp. But of course she knows perfectly well what "program" her services at the switchboard and teletype machine further. Far more than such a person as Commandant Rudolf Höss,* HELGA *unconsciously demonstrates, simply by her warmth and physical attractiveness, how human even professional murderers remain. She proves, indeed, that "human" is a far too equivocal word to be useful any longer.* HELGA's *favorite game, when she is not thinking about some man or other, is to daydream of living far away from this place—in the Lüneburger Heide, say. For she would like to be a happy, faithful wife; she wishes she did not have to repeatedly betray her fiancé, a handsome, utterly unimaginative crematorium drudge with the rank of lieutenant. But she is so completely under the spell of the* DOCTOR *that she overcomes formidable fears and scruples solely in order to come to his bed during the lunch hour. She hates him because she is helpless to resist his lascivious charm—and because she hates all evil and all unusual intelligence. Given her craving for purity and decency, she would even be repelled by the slaughter of the Jews if it had ever occurred to her that such a thing could be as reprehensible as adultery or listening to the BBC. But she is totally malleable, like most young girls; not only is she molten material in her lover's hands, but after the fashion of secretaries, she will parrot her boss of the moment even to his most personal likes and dislikes.*

Consequently, two years later, in 1945, she will quickly understand without in any way being an opportunist that what was done to the Jews was "not nice." But it will take a virile Jewish officer of the army of occupation to make that clear to her. Moreover, even in bed she will be careful not to admit that she knew what she was helping to do in Auschwitz, down to the most horrifying details. "Of course" she had no idea that people were being systematically killed there. And the American officer will believe her, not just because she is charming. He will in all seriousness think her avowal quite plausible—just as his fellow-countrymen on the judges' bench in Nuremberg could credit Julius Streicher when he maintained that he knew of no killings.

The DOCTOR enlisted the services not only of sweet young things without principles, but of sour, highly principled solid citizens— in keeping with Prince Talleyrand's incontestable observation that a married man with family will do anything for money. Whom God assigns a task, he also assigns a task force. The men who are now going to see HELGA are "fictional," but we are acquainted with them not only from the second scene of the first act. We have known them a long time, for we see them daily either on the roller coaster of the German Wirtschaftswunder or in our own bathroom mirror.

Let us take the man in uniform: Lieutenant Colonel Dr. FRITSCHE is pallid and bespectacled, resembling his superior Heinrich Himmler as an amateur photo resembles a portrait by a master. His job is to allocate the healthy "inmate material" of both sexes from the transports among the industrial plants which have settled in the immediate vicinity of Auschwitz, receiving a receipt in return. A few months later, after honorable firms such as I. G. Farben have mercilessly drained these workers of all strength, FRITSCHE takes back the worn-out human wrecks, returns the receipt, and delivers them to the gas chambers. Herr FRITSCHE has never felt any compunctions about this work, for he took his doctorate in jurisprudence and knows that nothing is being done illegally. The whole procedure is according to official decree. He has never had the impulse to beat a prisoner, and he hopes that his subordinates use the lash only if prisoners make themselves legally eligible for corporal punishment by malingering or laziness. All illnesses are considered malingering unless the prisoner proves otherwise by dying.

Herr FRITSCHE on principle neither sees nor hears the infliction of corporal punishment. He also avoids looking at the crematorium, for he sometimes fears "going soft and relapsing into our bourgeois notions." To offset such fits of weakness, he takes long walks accompanied by two wolfhounds, and reads the Nazi Party political education pamphlets, though politics scarcely interests him. He went through the university at the cost of considerable self-denial, married a girl without money, and consequently is anxious to do well in his career financially. But he would never enrich himself illegally; the gold watch once belonging to a cremated Amsterdam Jew has arrived on his wrist in a strictly official manner. Since the Führer has recently castigated all legal experts as stupid simpletons, Dr. FRITSCHE no longer cherishes hopes of becoming a judge. A lawyer's career seems to him totally absurd. Not that he would be conscious of the grotesquerie of people of his sort sitting in judgment on a man who has stolen a bicycle, for example—a situation frequently to be enacted in West Germany after 1950. But Lieutenant Colonel FRITSCHE tells himself that after Final Victory modern legal practice will hardly admit more than two punishments: death, or transportation for service in the occupied Eastern Territories. Greater Germany will not want to be burdened with superfluous mouths in prisons. Reasoning thus, Herr FRITSCHE talks of a subject which greatly pleases his family: the broad lands in the Ukraine (temporarily lost again, alas) which he will certainly receive for his services. Naturally, he knows nothing whatsoever about farming. He lacks the ability to come to grips with any living thing—including HELGA, for example. He even keeps a safe distance from horses, for fear of being kicked. In 1952 he will be a financial expert for one of the most prominent German building and loan companies and by 1960 a judge in a State Superior Court, and eligible for a pension—having changed his profession after a heart attack and put up with a temporary cut in salary out of concern for his family's security.

It has grown somewhat brighter, insofar as that is possible in the fog and pall of smoke. While HELGA is making coffee, FRITSCHE appears in winter coat, warm cap and earmuffs, and starts to enter

the guardroom to warm up. From the left a savage-looking
OFFICER, *equipped with steel helmet, whip, lantern and wolfhound,*
approaches him.

OFFICER: Lieutenant Colonel—report!

He ties the dog to the bench.

FRITSCHE: So early in the morning? What's up?
OFFICER: Quite a surprise at the outer platform, sir.
    The Pope in person has sent us a priest . . .
FRITSCHE: What's this about the Pope?
OFFICER: The Pope has sent a priest along
    to keep the baptized Jews company.
    These Jews are from Rome, you know. He was
    sent right with them, as their pastor, of course.
    And . . .
FRITSCHE: And what?
OFFICER: And some damned moron in Rome
    put the man aboard with the rabble,
    right in the middle of the lot,
    in the middle of a freight car, although
    the fellow's wearing a cassock, is an Italian, not a Jew,
    and even said to be related to the Pacellis.
FRITSCHE: Goddam! Goddamned idiocy!
OFFICER: He spoke to me. It was still dark.
    Lucky I didn't set the dog on him right off.
FRITSCHE: Where is he now?
    Has he seen anything of the camp?
OFFICER: No, not yet. He's still out there on Platform One.
    I turned him over to the military police
    who took charge of the transport from Passau on,
    and to the railroad men. They're to take him back.
    He's having some breakfast with them now and . . .
FRITSCHE: What a mess! Don't guard him too closely.
    He must be allowed to move around
    fairly freely on the outer platform,
    so that he doesn't get too nosy and
    make trouble for us, like the Red Cross people.
OFFICER: I'm afraid, though, that he's
    seen too much on the train already.
FRITSCHE: Come on in. We need a drink after this shock.

They cross the small garden. FRITSCHE *knocks rather timidly.*

HELGA: Come in.

FRITSCHE (*embarrassed*): Uh, *Heil und Sieg.* May we
    warm up here for a minute, Fräulein Helga?

HELGA: Of course, good morning. Cold, isn't it?
    Help yourself, Heinz—here are cigarettes.
    Herr Fritsche, please help yourself.

OFFICER (*taking a cigarette*):
    Thank you, Helga, how are you?
    I don't need a drink now—I'm off duty.

HELGA: What about you, Herr Fritsche? Coffee?

FRITSCHE: No thanks, better a brandy—I'm due at the platform.
    (*To the* OFFICER, *while* HELGA *folds blankets.*)
    We have to get that priest out of here.
    I'll telephone Berlin at eight sharp.
    Does the man want to go back to Rome?
    He's all we needed!

OFFICER: He wants to go to Breslau, at our expense.
    He says he's supposed to visit the Bishop there.
    Then he's going to see the Nuncio in Berlin.

FRITSCHE: What's that? Does he mean to make a complaint?

OFFICER: No, he's said nothing about that.
    He used to work there.
    Of course he was furious at the idiots
    in Northern Italy or Rome
    who shipped him off like some Jewboy.
    But he's calmed down now.

FRITSCHE: The man responsible for the slip-up
    will soon have the pleasure
    of getting a good look at Russia from the front lines.
    An irresponsible moron!
    To pick this of all times, when our situation
    in the south is so precarious,
    to act down there as if it were the Ukraine!
    Incredible, when only recently the Führer
    made a point of warning that the Church
    is not to be attacked before the Final Victory!
    And Himmler—have you heard about that?

OFFICER: No, sir.

FRITSCHE: Himmler recently had his mother buried
    with the blessings of the Church! Pretty rich, eh?

All right then—get that black crow out of here!
Ship him off to Berlin—there they know
how to behave toward an envoy from the Vatican.
Well—another drink to make up for the shock.
Helga, please pour me some consolation.

HELGA: I'm always the one to console—who consoles me?

FRITSCHE: Ah, that's good—I'll call Berlin later.
Well, Heil Helga, and thank you.

HELGA: See you later.

OFFICER: I'll go along, I want to get some sleep.

HELGA: Heil, Herr Fritsche. Heil, Heinz—sleep well.
I have to catch up for last night, too . . .

She yawns and laughs. FRITSCHE *and the* OFFICER *go out.* HELGA
*switches out the desk lamp and raises the blackout shades on the
window at the rear. A circular saw whines; this noise from one
of the camp workshops from time to time forms the background
for significant remarks of the* DOCTOR.

*From the right, jumping gallantly over the beds of the small
garden and up the two steps to the door, swagger stick in hand
and a book under his arm, the "handsome devil" appears. He
lithely enters the room, tall and slim, laughing and genial, crafty
and engaging.* HELGA *is frightened to the bone, but the audience
senses that she loves this fear more than her soul's peace. She starts
back, but he has already pulled her to him and kisses her on the
mouth between phrases.*

HELGA: You! Go away, let me be, you devil.
I hate you, I *hate* you—stop!
People can see us—don't!
The window—you beast—go back to your Jewess!

*After his first kisses she tries to push him away. He laughs softly
and tenderly; they wrestle a bit, and while she flails about, resent-
fully but hopelessly, he clamps her in his arms as in a vise.*

HELGA (*tormented, weak, already snuggling close to him as he bites
her ear*): You'll get us all in trouble—all three of us.
Go sleep with the prisoners, till you're hanged for it.

DOCTOR (*with tender irony, which at last forces her to smile*):
Jealous of that poor woman?
Do I make a fuss because at night
you do your duty as a bride-to-be
with Günter, and only have time for me at noon.

Today, at noon? Who comes knocking at my door,
who slips into my hut to ask—that's
the only reason—just to ask whether
Herr Doktor can lend her *Anna Karenina?*

HELGA: You don't need me, you have the Jewess now.

DOCTOR: But you'll only be coming, my puss,
to ask whether I have that trashy book . . .
there's no harm in that.
How would you know that I just
happen to be taking a shower?

HELGA (*frees herself; moves three steps away from him*):
Let me alone—people can see.

DOCTOR: Quite right—let's keep away from the window.

He picks her up; she kicks out and he whirls her twice around in a circle:

Why, you're wearing stockings, for the first time!

HELGA (*now passively clinging to him*):
It's so cold this morning. Oh, you—

He quickly lays her down on the cot and props his left knee between her feet.

DOCTOR (*tenderly*): I'm looking forward to this afternoon.
Look here . . .

He takes a string of pearls from his pocket and dangles it above her face. She pays no attention to it, but says tormentedly:

HELGA: He'll report you! He'll kill us.

DOCTOR: Nonsense! Your Günter has quite enough
of killing, in the normal course of things.
He's on duty at the crematorium this afternoon
while we'll be keeping warm in our bed.
Why not? You'll be so timid and so small,
my little naked puss—
(*softly*) and then all at once wild,
so wild that you'll be able to forget
whom you're being wild with.
Look here.

He swings the necklace.

HELGA: You're horrible.

DOCTOR: Doesn't the necklace excite you? I found the pearls
    yesterday morning when we scooped out
    a fat Jewish oyster.
    I'll give them to you for your wedding.
HELGA: I don't want any of those things.
    What would I tell Günter?
DOCTOR: Just say you inherited them.
    We'll consecrate the necklace this afternoon.

He stands up, paces the room nervously, says ironically but winningly:

    Then you needn't be shy
    in broad daylight. I'll dress you in the pearls.
    Besides, your left hand will be wearing something too:
    your engagement ring.
HELGA: It's worse when you make fun of me!
    I don't want to, I don't want to any more,
    I don't want to!
DOCTOR (*calmly*): It's good for you—I see that by the way you
        look:
    like a dirty mirror after it's been polished.

She shakes her head vehemently, and smiles involuntarily; then she embraces him and draws him down on to the bed.

HELGA: You're a devil!
DOCTOR: How do *I* look after we've had our fun?
HELGA: Very peaceful, no longer nervous, and
    not so wicked—especially not so wicked.
DOCTOR: Wicked? What do you mean by that?
HELGA (*embracing him more tightly*):
    That easy laugh of yours
    is no more real than my faithfulness to Günter—
    and than my love for you, this abominable love!
    I really don't know whether I love you at all.
    Sometimes I'm mad about you, but then—
    then the hate comes back, then I hate you
    with all my heart, I really do . . .
    Please, let's be honest—I'll break the engagement.
DOCTOR: But you sleep with him every night!
HELGA (*beginning to cry*): Stop it—not every night!
    And only so that I can be with you afternoons.
    Why do you send me away again every time?

I don't want to know whether I love you.
All I know is that I'm helpless to resist you.
I must be with you. Please, let's get married . . .

DOCTOR (*has gradually been freeing himself from her embrace.
Now he stands up and resumes his restless pacing*):
Marriage, propagating children—good God!
That's the one sin I won't commit,
never, I swear that.
Stick to your Günter, sweetheart.
My climate is too harsh for you.
Günter is better.
Present the Führer with soldiers and
joyfully fecund girls.
(*Sardonically, his irony directed at himself.*)
By the time your daughters are nubile
I'll have seen enough twins here
to learn how they're begotten. And then
I'll prescribe for our blond beasts,
our master race, the recipe for twins,
so they can multiply like rats.
I'll have my name in encyclopedias—
that's my last ambition, and the silliest.
Isn't that enough for you, my pet?
Do I myself have to plow, harrow, and sow
in marriage? I'm already doing enough
to perpetuate racially pure humanity.
I cremate life,
I create life—
and always I create suffering.
Some suffer when I steer them into the gas,
others because I turn them back to life.
But Uncle Doctor, my puss, is far too fond
of his own children to expose them to
history's tender mercies.
(*He draws her close to him and says almost passionately*)
Don't worry, in our tumbles
I'll see to it you do not get knocked up.

HELGA: Please stop, you make me feel so queer. Oh . . .
(*Softly, so haltingly that she barely brings out the words.*)
Tell me, why did you pick on just this Jewess
whose—who had two children. Does she know
that you're the one who sent her children . . .

DOCTOR (*releases her, but remains undisturbed. In a matter-of-fact tone*):
> I don't care to talk shop with you.
> Enough of your infantile jealousy . . . Oh,
> some nice rolls. Small and fair-skinned like you,
> and just as tasty. I'm hungry.
> (*He kisses her, takes a roll, eats, and starts toward the door.*)
> We have some Italians to sort out.

HELGA (*blocks his way; for the first time she shows a degree of firmness, but it does not last long*):
> I won't be jealous if you'll tell me
> why you chose this woman of all people . . .

DOCTOR (*impatiently*):
> It stimulates me, that's all, it stimulates me.

HELGA (*silly and feminine*):
> I suppose I don't stimulate you enough?

DOCTOR: Little fool—my little sugarbun, I mean.
> Can't you understand? I want to find out
> whether this woman will go on sleeping with me
> after I've told her where her children went—
> and that I am the lord of life and death
> in this place. That's what I want to find out.

HELGA (*moving away from him*): How cruel you are. Let her live.
> The least you can do is let her live . . .

DOCTOR: What good would it do her, with her family dead?

HELGA (*loudly, indignantly*): But that's what she hopes for.
> That's why she comes. That's the only reason!
> Any woman would—I would, anyway.

DOCTOR: Maybe that is why she came at first.
> Perhaps just for a hot bath and
> a bite of supper—that may be.

HELGA: What do you get out of it, if you know that!

DOCTOR (*smiling*): Things aren't quite so simple any more.
> Now she also comes . . .
> (*He laughs and breaks off.*)

HELGA: You make me more uneasy all the time. You know—
> (*Haltingly forces out the words:*)
> If you're the same to her as—as to me,
> then she simply can't help loving you
> even if she curses you—and herself
> to all eternity.

DOCTOR: Eternity!

HELGA: I'll never come to you again, never.

DOCTOR (*kisses her, smiles*): Fine, then, as usual—half past one.
    We'll play pretty pussycat, all right?

HELGA (*screams, tears in her eyes*):
    Never again, I said, never again.

DOCTOR (*takes her in his arms again, softly, tenderly*):
    Get some sleep first. Don't bother to knock.
    Look around. If anyone is following you,
    just walk right on—once round the house
    and in at the door.

HELGA (*humbly*): I'll have to think it over carefully.

DOCTOR (*smiling*): We'll think it over together. So long.

HELGA *has accompanied him to the door. He is now standing outside the hut. He bites off a piece of the roll and speaks the above last words to her. Unobserved by either of them, a dim wall of deportees has assembled upstage left. They are without their baggage—this always had to be left behind in the cars. (We diverge from the historical facts in one respect: the women and children are here not separated from the men, whereas in actual practice families were forcibly parted right on the platform, before they were "selected" for gassing or labor.)*

Each time deportees are led down the ramp to the right, we hear "incidental music": the low, gentle rumble of a concrete mixer. From the right a police whistle sounds—about at the spot where the glow of the fire is visible. This last should not be reproduced naturalistically. A Kapo moves away from the group waiting in the background, silently counts six deportees of all age groups, and sends them down the ramp to the right. For a moment HELGA *and the* DOCTOR *look at these first victims, who creep forward, almost paralyzed with fear, until they disappear at upstage right. Then the glow of the fire flares up; the concrete mixer grinds more softly. The monotony of its sound is in keeping with the stereotyped procedure of the killings.* HELGA *is now in a hurry to get away. Suddenly she points to the left and says:*

HELGA: Look—over there—look!
    Back there—the priest.

DOCTOR (*takes two steps away from her to the right*):
    Well, what about it? Take your nap now, Helga.

HELGA: No, listen—Fritsche gave orders
  that the priest—I guess it must be that one—
  wasn't to set foot inside the camp.
  He was deported by mistake!
DOCTOR (*turning around*): They all were. What's the difference!
HELGA: It seems he's not a Jew.
DOCTOR: I decide who's a Jew—as Göring says.
  So long—I know all about it.
HELGA: See you soon . . . How strong the smell is today. Horrible.
DOCTOR: The smoke can't rise on account of the fog.
  Sweet dreams, sugarbun.

HELGA *quickly goes across the garden. She turns to the left around
the hut, her head briefly appearing behind the window, and then
disappears. The* DOCTOR, *tapping his swagger stick against one
of his extremely smart, supple riding boots, looks at* RICCARDO
*who stands with Signora Luccani, her father-in-law and the chil-
dren.* RICCARDO *can just barely be discerned. We hear the sharp
noise of an approaching truck. The oppressive "light," the gaseous
smoke and the glow of fire, concentrate the gaze upon the* DOCTOR
*who stands with his back to the audience, legs wide apart, but
nevertheless graceful. He stares fixedly at* RICCARDO, *who glances
over once, shyly and timidly, as though he felt the look, and then
quickly takes the Luccanis' small daughter in his arms.*

DOCTOR: You there! Your Holiness.
  The one in black over there—come here.

Signora LUCCANI *draws her son closer to her. All the deportees
look at the* DOCTOR *except* RICCARDO. *It has become very quiet.*

  Get a move on, come here!

Impatiently he goes upstage, left, toward the group, beckoning to
RICCARDO, *who can now no longer evade him. Carrying the little
girl in his arms,* RICCARDO *hesitantly steps forward out of the line.
The* DOCTOR *silently retraces his steps, going as far as possible
downstage, right, signing to* RICCARDO *to follow him. Uncertainly,*
RICCARDO *follows. Signora Luccani watches him walking away with
her child and screams wildly.*

JULIA: Don't go away. Stay here, stay with us!

*She weeps. Her father-in-law takes her arm reassuringly and talks
to her. At her scream,* RICCARDO *stands still and looks back. He
is frightened.*

DOCTOR (*threateningly, as if speaking to a dog*): Come here, I say.

RICCARDO *again follows him a short distance. They now stand face to face, far downstage.* RICCARDO's *forehead and face are bleeding. He has been beaten.*

DOCTOR (*in a sarcastically friendly tone*):
    That pretty brat your own?
RICCARDO (*with pent fury*): The Germans beat her father to death.
    They thought it funny because he wore glasses.
DOCTOR: Such brutes, these Germans.

With his stick, which he handles with the air of a dandy, he gives RICCARDO *a brief and almost comradely tap on the chest.*

    Where is your yellow star?
RICCARDO: I threw it away because I wanted to escape.
DOCTOR: What's this about your not being a Jew?
    On the railroad platform, I am told, you claimed
    the Pope assigned you to care for the Jews.
RICCARDO: I said that only to escape.
    They believed me and let me go.
    I am a Jew like the others.
DOCTOR: Congratulations. A subtle Jesuit trick.
    How is it they caught up with you again?
RICCARDO (*contemptuously*): Nobody caught me.
    I joined my companions of my own accord,
    when nobody was looking.
DOCTOR (*scornfully*): My, how noble!
    We've needed volunteers. Priests too.
    Just in case someone should die here.
    The climate can be nasty in Auschwitz.
    Of course you're not a Jew . . .

RICCARDO *does not answer. The* DOCTOR *sits down on the bench. He says sarcastically*:

    A martyr, then.
    If that's the case, why did you run away?
RICCARDO: Wouldn't you be afraid if you were sent here?
DOCTOR: Afraid of what? An internment camp.
    Why should a man so close to God as you
    be afraid!
RICCARDO (*insistently*): *People* are being burned here . . .
    The smell of burning flesh and hair—

DOCTOR (*addressing him more as an equal*):
> What foolish ideas you have.
> What you see here is only industry.
> The smell comes from lubricating oil and horsehair,
> drugs and nitrates, rubber and sulphur.
> A second Ruhr is growing up here.
> I. G. Farben, Buna, have built branches here.
> Krupp will be coming soon.
> Air raids don't bother us.
> Labor is cheap.

RICCARDO: I've known for a year what this place is used for.
> Only my imagination was too feeble.
> And today I no longer had the courage—to go along.

DOCTOR: Ah, then you know about it. Very well.
> I understand your ambition to be crucified,
> but in the name of God the Father,
> the Son and the Holy Ghost,
> I intend to have a little sport
> deflating your self-importance.
> I have something quite different in mind for you.

RICCARDO *has placed the child he was carrying at his side. She snuggles close to him.*

DOCTOR (*to the child*): Uncle Doctor has some candy for you.
> Come here!

He takes a bag from his pocket. The child reaches out eagerly.

THE GIRL (*shyly*): Thank you.

The DOCTOR *picks up the little girl and attempts to seat her on the bench. But the child scrambles off and clings to* RICCARDO.

DOCTOR (*scornfully*): So affectionate!
> (*Pleasantly, to the child.*) What's your name?

The child does not answer.

> A pity the little girl has no twin brother.
> Research on twins is my special hobby.
> Other children here never live
> more than six hours, even when we're rushed.
> Nor their mothers either—we have enough workhorses
> and we're sufficiently accommodating
> to gas children under fifteen
> together with their mothers.

It saves a lot of screaming. What's wrong?
You did say you knew what we do here.
RICCARDO (*hoarse from horror*): Get it over with.
DOCTOR: Don't tell me you want to die right now!
You'd like that, wouldn't you:
inhaling for fifteen minutes, and then
sitting at God's right hand as saint! No!
I cannot give you such preferential treatment
while so many others
go up in smoke without that consolation.
As long as you can *believe*, my dear priest,
dying is just a joke.

A scuffle in the background; the deportees are being made to move forward. The line advances. Signora Luccani tries to break out of it, to go to RICCARDO. *She screams*:

JULIA: Let us stay together.
I won't.—My child!

A Kapo runs up and tries to push her back into the line. LUCCANI *clumsily intervenes.*

LUCCANI: Don't! Don't hit the women. Don't hit their children.

The little GIRL *tries to pull* RICCARDO *over to her mother.* RICCARDO *hesitates. The* DOCTOR *interferes.*

DOCTOR: Let her go!
(*To* JULIA.) What's this weeping over a brief separation?

The deportees move forward; old LUCCANI *tries to stay back, is pushed on. He calls out in a feeble voice*:

LUCCANI: Julia—Julia—I'm waiting—do come.

He is pushed out of sight. The whole group, including the MANU-FACTURER, *who is supporting old* LUCCANI, *and a pregnant woman, disappear off right. The back of the stage is left empty. Soon the cement mixer falls silent.*

JULIA (*pleading with the* DOCTOR):
Let us stay with the priest! You can see
how attached the child is to him.
He calmed us so on the train. Please,
let us die together, the priest and us—

DOCTOR (*to* JULIA): Now, now, nobody's dying here.
  (*To* RICCARDO.) Tell the woman the truth!
  That those are factory chimneys over there.
  You'll have to turn out work here, work hard.
  But nobody will do you any harm.
  (*He strokes the little boy's hair reassuringly.*)
  Come along, my boy. It's time for lunch,
  and there's pudding for dessert.

JULIA (*a moment before half-mad with fear, is now full of
  confidence in the* DOCTOR):
  Do you know where my husband is?
  Where my husband was taken to?

DOCTOR: Run along now. Here, take your sister with you.
  Your husband? Still in Rome, I think.
  Or perhaps in another camp.
  I don't know everybody here.
  (*To* RICCARDO.) Let go—give the woman her child!
  (*To* JULIA.) Here, take your little girl.
  The priest and I have some things to discuss.

JULIA (*to* RICCARDO): Stay with us, please stay!
  You disappeared so suddenly this morning,
  were gone so long.
  I was so relieved when you returned.

RICCARDO (*strokes the little girl, kisses her and gives her to her
  mother*): I'll come afterwards—I'll come,
  as surely as God is with us.

DOCTOR: Please, now—in fifteen minutes
  your friend will be with you again.

He beckons to the Kapo, who herds the family along.

  Those who don't keep up
  get nothing more to eat.
  Hurry—move on!

All go out except the DOCTOR *and* RICCARDO. RICCARDO *sways.
The* DOCTOR *addresses him patronizingly*:

  You're very tired, I see.
  Do sit down.
*He points to the bench and walks back and forth with little tripping
steps.* RICCARDO, *exhausted, sits down.*

RICCARDO: What a devil you are!

DOCTOR (*extremely pleased*): Devil—wonderful! I am the devil.
     And you will be my private chaplain.
     It's a deal: save my soul.
     But first I must see to those scratches.
     Oh dear—however did it happen?

While the DOCTOR *goes into the hut,* RICCARDO *remains seated on the bench, holding the bloodstained handkerchief to his forehead to check the flow. The* DOCTOR, *in the doorway, calls*:

     Come here. I have great plans for you,
     Chaplain.
RICCARDO: What do you want of me?
DOCTOR: I mean my offer seriously.
     Do you really know what awaits you otherwise?

He goes inside the hut, and is rummaging in a medicine chest. RICCARDO *has dragged himself up the steps. He drops into the nearest chair. The* DOCTOR *applies a dressing and adhesive tape to his wounds, meanwhile saying reassuringly, and almost seriously*:

     Not long ago the brutal idiots here
     had their fun with a certain Polish priest
     who said he wanted to die in place
     of another prisoner—a man with a family.
     A voluntary offering, in short, like yours.
     They kept him in a starvation cell ten days,
     then even put a barbed wire crown on him.
     Oh well, he had what he wanted, what your kind wants:
     suffering in Christ—and Rome
     will surely canonize him some day.
     He died as an individual,
     a fine, old-fashioned, personal death.
     You, my dear friend, would be merely gassed.
     Quite simply gassed, and *no one,*
     no man, Pope or God, will ever find out.
     At best you may be missed
     like an enlisted man on the Volga,
     or a U-boat sailor in the Atlantic.
     If you insist on it, you'll die here
     like a snail crushed under an auto tire—
     die as the heroes of today do die, namelessly,
     snuffed out by powers they have never known,
     let alone can fight. In other words, meaninglessly.

RICCARDO (*scornfully*):
Do you think God would overlook a sacrifice,
merely because the killing is done
without pomp and circumstance?
Your ideas can't be as primitive as that!

DOCTOR: Aha, you think God does not overlook
the sacrifice! Really?
You know, at bottom all my work's concerned
entirely with this one question. Really, now,
I'm doing all I can.
Since July of '42, for fifteen months,
weekdays and Sabbath, I've been sending people to God.
Do you think He's made the slightest acknowledgment?
He has not even directed
a bolt of lightning against me.
Can you understand that? *You* ought to know.
Nine thousand in one day a while back.

RICCARDO (*groans, says against his better knowledge*):
That isn't true, it can't be . . .

DOCTOR (*calmly*): Nine thousand in one day. Pretty little
vermin, like that child you were holding.
All the same, in an hour they're unconscious or dead.
At any rate ready for the furnace.
Young children often go into the furnaces
still alive, though unconscious. An
interesting phenomenon. Infants, especially.
A remarkable fact: the gas doesn't always kill them.

RICCARDO *covers his face with his hand. Then he rushes to the door.*
Laughing, the DOCTOR *pulls him back.*

DOCTOR: You cannot always run away.
Stop trembling like that. My word of honor,
I'll let you *live* . . . What difference does it make
to me, one item more or less
puffing up the chimney.

RICCARDO (*screams*): Live—to be *your* prisoner!

DOCTOR: Not my prisoner. My partner.

RICCARDO: I assure you, leaving a world
in which you and Auschwitz are possible,
is scarcely harder than to live in it.

DOCTOR: The martyr always prefers dying to thinking.
Paul Valéry was right. The angel,

he said—who knows, you may be an angel—
(*laughs*) is distinguishable from me, the devil,
only by the act of thought that still awaits him.
I shall expose you to the task of thinking
like a swimmer to the ocean.
If your cassock keeps you above water
then I promise I'll let you fetch me
back home into the bosom of Christ's Church.
(*Laughs.*) Who knows, who knows. But first you have to
     practice
the celebrated patience of Negation.
First you can watch me for a year or so
conducting this, the boldest experiment
that man has ever undertaken.
Only a theological mind like my own—
(*he taps* RICCARDO's *clerical collar*)
I too once wore the iron collar for a while—
could risk loading himself with
such a burden of sacrilege.

RICCARDO (*beating his forehead in despair, cries*):
Why . . . why? Why do you do it?

DOCTOR: Because I wanted an answer!
And so I've ventured what no man
has ever ventured since the beginning of the world.
I took the vow to challenge the Old Gent,
to provoke him so limitlessly
that He would have to give an answer.
Even if only the negative answer
which can be His sole excuse, as
Stendhal put it: that He doesn't exist.

RICCARDO (*bitingly*): A medical student's joke—for which millions
are paying with their lives. Can it be
that you are not even a criminal?
Are you only a lunatic? As primitive
as Virchow when he said he had dissected
ten thousand cadavers and never found a soul?

DOCTOR (*offended*): Soul! Now *that's* what I call primitive!
What utter flippancy to be forever
taking cover behind such empty words!
(*He imitates a priest praying.*)
Credo quia absurdum est—still?
(*Seriously.*) Well, hear the answer: not a peep

came from Heaven, not a peep
for fifteen months,
not once since I've been giving tourists
tickets to Paradise.

RICCARDO (*ironically*): So much sheer cruelty—merely to do
what every harmless schoolmaster manages
without all this effort,
if he happens to be stupid enough
to want to prove that the Incomprehensible
isn't there.

DOCTOR: Then do you find it more acceptable
that God in person is turning the human race
on the spit of history?
History! The final vindication
of God's ways to man? Really?
(*He laughs like a torturer.*)
History: dust and altars, misery and rape,
and all glory a mockery of its victims.
The truth is, Auschwitz refutes
creator, creation, and the creature.
Life as an idea is dead.
This may well be the beginning
of a great new era,
a redemption from suffering.
From this point of view only one crime
remains: cursed be he who creates life.
I cremate life. That is modern
humanitarianism—the sole salvation from the future.
I mean that seriously, even on the personal level.
Out of pity, I have always buried
my own children right away—in condoms.

RICCARDO (*attempts mockery, but shouts in order to keep himself
from weeping*): Redemption from suffering! A lecture
on humanism from a homicidal maniac!
Save someone—save just a single child!

DOCTOR (*calmly*): What gives priests the right to look down on
the SS?
We are the Dominicans of the technological age.
It is no accident that so many of my kind,
the leaders, come from good Catholic homes.
Heydrich was a Jew—all right.
Eichmann and Göring are Protestants.

But Hitler, Goebbels, Bormann, Kaltenbrunner . . . ?
Höss, our commandant, studied for the priesthood.
And Himmler's uncle, who stood godfather to him,
is nothing less than Suffragan Bishop in Bamberg!
(*He laughs.*) The Allies have solemnly sworn
to hang us all if they should catch us.
So after the war, it's only logical,
the SS tunic will become
a shroud for gallows birds.
The Church, however, after centuries
of killing heretics throughout the West
now sets itself up as the exclusive
moral authority of this Continent.
Absurd! Saint Thomas Aquinas, a mystic,
a god-crazed visionary like Heinrich Himmler,
who also babbles well-meant nonsense,
Thomas condemned the innocent for heresy
just as these morons here condemn the Jews . . .
But you do not cast him out of your temple!
The readers that they use in German schools
in centuries to come may well reprint
the speeches Himmler made in honor of
the mothers of large families—why not?
(*He is royally amused.*)
A civilization that commits
its children's souls into the safeguard
of a Church responsible for the Inquisition
comes to the end that it deserves
when for its funeral pyres it plucks
the brands from our furnaces for human bodies.
Do you admit that? Of course not.
(*Spits and pours a glass of brandy for himself.*)
One of us is honest—the other credulous.
(*Malignantly.*)
Your Church was the first to show
that you can burn men just like coke.
In Spain alone, without the benefit of crematoria,
you turned to ashes three hundred and fifty thousand
human beings, most of them while alive, mind you.
Such an achievement surely needs the help of Christ.

RICCARDO (*furious, loudly*):
I know as well as you—or I would not be here—

how many times the Church has been guilty,
as it is again today. I have nothing more to say
if you make God responsible
for the crimes of His Church.
God does not stand *above* history.
He shares the fate of the natural order.
In Him all man's anguish is contained.

DOCTOR (*interrupting*): Oh yes, I also learned that drivel once.
His suffering in the world fetters the evil principle.
Prove it. Where—when have I ever been fettered?
Luther did not fool himself so badly.
Not man, he said, but God
hangs, tortures, strangles, wars . . .

Laughing, he slaps RICCARDO *on the back*. RICCARDO *shrinks
from him.*

Your anger amuses me—you'll make a good partner.
I saw that right off. You'll help in the laboratory,
and at night we'll wrangle
about that product of neurosis
which for the present you call God
or about some other philosophical rot.

RICCARDO: I don't intend to act your court jester,
to cheer the hours when you are
face to face with your own self.
I have never seen a man so wretched,
for you know what you do . . .

DOCTOR (*painfully jarred*):
Then I must disappoint you once again.
Just as your whole faith is self-deception
and desperation, so is your hope
that I feel wretched. Of course
boredom has always plagued me.
That is why I find our dispute so refreshing,
and why you are to stay alive.
But wretched? No. At present I
am studying *homo sapiens*. Yesterday I watched
one of the workers at the crematorium.
As he was chopping up the cadavers
to get them through the furnace doors
he discovered the body of his wife.
How did he react?

RICCARDO: You do not look as if this study
        made you especially cheerful . . .
        I think you too feel
        no easier than that worker.
DOCTOR: Don't I? Well then, I still have my books.
        Napoleon, as you know, remarked to Metternich
        he did not give a damn about
        the death of a million men. I've just been
        investigating how long it was before
        that scoundrel became the idol of posterity.
        Quite relevant, in view of Hitler's . . .
        Of course, that disgusting vegetarian has not,
        like Napoleon, seduced all of his sisters.
        He's quite devoid of such endearing traits.
        All the same I find him more likable—

He picks up a book; the name "Hegel" is on the cover.

        than the philosophers who squeeze
        the horrors of world history
        through countless convolutions of their brains,
        until at last they look acceptable.
        I was recently rereading Nietzsche,
        that eternal schoolboy, because a colleague of mine
        had the honor of delivering to Mussolini
        Herr Hitler's present on his sixtieth birthday.

Laughs piercingly.

        Just think: The complete works of Nietzsche
        on *Bible* paper.
RICCARDO: Is Nietzsche to blame
        if weak-headed visionaries, brutes and murderers
        have stolen his legacy?
        Only madmen take him literally . . .
DOCTOR: Right, only madmen, men of action.
        It suits *them* perfectly that Nietzsche
        looked to the beasts of prey for his criterion
        of manly virtues—
        presumably because he himself
        had so little of the beast in him,
        not even enough to lay a girl.
        Grotesque: the Blond Beast, or,

The Consequences of Crippling Inhibitions,
comes down to: a massacre of millions.
(*He chuckles.*)
No, what captivated Hitler was certainly not
the finest critical mind in Europe.
What Hitler fell for was the Beast, the
beautiful beast of prey.
No wonder, when the inventor of that monstrosity
wrote in language so intoxicated,
and with such sovereign arrogance, it seemed
he had champagne instead of ink in his pen.
(*Abruptly.*)
You can have champagne here too, and girls.
This afternoon when those people there,
the ones you came with,
burn up in smoke,
I shall be burning up myself
between the legs of a nineteen-year-old girl.
That's one amenity that beats your faith
because it's something a fellow really has,
with heart, mouth and hands.
And has it here on earth, where we need such things.
But of course you know all that . . .

RICCARDO (*casually*): Oh yes, a fine amenity . . .
only it doesn't last too long.

DOCTOR (*draws on his gloves, smiles with something close to triumph*): We understand each other splendidly.
You'll have two nice girls in the laboratory.
I suppose the newest books will interest you more.
Habent sua fata divini—the saints
fall on their faces.
The light of reason falls on the Gospels.
I made a pilgrimage last year to Marburg,
to hear Bultmann. Daring, for a theologian,
the way he throws out the clutter in the New Testament.
Even evangelism no longer asks men to believe
the mythical cosmogony of the past.

During these last sentences the rumble of the cement mixer resumes. As yet, no more deportees are visible. But upstage, far right, the glare of a mighty fire rises once more, high and menacing. Shrill whistles. RICCARDO *has leaped to his feet. He wrenches the*

*door open and runs outside. He points to the underworld light and
cries out contemptuously, as the* DOCTOR *slowly follows him—*

RICCARDO: Here—there—I'm in the midst of it.
    What need have I of believing
    in Heaven or Hell.

He comes closer to the DOCTOR, *speaks in a lower voice.*

    You know that. You know that even St. John
    did not see the Last Judgment as a cosmic event.

Loudly, flinging the insult at the DOCTOR.

    Your hideous face
    composed of lust and filth and gibberish
    sweeps all doubts away—all. Since
    the devil exists, God also exists.
    Otherwise *you* would have won a long time ago.
DOCTOR (*grips his arms, laughs ebulliently*):
    That's the way I like you. The idealist's St. Vitus dance.

He grips him by both arms as RICCARDO *attempts to run off to
another group of deportees who have appeared and are now
standing silently, with only a* KAPO *prowling around them. The
DOCTOR forces* RICCARDO, *whose strength quickly deserts him,
down on the bench.* RICCARDO *covers his face with his hands, resting
his forearms on his knees. The* DOCTOR *places his foot on the
bench beside* RICCARDO *and says chummily*:

    All tensed up. You're trembling. So scared
    you can't stand on your feet.
RICCARDO (*shrinks back because the* DOCTOR's *face has come too
    close to him. Sick at heart, he says*):
    I never said that I was not afraid.
    Courage or not—in the end
    that is only a question of vanity.
DOCTOR (*while* RICCARDO *scarcely listens, for he has his eyes fixed
    on the waiting victims*):
    I gave my word that nothing would be done to you.
    I need you for a purpose of my own . . .
    The war is lost; the Allies will hang me.
    You find me a refuge in Rome, a monastery.
    The Commandant will even thank me

      if I personally return to Rome
      the Holy Father's guest, whom we
      did not exactly invite to come here. Agreed?
      One moment.

He goes toward the hut, looks around.

RICCARDO (*as in a dream*): To Rome? I am—to go back to Rome?
DOCTOR: We'll have a fine drive to Breslau.

He goes to the telephone in the hut, dials, listens, hangs up, meanwhile saying, half to RICCARDO, *half into the receiver*:

      With a girl as blond as sunlight
      and our own personal deputy of Christ.
      Helga, hello! Helga? Asleep already . . .
      And you'll be back with Pius.

He leaves the hut. RICCARDO *is shaking with emotion.*

RICCARDO: No—never! You only want me to try to run away.
      I would not get a hundred yards. You want
      to say I was shot trying to escape.
DOCTOR (*takes out his wallet and shows him a passport*):
      Only natural for you to mistrust my offer.
      But look at this. Is this a passport from the Holy See?
RICCARDO: So it is—where did it come from?
DOCTOR: Only the personal data are missing.
      I'll fill those out as needed. Now our agreement:
      You find me a place to stay in Rome
      until I can escape to South America.
RICCARDO: How can you hope to desert?
      Rome is occupied by the German army.
DOCTOR: For that very reason it's so easy
      for me to make a pilgrimage there.
      With a perfectly legitimate travel order.
      I'll be there in a week—then with your help
      I go underground. Agreed?

RICCARDO *remains silent.*

DOCTOR (*impatiently, insistently, persuasively*):
      Why—are you still thinking only of yourself,
      of your soul, as you call it?
      Go to Rome and hang your message
      on St. Peter's bell . . .

RICCARDO (*haltingly*): How could I tell the Pope anything new?
  Details, of course. But that the Jews
  are being gassed in Poland—the whole world
  has known that for a year.
DOCTOR: Yes—but the Deputy of Christ
  should speak out. Why is he silent?
  (*Eagerly.*) You couldn't yet have heard the news:
  last week two or three bombs
  which killed nobody, fell in the Vatican gardens.
  For days that's been the great sensation
  all over the world!
  The Americans, the British, and the Germans
  are all desperately trying to prove
  that they could not have been the culprits.
  There you have it again: the Pope is sacred
  even to heretics. Make use of that.
  Demand that he—what's wrong with you?
  Sit down.

He grips RICCARDO's *shoulder.* RICCARDO *has collapsed on to the bench.*

  You're whiter than the walls of a gas chamber.

Pause.

RICCARDO (*on the bench, with effort*):
  I *have* already asked the Pope to protest.
  But he is playing politics.
  My father stood by me—my father.
DOCTOR (*with infernal laughter*):
  Politics! Yes, that's what he's good for,
  the windbag.
RICCARDO (*for a moment seems to be elsewhere. Then,
    still lost in thought*): Let us not judge him.

During these last sentences the cement mixer has stopped. Upstage right, from the direction of the fires, comes the shrilling of whistles. The KAPO *drives the waiting victims off to the right—the procedure should be exactly the same as the last walk of the Luccanis and the other Italians. The* DOCTOR *blows his whistle to summon the* KAPO; *the deportees have vanished down the ramp; the reflection of the flames leaps very high.*

KAPO (*comes back, stands at attention*): Major!

DOCTOR (*indicating* RICCARDO):
> This fellow goes along to the crematorium.
> No jokes with him, understand.
> He is my personal patient.
> He's to work there.
> (*Ironically, to* RICCARDO.)
> I will not forget you, Father.
> You'll have plenty to eat,
> and a normal workday of about nine hours.
> You can engage in studies there,
> theological studies. Find out about God.
> In two weeks I'll take you into the laboratory,
> as my assistant, if you wish.
> I'm sure you will.
> (*To the* KAPO.) On your ashes: not a hair,
> not a hair of his head is to be touched.
> I'll talk to your superior later.
> Now beat it.

KAPO: *Jawohl, Sturmbannführer!*

He goes off, right, with RICCARDO, *down the ramp. The* DOCTOR *stands motionlessly watching them.*

CURTAIN

Scene Three

The same set. It is again early in the morning, about a week later. Snow is falling. We hear the cement mixer. HELGA *is standing in the guardroom, holding a hand mirror and combing her hair.* FRITSCHE *enters accompanied by civilians carrying briefcases: Baron* RUTTA *and Chief Engineer* MÜLLER-SAALE.

FRITSCHE: So early, gentlemen! I'm sorry
> I cannot take you to the officers' mess yet. Please.

He lets the civilians precede him.

RUTTA: We have all day, Major, and we are
    looking forward to being shown around.
    Herr Müller can go over the contract with you.
    Once you've checked its details, we can have it
    all wrapped up by lunchtime.

FRITSCHE (*at the door of the guard hut*):
    We'll find a table here, and something to drink.
    All at once it's winter. I don't
    like to think about our Eastern Front.

He knocks and opens the door rather shyly.

HELGA: Come in.

FRITSCHE (*embarrassed*): Please, step in . . . I have visitors from
        Essen.
    The gentlemen will be going over to the mess—
    we just wanted to have a drink together.
    They've had a long drive. Please come in.

RUTTA (*courteously*): Are we a bother? I hope
    you've rested well? Good morning.

HELGA: I was on night duty, not much sleep—it's all right.

MÜLLER: Heil Hitler, Fräulein. Good morning.

FRITSCHE: Herr von Rutta and Herr Müller-Saale—
    This is Fräulein Helga, our loveliest assistant,
    if I may say so. We're on duty
    and freezing, Helga dear.

RUTTA (*with exaggerated gallantry*):
    We know each other! From Berlin, don't we?
    Where was it that we met? How delightful . . .

HELGA: In Falkensee, at the tavern there—of course.

RUTTA: Why yes! And now you're in Auschwitz.
    Do you enjoy your new job?

HELGA: A job's a job.
    But my fiancé is here too.

MÜLLER: Aha, so it was love that lured you here.
    An enviable fellow, your fiancé.
    No doubt about it.

HELGA: Shall I make coffee—or would you prefer schnapps?

RUTTA: So kind of you, Fräulein Helga.
    Herr Müller will have schnapps, if I know him . . .

MÜLLER: You wouldn't be wrong. It's turned
    damnably cold overnight.

RUTTA (*laughs pointlessly*): As for me, though I'm no wet blanket
    I really would prefer a cup of coffee.
HELGA: Gladly. The water will be hot in a minute.

FRITSCHE *gives her a rather inane smile; he is trying to be gallant,
but does not know how. She puts out glasses and cups. The men
take off their coats;* RUTTA *has been wearing a fur coat and wool
leggings.* MÜLLER-SAALE *takes a file from his briefcase,* RUTTA *a
set of blueprints which he spreads out on the bench. He indicates*
HELGA.

RUTTA: Congratulations, Herr Fritsche! I hardly
    expected to find such attractions in Auschwitz.
FRITSCHE (*smiling as if* HELGA *were his fiancée*):
    Yes—Strength through Beauty!

The telephone rings. HELGA *lifts the receiver.*

MÜLLER (*half-humorously, half-seriously, as* HELGA *goes to answer
    the telephone*): After working hours, I should think,
    that's a sight for sore eyes, isn't it?
HELGA: Inside Platform One, yes. He's here. Certainly.
    Herr Fritsche, for you.
FRITSCHE (*still utterly vapid and humorless, listening to*
    HELGA *at the telephone*):
    Yes, we're lucky—a few of the gentler sex . . .
    Excuse me . . . Thank you, Fräulein Helga.

He takes the receiver as RUTTA *is spreading the map out on the cot.*

    Fritsche speaking. Yes sir, Commandant. *Gerstein?*
    Oh, *he* is to fetch him?
    But I have visitors from Essen—
    I can't go for the priest.
    I suggest we have him brought here
    and Gerstein himself can take charge of him.
    Yes, sir. Of course. The whole thing was totally unnecessary.
    Incredible carelessness.
    Just what I said right off. Thank you, sir.
    (*He hangs up, murmurs:*) A fine mess.
    (*Abruptly, turning toward the cot, respectfully:*)
    By God! The fuse plant!
RUTTA: Ideal, isn't it? Capacity
    five hundred thousand fuses every month.

When in your opinion can Krupp
begin production here in Auschwitz?
You certainly should have enough labor.

FRITSCHE: More than enough! One moment, please.

He listens to sounds from outside. All listen. HELGA *brews the coffee. A distant loudspeaker comes on:* "Attention, an announcement: Inmate Riccardo Fontana No. 16670 is to report at once to the guardroom at Inside Platform One. End of Announcement."

That is a priest from Rome, an Aryan.
The Church sent him along with the Italians
since some were Catholic. Now he's to be released.
We've had him here ten days—just by mistake.

MÜLLER (*incredulously*): And now you're releasing him, just like
that?
Isn't that pretty risky?

FRITSCHE: We'll saddle his conscience with hostages,
two Polish priests we have as inmates here.
If he talks—they die.
He'll keep his mouth shut all right.

RUTTA: Ah! Yes, they use hostages
in Essen too: French or Belgian workers
whom we cannot refuse a visit home
must give a hostage to the firm,
a fellow-countryman.

MÜLLER: That does the trick, just like in Schiller's poem.

Everyone laughs.

FRITSCHE (*stupidly*): Haha, Damon and Pythias—I see.
But can the workers from the East—Polacks,
Ukrainians, also go home on leave?

MÜLLER: What a fine mess that would be! Naturally not.

The coffee is now ready. The announcement comes through on the loudspeaker again. While MÜLLER-SAALE *chats with* HELGA, FRITSCHE *makes a telephone call.*

MÜLLER: What part of the country are you from, Fräulein Helga?

FRITSCHE (*to* RUTTA *as he lifts the receiver*):
Excuse me, Baron . . . yes? This is Sturmbannführer Fritsche.
Bring Bundle 16670 to the guardroom Inside Platform One—
a cassock. What's that? You know, the thing a priest wears.
Can't find it that quick? Are you crazy, 16670 was delivered

last week. I made a special point that that piece was to be put aside. Kindly look around. I should think so. Good. At once.

MÜLLER: Is your mother Saxon? Or did someone from Saxony teach you to brew perfect coffee like this?

HELGA: Glad you like it. We make pretty good coffee in Hamburg too.

RUTTA: Really tip-top. Herr Müller, please read the draft aloud to us, will you? Then we'll go to Herr Fritsche's office . . .

MÜLLER (*reading aloud*):
Very well, then, to make it short and sweet:
subject of the contract, the Auschwitz building,
one hundred and twenty by one hundred eighteen meters,
will be leased by the SS to Friedrich Krupp.
Secondly: the electrical substation,
to be built and equipped by Krupp,
will be transferred to the SS administration.

FRITSCHE: Transferred to us?

RUTTA: Only the substation, Herr Fritsche. The machines, am I not right, Herr Müller, remain Krupp property?

MÜLLER: Yes. Point Three: machines
remain the property of Krupp.
Fourth: a year's notice is required
to terminate the contract.
I think it just as well, Major,
if we say nothing in the contract
about the daily fee Krupp pays the SS
per inmate?

FRITSCHE: Of course not, Herr Müller, of course not.

RUTTA: For the rest, our Lieutenant Colonel—
I mean Herr Doktor von Schwarz of Army High Command—
looked the plans over last week and approved them.

FRITSCHE: Fine. I guess that's it. One more cigarette,
then I must go.

They smoke and drink.

RUTTA: Many thanks. My colleague, Streifer,
of I.G. Farben was not exaggerating,
God knows, when he praised the exemplary
cooperation of SS and industry
in Auschwitz.

FRITSCHE: Yes. Siemens, too, is using forced labor
from some of the camps.

MÜLLER: Back in September Alfried Krupp von Bohlen
wanted to send a man to Auschwitz.
And Herr von Bohlen knows that his Breslau office,
which is in charge of technical affairs,
has kept in closest contact with Auschwitz.

RUTTA (*abruptly*): The people here are easy to control!

FRITSCHE: Here, yes! But how does Krupp keep in check
the twenty thousand foreigners in Essen?

RUTTA: They're fairly docile. If not—there's the Gestapo,
Mother's little helper. They pick up
a few troublemakers every now and then.
We even allow a certain amount of correspondence.
Not to the East, of course. Their mail
has to be burned twice a week.
They're quite a bother, that rabble.
A pity we have to make do with them.

They laugh; HELGA *does not join in. Outside, wearing a steel helmet, looking about tensely,* GERSTEIN *has appeared. He peers sur-
reptitiously into the hut, and hesitates. His expression is gloomy
and depressed—he knows this is to be the greatest risk he has yet
taken. Now he forces himself to assume an expression of calm
superiority, knocks, enters, salutes.*

GERSTEIN: Major—the Commandant has sent me to you.
Am I intruding? I have orders
to fetch a certain Father Fontana from here.

FRITSCHE (*amiably*): Heil Hitler, Gerstein . . . Excuse me,
gentlemen.
I'll be along shortly. Fräulein Helga, will you
be so kind as to show them the way.
I know all about it, Gerstein.

HELGA: Yes, I'm due there, anyhow. Good morning, Herr Gerstein.

GERSTEIN: Ah, Fräulein Helga, how are you—good morning.

RUTTA: Well, many, many thanks, Herr Fritsche.

MÜLLER (*while the three are helping one another into their coats*):
It's been nice in your wigwam, Fräulein Helga.
I wouldn't mind having you make my coffee
every morning. Heil Hitler!

RUTTA (*to* GERSTEIN): Heil Hitler.

GERSTEIN: Heil Hitler.

HELGA (*calling back as she goes*):
> There's some coffee left, Herr Gerstein.

FRITSCHE (*to the civilians*): I'll be right along.
> (*To* GERSTEIN.) The black crow will be along soon.
> Our Doctor, it's incredible, amused himself
> putting the priest to work at the crematorium.
> As a dentist—just for a joke! He wants, he says,
> to give the priest this chance for a second communion.
> It's all the Doctor's fault that the man
> ever set foot inside the camp.
> I wanted to send him straight back home.

GERSTEIN: Where is the Doctor now?

FRITSCHE (*laughs disapprovingly*): He was going strong last night.
> Still sleeping. Everyone's sleeping late. I could have used
> a few extra hours sleep myself. We threw
> a farewell party for Höss last night—
> (*confidentially*) till four in the morning. You know about
>   that?

GERSTEIN: Yes, of course. But they don't hold it against him.

FRITSCHE (*sniggering*): The Doctor says that from now on Höss
> can wear the Iron Cross with fig leaves and balls.
> Seriously, though, he's getting a promotion.
> He's to be inspector of all the camps in Germany.
> All the same, it was going pretty far
> for the Commandant to shack up with a Jewess.
> You know, that was his consolation—
> since he inspected the ovens every day.
> At bottom he's a *terribly* good fellow.

GERSTEIN (*without sounding in the least sardonic*):
> Yes, Höss has a heart. You'll miss him.
> He's right at his post today, as always.
> (*As casually as possible.*)
> Has the Jewess been liquidated?

FRITSCHE (*eagerly*): No—imagine that—she's still alive. Odd, eh?
> I suppose that Kaltenbrunner
> means to keep the dame on ice
> so that he has a hold on Höss for good.
> Oh well, you'll bring the priest over?

GERSTEIN: To you, Major?

FRITSCHE (*rejecting that suggestion*): No, not to me! I want
> (*firmly*) nothing at all to do with this affair.

Take him to Höss. See that the fellow signs a statement
that he's seen nothing in the camp but flower beds.

GERSTEIN: He'll sign anything to get out of here.

FRITSCHE: Nobody's ever been released before.

GERSTEIN: I've wondered about that myself. Oh well,
I suppose they know what they are doing.
I happened to be at the phone when the Nuncio called.
Then I went straight to Eichmann, who
was just as much upset as I was.

FRITSCHE: Terribly reckless of the Doctor
to let that black crow come in here at all.
He really goes too far, I think. Last night
he did a take-off of Ley and Heydrich. I found it disgusting.
After all, there's a limit to everything.

GERSTEIN: Heydrich—well, that certainly is tasteless.
Ley is really a marzipan pig, but Heydrich!

A KAPO, *timorous and careworn, brings a bundle of clothing tied
with string, to which a number is attached:* 16670. FRITSCHE *and*
GERSTEIN *leave the hut. The* KAPO *takes the bundle inside. A
factory siren screeches.* FRITSCHE *looks at his watch and sets it.*

FRITSCHE (*laughing*): Marzipan pig is right. And always soused.
The cassock! Just drop it in the hut.
Well then, Gerstein, the black crow . . .

KAPO: Yes sir.

FRITSCHE: . . . will be along in due course. After all,
we're a good two kilometers from the crematorium.

GERSTEIN: And still the smell of flesh is so sharp?
What do the local people say?

FRITSCHE: They know what's up, of course.
What you smell now doesn't come from the furnaces.
That's from the open burning pits.
We can no longer manage with furnaces alone.
I must go now, I really don't want
to have *anything* to do with this affair.
It can only lead to trouble.

CARLOTTA *shyly passes by the two men in uniform. Carrying a pail
of water and a scrubbing brush, she approaches the hut, enters,
and begins scrubbing the floor on her knees. She sees* HELGA'S

*hand mirror lying on a chair. Still on her knees, she pushes her
kerchief back slightly and examines her shorn hair, her dirty,
haggard face. This seems to have been her first opportunity to
do so since the deportation. She begins crying silently. Later,
when GERSTEIN enters the hut, she makes an effort not to show that
she has been crying.*

FRITSCHE: Please tell them in Berlin that I
    had not a thing to do with it.
    I guessed right off he wouldn't stay here.
    (*He points to the bundle of clothes.*)
    That's why I did not have his costume there
    thrown on to the big heap. (*As he walks off.*)
    So then, it's not my fault. Heil, Gerstein.
    And feed him up a bit at the canteen.
GERSTEIN: Thanks, Heil Hitler, Major, many thanks.
    (*Gritting his teeth.*) Asshole!

*His nervousness keeps him pacing about. He lights a cigarette,
then notices the girl scrubbing and goes into the hut, trying to
flee from his own uneasiness. As he enters, the girl shrinks away;
her every movement betrays her terror of any man in uniform.
GERSTEIN takes a piece of bread wrapped in newspaper from his
pocket, unwraps it and offers it to CARLOTTA.*

GERSTEIN: Where do you come from? Here, eat this.
    Have you been here long?
CARLOTTA (*not standing or taking the bread*):
    From Rome—no, thank you, for a week.
GERSTEIN: From Rome? Then you know the priest,
      Father Fontana?
    Go on, take the bread.
CARLOTTA: We all know him.
    (*Refusing, for fear of a trick.*)
    Why do you give me bread?
GERSTEIN (*placing the bread on the chair*):
    Why? You're hungry, aren't you?
    Would you like me to send a letter out for you?
CARLOTTA (*after a pause, coldly*): No, thank you.
GERSTEIN: You don't trust me.
    But give a message to the Father.
    He's being released to go back to Rome.

CARLOTTA (*overjoyed, then abruptly sad*):
>   Released? He, too. But of course he
>   doesn't really belong—to us.

GERSTEIN (*takes a sheet of paper and an envelope from the type-
>   writer table, unscrews his fountain pen, and lays all these
>   objects on the chair*):
>   Write in here, so that no one will see.
>   The Father will take the letter to Rome.

CARLOTTA (*continuing to refuse, but with a touch of Italian
>   pathos; her voice at the end subsides into tears*):
>   I have no one to write to!
>   My fiancé died in Africa—for Germany,
>   at the capture of Tobruk. To prove your gratitude
>   you Germans have deported
>   my parents and me, my sister and her children.
>   Don't offer me bread—tell me, are they . . . dead?
>   Tell me that. We arrived on October 20th.
>   We were separated on the platform.
>   Only a hundred or so entered the camp here.
>   The others were taken away in trucks.
>   Where? Trucks with Red Cross markings.
>   You must know where they were taken!

GERSTEIN (*helplessly*): I'm not one of the camp guards, really not.
>   I don't know. I never go inside.

*The cement mixer begins to grind. She listens for a moment to the
sound. He attempts to distract her.*

>   Your fiancé wasn't Jewish. Then write
>   to his parents. Ask them to try, through the Vatican . . .

CARLOTTA: No. It's because of my in-laws
>   that I became a Catholic.

GERSTEIN: You regret that—why?

CARLOTTA: Catholics, Catholic Fascists were the ones
>   who handed me over to the Germans,
>   who took away my last picture of Marcello
>   and my engagement ring. Perhaps that was
>   my punishment for deserting my own people
>   and going over to the Catholic Church.

GERSTEIN: You must not say that! Catholics
>   are being persecuted too. Many priests
>   in Poland and in Germany have been murdered.
>   And Father Riccardo, coming with you voluntarily . . .

CARLOTTA (*still hostile*): There are just a few like that. Exceptions.
GERSTEIN: Of course. And yet—the majority of Italians,
the great majority, are against this terrorism.
Both Church and people.
CARLOTTA (*ostentatiously turning back to her work*):
Against this terrorism—like you, I suppose.
But do nothing or little against it, like you.
Christians! They're all Christians.
Marcello—he was a Christian. He could
respect a different religion, and let me keep mine.
But I listened to his parents instead—
they were after me to become a Catholic.
(*Bitterly.*) As a Catholic I felt safe in Rome.
That's the only reason I did not hide.
Can't you please find out
whether my family is still alive?
GERSTEIN: Really, I have no way to.
At least write down your name for Father Riccardo.
CARLOTTA (*suddenly taking heart*):
I'd like to write a letter after all.
Thank you. And forgive me.

She crouches on the floor and begins hurriedly writing, using the chair for a desk. Later, alone in the hut, she cries again and tears up what she has written. She puts the scraps of paper into the pocket of her smock.

GERSTEIN (*smiling at her, goes to the window, says rapidly to himself, but quite loudly*):
Here he comes—why, it's Jacobson!

He wrenches open the door and rushes to meet JACOBSON. JACOBSON, *at the shock of finding him here, is incapable of doing more than cry out his name, while his skeletal face widens in a smile that threatens at any moment to disintegrate into sobs.*

JACOBSON: Gerstein! You!
(*Softly.*) Sometimes I hoped for this.
GERSTEIN (*has retreated three steps to close the door to the hut*):
Good God, Jacobson! You here. I thought
you were in England. Where were you caught?
Why, you had Riccardo's passport.
JACOBSON: At the Brenner.
They looked too carefully at the passport photo.

But I stuck to my story
through thick and thin.
Otherwise they would have killed me outright.
I kept insisting that I was the priest.
You understand, my name here is Father Fontana.
I *am* the priest, you see.

As he speaks, he looks around several times to make sure he is not being overheard. One can sense that he has almost completely identified with his part, which is his sole salvation. Feverishly and hoarsely:

I work at the outer platform sorting the belongings
of those who have been gassed. Sometimes I find
jewelry that I swap with the railroad men
for bread. That's why I'm still alive.
And because I hate. I want to get out.
Otherwise I would long ago
have run into the wire.
And now you've sent for me!

GERSTEIN: Not you, Jacobson!
(*Despairingly.*) Don't you see: Riccardo Fontana's in the
camp.
I've come on his account.
How could I have dreamed
that you were here.

JACOBSON (*not understanding*): What's that? The Father here?
But he's no Jew. How could he . . .

GERSTEIN: They deported the Jews from Rome,
and he went with them, of his own volition.
He's been in Auschwitz for a week.
Now they're releasing him.

JACOBSON (*incredulous—then with an effort to respond
generously*): Released—from Auschwitz? Incredible!
But . . . I'm glad for the priest's sake.

GERSTEIN: To think that we should meet here, Jacobson!
How painful it is to be powerless to free you.

JACOBSON (*unable to hide his mounting bitterness*):
Yes, I am no priest, Gerstein.
A priest is worth an ultimatum.

GERSTEIN (*gives a short, harsh laugh*): Ultimatum? From whom?
Believe me, this order for Riccardo's release
is only something I've invented.

JACOBSON: Then invent another—to get that girl,
 or me or any of us wretches out of here.
GERSTEIN: You know I can't, Jacobson.
 I'm only a lieutenant, nothing more.
 At this moment I stand closer to the brink
 of death than you, Jacobson!
JACOBSON (*looking away*): Forgive me—you wear that uniform.
GERSTEIN: How else could I have come here?
 That I can never shed this uniform
 is my part-payment of the debt of guilt
 that burdens all of us. Our resistance movement . . .
JACOBSON: Resistance? Why, Gerstein, can't it even
 tear up the railroad tracks to Auschwitz?
 Why doesn't your resistance show itself?
 (*Softly, fervently, despairingly.*)
 Or are you still a lone wolf?
 How can you people go on living, knowing
 what day after day, for an entire year,
 has been happening here?
 You live, you eat, you beget children—
 and you know—you all know about the camps.
 (*He grasps* GERSTEIN's *shoulders, his voice tearful*:)
 Make an end, make an end of it, somehow!
 (*Disjointedly.*)
 Why don't the Allies drop arms for us?
 God knows, Gerstein, I don't mean to accuse you;
 it's only thanks to you that I'm alive . . .
 It's only that—I was numbed enough to forget.
 Seeing you has made me realize
 there's still a world outside the camp.
 Gerstein, you can do something for me, after all.
GERSTEIN: If there's anything . . .
JACOBSON (*rapidly*): Just say I claimed to be the priest
 and then attacked you when—the real priest came.
 Shoot me.
GERSTEIN: Jacobson!
JACOBSON (*pleadingly*): Shoot me, Gerstein.
 Say I attacked you—they'll believe that.
 Please, Gerstein, do this for me. I no longer
 have the courage to run into the fence—
 the current doesn't always kill at once.

GERSTEIN: You've survived for a whole year—surely
    you'll make it to the end. Jacobson—
    just one more year—at most one year.
    Then the Russians will be here to free you.

JACOBSON: A year!

GERSTEIN: They've already retaken the Ukraine.

JACOBSON: Gerstein, why won't you do it? Why not?

GERSTEIN *shakes his head, unably to reply.* JACOBSON *turns away.*

    Then I'll go, so that I don't
    put you and the priest in greater danger.

GERSTEIN (*helplessly, deeply moved, stops him*):
    Not this way, Jacobson, don't leave this way.

JACOBSON: Four thousand, five thousand—some days
    even more are gassed here.
    Nothing frightens me any longer except
    the world that permits such things.
    (*More composed and matter-of-fact.*)
    And the most devilish thing of all is
    that if one man escapes he dooms
    ten others to the hole. That happened once,
    and ten were sentenced to death by starvation.
    We listened to their crying for a week.
    Father Kolbe was the last to die, they say.
    It's knowing that which held me back
    a while ago, when I could have escaped—
    out there on the platform—in one of the cars
    that take the shoes
    of those they've gassed to Breslau.

GERSTEIN: They think the priest is being freed
    officially. There'll be no reprisals,
    except for me, if ever the truth comes out.

RICCARDO, *shocked speechless at seeing* GERSTEIN *here, has appeared behind* JACOBSON, *whom he does not immediately recognize.*
RICCARDO *has been terribly marked by the work he has had to do
at the crematorium for the past week.*

GERSTEIN: Riccardo!
    The Nuncio sent me to take you back.

RICCARDO: Gerstein! You should not have tried to find me.
    Jacobson—you!

JACOBSON: How could you come here, Father?
  I'm living under your name, you know.
RICCARDO: Jacobson—forgive me, I thought
  you'd come through safely that time.
JACOBSON: To come here voluntarily, unarmed—
  whom did you think you could help?
GERSTEIN (*insistently, since* RICCARDO *has obviously not
  understood*): Riccardo, you are being released!
RICCARDO: Released?

*Suddenly done in, he sits down on the steps leading up to the
guardroom.*

> I can't go on.
> I've already told myself a hundred times
> that it was sheer presumption to come here.
> I can't bear it, I can't bear it.

He cries silently; none of the others can speak.

> For the past week
> I have been burning the dead ten hours a day.
> And with every human body that I burn
> a portion of my faith burns also.
> God burns.
> Corpses—a conveyor belt of corpses.
> History is a highway paved with carrion . . .
> If I knew that He looks on—
> (*With revulsion.*) I would have to—hate Him.

GERSTEIN (*uncertainly, pulling* RICCARDO *to his feet*):
  None of us understands Him any longer.
  But now at least He wants to save you, Riccardo.
RICCARDO (*wearily*): How do you know that? And why me?
  I was not speaking of myself—the families . . .
  (*Murmuring disconnectedly.*)
  I am—I would be frightened of rescue
  by Him . . . The Monster that devours its young.
JACOBSON (*speaking more vigorously and resolutely*):
  Father, speak for us, help us!
  Tell the Pope that he must act.
RICCARDO: I could never get to the Pope again.
  (*Suddenly.*) What were you thinking of—return to Rome?
GERSTEIN (*feverishly*):
  You have to survive, Riccardo—to live, somewhere.

RICCARDO: Live? No one can
    come back from here to go on living.
    (*Points to* JACOBSON.)
    And what about him? And all the others?
    I came here with a mission; that must sustain me.
    Whether it's meaningful, I'm no longer sure.
    I do not know. But if it's not,
    my life, too, is no longer meaningful.
    Let me be.

JACOBSON: Father, if you do not go along
    you will endanger Gerstein. He only
    invented the order for your release.

GERSTEIN: You shouldn't have said that.

JACOBSON: I did to get him out of here—now hurry!

RICCARDO (*starts convulsively*):
    So—I rather thought as much. Gerstein,
    you used to go about things
    so cautiously, for all your daring . . . (*Despairingly.*)
    Why this insanity now, to come for me?

GERSTEIN (*gloomily*): Because I have you on my conscience.
    I turned you first onto this fatal path.

RICCARDO (*quickly going up to him*):
    What would I have on my conscience, if I weren't here?
    And shall I shrink from it now that I am? No,
    God knows it's not your fault that I am here.
    But it is not my fault either, is it,
    if something happened to you through my staying?
    Please understand, I have no right to go.
    Why lead me into temptation—that makes it worse.
    You see I hardly have the necessary strength.
    (*Softly.*) I'm doing penance, as I must.

GERSTEIN (*excitedly*): You've done your penance long ago.
    You've just come from the fires, Riccardo.

RICCARDO: Gerstein, please, take *him* with you.

JACOBSON: Me?

GERSTEIN: And suppose he is killed?

JACOBSON (*firmly*): Father, I won't accept that.

RICCARDO: Jacobson, I'm not staying in your place.
    It's not a question of me or of you.
    I am here to represent the Church.
    I could not go even if I wanted to.
    God knows, I did want to.

You will owe me nothing, Jacobson.
If you don't go, then no one will at all.

While GERSTEIN, *who feels it is unendurable to leave the two behind, stands by passively, although with dark forebodings,* RICCARDO *says slowly, with heavy pauses*:

Put on my cassock one more time—
if Gerstein agrees . . .

JACOBSON: I can't accept that—not from you,
and certainly not from him.

He indicates GERSTEIN, *and the two wait for* GERSTEIN *to reply.*
GERSTEIN, *to hide his fear of such a risk, fends off the decision.*

GERSTEIN: I say nothing. Decide it for yourselves.

RICCARDO: You can do all the things that I cannot.
You can use a gun, can sabotage.
It's not a case of simply saving your life.
Gerstein is not going to set you free
so that you can hide out till the end of the war.

GERSTEIN (*unable to forebear commenting*):
The practical side—do any of the high camp officers
know either of you personally?

JACOBSON: No.

RICCARDO: Only the head doctor knows me.

GERSTEIN (*starts back, aghast*): The Doctor!
No! If the Doctor knows you, Riccardo,
that makes our game so much more difficult
that we must ask ourselves: can we afford to risk it.
His house is at the entrance to the camp.
He's too much for me.

RICCARDO (*undeterred*): The Doctor—and nobody can prove
that you knew me, Gerstein,
or that you already knew Jacobson.

GERSTEIN (*with extreme impatience*): Yes, that's *my* outlook.
(*He indicates* JACOBSON.) But what chance has he
if the Doctor finds him with me.
We'd only be endangering Jacobson.

Pause. Both look at JACOBSON. *He hesitates, then says softly—*
than stay on with the railroad squad until the time

JACOBSON: Rather one more risk—even if I lose—
they automatically count me off for gassing.

Gerstein, I swear to you, those bandits
will never learn from me that you knew me.

GERSTEIN: I'm not worrying about myself now,
but about you. Make up your mind:
Either back to your work—
for there on the platform you might possibly
come through after all—→
and in that case I'll tell the Commandant
that the priest refused to give his pledge
to keep his mouth shut after his release,
and therefore it's all off—
or else we go straight to the gate,
to the Commandant—a course that may
lead us right into the Doctor's arms.
You know what that would mean.
The odds are about fifty-fifty.

JACOBSON: But what would happen to you then?

GERSTEIN: I'll talk myself out of it. Perhaps. Probably.
Decide for yourself alone.

JACOBSON (*quickly, firmly*): Then I will try it.

From this point on to the end GERSTEIN *reacts swiftly, unsenti-
mentally and consistently, although he has no hope at all.*

GERSTEIN: Good. Let's try it.
The cassock's in the hut. Get into it!

RICCARDO (*with forced dryness*):
Is my breviary there? Let me have that.
Then I'll go . . . Carlotta!

RICCARDO *and* GERSTEIN *enter the hut.* JACOBSON *hangs behind,
suddenly frightened.*

CARLOTTA (*warmly*): Father, you're going free!

GERSTEIN (*insistently to* JACOBSON): Come in, hurry, Jacobson.

RICCARDO: I'm staying with the rest of you, Carlotta.
Your father is still living. I saw him
last night at roll call . . .

GERSTEIN (*to the still hesitant* JACOBSON, *irritably*):
Change your clothes, man, change your clothes!

CARLOTTA: How did he look? And my mother,
my sister, the children . . .

JACOBSON *now removes his jacket and puts the cassock on over a
dirty, torn undershirt. While* RICCARDO *takes the breviary and*

rosary from the pocket of his cassock, he tries to hide his face from
CARLOTTA—*he knows that her mother and sister have already
been cremated.*

GERSTEIN: I'll take your letter with me—is it ready?
RICCARDO: No, Carlotta, I don't see the women.
    Your father is holding out bravely.
CARLOTTA (*fumbles the scraps of paper from the pocket of her
    smock*): Thank you, I . . . could not write the letter.
    Take these, please—so that
    they aren't found on me.
GERSTEIN (*helplessly*): The Father is staying with you.

RICCARDO *offers* CARLOTTA *the rosary.*

CARLOTTA (*embarrassed, does not want the rosary, but also does
    not want to reject him*): No, Father, no—keep it for yourself.
    You're staying?
RICCARDO (*who does not understand her refusal, smilingly places
    the rosary in her hand*): Yes.
GERSTEIN (*to* RICCARDO, *in fear*):
    If we run into the Doctor, Riccardo,
    you'll see us both again—there—tomorrow.

Silently, RICCARDO *shakes hands with* GERSTEIN. JACOBSON, *already
wearing the cassock, grips* RICCARDO's *shoulder.*

JACOBSON: Thank you.
    (*Fanatically.*) Hold out. We'll come. We will avenge you.
RICCARDO (*trying to smile*): Then you'd better hurry . . .
    Goodbye Gerstein. Don't let my father know
    where I am. Tell him my life
    has been fulfilled.
    You know the truth.
    Carlotta!

*He leaves quickly; just outside the hut he makes a broken gesture
that betrays the depths of his emotion.* GERSTEIN *accompanies him
to the door, then turns around. A long silence.*

GERSTEIN (*urgently to* CARLOTTA):
    Don't let yourself fall sick. Keep fit for work.
    Above all keep fit for work.
    They cannot finish off all of you.
JACOBSON: I feel ashamed
    because I am going and you stay.

CARLOTTA: I'm glad for you anyhow.
JACOBSON: Stave off despair. If you start
   weeping here, you're lost.

CARLOTTA *nods mutely to him and goes out quickly to refill her pail, but chiefly to make their departure easier. With spasmodic self-control,* GERSTEIN *raps out his instructions.* JACOBSON *has just drawn the black trousers over his striped ones and now kicks off his wooden sandals and puts on* RICCARDO's *shoes.*

GERSTEIN: We're going to the Commandant now.
   Talk as little as possible.
   You've been here a week, is that clear, one week.
   You must sign a statement
   pledging your silence by the lives of two priests.
   Do so. All right, let's go.
   Talk as little as possible.
   Remember, you were working at the crematorium.
   Let's try it.
JACOBSON: He was here a week? I have
   (*pointing to his forearm*) an altogether different number . . .
GERSTEIN (*gloomily*): No one will ask your number. Ready!
   (*Already at the door, he starts violently.*)
   Over there—the Doctor! Hurry past now.
JACOBSON (*in a harsh whisper*): He's coming here. Done for.
GERSTEIN (*in the same manner*): Pull yourself together.
   (*In tone of command.*) Walk ahead of me, Father.

The DOCTOR *approaches, wearing a jaunty fatigue cap and accompanied by a helmeted SS man who holds a submachine gun at the ready. Flexing his swagger stick between his hands, the* DOCTOR *plants himself in front of* JACOBSON *and* GERSTEIN. *He is smartly dressed, from the big, soft gloves to the high, supple boots and the wide black cape. The sound of a circular saw, very close by, has accompanied his entrance.*

DOCTOR: What's the hurry, Gerstein? How are things?
GERSTEIN: Heil Hitler, Major—I'm here to pick up
   Inmate Fontana, the priest.

Abruptly, making a pointless attempt at distraction, in a forced, confidential tone:

   Incidentally, Doctor, you've got a girl here . . .
   (*He looks around in embarrassment.*) She comes from Rome.

Where is she? Oh, she's gone for more water.
Her fiancé was killed fighting for Germany.

DOCTOR: Then he won't have to cry over her.

GERSTEIN (*in the jargon*): Keep the girl on ice, Doctor.

DOCTOR (*laughing*): I don't mind, if she's attractive,
    I'll take her into my private lab.
    A Roman girl who has survived our recent
    Feast of Tabernacles, our grand harvest-home,
    is certainly a rarity in the camp.
    But the reason I left my soft bed, Gerstein,
    was to say goodbye to our priest.
    (*Yawns widely.*)
    In a hurry, isn't he? Touching, touching.
    Since when do Hebrews belong to the One True Church?

GERSTEIN (*harshly, with a good pretense of assurance*):
    Hebrews? What do you mean by that?
    Major Fritsche told me . . .

DOCTOR (*irritated by the mention of Fritsche*):
    Oh, don't give me any of that Dr. iuris neutrum Fritsche.
    What business is it of Fritsche's!

GERSTEIN: I have orders from Lieutenant Colonel Eichmann . . .

DOCTOR (*scornfully*): Really!

GERSTEIN: To take this Jesuit, a diplomat from the Holy See
    who was sent here by mistake . . .

DOCTOR: By mistake—they're all sent by mistake.
    What does that matter?

GERSTEIN (*undeterred*): . . . to the Nuncio in Berlin.
    Well, here he is.

DOCTOR: Who? The Nuncio? Is he the Nuncio?
    (*With an elaborate bow to* JACOBSON.)
    Your Excellency—is it true that God is sick?
    It's said he's having those depression fits again—
    as he did the time his Church was burning up
    the Jews and Protestants in Spain.

GERSTEIN: This is Father Riccardo Fontana.

JACOBSON (*trying to play along*):
    I also think God suffers great grief now.

DOCTOR (*playing with his stick, enjoying every word*):
    Or maybe he has syphilis, like so many female saints
    who were prostitutes on earth—and sodomites
    like St. Francis. . . .

You've stuck your hand right in the shit this time,
Gerstein, old fox—I've seen through you
ever since our drive to Tübingen.
But Christians as ingenious as you are
delight me.

GERSTEIN (*indignantly*): Major, I will not stand for that.
I demand an explanation.

DOCTOR: So, you demand! You demand
that I make a fool of myself.
You think I am another Adolf Eichmann?
I'll make you pay for thinking me a fool, Gerstein.

GERSTEIN: I don't understand you at all.

DOCTOR: You understand perfectly well; I know the priest.

GERSTEIN (*to* JACOBSON): Do you know the Major, Father?

DOCTOR (*thrusting* JACOBSON *aside with his stick*):
I know the *real* priest, the real one.
When he arrived here a week ago
he wanted to convert me, then and there.
A charming master of ceremonies for Christ
who'll amuse me as my private chaplain
(*points to the glow of the fire*)
as soon as the incense from the furnaces
tickles his nose enough to make him puke
and spew all over his faith.
(*He taps* JACOBSON *in the face with his stick.*)
Tell me what's so attractive about this fellow
that you're determined to have him?
Nice, warm, Christian, brotherly love?

GERSTEIN: It's a cheap joke, Major,
to go on mocking me all the time
because I go to church. That's my affair.

DOCTOR: Really touching: a member of the Confessing Church
comes here to swindle a priest free
and instead smuggles a Jew out of camp.

GERSTEIN (*seemingly bitterly amused*): Smuggle? Ridiculous!
Smuggling an inmate past Höss in broad daylight!
I'm taking him to the Commandant now.
Of what are you accusing me?
Did I have the inmate summoned?
How am I supposed to know
if he is not the man they're looking for?

DOCTOR (*blows his police whistle; laughs malignantly*):
>How? How are you supposed to know?
>You'll get your chance to explain how . . .

CARLOTTA *returns with the pail of water and resumes her work inside the hut.*

GERSTEIN (*feverishly interrupting him*):
>Was I the one who insisted
>on taking the priest to the camp gate?
>I wanted to wait outside. It was only because
>Major Fritsche was busy with visitors from Essen—
>Fritsche asked me, and Höss too,
>to wait for the priest here at the platform.
>—By the way, there's that girl again.

He points to JACOBSON. *The* DOCTOR *has blown his whistle once more.*

>If you have any doubts . . .

DOCTOR: Doubts! I'm arresting you, Gerstein.
>All three of you were standing here just now
>and cooking up your little plot.
>I've bided my time patiently to hear
>how idiotic you expect us to be.
>Rome hasn't asked for the priest at all
>or you would never have swapped him for that fellow.
>There, his belt! Arrest him!

These last words are addressed to the guard. GERSTEIN *draws his pistol; it is impossible to say whether he intends to shoot. The guard knocks it from his hand and kicks it to one side. The guard grins.* GERSTEIN *hesitantly hands over his belt. Immediately after his last words the* DOCTOR *turns to* RICCARDO, *whom another guard has brought in.* RICCARDO *has come to a halt some steps away.* CARLOTTA, *inside the hut, senses the terrible events outside. She opens the door and begins scrubbing the three steps.* RICCARDO, *endeavoring to grasp the situation, scarcely pays attention to the* DOCTOR'*s chatter.*

>Well, well, hello, my dear Father. Have you now
>reconciled reality with the ideal
>there at the furnaces? This baptism of fire
>enters you in the ranks of the great testes veritatis.

I hope, as my private chaplain, you will show
appreciation for my giving you the chance
to study the Golgotha of Absolute Spirit
at closer quarters. A little stunned, eh?
Well, anyone who, like you,
sees history as a therapeutic process ...
(*He laughs challengingly.*)

RICCARDO (*calmly and contemptuously*):
You'll never win; that makes you so talkative.
Your kind can only triumph temporarily.
What have I been brought here for?

JACOBSON (*has come to the decision to give up quickly, so that*
GERSTEIN *at least may be exonerated. He steps forward*):
Wish to report that I tricked the lieutenant.
I pretended to be the priest.
Since he didn't answer, I reported to the guardroom.
He wasn't here ... didn't come, so ...

DOCTOR (*flies into a rage after this last sentence, which too*
obviously attempts to give information to RICCARDO):
One more word and you'll go into the furnace *alive.*
About face—about face, I say!
(JACOBSON *obeys.*)
Kneel—on your knees.
And now your face in the filth.

JACOBSON *lies on the ground, face down. The* DOCTOR *says*
triumphantly to GERSTEIN, *pointing to* RICCARDO:
I suppose he did not want to come?
Or didn't you want to take him?
(*Ironically.*) You know he is the man the Pope
blubbers over, night after night, in the Sistine Chapel.

GERSTEIN (*indicating* RICCARDO):
This is the first time I have ever seen him.
How should I know which is the real priest.
It isn't my affair to check on that.

DOCTOR (*looking at* CARLOTTA):
Oh well, let's see what the bit of skirt here has to say.
Come over here, you! Come here!
Oho, the Spiritual Exercises of
Ignatius Loyola. Crematorium reading!
Always used to be read aloud at the stake.

Reaching out quickly, he has snatched the breviary from RIC-CARDO's *pocket. With his other hand, he takes hold of* CARLOTTA, *who has approached falteringly.*

RICCARDO (*addresses her rapidly, then the* DOCTOR):
    Carlotta—*you!* We were deported together . . .
    Do you still remember me?
CARLOTTA (*trying to play along*):
    Father, it's good to see you're still living.
DOCTOR (*paying no attention, speaks to the girl while, stick tucked under his arm, he eagerly leafs through the* Exercises):
    You came from Rome, with your family? Are you Catholic?
CARLOTTA: Yes.
DOCTOR: Where's that passage about the girls . . . ?

Reads aloud, savoring the words; the background and the man himself give vividness to Loyola's text.

    The devil on the throne of fire and smoke
    lures as the tempter—yes, yes, we know.
    Aha, here it is: "I see with the eyes
    of imagination the tremendous glow of flame
    and the souls locked in the *burning* bodies.
    I smell with the sense of smell smoke, sulphur,
    excrement and rotting things."
    And that about the girls, Father, where is it?
    The sin of fleshly lust, my love of the flesh
    (*laughs*) of the world—you ought to be exposed
    to that, too, Father.
    Shall I put the two of you together?
    (*Abruptly to* CARLOTTA *as he closes the breviary.*)
    You've been cleaning here since seven o'clock?
    Were you on time today?
CARLOTTA (*frightened*): Yes, right on time.
DOCTOR: Your fiancé was killed?
CARLOTTA: Yes, at Tobruk.
DOCTOR: I see—what is—what was his name?
CARLOTTA: Marcello.
DOCTOR (*very rapidly*): So, you were here on time!
    But still you came later than the priest, eh?
CARLOTTA (*bewildered, does not dare to reply, stammers*):
    I—don't know—I was . . .

RICCARDO (*calmly, pointing to* JACOBSON, *attempting to help her*):
    He's asking whether the priest was here
    when you came, Carlotta.
DOCTOR (*infuriated*): Father, don't stoop so low!
    (*Casually to* CARLOTTA, *pointing to* RICCARDO.)
    Well then, when did your soulmate get here?
CARLOTTA: The Father—I don't know—I couldn't . . .

Although nothing really depends on her answer any more, the
DOCTOR, *out of pleasure in tormenting her, forces her to her knees
with an iron grip and then bends her over so that she is almost
on her back. He applies this force so unexpectedly that she cries
out.*

DOCTOR: Well—do you know or don't you?
CARLOTTA: I didn't look up, I was just—
    scrubbing the floor—I . . .
DOCTOR (*pulls her to her feet again, with smiling sadism*):
    Shall I send you where your family went?
    Look at the fires over there.
    And there—the fence—do you want me to
    chase you over there or over there?

At this casual mention of the end of her family CARLOTTA *collapses
psychically—this news is the last straw. Madness already in her
eyes, she whispers, an insane stammering.*

CARLOTTA: Dead—all dead—dead—all dead—dead . . .

While she stammers, the DOCTOR *says offhandedly—*

DOCTOR: Was he here first—or was it this one?
CARLOTTA (*looks at him in silence, her face wildly contorted.
    At last she stammers*): I don't know, I don't know, I don't
    know.

The DOCTOR *has let go of her. She retreats several steps toward
the guardroom while staring hypnotized at "the most cunning of
brutes" (Canaris's phrase for Heydrich)—his bestiality has now
come fully to the fore. Now she screams, screams like a woman in
labor, under anesthesia, all inhibitions gone. The actress may, if
she wishes, blurt out words at this point—perhaps the simplest,
the most cliché phrases might be used.*

    No—no—let me alone—no—don't . . .

At the first piercing outcry, which even takes the DOCTOR *aback, she flees in a single bound up the steps and into the hut. Her movement is so wholly natural, so utterly irrepressible, so lacking in the "alienation" of theater, that it completely smashes all our efforts heretofore to create theatrical stylization, to remove from actuality the atrocities of the Final Solution, which are still so close to us.*

CARLOTTA'S *screams pass over into spastic laughter. She tears off her kerchief, lashes aimlessly about with it, and throws it away. Her eyes dart frantically over the men. Rosary in her hands, she rushes into the guardroom, her harsh laughter like the cries of an animal as she looks into* HELGA'S *mirror. She crouches in a corner with the mirror, gasping in brief bursts of laughter and sobbing, and tries to put the rosary around her neck like a necklace. It slips from her hands. The* DOCTOR *has recovered. Mechanically, he opens his holster, murmuring—*

DOCTOR: Gone off her rocker.

He strides quickly and firmly into the hut to do what is always done with deportees whose nerves give out before gassing. Putting down the breviary, he picks up the rosary and holds it out to CARLOTTA. *An insane smile passes over her face, for he radiates that "most persuasive kindness" we have mentioned. Her madly flickering eyes look into his. She jumps up and tries to grasp his hand and the rosary. She utters a cry of release because she has found "him" again and wants to embrace him.*

CARLOTTA: Marcello! Marcello! (*Laughs madly.*) I was afraid you would never come back from Africa.
It's so long, Marcello—you've been gone so long.
DOCTOR (*evading her embrace, with compelling tenderness*):
Come along—come now—not here.

She follows without hesitation. He does not touch her, merely extends his arm to her—the gesture lightly, gracefully suggesting that she come with him. He moves backward toward the door, holding her gaze with his eyes. All this happens very quickly.

CARLOTTA (*passing in front of him, already outside on the last step, anxiously*): Marcello—Marcello!

Standing behind her in the doorway, he draws his pistol with an unexpectedly rapid movement and kills her with a bullet in the back of the neck. Without so much as a glance at the corpse, he replaces the pistol in the holster. At this moment, while the two guards are absorbed in what is happening, RICCARDO *stoops for* GERSTEIN's *pistol, picks it up, and aims at the* DOCTOR, *crying out—*

RICCARDO: Destroy him!

He is shot down by the submachine gun of the SS man standing behind him before he can release the safety catch or press the trigger. RICCARDO *drops to his knees, then slowly falls over backward. The guard picks up* GERSTEIN's *pistol. Grinning with the shock, he holds it out to the* DOCTOR. GERSTEIN *has covered his eyes with his hand for a moment.*

DOCTOR: Aimed at me? I guess he really meant it.
　　　Thank you, sergeant.
　　　(*Bending over* RICCARDO.)
　　　Hm, Father, shooting comes almost as hard as praying—
　　　in Auschwitz.
　　　Too bad, I was looking forward to
　　　debating with you for a few weeks more . . .
　　　Any nearer to God now?
RICCARDO (*straightens up, tries to say something, sinks back, murmurs almost inaudibly*): In hora mortis meae voca me.
DOCTOR (*mockingly, as he straightens up*):
　　　Amen. Did you really hear him calling—
　　　in the crematorium?
　　　(*Kicks* JACOBSON, *orders*:)
　　　Get up—on your way, to the campfire
　　　(*points to* RICCARDO:)
　　　and take that with you—go on, take it along.

JACOBSON *gets up.* GERSTEIN *has stooped over* RICCARDO *and opened the dying man's jacket, thus plainly showing whose side he is on. Without a word the* DOCTOR *pushes between* GERSTEIN *and* RICCARDO. JACOBSON, *on his knees, his hands under* RICCARDO's *arms, tries in vain to lift* RICCARDO.

GERSTEIN: He isn't dead. You are a physician—help him.
　　　(*Shouts*:) He's still alive!
DOCTOR (*without looking at* GERSTEIN, *coolly*):
　　　The fire is a good physician. It will burn out
　　　the Jew *and* the Christian in him.
　　　(*Beckons to the* GUARD *who saved him.*)
　　　Take this man to the Commandant.
　　　Watch out for him—I'll be along shortly.

GUARD: Yes, sir.

GERSTEIN, *after a last look at his friends, strides off swiftly to the left behind the hut, followed by the SS man. The other guard, with kicks and blows of his submachine gun, has tried to make* JACOBSON *stand up. But* JACOBSON, *exhausted and numbed with horror, remains in a half kneeling position,* RICCARDO'*s head in his lap. The sound of the circular saw is heard, very close.*

DOCTOR (*with biting impatience*): You'll have to help the cripple!
  (*Points to* CARLOTTA.) And get that cleared away too.
GUARD: Yes, sir.

Reluctantly, he takes RICCARDO'*s shoulders,* JACOBSON *takes* RICCARDO'*s feet. They go off right. The* DOCTOR *walks slowly to the left, where* GERSTEIN *was led away. After passing behind the windows of the guardroom, he remembers the* Spiritual Exercises, *returns, passes by* CARLOTTA'*s body, enters the hut, leafs through the book, smiles, tucks it under his arm, and leaves the stage like a professor after a lecture.*

The unemotional voice of an announcer on tape reads:

"On October 28, 1943 Herr von Weizsäcker, Hitler's Ambassador to the Holy See, writes to the Foreign Office in Berlin":

Here, as the glow of the flames sinks lower and lower, a different voice continues, the deliberate, refined voice of a well-bred elder statesman:

"Although the Pope is said to have been importuned from various quarters, he has not allowed himself to be carried away into making any demonstrative statements against the deportation of the Jews. Although he must expect our enemies to resent this attitude on his part, he has nevertheless done all he could, in this delicate question as other matters, not to prejudice relationships with the German government. Since further action on the Jewish problem is probably not to be expected here in Rome, it may be assumed that this question, so troublesome to German-Vatican relations, has been disposed of.
"On October 25 the *Osservatore Romano,* moreover, published a semi-official communiqué on the Pope's charitable

activities in which the statement was made, in the style typical of this Vatican newspaper—that is to say, involved and vague—that the Pope extends his paternal solicitude to all men without distinction of nationality and race. There is no need to raise objections to its publication, since hardly anyone will understand the text as referring specially to the Jewish question."

The unemotional announcer speaks again. The fire is out, the stage dark; we see only the dead girl close to the footlights.

"And so the gas chambers continued to work for a full year more. In the summer of 1944 the so-called daily quota of exterminations reached its maximum. On November 26, 1944 Himmler ordered the crematoria to be blown up. Two months later the last prisoners in Auschwitz were freed by Russian soldiers."

CURTAIN

Sidelights on History

It is rather unusual to burden a drama with an historical appendix, and I would willingly have omitted doing so. As a stage play the work requires no commentary. But the action does not follow the historical course of events in a step-by-step manner, like a journalist's account. Condensation has been necessary in the interests of drama. Consequently, the historical persons mentioned in the play, and those of their relations who are still living, are entitled to know what sources—often obscure ones—have led the author to view a given person or episode in this or that light. I must add that I have quoted here only a fraction of the material I have collected. Perhaps one day, if there seems to be general interest in the matter, I shall present it all in a separate historical study.

Naturally I examined those memoirs, biographies, diaries, letters, records of conversations and minutes of court proceedings which bear on the subject and which have already been made available. No bibliography of these well-known sources is needed. If I submit the following notes on controversial events and testimony, it is to demonstrate that as far as possible I adhered to the facts. I allowed my imagination free play only to the extent that I had to transform the existing raw material of history into drama. Reality was respected throughout, but much of its slag had to be removed.

Anyone who retraces the roads of historical events, littered as these are with ruins and corpses; anyone who reviews the contradictory, complacent or wildly distracted statements of the victors and victims; anyone who makes even the most modest effort to pick his way through the rubble and incidental circumstances of so-called historical events in order to reach the truth, the symbolic meaning—will find that the dramatist "cannot use a single element of reality as he finds it; his work must be idealized in *all* its parts if he is to comprehend reality as a whole."

Anyone in this day and age who ignores this precept of Schiller, anyone who does not "openly and honestly declare war on naturalism in art," must capitulate in the face of every newsreel—if only because the latter can present "the raw stuff of the world" far more drastically and completely than the stage. For the stage—Bertolt Brecht with his theory of alienation was not the first to discover this—remains true only if, as Schiller says in *Wallenstein,* "it itself frankly destroys the illusion it creates."

In regard to the following documentary material I may explain that I have done my best to arrange the often overlapping items in an order corresponding with the action of the play. Stricter organization proved unfeasible since the same facts often crop up in different scenes—but sometimes as contradictions or in diverse interpretations, as happens in the living flow of dialogue. What is offered here is not scholarly work and is not meant to be. But since neither the Vatican nor the Kremlin as yet permit free access to their archives, historians will have to wait before they can present a comprehensive account of these events. To intuitively combine the already available facts into a truthful whole becomes the noble and rarely realized function of art. Precisely because he is faced with such a plethora of raw material, as well as with such difficulties in collating it, the writer must hold fast to his freedom, which alone empowers him to give form to the matter.

Kolbe and Gerstein

After 1945 the German press carried many accounts of Cathedral Provost Lichtenberg[1] and his public espousal of identity with the persecuted Jews; but almost nothing was said about the martyrdom of the Polish priest, Father Maximilian Kolbe. Born in 1894 in the vicinity of Lodz, this Franciscan monk had been engaged in missionary work in Japan before the war. He died in August 1941

---

[1] After the play opened I learned that Provost Lichtenberg was not alone in publicly identifying himself with the Jews. The present Protestant Provost in Berlin, Dr. Heinrich Grüber, twice applied to the Nazis for permission to accompany deported Jews into the ghetto. With the help of men in the *Abwehr* (the military intelligence bureau under Admiral Canaris, who was a member of the Resistance) he tried to get into the camp at Guers. But this attempt failed and led to Grüber's own arrest.

in the starvation bunker at Auschwitz under the following circumstances. One of his fellow prisoners had escaped from the camp, although the consequence of such prison breaks was that ten other inmates were condemned to death by starvation. Ten men were arbitrarily counted off from the escapee's "block," among them a prisoner named F. Gajowniczek, who had a wife and children. He began to weep—and Kolbe stepped forward and asked permission to go to his death in this man's place. He offered the argument that he was no longer fit for work. Although this was obviously a pretext, even the SS must have been impressed. Prisoner No. 16670 was allowed to enter the starvation bunker in place of Prisoner No. 5659 (who survived the war). The prisoners were locked up naked in a completely empty, windowless concrete cell (some of them beaten so badly that their bones were broken). The building may be seen today; it has been allowed to stand as a memorial. The prisoners were even refused water. One report states: "Gandhi drank water during his hunger strikes. Survivors of lost caravans in the desert can describe what it is like to die of thirst . . . The torments of hunger degrade the victim into a beast, for human endurance has its limits—beyond those limits are only despair or sanctity."[2]

Father Maximilian was nevertheless able to offer consolation to his comrades in death. Borgowiec, the prisoner whose job it was to clean the death cells, testified that the SS men could not endure Kolbe's gaze. Once, when those who had already died were being carried out, the guards roared at Kolbe: "Look at the ground, not at us." He died too slowly to satisfy them; perhaps, too, his bearing forced them to concede him the final mercy—at any rate, they at last put him to death with an injection. One report says that he was the last of the group left alive; another, that two of his fellows briefly survived him.

In Rome, on May 24, 1948, information proceedings for the beatification of Father Maximilian were initiated.

From letters about Kurt Gerstein in the possession of his widow:

Churchwarden O. Wehr, Chief Representative of the Evangelical Church of Rhine Province for the Saar, writing on January 24, 1949, from Saarbrücken:

"The undersigned knew Kurt Gerstein for several decades dur-

---

[2] M. Winowska, *Pater Maximilian Kolbe* (Fribourg, 1952).

ing the period of Gerstein's involvement in Bible Circles for young people of secondary-school age. I can vouch for his decisive influence, as a Protestant youth leader, upon young men in the crucial years of their development. Throughout the period of the Church's struggle against the totalitarian aims of the National Socialist government, Kurt Gerstein adhered to a clear, unequivocal line. I happen to know that some of his articles were written in order to help young men maintain their inner integrity during the Nazi period. What is more, while employed as assessor at the Mining Bureau in Saarbrücken he made use of every opportunity to disseminate the confidential circular letters of the Confessing Church[3] throughout Germany. Some of this material, carelessly left in his office, proved his downfall. All efforts at that time (1936) by highly placed persons, including Minister [Hjalmar] Schacht, to prevent the arrest of this highly qualified assessor, were in vain. After his discharge from concentration camp he surprised me one day by announcing his plan to enter the SS. From my discussion with him at that time I can state the following:

"The immediate cause for this decision was the death of a relation of his (the daughter of Pastor Ebeling of the Evangelical Parish of Alt-Saarbrücken) in the Hadamar Mental Hospital. Fräulein Bertha Ebeling was put to death by gas at Hadamar. After I had officiated at the interment of the ashes, he informed me of his decision. He wanted to investigate, he said, what truth there was to the rumors circulating about such criminal actions, and crimes of other sorts. I expressed strong doubts about this plan of entering the camp of the demonic powers; he replied with passionate determination. Given the great drive that marked Kurt Gerstein's whole personality, and given his extraordinary abilities and talents, I felt he would succeed in reaching the place where he wanted to be: inside the *Reichsführung SS*. Events bore out this prediction. Thereafter he was perpetually on the move, full of ideas and plans for helping and hindering, until he formulated the bold plans of the autumn of 1944. In the course of some of his official journeys he called on me at various times and gave me reports of everything he had witnessed, including what he had

---

[3] A German Lutheran and Evangelical movement which came into being with the Confessing Synod in May 1934 when the Old Prussian Union (APU), now known as the Evangelical Church of the Union (EKU), met to draw up a program of resistance to Hitler's attempt to fill leading Church positions with trusted Nazis. See: Franklin Hamlin Littel, *The German Phoenix* (Garden City: Doubleday, 1960).—*Ed.*

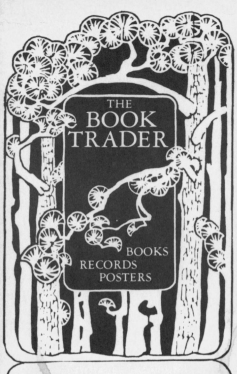

THE
BOOK
TRADER

BOOKS
RECORDS
POSTERS

501 South Street
Philadelphia 19147

215·925·0219

Open Every Day
10 AM to Midnight

seen of the gas camps in the East. He told me of the satanic, nihi-
listically cold cynicism of the big and small murderers and murderers' henchmen, and of his impressions of the despairing victims,
which haunted him from then on . . .

"A personality like Kurt Gerstein's is necessarily a twilight
figure. Or rather, viewed by the standards of the average man, he
must seem absolutely incredible. The uncanny mastery with which
he camouflaged his inward Christian being by an outward de-
meanor of the perfect SS man, with the sole aim of giving succor
to others, made a mockery of all ordinary standards. I could ad-
duce many examples of his skill in masking his real intentions. All
attempts to do justice to this man's innermost nature and aims
from the moralistic and politico-psychological angle are bound
to remain inadequate.

"He came to me at times for spiritual guidance, and from the
talks we had I never had any doubts whatever of the constancy
of purpose in the depths of his being."

Pastor Martin Niemöller, President of the Evangelical Church in
Hesse and Nassau, wrote to State Prosecutor Erbs in Frankfurt on
April 26, 1948:

"Before my arrest in July 1937 I had known Gerstein for many
years from his association with Bible Circles and the Confessing
Church. He was something of a 'peculiar saint,' but altogether pure
and unequivocal. His word could be trusted, and he always fought
for his convictions down to their ultimate consequences. I consider
him absolutely trustworthy and therefore believe it absolutely out
of the question that he was ever even tempted to support Nazism,
let alone its crimes. In my firm conviction he is a victim of his
consistent oppositional attitude, which he pursued to the logical
end. He was prepared to give up honor, family, and life for this
cause, and did give them up. I do not question a word of his own
account of himself, and am convinced that any such questioning
would do him an injustice."

Cathedral Capitulary Buchholz, who for years ministered to Catholics condemned to death before their executions in Plötzensee, in
a letter dated July 10, 1946:

"I made the acquaintance of Herr Gerstein through a former
political prisoner in Tegel, an industrialist whose name has unfortunately slipped my mind . . . Herr Gerstein personally assisted in

his release—if I am not mistaken, by disposing of the file. This man from Tegel invited me, in September 1944, to an evening at Herr Gerstein's apartment, where I met a number of other men, all of whom had either been subjected to disciplinary action on political grounds, or had passed through the Gestapo jails as political prisoners. My acquaintance assured me that all the men present were absolutely trustworthy and that all, especially Herr Gerstein, wished to hear from me details about the mass executions in Plötzensee. Most of them had heard only rumors about these. I thereupon told them in detail, with complete candor and without any holding back—especially about that terrible night in September 1943 when 186 political prisoners were executed by hanging . . . Gerstein then . . . listed the names and locations of the death camps and spoke of the 'daily quota achieved' in the various crematoria and gas chambers . . . All of us had some inkling of these matters, but these precise data were so monstrous that we were scarcely able to believe them . . . I subsequently had ample opportunity to observe how sincere Herr Gerstein was, for he paid me several visits, again and again finding release and relief in being able to talk these matters over unreservedly with a clergyman. I may add as proof of Herr Gerstein's true principles that he not only promised to do all he could for my political prisoners, but also brought to me suitcases full of food, cigarettes, etc., which I was able to pass on secretly."

In 1942 Bishop Otto Dibelius heard a report from Gerstein immediately after Gerstein's return from the death camps, and passed this information on to the Bishop of Upsala.

The proposal mentioned by Gerstein in the play (Act Three, Scene Two)—assuring the success of a *coup d'état* by issuing the false report that the SS had assassinated Hitler—is patterned after a plan by Count Stauffenberg, who attempted the assassination of Hitler on July 20, 1944. Field Marshal von Witzleben, however, forbade Stauffenberg to publish any such report, even as a temporary ruse.

Gerstein's courage and adroitness, which enabled him to carry on his well-nigh suicidal double game inside the SS for years, would suggest that in his attempt to tell the Nuncio about Treblinka he would have forced his way into the presence of Orsenigo personally. Given the urgency of his concern, his cunning and his determination, it appears unlikely that he would have allowed a subordinate priest to show him the door. But even Gerstein's widow does not know definitely whether her husband spoke to Orsenigo in person. Whatever the case, I have endeavored throughout this work to *underplay* the already almost incredible events of Hitler's war and the number of its victims. There is little prospect that in time to come, when all eyewitnesses are dead, the historical truth will be believed in its full ghastliness. In line with this policy of understating, we have softened the shameful ejection from the Papal Legation. I have endeavored to palliate and to adjust events to fit the human capacity for imagination. Thus I propound that the master of the house listened at least once to a human being plainly in distress. In the age of universal conscription soldiers are particularly likely to fall into conflicts similar to Gerstein's. Pius XII opened the door to them to the extent of at least granting mass audiences to thousands of German and Allied soldiers. We therefore shrink from assuming that of all persons the Ambassador of the Deputy of Christ in Hitler's capital would no longer receive a refugee in 1942, as he had done in 1939, but would have turned him away from his door. For many hapless individuals such a reception would have meant that they would no longer be able to recount the event—as by chance Gerstein was able to do. Moreover, the question is unimportant as far as the play is concerned. Here, in the play, Orsenigo stands for *the* representation of the Curia in Hitler's capital. Since as the Nuncio he had assumed the greatest responsibility, in this tragedy he must stand for all those dignitaries of the Church who held such opinions as did Count Preysing, the Bishop of Berlin and subsequently Cardinal, who declared that the "life and actions" of the interpreter of Hitler's racial laws were determined "by the principles of the Catholic Faith."[4] On the other hand Riccardo stands for those priests, mostly nameless, who instantly set love for neighbor above all utilitarian considerations—ultimately at the price of their lives.

Moreover, the unfolding of the drama would remain the same if I showed Gerstein visiting, for example, the rooms of Bishop Preysing's syndic. We know for certain that Gerstein paid such a

---

[4] Wilhelm Stuckart and Hans Globke, *Kommentare zur deutschen Rassengesetzgebung* (Munich, 1936).

visit to the bishop, after his return from Treblinka. He made his report "with the express request that the information be transmitted to the Papal See."

Historically speaking, Gerstein could only have provided the Vatican with detailed data on the procedures of the murderers and the number of the victims. The Vatican already knew that death factories existed. The Holy See had numerous informants; officially the Polish Government in Exile had been first and most active in providing the Vatican with such intelligence by a great variety of routes.

I shall never believe that Gerstein committed suicide. Anyone who has gone deeply into the story of this man, and has heard the strange reports that were sent to his widow from Paris, must conclude that Gerstein was one more of the still uncounted Germans and Frenchmen who were arbitrarily killed in France after the liberation in 1944. Not many of those resistance fighters who after the entry of the Americans took savage action against defenseless fellow countrymen and German prisoners truly deserved the honorable name of resistance fighters; that is a grim chapter that still awaits its chronicler. On April 11, 1952, the French Minister of Justice made it known that since the liberation of France 10,519 Frenchmen had been executed, only 846 of these after a proper legal trial.[5]

It is also possible, since none of his fellow prisoners can remember Gerstein, that he was hanged by hardcore SS men when they realized how committed he was to the "obligation of giving an accounting" to the Allies, a subject he had touched on in a letter to his father. This letter, first made public by Gert H. Theunissen in a documentary radio program on Gerstein, was written in Helsinki on March 5, 1944: "At some juncture you will have to stand up with the rest for your times, for what has happened in them. You and I would no longer understand each other and would no longer have anything meaningful to say to one another if I could not say this to you: Do not underestimate this responsibility and this obligation of an accounting. It may come sooner than people think. I am aware of this obligation, granted; I am gnawed by it."

In the autumn of that same year he wrote to his father: "It seems my destiny to think through to their ultimate consequences

---

[5] Gerald Reitlinger, *The Final Solution* (New York: The Beechhurst Press, 1953).

all these things between black and white, between good and evil—
to think them through and, please understand me rightly, to suffer
them through."

On the Concordat

Dr. Rudolf Pechel told me that the Nuncio was regarded in German oppositionist circles as an outright Fascist and adherent of
Mussolini. Nevertheless he listened benevolently to Pechel, who
came to him as an unofficial, confidential emissary to transmit a
request from some high-ranking military men. These officers
wanted the Nuncio to use his influence to see that no cleric particularly sympathetic to the Hitler regime should be appointed
chief Catholic chaplain to the German army.

The Nuncio had once acted forcefully of his own accord upon
hearing of crimes committed by the Gestapo in Poland. In November 1939 members of the army and "Protestant professors came
to the Papal Legation, tears in their eyes, to report atrocities."
Whereupon the Nuncio sent a very courageous protest to the Foreign Office and resolutely demanded an investigation. Unfortunately he deprived his intervention of its official character and
stressed that he was not acting as a Nuncio nor as the dean of the
Diplomatic Corps, but solely in his private capacity. Even then
Weizsäcker, as he was to do four years later in Rome, had advised
against "taking an interest in such cases in order not to damage
the cause one wishes to defend." The German government refused
to concede to the Nuncio in Berlin any authority in the territories
that Germany had incorporated during the war—hoping thereby
to blackmail the Vatican into public recognition of the new borders. Rome never recognized them. Consequently, as late as 1943
Weizsäcker politely returned to the Nuncio's pocket the subsequently famous letter of Cardinal State Secretary Maglione to
von Ribbentrop—a grave protest listing in detail all the crimes
against the Polish Church and demanding that they cease. At that
time over 1,000 Polish priests were prisoners in Dachau, and the
Vatican knew that many more of them had already been put to
death. How far the Nazis went in their altogether pointless harass-
ment of the Polish people also can be seen from one decree that
men under twenty-eight and women under twenty-five years of age
were not permitted to marry.

After 1945 Nuncio Orsenigo was *persona non grata* in the Vatican. Whatever the reason may have been, it is not to Orsenigo's discredit.

Orsenigo presumably could not have persuaded Pius XII to abrogate the Concordat with Hitler because it was Pacelli himself, in his role of Secretary of State, not Pope Pius XI, who was anxious for the quick conclusion of a Concordat with Hitler—as was Mussolini also, incidentally. Chancellor Brüning, who should have known better than most others, said in 1935 to Count Harry Kessler in Paris:

"Behind the agreement with Hitler stood not the Pope, but the Vatican bureaucracy and its leader, Pacelli. They visualized an authoritarian state and an authoritarian Church directed by the Vatican bureaucracy, the two to conclude an eternal league with one another. For that reason Catholic parliamentary parties, like the Center in Germany, were inconvenient to Pacelli and his men, and were dropped without regret in various countries. The Pope did not share these ideas."[6]

Nine years later Jesuit Father Delp was strangled in Plötzensee —while the head of his Church did not lift a finger to ask his Concordat partner Hitler to spare either Delp or other Germans of the priesthood. Shortly before his death Delp wrote (as quoted by Professor Friedrich Heer): "An honest . . . cultural history will have to include some bitter chapters about the churches' contributions to the creation of mass man, of collectivism, of dictatorial forms of government."[7]

Post festum, however, Pacelli, with an eye to future historians, imputed nobler motives to the conclusion of the Concordat. "Do you think I don't know that people have said and written," he said to the journalist Morandi in 1946, "that I never should have concluded the Concordat with the Third Reich? If Hitler so severely persecuted the Catholic Church in spite of the Concordat, consider what he would have presumed to do without the Concordat? Do you think that his henchmen would not have smashed right into the Vatican?"

In 1934, when relations between the Church and the Nazi party were so cordial that Hitler's SA (Storm Troopers) served as musicians and masters of ceremony for the display of the Seamless

---

[6] Harry Kessler, *Tagebücher 1918–1937* (Frankfurt am Main, 1961).

[7] Friedrich Heer, *Die Deutschen, der Nationalsozialismus und die Gegenwart* (Bielefeld, 1960).

Garment in Trier, it could scarcely be foreseen that Hitler would persecute the Church—or that nine years later he would be occupying Rome. (Though when it did happen Pacelli could be confident that the Vatican would not be occupied.) Pius XI, who in the very year the Concordat was concluded had already been informed of the terror against the Jews in Germany by the convert Dr. Edith Stein, although he never answered her letter, which was handed to him personally—Pius XI had at any rate said that the Concordat would be a platform from which protests could be made. In point of fact, little use was made of it, aside from the predominantly lame protests about purely ecclesiastical affairs which the Nuncio conveyed to Herr von Weizsäcker.

Moreover, consider how the eleventh Pius greeted Herr von Papen, whom Hitler had sent to Rome for preliminary discussions of the Concordat. At the very first audience the Pope told von Papen how "pleased" he was "that the German Government now had at its head a man uncompromisingly opposed to Communism and Russian nihilism in all its forms. Indeed, the atmosphere was so cordial that I was able to settle the details of a draft agreement at a speed quite unusual in Vatican affairs . . ."[8] Mussolini, who at that time had no very good opinion of Hitler and in particular mocked at his race theories, advised Herr von Papen to proceed with all possible speed. "The signing of this agreement with the Vatican will establish the credit of your Government abroad for the first time."[9]

After the war the situation was, as Friedrich Heer wrote in 1960, so delicate that "only a gigantic camouflage maneuver could save the reputation of official Christianity in Germany, or rather attempt to recover it." There arose "in the shadow of the ruins that mighty edifice, the living lie of German Christendom."[10] It was then, after 1945, that the Berlin representative of the Holy See was, as might be expected, driven into the desert as a scapegoat. Contrary to all custom, Pius XII even refused Orsenigo the usual obituary in the *Osservatore Romano* when the bishop, far from Rome, died in the early fifties. Even Ernst von Weizsäcker made an attempt to intervene in Rome in favor of the Nuncio, but without success.

Considerable light is thrown on the attitude of the bishops in

[8] Franz von Papen, *Memoirs* (New York: Dutton, 1953), p. 279.
[9] *Ibid.*, p. 280.
[10] Heer, *op. cit.*

1933 by an article in *Hochland,* February 1961. Herr von Papen writes, in regard to the opening ceremonies of the Reichstag after the elections on March 5, 1933, in the Garrison Church: "If today we read in Hitler's *Table Talk* that he had seized the state despite the curse of the two Confessions, and therefore, as a matter of principle, could not enter the Potsdam church, then that is . . . an historical falsehood. At that time he was certainly conscious of opposition from the churches, but there was no talk of any curse or enmity. He hoped to find a middle way."

On July 14, 1933, Hitler told a session of the Reich Cabinet: "This Concordat, whose contents do not interest me at all, nevertheless creates an area of confidence which will be very useful in our uncompromising struggle against international Judaism."

If Pacelli had been the great diplomat he is believed to be today (though Brüning's opinion of him is probably more accurate), he would scarcely have fallen into Hitler's trap so quickly. After all, he had had ten years in which to observe conditions within Germany. In June 1945 he asserted that the Concordat had prevented worse things. The wild rejoicing of the Catholic bishops in 1933–34, despite the fact that they could watch from close at hand Hitler's murderous treatment of his opponents within Germany, proves that this significance was imputed to the Concordat only in 1945, not at the time of its framing. For what did it prevent, since the Vatican never threatened with its abrogation in order to protect the Church in Poland or German Catholics from the Gestapo? Giovannetti tells how even Japan stubbornly fought to conclude a Concordat with Rome in 1942, for the same propagandistic reasons that caused the Allies, including Roosevelt personally, to try to prevent its conclusion.[11] Hitler even stated explicitly that *after* victory the Concordat would be dispensed with. Who can then claim that the Nazis would not have drawn back if during the war Pius had threatened them with the interdict? Would they have set against themselves thirty-five million Germans and the great majority of their allies who were members of a church which would have become "hostile to the state"?

The Vatican and the "Final Solution"

Whatever the reasons that led the Pope never to mention, *expressis verbis,* in his many speeches even the deportation of the Jews, it

---

[11] Alberto Giovannetti, *Il Vaticano e la guerra, 1939–1940* (Vatican City, 1960).

remains incomprehensible that His Holiness did not bestir himself to protest against Hitler when it was clear that Germany had lost the war, while at the same time Auschwitz was just beginning to reach its highest daily quota of killings. In June 1944, when Rome, and thus the Vatican, were already under the protection of American troops, two prisoners who in April had escaped from Auschwitz-Birkenau—Rudolf Vrba and Alfred Wetzler—spent five hours talking with the Papal Nuncio in Slovakia. They gave him a detailed account and drawings of the camp, the gas chambers, and the access railroads. This report was published as early as August in Geneva, and as a result was later secretly read in Germany—by an editor named Ursula von Kardorff, for one. The monstrous horrors contained in the report were soon confirmed and supplemented by a different source: on July 24, 1944, Allied reporters shocked the world with new revelations about the camps. The British journals *London Illustrated News* and *Sphere* even published special issues on Maidanek near Lublin. The photographs of human bones, of gas chambers, of the camp crematorium with its five ovens, of filing cases and of the clothes of gassed women and children, threw Hitler into "a fit of fury against the slovenly, cowardly dogs of the *Sicherheitsdienst* who did not destroy all trace of the two camps in time." So Fritz Hesse learned from Hitler's intimate, Hewel.[12] Not even these photographs could spur the Vatican to make a protest, although it had to assume that of the 380,000 Hungarian Jews who had been deported to Auschwitz from May 15 to June 30, many could not yet have been gassed, though their turn would soon come. And in fact, as Reitlinger reports, it was not until July 1944 that "the full capacity of all four crematoria" in Auschwitz, and the much more "practical" open burning pits, were employed to burn the bodies of the gassed and shot Hungarians.

But as early as May 15 the Papal Nuncio, Monsignore Angelo Rotta, had "warned" the Hungarian Premier "on the first day of the deportations that the whole world knew what they really signified." It took until June 25 before Rotta handed Horthy a message from the Pope which made considerably more of an impression upon the Regent than the "remonstrances of the Hungarian bishops, who attacked less the principle of the deportations than the cruelties that accompanied them. The pastoral letter of Archbishop Cardinal Prince Seredi, for instance, was a long-winded

---

[12] Fritz Hesse, *Das Spiel um Deutschland* (Munich, 1953).

affair, which failed to name the deportations for what they really were. Its publication was delayed and finally withdrawn on July 8, on an assurance that the Budapest deportation had been countermanded. This and other evidence, collected by Eugene Levai, suggests that the bishops were only ready to exert their power from the pulpit when deportation threatened the Magyarized Jews, among whom there were many converts. Nor should it be forgotten that the uninhibited collaboration of the [Hungarian] *gendarmerie* would have been impossible, if the church in Hungary had consistently denounced anti-semitism in the past."[13]

Even this extremely belated message from Pius XII, which was not even directed to Hitler himself, thus produced a promise to the Nuncio that baptized Jews would no longer be deported. This proves again how high the Pope's credit stood. For his message, Reitlinger continues, "was the beginning of a world-wide bombardment of the Regent's conscience."[14] The deportations from Hungary stopped when little more than half of the Jews had been carried off. Cordell Hull, the American Secretary of State, threatened Horthy with reprisals. The King of Sweden and the International Red Cross offered to help the Hungarian Jews to emigrate. And on July 7 Mr. Eden protested in the House of Commons against the planned extermination of the Hungarian Jews. "All these protests from the outer world had rekindled in Himmler's breast his most characteristic dream that international charity could be harnessed to the waning German war effort. And to realize that dream there was the Eichmann commando, which, ever since its arrival in Hungary, had been bargaining with Jewish lives."[15] Thus Reitlinger concludes this chapter.

The Hungarian police conducted the deportations virtually alone, since Eichmann's commando consisted of only a few men. The savagery with which the police proceeded against their own fellow countrymen can be seen in the account of Edith Bruck. Her father was one of those Jews who counted on his war record to save him; when his family was being brutally expelled he showed his decorations from the First World War, in the misplaced hope that they might save him from delivery to the Germans, with whom he had fought shoulder to shoulder.

[13] Reitlinger, *op. cit.*, pp. 431 f.
[14] *Ibid.*, pp. 434 f.
[15] *Ibid.*, p. 434.

In view of the successful protest of the Slovaks against the deportations, Mr. Reitlinger raises the question: "But is one really to believe that Himmler could apply no pressure to this pocket-government?" He could easily have applied pressure to the government, I should say, but not to the Papal Nuncio who in 1942 actually saved the remnant of the Slovakian Jews after some 52,000 had already been deported, of whom only 284 survived to the end of the war.

The Vatican, the bishops in Germany, and the Papal Legations were in fact the only authorities Hitler continued to respect following the unwelcome entry into the war of the United States. In 1940 Hitler, after a talk with Mussolini, expressly forbade Rosenberg to commit any provocations against the Vatican, and in August 1941 he ordered the euthanasia program halted because of protests from the churches. "It is probable," Reitlinger writes, "that on no question was Hitler's personal dictatorship more severely challenged than this one—on which he acted with quite disgusting cowardice."[16]

We can understand Hitler's deference better when we read the following homily which appeared in November 1937 in *Angriff,* "the daily newspaper of the German Labor Front," and which later served as introduction to a pamphlet published in 1938 by the Central Publishing House of the NSDAP (National Socialist Party), which bore a portrait of Secretary of State Pacelli on the title page:

"Why is the Vatican so important to us? The Vatican again! What for? Why make so much fuss over that ridiculous little corner of the earth in the capital of the one-time Roman Empire? Many a reader of the National Socialist Press asks that question. Roosevelt, Ibn Saud, Chamberlain, Dimitroff, Herriot, above all the Duce, are the men of today upon whom world politics and the politics of the Reich depend. But these Roman prelates, these sneaky nuncios and incense-wreathed cardinals—sheer farce!

"This view is based on a mistaken notion. Chamberlain and Herriot, Roosevelt and Dimitroff are very influential persons. Today they are important. Tomorrow no one will give a damn about them. But the men around the Pope, those close-mouthed prelates of the Roman Curia with their bejeweled crucifixes, do not change. They remain the same for decades; when they are replaced, they

---

[16] *Ibid.*

are replaced by others from the same school; and they all follow
the same policies, century after century. They rule nearly four
hundred million 'faithful' throughout the world; they control an
amount of property of inconceivable proportions distributed over
the whole globe; they influence a press such as no Great Power
possesses . . . We can say that an understanding of this eternal
enemy is more crucial to the building of the German racial community than an understanding of any other secular big power. We
National Socialists know better than anyone that the faith that
moves mountains makes history—not money, not economic laws,
and not weapons alone. Therefore we can recognize the importance of a power which has a different faith from ours. We saw
this once again during the election campaign for the return of
Austria to the Reich. Radio Moscow and Radio Vatican with one
accord tried to sabotage those elections, and denounced in the most
unworthy fashion the understanding attitude of German princes of
the Church. In vain! But they have not yet given up their game
and are again agitating against German policy inside and outside
our country. Therefore, increased watchfulness!"

Monsignore Giovannetti, Member of the Papal Secretariat of State,
in his book, *The Vatican and the War* (1960) corroborated with
many examples "the importance attributed to the Holy See by all
sides during the war. In Switzerland in those days one could
properly speak of a veritable battle for the conquest of the Vatican
on the part of both belligerent blocs. It was a battle for the Pope—
a diplomatic struggle for the favor of the Vatican."

Robert E. Sherwood reports: "As a measure for coping with the
serious Catholic opposition to aid for the Soviet Union, Roosevelt
decided to send Myron C. Taylor, his special Ambassador to Pope
Pius XII, on another mission to Rome. Even this move raised
difficult religious issues, for there were many Protestants, including
some important church leaders, who were deeply alarmed by any
signs of collusion between the White House and the Vatican . . .
There were some impatient people who thought that the President
exaggerated the strength of Catholic sentiment, but it was his way
to tread with extreme wariness wherever religious sensibilities
were involved; he knew a lot more than his advisers did about
these sensibilities."[17] In September 1941 Harry Hopkins had

---

[17] Robert E. Sherwood, *Roosevelt and Hopkins* (New York: Harper & Brothers,
1948), p. 384.

written to the British Minister of Information: "We are having some difficulty with our public opinion with regard to Russia. The American people don't take aid to Russia easily. The whole Catholic population is opposed to it, all the Nazis, all the Italians, and a lot of people who sincerely believe that Stalin is a great menace to the world . . . The exhibition of the Russian Army has certainly made all of our military people look a little ill. Anglo-Saxons have a hard time believing that anyone can fight except themselves."[18]

In this matter, Hitler's instincts were better than Roosevelt's; and he knew that the Pope did not possess anything like the personal stature commensurate with his tremendous prestige throughout the world. Nevertheless he sent his Secretary of State for Foreign Affairs as ambassador to the Holy See. And even the arrogant Ribbentrop found it useful—at the beginning of November 1943, when a number of bombs of unknown origin fell into the garden of the Vatican—to telephone Consul Moellhausen in Rome and instruct him to persuade the Pope to protest the bombing. Since Ribbentrop knew Pius personally and also knew that he was not even denouncing the arrest and deportation of the Jews, he added that the Pope's usual "vaporous" talk (*"säuselndes" Gerede*) would of course be worthless; he must speak more precisely. Goebbels, with his Jesuit education, who regarded the power of the Vatican in wartime at least as realistically as Hitler, expressed regret on November 9, 1943 that "unfortunately the *Osservatore Romano* assumes only a very moderate attitude concerning this event."[19] He added: "Obviously the Pope does not want to forego the possibility of acting as mediator between the Reich and the western enemy powers, at least not for the present, although there isn't the slightest occasion for such mediation at the present moment."[20] He had earlier dictated the statement that the dropping of a few enemy bombs on Vatican City "still creates a world sensation. Under the pressure of commentary in the neutral press the English have been compelled to deny any guilt and to attempt to blame us."[21]

A few bombs which hurt no one created a world sensation! Werner Stephan, who worked in the Press Department of the Propaganda Ministry from 1933–45, relates that when Bishop

---

[18] *Ibid.*, p. 372.
[19] Joseph Goebbels, *Diaries, 1942–1943* (Garden City: Doubleday, 1948), p. 503.
[20] *Ibid.*
[21] *Ibid.*

Galen of Münster was delivering his fiery speeches against the crimes of the Nazis, Goebbels, who had a speaking engagement in Münster, did not dare present himself in that city. "He would have had to come as executor of an order from Hitler for the arrest of the refractory bishop. That would have made an effect at a mass meeting of Party members and susceptible fellow-travelers. But Goebbels could never ignore the other side: Galen would have become a martyr whose fate *might have inspired millions to uncompromising commitment against the totalitarian régime.* The Propaganda Minister knew only too well what this particular opponent could accomplish."[22] Why, we may ask again, did not the Pope place this power in the service of humanitarian action? Perhaps never before in history have so many human beings paid with their lives for the passivity of a single statesman.

"The question of the absence of any threat to excommunicate the instruments of Hitler's extermination policies is a graver one, and frankly I am inclined to think that the fact the victims were Jews was one of the reasons why this threat was never made. Here again, however, neutrality and diplomatic immunity had become an obsession, and I do not think this need have happened had there been a better Pope," Gerald Reitlinger has written to the author.

In 1938 Goebbels warned the people in his Ministry against withdrawing from the Church, and in a speech to the heads of the propaganda bureaus he emphasized that he himself had had all his children baptized. Even during the war he would give his secretary time off to attend church when he needed her services on Sunday mornings. On Easter Sunday 1943 he entered in his diary: "The SD has taken the so-called Clemens Chapel away from the Catholics of Berlin. Pape wrote me a letter about it and urged me to return the chapel to the Catholic Congregation. I did this immediately and bawled out the SD for taking action in direct violation of my directives."[23]

Hitler and the most powerful men in his government, Himmler, Göring, and Goebbels, were too cunning to provoke the Vatican during the war by inflicting annoyances on the Church in Germany. In his *Table Talk* Hitler might make the most contemptuous remarks about the church, but he as well as Göring wrote conciliatory letters to protesting bishops. For, as Friedrich Heer writes,

---

[22] Werner Stephan, *Joseph Goebbels—Dämon einer Diktatur* (Stuttgart, 1949).
[23] Goebbels, *op. cit.*, p. 344.

the clergy's objections "stayed within the bounds of allegiance to the legitimate, God-willed authorities, within the bounds of allegiance to Führer and Chancellor. In spite of everything, the masses of the believing people were placed at his disposal for his crusade against Bolshevism and were led into battle by the army chaplains of both religious confessions."[24]

The fact that Hitler had many a nameless priest murdered evidently did not seriously disturb his accord with the Vatican. I again quote Friedrich Heer: "Clergy and laymen, priests and men in political life, who ventured to think and practice resistance, could count on the sympathy of their church leaders neither in prison nor on the scaffold. The Christian resistance to Hitler, accordingly, from the very start assumed the character of the odd, the exceptional, the undesired, of disobedience!"[25]

Bormann alone, spiteful and not very intelligent, tended to issue decrees during the war that were bound to annoy even the patient Vatican. But highly as Hitler esteemed this "most loyal Party comrade" of his, he would call Bormann to heel whenever this deputy ventured one of his forays against the Church. The secretary for ecclesiastical affairs in the Foreign Office said that during the war Hitler intervened personally three times to cancel anti-Church measures.

Herr von Papen also speaks of this matter: "The sermons of the bishop of Münster, Count Galen, travelled around from hand to hand, and I discovered from Lammers[26] that he had shown them to Hitler. It was therefore not difficult to approach him about this difficult situation. Hitler showed understanding for my explanations but, as on a number of previous occasions, placed the whole blame on the hotheads of the party. He had, through Bormann, issued a firm edict that this 'nonsense' was to be discontinued: he would brook no conflicts in the internal situation."[27] This was not hypocrisy; the decree took effect. Even Himmler, who had once boasted to Frau von Weizsäcker, "We shall not rest until we have rooted out Christianity,"[28] was cunning enough to concentrate his destruc-

[24] Heer, *op. cit.*

[25] *Ibid.*

[26] Hans Lammers, Chief of the Reich Chancellery, sentenced in April 1949 to twenty years imprisonment by a U.S. military tribunal at Nuremberg for his part in drafting anti-Jewish decrees, but released at the end of 1951. See: William L. Shirer, *The Rise and Fall of the Third Reich* (New York: Simon and Schuster, 1960), p. 965.—*Ed.*

[27] Von Papen, *op. cit.*, p. 481.

[28] Ernst Heinrich von Weizsäcker, *Memoirs* (Chicago: Regnery, 1951), p. 281.

tive instincts upon groups of people whose extermination would not damage relations between the Hitler régime and the Holy See: Jews, Slavs, gypsies, Jehovah's Witnesses, Communists. The Berlin Nuncio repeatedly intervened with Herr von Weizsäcker on behalf of persecuted Polish priests, sometimes with success. The Polish clergy, moreover, was regarded as more trustworthy. While the oppositionist priests from Poland were sent to concentration camps and often, like Father Kolbe, were horribly tortured, Gauleiter Forster of Danzig recommended to the Führer that those Poles who were "worth Germanizing" should not be placed under the care of priests from the Reich but should continue to be served by their Polish clergy. "For under the pressure to which the Polish priests feel themselves to be exposed, they are susceptible to any influence and even inquire at the end of every single week, at the district magistrate's office, what they shall preach about in church. It would be still better, in his opinion, to win the Polish bishop over to a close contact with the Gauleiter, so that through him the required subjects and instructions could be passed on to the priests. In this way it might be possible to assure peace and order through the country during this period of transition."[29] Hitler issued a warning against expecting too much of such a program; even Charlemagne, he said, had tried without success to use bishops to win the Church over to a "German" policy.

The Italian Foreign Minister, Count Ciano, who said of Himmler that he was "the only man who really has his finger on the pulse of the German people," also evidently did not regard Himmler's remarks on the Vatican and Pacelli in May 1939 as hypocrisy: "Himmler talked at length about relations with the Church. They like the new Pope and believe that a *modus vivendi* is possible. I encouraged him along these lines, saying that an agreement between the Reich and the Vatican would make the Axis more popular."[30] In point of fact, Himmler, of whom Reitlinger has said that he could neither lie nor let his imagination go without becoming ridiculous, probably meant that sincerely at the time, and not *only* out of sheer opportunism. After all, he had given his mother a church funeral in 1943, permitted SS officers to partake publicly of Communion, and possibly spoke of the extermination of Christianity only out of inner weakness and because certain Party

[29] *Hitler's Table Talk* (London: Weidenfeld and Nicolson, 1953), pp. 472 f.

[30] *The Ciano Diaries 1939–1943*, edited by Hugh Gibson (Garden City: Doubleday, 1946), p. 86.

circles—whom Hitler scarcely permitted to influence his actions—liked to hear that sort of thing. When in the winter of 1942 the proposal arose for secretly gassing Poles ill with tuberculosis, Himmler allowed himself to be dissuaded by the consideration that the Church would not remain silent and that "the intended procedure will provide excellent propaganda material for our enemies, not only among the Italian doctors and scientists but also among the entire Italian nation as a result of their strong Catholic ties."[31]

He knew at any rate what was unpopular—the extermination of the Jews and the mentally ill; and *because* they were unpopular, he at first desired neither of these actions which were later initiated under his command. But he bowed to Hitler's orders, though not without protest, and would undoubtedly have murdered priests too if Hitler had so commanded. Then again, he said after the attempted assassination of July 20, 1944—whose failure to kill Hitler he deeply regretted—that he could only salve his guilty conscience toward the Führer somewhat by exceptional cruelty toward the conspirators. And in 1944 he said to his personal physician, before whom he made no attempt to play a part: "We should not have let ourselves attack the Church, for it is stronger than we. When I am dead, let those priests pray for my soul too."

To my mind Himmler's personality has been best grasped by the Oxford historian H. R. Trevor-Roper, who as an Allied intelligence officer immediately after the war had the opportunity to question personally or to study at first hand the testimony of the subsequently condemned (or released) Nazi leaders, as well as that of their aides and secretaries. He writes:

"In a civilized world, it is true, such men are seldom tolerated; but if we look back at the cataclysmic periods of society, at periods of revolution and violent social change, his prototype is there. It is the Grand Inquisitor, the mystic in politics, the man who is prepared to sacrifice humanity to an abstract ideal. The Grand Inquisitors of history were not cruel or self-indulgent men. They were often painfully conscientious and austere in their personal lives. They were often scrupulously kind to animals, like the blessed Robert Bellarmine, who refused to disturb the fleas in his clothes. Since they could not hope for theological bliss (he said), it would be uncharitable to deny them that carnal refreshment to which

---

[31] Alexander Mitscherlich and Fred Mielke, *Doctors of Infamy: The Story of the Nazi Medical Crimes* (New York: Schuman, 1949).

alone they could aspire. But for men who, having opportunities of worshipping aright, chose wrong, no remedy was too drastic. So the faggots were piled and lit, and the misbelievers and their books were burned, and those gentle old bishops went home to sup on whitefish and inexpensive vegetables, to feed their cats and canaries, and to meditate on the Penitential Psalms, while their chaplains sat down in their studies to compose their biographies and explain to posterity the saintly lives, the observances and austerities, the almsgivings and simplicity, of those exemplary pastors, knowing (as Cardinal Newman said) that it is better that all humanity should perish in extremest agony than that one single venial sin should be committed.

"Such a comparison perhaps seems fanciful; but nature is fanciful in designing the human mind, and times of revolution do throw up into positions of eminence men who, in stable periods, remain unobserved in gaols and monasteries. Himmler himself, everyone is agreed, was an utterly insignificant man, common, pedantic, and mean. He was greedy of money and incapable of thought; and yet he could not resist the temptation to speculate, to lose himself in the *O Altitudo,* and entangle himself in the theological minutiae, of the pure Nazi doctrine. Hitler himself, in one sense, was not a Nazi, for the doctrines of Nazism, that great system of Teutonic nonsense, were to him only a weapon of politics; 'he criticised and ridiculed the ideology of the SS'; but to Himmler they were, every iota of them, the pure Aryan truth, which if a man keep not pure and undefiled, he shall without doubt perish everlastingly. With such narrow pedantry, with such black-letter antiquarianism, did Himmler study the details of this sad rubbish, that many have supposed, but wrongly, that he had been a schoolmaster. He gave Speer the impression of being 'half schoolmaster, half crank.' During the war, while Goebbels was demanding total mobilisation, Himmler was employing thousands of men and millions of marks in the projects of a religious maniac. In one department of his foreign intelligence service, a school of eager researchers studied such important matters as Rosicrucianism and Freemasonry, the symbolism of the suppression of the harp at Ulster, and the occult significance of Gothic pinnacles and top-hats at Eton. The SS scientific laboratories laboured infelicitously to isolate pure Aryan blood. An explorer was sent to Tibet to discover traces of a pure Germanic race believed to preserve the ancient Nordic mysteries in those unvisited mountains. Throughout Europe excavators sought for relics of authentic German *Kultur*. When the German army prepared hastily to evacuate Naples, Himmler's only demand was that it should not omit to carry with it the vast stone tomb of the last Hohenstaufen Emperor. Meanwhile, rich business men, if they wished to join his exclusive Circle of Friends, had to buy admission by subscribing perhaps a million marks to the *Ahnenerbe,* a 'scientific' institute that made expensive researches into Aryan origins. Even in April 1945, when the whole Reich was tumbling in ruins, Himmler was contemplating the colonisation of the Ukraine with a new religious sect recommended by his masseur, and in conversation with Count Bernadotte (having just maintained that he was the only sane man left in Germany), interrupted the discussion of war and peace to digress for an hour on runes. He was particularly interested in runes, the uninterpreted script of the Northmen of the Dark Ages. Studied with the eye of faith, they might, he believed, yield resemblance to Japanese ideograms, and thus prove the Japanese to be Aryans after all.

"In such a character no grain of subtlety is discernible. Himmler was an elementary believer. His fanaticism was not the difficult birth of fear and weakness, nor his hesitation the consequence of doubt. Doubt had not yet nibbled at the infantile serenity of his cosmic acceptances." [32]

Himmler's closest confidant, Schellenberg (with whom he had been discussing treason since 1942 without ever calling it by its true name even in their most intimate moments), states, in confirmation of this view of the man: "Himmler owned an extremely large and excellent library on the Jesuit Order and for years would sit up late studying the extensive literature. Thus he built up the SS organization according to the principles of the Jesuits. *The Spiritual Exercises* of Ignatius of Loyola served as the foundation; the supreme law was absolute obedience, the execution of any order whatsoever without question. Himmler himself, as Reichsführer of the SS, was the general of the order. The structure of leadership was borrowed from the hierarchical order of the Catholic Church. He took over a medieval castle, the so-called Wevelsburg at Paderborn in Westphalia, and had it repaired so that it might serve as a kind of 'SS monastery.' Here the general of the order would hold a secret consistory once a year, attended by the top leadership of the order. They would take part in spirit-

[32] H. R. Trevor-Roper, *The Last Days of Hitler* (New York: Macmillan, 1947), pp. 19–22.

ual exercises and practice sessions in concentration. In the large meeting hall each member had his particular chair with his name engraved on a silver plaque. No doubt these mystical leanings of Himmler go back in part to his attitude toward the Catholic Church, which might be called 'hate-love'; in part to his strict upbringing by his father with its stern Catholic code of conduct, from which he fled into a reckless romanticism . . ."[33]

What was Hitler's position toward the Vatican during the war? I offer a few additional sidelights on that. "High dignitaries of the Church in Germany," Professor Eugen Kogon writes, "were never sent to a concentration camp. On one occasion a canon of the Olmütz cathedral chapter was selected as suffragan while he was at Buchenwald. He was immediately released by the SS."[34]

The protests of the Bishop of Münster annoyed Hitler extremely. He declared that after the final victory Galen would be "sent before the firing squad." He also remarked ironically that if the Bishop did not succeed in being called to the Collegium Germanicum in Rome before the end of the war, there would be an accounting with him down to the last farthing—*after* the war. But Hitler contained his fury. Except within his intimate circle, he camouflaged his dislike for the Church as long as the clergy did not obstruct him politically. He had early said to von Papen that Rosenberg's *Myth of the Twentieth Century* was not worth the paper it was printed on. He himself always merely smiled at the idea of replacing the Catholic Church by a new German Nazi church. In a few centuries, he believed, the Church would disintegrate of its own accord. He wanted to accelerate this process after the war by following the example of the United States and according the Church—which in 1942 still received some 900 million marks from the Reich—only scanty financial support. Then, he said, the Church would eat out of his hand. Hitler vetoed Heydrich's diabolical plan of sending talented Hitler Youth leaders in the guise of pious would-be priests into theological seminaries so that in later years they could shatter the clergy from within and deliver it into the hands of the Party. Perhaps Hitler was not certain that he would be able to keep these young double agents permanently on his side.

---

[33] Walter Schellenberg, *The Labyrinth: Memoirs of Walter Schellenberg* (New York: Harper, 1956).

[34] Eugen Kogon, *The Theory and Practice of Hell* (New York: Farrar, Straus, 1950), p. 41.

There is ample documentary evidence for the attitudes of Hitler, Göring, and Goebbels during the war. Here is an excerpt from the Propaganda Minister's diary of March 1942: "Göring also addressed a sharp letter to Bishops Galen of Münster and Berning of Osnabrück. He reminded them of their oath, pledged to him, of fidelity to the state, and reprimanded them severely for their treasonable attitude. While I was with him, the answers to this letter happened to arrive. They are relatively meek. The bishops try to alibi and with involved turns of speech to prove that they kept their oath. Göring naturally won't accept that. I suggest to Göring that he write another letter, especially to Galen, charging him to his face with having created the greatest unrest in the Reich by his claim that seriously wounded soldiers were being liquidated, and pointing out that his utterances are being used by the English propaganda services against the National Socialist regime. On the one hand it must be recognized that certain measures of the Party, especially the decree about crucifixes, have made it altogether too easy for the bishops to rant against the state. Göring, too, is very much put out about it. His whole attitude toward the Christian denominations is quite open and above board. He sees through them, and has no intention whatever of taking them under his protection. On the other hand he agrees with me completely that it won't do to get started now, in wartime, on so difficult and far-reaching a problem. The Führer, too, has communicated the same point of view to him, as he has done to me time and again. In this connection the Führer declared that if his mother still lived, she would undoubtedly go to Church today, and he could and would not hinder her . . ."[35]

This was at the height of Hitler's power, when all Europe aside from England was at his mercy. A few months later he said to Himmler (who, relieved by Heydrich's assassination, wanted to be somewhat more cautious "in the Church question also"): "If filled churches help me to keep the German people quiet, then in view of the burden of the war there can be no objection to them." Hitler's opportunism went so far as to place the Oberammergau Passion Play in the service of anti-Semitism. He said in 1942: "One of our most important tasks will be to save future generations from a similar political fate [to that of Germany from 1918–33] and to maintain forever watchful in them a knowledge of the

[35] *Goebbels, op. cit.,* pp. 141 f.

menace of Jewry. For this reason alone it is vital that the Passion Play be continued at Oberammergau; for never has the menace of Jewry been so convincingly portrayed as in this presentation of what happened in the time of the Romans. There one sees in Pontius Pilate a Roman racially and intellectually so superior, that he stands out like a firm, clean rock in the middle of the whole muck and mire of Jewry."[36]

Although I did not doubt the figures which Gerstein presented in his report[37], I have replaced them by the smaller and therefore more credible ones (as throughout the play) which had already reached the Allied press by this time. Thus on January 21, 1943, Gerhard Riegner, the representative of the World Jewish Congress stationed in Berne, reported that 6,000 Jews were being killed daily in Poland. This report led to a public protest demonstration in New York's Madison Square Garden. As early as August 1942 Riegner had informed Washington of Hitler's plan for extermination of the Jews, and in November he corroborated this report by four new affidavits to Secretary of State Sumner Welles. Still earlier, on July 21, 1942, President Roosevelt had written to Dr. Wise on the occasion of a demonstration in Madison Square Garden: "The American people not only sympathize with all victims of Nazi crimes but will hold the perpetrators of these crimes to strict accountability on a day of reckoning which will surely come." Incidentally, on September 30, 1942, Hitler publicly repeated his "pledge" to "eradicate" the Jews in Europe. On December 17, 1942, the Allies solemnly declared that atonement would be exacted for the massacres.

Gerstein's descriptions of the gassing operations in Belzec have here been supplemented by details from the famous report of Hermann Friedrich Graebe, who as manager of the Solingen construction firm of Josef Jung witnessed a mass shooting of Jewish families in Sdolbunov in the Ukraine on October 5, 1942. (See Poliakov-Wulf, *Das Dritte Reich und die Juden*.) Such shootings at pits and quarries, such as the one on the outskirts of Kiev where 34,000 persons were liquidated on September 28 and 29, 1941, were no more kept secret from many members of the army

---

[36] *Hitler's Table Talk*, p. 563.
[37] See: Léon Poliakov and Josef Wulf, *Das Dritte Reich und die Juden* (Berlin, 1955); and *Vierteljahreshefte für Zeitgeschichte*.

than from the native populace. In fact, in the Ukraine and the Baltic countries volunteers were often recruited from the population to take part in round-ups and shootings under German leadership. The diaries of Ernst Jünger also contain entries about the ugly rumors that reached him (see the entries for March 6, 1942; December 31, 1942; April 21, 1943). The stories reached most Europeans—to the extent that they were keenly interested in these matters. Details were also made public by Thomas Mann on September 27, 1942, over the BBC radio, in one of his monthly, deeply moving eight-minute speeches. That same month in America a book came out containing the first twenty-five of these radio broadcasts of Thomas Mann, which had started in October 1940. The speech of November 1941 mentions the mass murder of Jews and Poles. In January 1942 Mann stated that Jews from Holland had been gassed. The Dutch government-in-exile later published details, the number of victims and the scene of the crime: Mauthausen; these were repeated by Thomas Mann in June 1942 in his radio speech, and printed in the above-mentioned book. Auschwitz was not yet known as a center of the extermination program, although the New York German newspaper, *Neue Volkszeitung,* as early as July 14, 1941, and March 14, 1942, carried reports on the "torture hell" of Oswiecim. Later, on December 13, 1943, a bulletin of the Jewish Telegraph Agency in London spoke of 580,000 Jews killed in Auschwitz. Six months later, on June 2, 1944, this agency estimated the number of Jews murdered in Auschwitz by the middle of 1942 as 800,000. Since the victims were Jews, such bulletins failed completely to excite the horror they merited among the Christian belligerents on either side, reserved as it was for the daily events of the war. A nation at war has enough problems of its own—that serves as some explanation. But without question Hitler's public "pledge" to "eradicate" the Jews, which was often repeated, should have been taken as no idle threat. And without question every personage of rank and influence beyond the German borders, as well as inside Germany, knew that "eradication" was going on legally and continually and that deportation trains were bound for a void. In October 1943, for example, American newspapers published the fact that 4,000 children between the ages of two and fourteen, sixty in a single car, had been separated from their parents in France and sent to the East to an unstated "destination."

On June 22, 1943, Jan Ciechanowski, Ambassador of the

Polish Government-in-Exile in Washington, received Lieutenant Jan Karski, secret envoy of the anti-communist underground in Poland, who was being sent to London and the United States for the second time to transmit information and eyewitness reports to the appropriate civilian and military officials. He was also received by President Roosevelt for whom he sketched a picture of "the concentration camps in which mass murders were an everyday event. He spoke of Oswiecim [Auschwitz], Maidanek, Dachau, Oranienburg, and the women's camp at Ravensbrück, and gave the President a nerve-shattering description of his own visit— disguised as a policeman—to the two murder camps, Treblinka and Belzec, where Jews were gassed in railway trucks. 'I am convinced, Mr. President,' continued Karski, 'that there is no exaggeration in the accounts of the plight of the Jews. Our Underground authorities are absolutely sure that the Germans are out to exterminate the entire Jewish population of Europe. Reliable reports from our own informers give the figure of 1,800,000 Jews already murdered in Poland up to the day when I left the country. . . . I was instructed by the leaders of our Underground to tell the British and American military authorities that only through direct reprisals, such as mass bombing of German cities, after dropping millions of leaflets telling the Germans that they were being bombed in reprisal for exterminating Jews, could this mass extermination be stopped or at least limited.' "[38]

In fact, during the summer of 1943 the Allied bombers did drop leaflets on Germany informing the German people of the extermination of the Jews, and supplying many details, such as the discovery of the mass graves in Kharkov. Leaders of the *Jungvolk* organization, that is to say, children of the ages of twelve to fourteen, were often assigned the task of picking up and burning these leaflets.

Presumably this report of Karski's, along with other, considerably earlier accounts, prompted the President's appeal to the Pope. Through his special ambassador Myron C. Taylor and through other channels Roosevelt asked Pius XII to make an *ex cathedra* pronouncement calling upon Catholics to oppose Hitler's atrocities. The author has asked the Polish ambassador to Washington whether he communicated Karski's report to the Vatican. In a letter to the author, the ambassador replied that he had trans-

---

[38] Jan Ciechanowski, *Defeat in Victory* (Garden City: Doubleday, 1947), pp. 182 f.

mitted the report not only to the Apostolic Delegate in Washington (who is today Secretary of State, Cardinal Cicognani), but also to the Congress of the United States, and to American cardinals, bishops, and universities. Moreover, until his recall on July 5, 1945 he repeatedly transmitted this and new information from Poland to the above-mentioned persons and institutions. From May 1941 on, even before Karski's visit, Ambassador Ciechanowski had done all in his power to acquaint Washington with the situation.

Golo Mann[39] asserts that during the war the Allies knew nothing of the gas chambers in Austria and Poland—although his father publicly denounced the gassings in Mauthausen as early as 1942. In making this statement, Professor Mann—quite unconsciously, of course—continues the attempt of the British and Americans to find an excuse for themselves for all the years in which they ignored the most reliable information on the mass murders. Their horror and rage when they opened up the camps in 1945 sprang partly from their own guilt in the matter. Who can tell how many of the Jews fell victim to the "Final Solution" because other countries so heartlessly and needlessly refused to admit them? Not that this in any way excuses the mass murders, of course. But it was a tragedy in itself. When in January 1944 a half-Jew warned the Berlin journalist Ursula von Kardorff of the "fearful judgment" which would be meted out to the Germans after the war by the Allies, she noted in her diary: "Certainly we have taken a horrible guilt upon ourselves, but surely the others have done so also— the Americans and English who made entry so hard for the fleeing Jews. They have little call to sit in judgment like Pharisees. Bärchen asks: 'Where were the others when the Jews had to leave Germany after November 9, 1938? Who placed so many obstacles in the way of their immigration that many abandoned the attempt and so after the outbreak of the war were exposed to such inhuman treatment?' She told of her repeated vain attempts to find a way for a Jewish girl friend, whose brothers were already in America, to emigrate. She went from consulate to consulate, armed with recommendations from diplomats and influential journalists. She waited in line for hours in front of the American Consulate. She did this for three successive days, only to have an American secretary say to her that she was quite astounded at a

[39] Golo Mann, *Deutsche Geschichte des 19. and 20. Jahrhunderts* (Frankfurt am Main, 1960).

German woman's attempting to do something for a Jewess; after all, that was forbidden.

"I don't know whether we convinced Dr. Meier; he is in despair because his Jewish father starved to death in a camp near Darmstadt. I cannot blame him for hoping that we will be punished. At the front, the best young men of the nation are dying for a victory which I dread—for if Hitler wins, we are lost. And what if he does not win?"[40]

In 1955 Professor Mann, discussing the last months in the life of the resistance leader Carl Goerdeler,[41] the winter of 1944, wrote: "One is ashamed of one's own attitude during those months, ashamed of Germany, of the Allies. . . ." And concerning Goerdeler's famous letter to Field Marshal Kluge:[42] "If only the Anglo-Americans had known at the time that such letters were being written by prominent men in Germany! If only they had seriously tried to know, and had drawn serious conclusions from the facts!"

As regards the extermination of the Jews it required no special effort to know the facts; the Allies were told, again and again, until they no longer wanted to listen. Ambassador Ciechanowski writes of the summer of 1942: "The incredible details of the system of human extermination started by Hitler's gang were as yet unknown to Americans at large. But the Polish Government was being fully informed about all these happenings owing to the perfect system of daily contact which it had successfully set up with the Polish Underground.

"From information I was receiving and constantly communicating to the American Government and to the press, and describing in my numerous speeches in many American cities, the monstrous pattern of Hitler's mass extermination of Polish Jews and of Jews brought to Poland from other countries was becoming clearly evident. The Polish Underground insistently demanded that our government present these facts to our allies and especially to the American Government.

---

[40] Ursula von Kardorff, *Berliner Aufzeichnungen aus den Jahren 1942 bis 1945* (Munich, 1962).

[41] Former mayor of Leipzig, executed in February 1945 as one of the chief plotters against Hitler in the abortive attempt on Hitler's life of July 20, 1944.—*Ed.*

[42] Field Marshal Günther Hans von Kluge, a central figure in the plot against Hitler, was enlisted into the conspiracy by Goerdeler as early as November 1942, but at the decisive moment refused to join the revolt. Committed suicide by swallowing poison in August 1944 to escape arrest. See: Shirer, *op. cit.*—*Ed.*

"General Sikorski was working on it overtime in London and I was following up his requests to the President, the State Department, and the Combined Chiefs of Staff . . ."[43]

Ciechanowski, who incidentally has also written the most macabre description of the desperate search for the Polish army officers who had seemingly vanished without a trace, and who reveals the fact that a quarter of a million Polish Jews were carried off to Siberia—Ciechanowski relates that as early as 1942 he went to Roosevelt to appeal for retaliatory measures and a protest by the Great Powers against the massacres. His efforts were in vain. "The general lack of understanding of German barbarity and a certain basic kindheartedness toward the Germans were most striking at the time. They appeared suddenly in some of my contacts with American officials and representatives of American public opinion. . . . The average American, and even officials who had every means of being fully informed, practically refused to believe the Germans capable of the horrors which they were committing."[44]

According to Ciechanowski, friendliness toward Germany decidedly increased in America as late as 1944, a full year after Karski's call upon the President. Ciechanowski suggests three reasons for this. First: "As victory was becoming more and more certain, the natural sporting instinct of the American people was beginning to reassert itself." Secondly: "The elections were approaching. The numerically strong and well-organized group of Americans of German descent constituted an influential body in the electorate." Thirdly: Germanophile sentiment increased "because of increasing fear of Russia and of Communism. The idea was spreading that Germany, after having been purged of Nazism, might be used as a convenient barrier against Soviet expansion."[45]

It is dishonest to close one's eyes to the fact that the Jews as a body could not hope to receive from any nation—with the possible exception of the Danes—nor from the Vatican or the Red Cross, the kind of support which would have been accorded to persecuted non-Jews. That is a horrifying truth. Herr von Kessel, who testified at Nuremberg in defense of Weizsäcker, was asked in court:

Question: Since you worked for a considerable time both with the International Red Cross and at the Vatican, I should like to

---

[43] Ciechanowski, *op. cit.,* p. 117.
[44] *Ibid.,* p. 119.
[45] *Ibid.,* pp. 285 f.

ask you to sum up your testimony by stating your opinion on two questions. Have these two great humanitarian organizations ever protested on principle to Hitler against the anti-Jewish measures?

Answer: No, neither of them.

Question: Can you describe concretely whether the Red Cross ever considered such a plan?

Answer: Yes. A member of the Committee of the International Red Cross met me one day in Geneva and said: A terrible thing has happened. A woman member of the Committee demands that we make an official protest against the persecutions of the Jews in Germany. How can we do that? Switzerland is encircled by National Socialist territory. If we protest, Hitler will abrogate the Geneva Convention and we will have to stop all our work, for the prisoners of war, for the occupied territories, for the civilian internees, and all those in distress. We are in a frightful quandary, he said. . . . A few days later I met the same man again and he said: Thank God, after hours of discussion the motion to protest officially was finally rejected. It is a terribly difficult decision for us all, but at least it means we can continue our work.

Would the Red Cross have steered so prudent a course if, for example, it had been informed that in Germany—as in Japan— Allied pilots shot down after dropping incendiary bombs on civilians were being killed like the Jews?

On December 13, 1942 Goebbels noted in his diary: "The question of Jewish persecution in Europe is being given top news priority by the English and Americans. . . ."[46] On December 14: "Jewish rabbis in London have held a great protest meeting. The theme was, 'England, Awake.' " On December 15: "The Jews in London proclaimed a day of mourning for the atrocities allegedly committed on Jews in Poland by us. . . . Sentiment has turned very much against us in Sweden and in Switzerland."[47]

Emanuel Ringelblum in his chronicle of the Warsaw Ghetto set down June 26, 1942 as the "Great Day" on which the world public was for the first time informed of the extermination of the Jews in Poland. "This morning the English radio reported on the fate of the Polish Jews. . . . For months it has been an added agony to us that the world remains deaf and dumb to our unprecedented tragedy. We blame Polish public opinion and the agents

---

[46] Goebbels, *op. cit.,* p. 241.

[47] *Ibid.,* pp. 243 f.

who are in touch with the Polish Government-in-Exile." This chronicler, who was killed along with his family in March 1944, continues: "Why did they not inform the world that the Jews in Poland are being exterminated? Have they deliberately concealed our tragedy, so that theirs will not be overshadowed? . . . Today's broadcast drew up the balance sheet: it gave the figure of 700,000 Jews killed so far."[48]

The historian Léon Poliakov, now living in Paris, who translated Ringelblum's chronicle into French, has written to the author attesting that "in June 1942 the information on the annihilation of the Jews in Poland was officially communicated to the Vatican also."

From 1939 to 1946 the Vatican maintained an extensive information and intelligence service for the benefit of refugees and prisoners of war, as we are informed by the *Aperçu sur l'Œuvre du Bureau d'Informations Vaticans,* published in 1948 by the Tipografia Poliglotta Vaticana. Books about Pius XII and the Vatican often make the point that the Holy See is the best-informed institution in the world. Thus Bernard Wall writes: "Priests are situated in places where no secret service agent of any of the great powers has ever been. They meet people of every class of society. As celibates without family responsibilities they can devote themselves whole-heartedly to their work. . . . There are plenty of priests behind the Iron Curtain. There are priests still in prisons and concentration camps, and others who have been liberated only recently. All this information reaches Rome, where it is carefully docketed and filed. . . . Hitler's attack on Russia was no great surprise to the Vatican; the Jesuits had received word of the preparations through the Polish Father Provincial of their order."[49]

The best informant of the Pope during the war is said to have been the Archbishop of New York, Cardinal Spellman, who traveled all over the world as an American military chaplain and repeatedly stopped off in Rome. In his book on the Vatican Herbert Tichy wrote in 1949: "Probably the Vatican was then—not only as a result of Spellman's efforts—amazingly well-informed about most of the secrets of the belligerent Powers. In February 1943, two and a half years before Hiroshima, the Pope made a reference to the atom bomb in an address to the Papal Academy.

---

[48] Quoted from *Der Spiegel,* 1960.

[49] Bernard Wall, *Report on the Vatican* (London: Weidenfeld and Nicolson, 1956).

'We know,' he said, 'that a uranium atom disintegrates when it is bombarded with neutrons, releasing two or more neutrons which in their turn can shatter more uranium atoms and so generate a wave of energy. A cubic meter of uranium oxide can raise a billion tons to a height of twenty-seven kilometers. . . . It is important that the release of such inconceivable force be chemically controled, to prevent the destruction of our planet.' "[50]

In his memoirs Weizsäcker would have us believe that not only Ribbentrop but Hitler as well sent him to the Vatican solely in order to be rid of him. This was the most convenient postwar version of the facts. It is not credible. Hitler was disturbed by rumors that Mussolini would not be able to hold power much longer. Out of courtesy toward Mussolini he had vetoed plans for setting up a security service in Italy. He scarcely trusted his ambassador at the Quirinal to handle the situation diplomatically, or to supply him with the required intelligence. For these reasons alone he probably felt it reassuring to have Weizsäcker in Rome. But there was also another reason. Goebbels speaks of his deep concern with the question, which he also laid before Hitler, of whether "something might not be done" with this particular Pope in regard to mediating a peace. In view of this, we cannot believe that Weizsäcker was sent to the Holy See merely to play boccia. By the end of 1943 he himself may already have resolved never to negotiate a compromise between Hitler Germany and the Western Powers, but to attempt to reach a peace only for a Germany without Hitler. On December 29, 1943 he wrote to a confidant in Germany: "Carl Friedrich is well. I suppose he could be somewhat more active, and I have told him so. But of course Carl is in his way, or at least in the way of success for his efforts. I suppose nothing can be done about that, can it?" "Carl Friedrich" was the code name for the Pope, "Carl," for Hitler.

Professor Robert Leiber has said: "For understandable reasons Herr von Weizsäcker, as long as he held the office of ambassador, was extremely reticent about events in Germany."[51]

This corresponds with what I have been told by one of the few surviving associates of Admiral Canaris, who twice during the war in talks with the Vatican brought up the subject of the extermination of the Jews. In this he was exceptional; most members

---

[50] Herbert Tichy, *Auf Einem Hügel der Ewigen Stadt* (Vienna, 1949).
[51] Article in *Stimmen der Zeit*.

of the German resistance movement, including Weizsäcker, refrained from telling the world about the crimes being committed in the name of Germany, for they did not wish to demolish abroad all willingness to compromise. They had in any case been made to learn that the world by and large identified the Germans with the Nazis. But just as they wished the fighting fronts to be held after the overthrow of Hitler, so that Germany would still be in a position to negotiate, they also wanted to avoid news of the crimes to spread abroad beyond what was already known, so that Germany would not be completely ruled out as a negotiating partner.

The English and Americans are still blamed for having shown too little inclination to meet the German opposition halfway. But no mention is made of the cunning trick which Heydrich and Schellenberg played on the British Secret Service in the "Venlo Incident."[52] After that bitter experience, how could the English have any faith in the prospect of high-ranking German officers overthrowing the Hitler regime?

From the artist's viewpoint, Weizsäcker's many-faceted, enigmatic character is one of the most fascinating in contemporary history. Rather than do him the injustice of dealing with him as a secondary figure, I have preferred to omit him from the play altogether.

He was one of the first to hear about the mass-murder of the Jews—Admiral Canaris, Chief of Military Counterintelligence, was his informant. He continued to be on intimate terms with Canaris, who was certainly one of the four or five best-informed Germans of the Hitler era. When arraigned before Freisler,[53] Trott zu Solz[54] named Weizsäcker, knowing him to be safe in the Vatican, as head of the Foreign Office plot against Hitler. But in spite of this and many other proofs of his oppositional work, Weizsäcker often acted in an utterly merciless way. For example, when the Swedish Ambassador came to him with the proposal that Sweden take in Jews who had been deported from Norway to

[52] On November 8, 1939 a bomb exploded at Munich's Bürgerbräukeller minutes after Hitler had left it. The following day Schellenberg, posing as spokesman for a group of German generals intent on overthrowing Hitler, lured two British intelligence agents to Venlo, Holland, where they were kidnaped and taken to Germany to be accused of complicity in the bombing. See: Shirer, *op. cit.*, pp. 652 f.—*Ed.*

[53] Roland Freisler, president of the dreaded People's Court, a man Shirer describes as "perhaps the most sinister and bloodthirsty Nazi in the Third Reich after Heydrich." See: Shirer, *op. cit.*, pp. 1023, 1070.—*Ed.*

[54] A leading member of the Kreisau Circle and the July 20, 1944 conspiracy; hanged on August 25, 1944.—*Ed.*

Auschwitz, Weizsäcker informed Ribbentrop that he had flatly refused even to discuss the question. Poliakov and Wulf have printed documents of September and October 1942 showing that Weizsäcker pressed the Hungarian Ambassador to consent to the "resettlement" in Eastern Europe of Jews who might tend to "stir panic." Luther, who was the driving force in the Foreign Office behind the deportation of Jews from various countries of Europe, always submitted "the measures to be undertaken by us" to Weizsäcker "for his approval." Weizsäcker himself writes that in order to leave no stone unturned, as early as the autumn of 1941, when he first learned of the massacres, he "appealed to Ribbentrop at his headquarters to take energetic action against these atrocities in general. I never learned what his reactions to this were. For me the Jewish problem as a whole merged into the greater general problem: what was the quickest way of obtaining peace without Hitler?"[55] To know that the Jews in the East were being murdered en masse, to hand in a protest against the killings and, when it was not answered, to make no further inquiry for two full years, meanwhile becoming involved in the issuance of orders for deportations to the East, or even pressing foreign diplomats to ship their Jewish fellow-countrymen to the East—is that normal conduct? "To be misunderstood," Weizsäcker imperturbably sums up his work in Berlin, "is one of the risks attached to the diplomatic career. And to anyone who could not of himself understand what I was doing I really had nothing further to say."[56]

Weizsäcker writes that "from the late summer of 1938 on I took the unwavering position that Hitler must be eliminated." But on May 20, 1942, in the Kaisersaal of the Frankfurt Römer, speaking not to twelve-year-old Hitler Youths but to diplomats who had just returned from America, he said—to the utter dismay of Chief of Staff Beck [one of the leading oppositionists]: "If you have withstood the barrage of enemy propaganda and lies across the ocean, and if you have observed how our enemies are waging a war of words, you will see here and now that we in Germany are waging a war of deeds. You will not encounter any 'American way of life' here; here the good old German way of facing facts still prevails. Among us there are no committees eternally conferring; among us the Führer principle reigns. We have no 'fire-

[55] Von Weizsäcker, op. cit., p. 271.
[56] Ibid., p. 280.

side chats'; rather, what you will find here are initiative, resolution, commands, aggressiveness and blows against the enemy. . . . What matters to us is what the Führer commands; his will is our will, his faith in victory is our faith in victory."

As early as September 1941 Weizsäcker gave Ribbentrop to understand that he would like to be transferred to the Holy See. A year after the speech cited above, he presented his credentials in Rome. His motives, as he later explains them, was that he felt the Vatican provided "the greatest opportunities for influence and at the same time was a good lookout post." He also thought that the Curia had become "quite without interest to our leadership." We may well be skeptical of the latter, so long as the conversations of Pius XII with Hitler's Ambassador continue to be kept secret "in accordance with the good custom of the Curia." Goebbels, at any rate, did not regard Weizsäcker's position at the Holy See as a sinecure, and Weizsäcker himself remarked, when paying his farewell visit to Hitler, that he was going, so to speak, into enemy territory. We can see from Goebbels' diary that just at this particular time the Propaganda Minister was far from placing a light evaluation on the Vatican. He said to Weizsäcker that he "would not consider himself capable of filling" the latter's post of ambassador to the Holy See. Weizsäcker replied: "But I should consider you capable of that"—"and our conversation ended in malicious laughter on both sides."[57] Even the "admonitory" comments of the Pope at their first meeting, after Weizsäcker had presented his credentials, were "never published, contrary to the usual custom." Weizsäcker seems at least to be suggesting that there was a great deal behind this silence.

The Jesuit Father Professor Leiber, an intimate of the Pope, published an article in *Stimmen der Zeit* (March 1961) on *Pius XII and the Jews in Rome*. This was in connection with the publication of a volume of photographs, *Der gelbe Stern*, in which Weizsäcker's letter of October 28, 1945 (quoted at the end of the play) was reprinted. I should like to make a few comments on Professor Leiber's article:

Weizsäcker was glossing over the facts when he wrote: "Since further action on the Jewish problem is probably not to be expected here in Rome . . ."

Father Leiber is not the only one to attest that the persecution

---

[57] *Ibid.,* p. 285.

of the Jews "lasted until the German withdrawal from Rome on June 4, 1944." Pius XII's failure to act was, therefore, not just a temporary matter. Rather, for nearly nine months he looked on in silence while the victims were being loaded on trucks in front of the very door of the Vatican. Let us consider the strategic situation at the time. On October 13, 1943 the Badoglio government declared war on Hitler. On October 16 the Americans crossed the Volturno. There was no longer any reason for the Vatican to still be seriously afraid of Hitler. The author was repeatedly assured at the Vatican that no one there really expected Hitler to commit the folly of occupying the Vatican and taking Pius XII into a kind of Babylonian Captivity, such as had befallen the fourteenth-century Popes at Avignon—for all that a few timid souls allowed themselves to believe those rumors. Not for fifteen minutes did the Vatican seriously discuss a proposal that the Curia move to South America for the duration of the occupation of Rome. When among his intimates Hitler vented his rage and disappointment at the arrest of Mussolini—so short a time after he had met with the Duce—he actually considered for a moment "while seizing the responsible men in Rome also to take on the Vatican." It was reported to the Führer's Headquarters that the Vatican had plunged into feverish diplomatic activity. Himmler (according to Schellenberg), Goebbels and Ribbentrop (as Goebbels writes) were "most vigorously opposed to anything of the sort. I do not think it is necessary to break into the Vatican, while on the other hand I consider that any such measure would have singularly dire consequences for the world-wide effectiveness of our actions." That same day Goebbels appended the following note to his diary entry: "In any case everyone, including the Führer, now agrees that the Vatican must be excepted from the measures we intend to take." Before the Germans occupied Rome in September, the Vatican officially inquired, through Weizsäcker, whether its rights would be guaranteed. Hitler answered this inquiry affirmatively. After the entry of the Germans, General Stahel, the commandant of the city, got in touch with the Vatican and posted guards who "had orders to prevent any violation of Vatican territory." Presumably this step also made it difficult for fugitives to break through to the protection of the Vatican unless the Papal authorities had been forewarned of their arrival.

Rahn, the German Ambassador to the Quirinal, who in his memoirs considerably exaggerates the importance of his efforts to protect the Vatican from Hitler, concluded his report at the Führer's Headquarters on the situation in occupied Rome as follows: " 'By the way, I forgot to mention that I have concluded a little special concordat with the Vatican through General Stahel.' Bormann, the bitter enemy of the Catholic Church, blew up, and Hitler looked at me in surprise. In the style of a businessman's account of a deal, I then gave a report on the contributions the Vatican had made to the restoration of quiet and order in Rome, which the two security detachments—all we had available—would scarcely have been able to accomplish alone. For my part I had naturally been forced to guarantee that the Pope's person, the Roman clergy and the property of the Church were protected under all circumstances. 'It is strictly business,' I concluded, 'and the balance is at least as much in our favor as in the Vatican's.' I seemed to have chosen the right tone. Hitler said: 'Yes, those Roman gentlemen understand business.' "[58]

Most Italian Jews had fled to the American troops in southern Italy in time. Among the Papal relief organizations, the St. Raphael's Society arranged the emigration to America of 1,500 Jews; 4,000 were hidden in various religious houses.

Professor Leiber writes that against the background of these relief measures, Weizsäcker's letter to the Foreign Office takes on another aspect. But that Herr von Weizsäcker felt the deportations to be "embarrassing," is embarrassing to read. His letter so plainly reveals gratification that the Pope did not protest that no one would ever suspect the writer to have been a resistance fighter against Hitler. How could anyone in Berlin have become suspicious of Weizsäcker (who incidentally does not devote a single line in his memoirs to the deportations of the Jews from Rome) if his letter had made the "indignation" of the Pope seem even more dramatic and had created the impression that Pius XII was ready to proceed with the utmost resolution against the murderers? But in fact Weizsäcker did the opposite.

By his ironical allusion to the heartless drivel in the *Osservatore Romano* he so completely reassured Berlin that the Germans continued to hunt Jews in Rome for eight months, whenever the impulse struck them. The letter also says a great deal for the Ambassador's diplomatic skill in handling the Holy Father. That Weizsäcker should have sent this letter to Berlin at all becomes even less understandable when we read that ten days earlier, at

[58] Rudolf Rahn, *Ruheloses Leben* (Düsseldorf, 1949).

the beginning of the arrests, he spontaneously wrote to the Foreign Office to say that the Curia was deeply concerned, that the Pope was being forced out of his reserve and that the enemy's propaganda would stir up "dissension between us and the Curia." Why, then, did he reverse himself and make a point of erasing Berlin's last fear of Pius XII?

It is only too easy to suggest that he wanted to convince Berlin of the effectiveness of his mission at the Vatican since this change of attitude on the part of the Pope would naturally have to be ascribed to his influence. But is there any other explanation—since one must assume, after all, that Weizsäcker was actually opposed to the deportations? As we have said, Canaris had told him about the mass murders of the Jews as far back as the autumn of 1941 —for which reason he can scarcely have believed his own phrase about "used for labor in Italy itself." He did, after all, follow the Allied news reports. As was well known, more women and children than men had been taken away. To work? It seems improbable that he did not know that the order for the arrest of the Jews, which SS Chief Kappler received from Berlin, explicitly spoke of "liquidation" of the Jews. Consul Moellhausen of the Embassy at the Quirinal had received a reprimand for using the word "liquidate" in an official telegram. Whereupon he told Weizsäcker's closest associate, Embassy Secretary von Kessel, about his intervention on behalf of the Jews. Both men took comfort in the thought that the Jews would be able to buy themselves off by paying ransom and thus would at least "be physically spared."

At the Nuremberg Trials von Kessel, who undoubtedly had told Weizsäcker about this, testified in court: "If he (the Pope) did not protest, he failed to do so because he told himself, quite rightly: If I protest, Hitler will be driven to madness; not only will that not help the Jews, but we must expect that they will then be killed all the more. . . ." During the arrests in 1943 von Kessel thought differently. It is said in the Vatican nowadays that he was the *only* unequivocal and resolute anti-Nazi in the German Embassy. And he did, indeed, take positive action, together with Gerhard Gumpert, legation secretary of the Economic Section of the German Embassy at the Quirinal. Gumpert arranged with Kessel for Pancrazius Pfeiffer, Father General of the Salvatorian Order, to bring a letter to the German commandant of the city which threatened that "for the first time since the beginning of the war" the Pope would issue an un-neutral statement. Bishop Hudal promptly signed this letter without consulting his superiors. As rector of the German Catholic Church in Rome, Hudal requested "that in Rome and vicinity these arrests be instantly stopped; otherwise I fear that the Pope will take a public stand against them, which would inevitably serve anti-German propagandists as a weapon against us Germans." This letter alone (we cannot compare it with anything from the pen of an Italian bishop because no Italian bishop ever protested openly against the persecution of the Jews) should be enough to shield Bishop Hudal from the condemnation hurled at him only because he, like almost all the clergy, was duped by Hitler for a while. A further point in his honor: he hid Jews in the monastery dell'Anima.

Gumpert quoted from this letter of the bishop's when he wrote to the Foreign Office in Berlin. Weizsäcker, too, alluded to it in his letter to Berlin of October 17, 1943. But in that famous letter he did not—as Gumpert said he did when testifying in his behalf—"emphatically demand the immediate cessation of deportations of the Jews." And add to that the fact that ten days later Weizsäcker sent his reassuring letter to the Foreign Office; language lacks the polite euphemism to describe such conduct.

He even "advised" the Vatican in a way which played into Hitler's hands. Gumpert made a statement concerning that at Nuremberg: "Later, when I bade goodbye to Weizsäcker because I was being transferred to the Embassy in Northern Italy, he spoke of this incident once more and said in so many words: 'That was another stinking mess.' In reaction to the reports, he said, they had got cold feet in Berlin and stopped the deportations immediately. He added: 'I can also tell you that at the time I spoke very confidentially with Montini [the present Pope; then Undersecretary of State] and advised him that any protest by the Pope would only result in the deportations being really carried out in a thoroughgoing fashion. I know how our people react in these matters. Montini, incidentally, saw the point.' "

What we have here is a morass. Weizsäcker's closest collaborator, von Kessel, tries to force the Vatican to drop its reticence. When at least one German bishop takes him up on his suggestion, Weizsäcker temporarily makes the bishop's demand his own. He threatens Berlin with an ultimatum by the Pope; this obviously means that he regards such an ultimatum as a deterrent. But simultaneously he tells the Pope's closest associate that a statement by the Holy Father "would only result in the deportations being really carried out in a thorough-going fashion." And Montini, or as the case may be, the Pope, are only too glad to hear that, although they know, although every child in Rome knows, that the first Jews were already being loaded into the boxcars; that the round-ups are going on regardless; and that Weizsäcker's words are therefore —to put it mildly—sheer twaddle.

Finally, by the following weekend (October 25-26), when the *Osservatore Romano* reports that "the Pope's universal and fatherly works of mercy . . . know no limits," the first 615 Roman Jews had already arrived in Auschwitz, and 468 of them were already in the crematorium.

Father Leiber says that Pius XII did not protest because he thought "in more comprehensive terms." When Father Leiber reports that in Rumania, for example, deportations had been stopped after the Nuncio there intervened, this only confirms the main thesis of this play: that Hitler drew back from the extermination program as soon as high German clerics (as in the case of euthanasia) or the Vatican, represented by a Nuncio, forcibly intervened. *Then* Hitler drew back—in every, every single case. Therefore Leiber's conclusion—that by its very support of these isolated measures of assistance a strong pronouncement from the most prominent of all Christians would "very likely have condemned these efforts to failure"—strikes us as wholly unconvincing. The contrary is true!

Moreover, in reading Professor Leiber's otherwise objective article we must not fall under the impression that the SS in Rome terrorized the clergy. The SS was well aware that many religious houses also served as hiding places for Jews and other fugitives. They even knew that the Italian general Bencivenga was operating a radio in the Lateran, and that an American agent with broadcasting apparatus was at times located in the Deutsches Haus on the Campo Santo Teutonico. But in spite of this arrant misuse of ecclesiastical buildings, Kappler was careful not to invade extra-territorial property. To be sure, there were some exceptions. For example, Professor August Bea, Rector of the Pontifical Bible Institute, complained to Weizsäcker that in October 1943 five SS men had come looking in his Institute for a "formerly Jewish" servant.

The worst invasion of a Papal institution, and the one that had the most serious consequences, was committed by a gang of Italian Fascist militia under their brutal bandit chieftain Koch, who was executed after the war. These Italians are also said to have made the attack upon the Monastery of St. Paul's-outside-the-walls, which Father Leiber ascribes to the German SS.

The foreign press, reporting the atrocities in Rome, was apparently so dismayed at the Pope's passivity that it had perforce to invent the ridiculous story that the Germans were holding the Holy Father in virtual captivity. However, during that same month of October the *Osservatore Romano* prominently published its official statement. "This expressed gratitude to our troops for having respected the Papacy and the Vatican City," Weizsäcker said with satisfaction. "We also promised in this *communiqué* that we would maintain the same attitude in the future."[59]

Such was the statement in *Osservatore Romano* in that month of terror, October 1943. Herr von Weizsäcker could certainly not have found a better place for his reply to the world press which was heavily exercised over the events in Rome.

Weizsäcker remained in office to prevent worse things from happening; the Pope remained silent, as Leiber writes, to prevent worse things from happening. A strange justification when we cannot conceive anything worse than what was actually happening— the most ruthless manhunt in human history. Leiber, and Giovannetti also, maintain that a Pope may not concretely and in detail reprehend the misdemeanors and crimes of one side in a war since his doing so would be exploited by the other side for propaganda. But in fact Pius XII pointedly and precisely condemned incidents which really concerned him. For example, he wrote personally to Roosevelt about the bombing of Rome and protested against the destruction of San Lorenzo. He also made a protest against the extraordinarily cowardly and senseless bomb-throwing on the Via Rasella which killed thirty-three German soldiers, most of them South Tyroleans who were not gladly wearing Hitler's uniform anyhow, and ten Italians, six of them children. But why did he not condemn the criminal vengeance taken for that act: the murder of 335 hostages, or the hunting down of the Jews? But above all, how could a protest against the extermination of the Jews be interpreted as a partisan intervention in the war? What had Hitler's genocidal measures to do with the Second World War? They were possible and undertaken at that time only because the German Army had already subjected the whole Continent to Hitler. But did the extermination program decide a single battle?

[59] Von Weizsäcker, *op. cit.*, p. 290.

Was Auschwitz or were the gigantic mass graves of murdered civilians battlegrounds? Both sides committed nefarious crimes in the air war against open cities; both sides let prisoners starve or killed them outright. In such cases it was appropriate to react as Pope Benedict XV did in the First World War, that is, as Leiber writes, "to enter a protest against injustice and violence wherever these might occur." Though that too should have been done in unequivocal, not in cryptic phrases. But neither the "Final Solution" nor the "euthanasia program" are to be taken as the misdeeds of a Power at war. Nothing can better further the creation of a pro-Hitler legend than to include his plan for gassing an entire race within the general framework of belligerent actions—thus dismissing it as one of the unfortunate crimes which have always accompanied warfare. And does not Pacelli's excommunication of active Communists (which his wise and very humane successor may well feel to be an unfortunate legacy) prove that Pius XII could, when he wanted to, speak out quite plainly in the political realm?

When Father Leiber suggests that "Providence entrusted the guidance of the Church through the war years not to Pius XI, but to Pius XII" for the very reason that Pacelli, in contrast to his spirited predecessor, could not easily be moved to take a public stand, a layman in matters of faith can only stand amazed at such insight into the scheme of Creation.

And yet the question forcibly arises: was it not an unprecedented tragedy for Christendom and for the victims of Hitler that Pius XI was called from the scene just on the eve of the war? During the election of his successor, several cardinals are said to have been opposed to Pacelli. According to Cardinal Tardini, they are reputed to have said: "Pacelli is a man of peace and the world now needs a Pope of war."

If only those cardinals had won their point! We cannot read without emotion of one of the last audiences which Pius XI, already failing, gave shortly before his death to Prime Minister Chamberlain and Lord Halifax. The London *Times* reported on February 11, 1939: "And then the Pope—speaking slowly and gently in clear, scholarly English—told them exactly what he thought of reactionary régimes and of the duties of democracies; of racial persecution and of the pressing need of helping refugees. . . . He pointed to a diptych containing portraits of Sir Thomas More and Cardinal John Fisher—two Englishmen, he said, who were often in his thoughts. 'I often sit here thinking of the English.

I am happy to believe . . . that these two Englishmen stood for what is best in the English race; in their courage, their determination, their readiness to fight—to die, if need be—for what they knew to be right. I like to think, indeed, I am sure, that those qualities—the courage and the readiness—live on still among the English. You agree with me?'

"None spoke, held by the words of the old man. . . . The Pope talked on—not lecturing them, rather leading their thoughts to the problems and struggles before them. The problems were many, greater perhaps than other ages had to face. They had a hard task—'But you know better than I do what is in the English race.' "

That was a legacy, an unmistakable *avis au lecteur* directed at Hitler, who was just on the point of marching to Prague. Who would ever have heard such direct words from Pius XII, who immediately after Hitler's arrival at the Hradschin Palace said to Count Ciano that he intended to establish a more conciliatory policy toward Germany than his predecessor. Then there is Pacelli as Chancellor Brüning knew him; when Brüning forbade the Nuncio to interfere in German internal affairs, Pacelli began to weep. In all the deliberately cryptic speeches of this incessant speechmaker of a Pope one cannot find any sentences that approach in pithiness the words of Pius XI when that Pope was already marked by death. After the latter's death, Mussolini exulted: "So that stubborn old man is dead now!" And he was just as pleased with Pacelli's election as were the Nazis.

At the time of Pacelli's death in 1958, the Paris Jewish newspaper *L'Arche* published an extraordinarily bitter essay, *Les Silences de Pie XII,* which differed radically from the usual obituaries and went so far as to maintain that one of the reasons for the silence of Pius XII had been the medieval anti-Semitism of the Catholic Church. The author, Rabi, based his thesis on the attitude of the French clergy and of the Vatican toward the anti-Jewish laws of Vichy France. The Church, he wrote, had opposed in the name of Christian love the physical persecution of the Jews, but in the name of justice had approved social discrimination against them. Thomas Aquinas was quoted in that connection. . . .

In *The Deputy*, on the other hand, there is no imputation that Pius XII and his clergy had anti-Semitic feelings. I have wanted to keep only to provable facts. Thus I quote here from the report of the Italian banker Angelo Donati, to whom many Jews owe their rescue, and do not cite the bitter personal experiences which that brave man had with a number of priests during the period of the persecutions. Those episodes are fully balanced by the numerous examples of help rendered by other clerics. On the other hand, I must refer to Donati's report to the Centre de Documentation Juive Contemporaine (Document CC XVIII-78) concerning the official attitude of diplomats of the Holy See. In the autumn of 1942 Donati had handed to the Pope, by way of the Father General of the Capuchin Order, a note on the situation of the Jews in Southern France. He asked for Papal assistance. None was forthcoming.

In August 1943 the British Ambassador to the Holy See, Sir D'Arcy Osborne, told him that in the course of the year he had repeatedly sent requests to the Pope to issue a formal condemnation of the German atrocities. Osborne told Donati that after the Papal Christmas Message of 1941, which in general terms deplored all horrors of the war, Secretary of State Cardinal Maglione said to him at a reception: "You see, the Holy Father has given consideration to the recommendations of your government." Osborne replied that such an all-embracing indictment, which might just as well be directed against the bombing of German cities, was *not* what the British Government had in mind.

These reports are confirmed by other sources. See especially *Foreign Relations of the United States, Diplomatic Papers 1942, Volume 3*, Washington, 1961.

While the *Osservatore Romano* was condemning Stalin's aggression against Finland in language ("coldly calculated crime, law of the jungle, the most cynical aggression of modern times") whose severity contrasts radically with its noncommittal article on the deportations of the Jews from Rome and with the Holy Father's vague laments about the war; while Cardinal Maglione was saying to Sumner Welles as late as the spring of 1940 that Germany had so far come out the loser in all diplomatic negotiations with Russia, and was voicing Italy's fears that Stalin might make further advances even into the Balkans, the moment soon came when in the face of Hitler's crushing victories even the Vatican began to regard the Russians as the lesser evil. We learn this from the Pope's personal physician and also from the statement that Maglione made to Princess Colonna at Christmas 1941. Even Mussolini welcomed with relief, indeed with joy, Hitler's defeat on the outskirts of Moscow. Ciano, however, very soon noted in his diary: "Alfieri (the Italian Ambassador in Berlin) writes that the failures on the Russian front, and the consequences which follow from them, have already exceeded the limits within which they might have been useful to us."

The Vatican, as always, saw things in a considerably more sober light than a good many of the bishops or than, say, the Turkish Foreign Minister, who exclaimed immediately after receiving news of Hitler's surprise assault on Russia: "This is not a war—it is a crusade!" Spurred on by Papen, this same Foreign Minister was immediately ready to call upon the British Prime Minister, through the British Ambassador, to bury the hatchet in Europe in order to "stand together with one mind against the Power whose program is the annihilation of the West." That attempt failed. On the following day Churchill told the world: "The Nazi regime is indistinguishable from the worst features of Communism. . . . It excels all forms of human wickedness in the efficiency of its cruelty and ferocious aggression. . . . We have but one aim and one single, irrevocable purpose. We are resolved to destroy Hitler and every vestige of the Nazi regime."[60]

Herr von Papen, who ignores the question of whether the Russians would have marched to the Elbe if Hitler had not attacked them, states that with this speech the Prime Minister "inaugurated the policy which . . . has led to the present condition of Europe" —an opinion that enjoys growing popularity nowadays and which as early as 1959 was shared by all those who condemn Churchill and Roosevelt for not having been so astute as to defend the Christian West by making common cause with the engineer of Auschwitz.

Franz von Papen, Vice-Chancellor and later Ambassador, was undoubtedly never Hitler's friend and was seldom admitted to his confidence. In fact, Hitler had von Papen's closest associates murdered even before the outbreak of the war. Yet von Papen, as a good Catholic, was nevertheless persuaded that his nephews, killed on Hitler's battlefields in Russia, had "fallen in the struggle against irreligion and the powers of darkness." That sort of thing is still another proof of how valuable it was for Hitler to maintain his peace with the Vatican, or at least its outward semblance. People like von Papen simply laughed at Roosevelt when, as Giovannetti puts it, "the President subsequently repeatedly assured the Pope

---

[60] *The Unrelenting Struggle: War Speeches by the Right Hon. Winston S. Churchill,* Charles Eade, ed. (Boston: Little, Brown, 1942), p. 172.

that there was a strong possibility that Bolshevism might be converted to democracy and abandon its Marxist-Leninist demand for world revolution."[61]

But there was something that seemed even more terrible than the Nazis or the Russians—the specter of a new agreement between Hitler and Stalin. It is unlikely that we shall ever learn precisely how substantial were the approaches the two parties made to one another. Probably most of the stories of such overtures were sheer rumor or ruse. Hitler himself mistrusted most of these offers. Herr von Papen, who early realized that Gemany alone could not defeat Russia, in the spring of 1942 sent an emissary from Ankara to some of the Pope's intimates, only to be told that they saw no prospect of persuading the western Allies to engage in peace negotiations. And von Papen commented: "The war situation was such that there were strong fears that Stalin, who was already demanding a second front, might reach some compromise with Hitler. For this reason alone, no thought of peace talks could be entertained. Our efforts were therefore to no purpose."[62]

As late as August 1943 Hassell noted: "If Hitler makes an agreement with Stalin, the resulting evil will be inconceivable. It would be different with a decent, politically mature Germany." And according to Fritz Hesse, it was only after hearing Schulenburg's sensational information that Hitler was on the point of reaching an agreement with Stalin through the mediation of the Emperor of Japan, that Count von Stauffenberg abruptly decided "to abandon his original plan and to carry out the assassination and the *putsch* at once . . . and not to wait until . . . the bloodsucking monster had once again regained strength by this treacherous gamble with fate and would be able to maintain himself in power and drench the earth with German blood."[63]

Which steps the Pope, out of fear of Stalin, let himself be persuaded to take toward arranging a peace between Germany and the West will probably never be determined now because, ludicrously enough, since 1945 it has been regarded as "impossible" for anyone to admit that he ever dreamed of making peace with Hitler—for the sake of peace. As if the opposition circles in Germany ever enjoyed, during the war, the prestige abroad which was attributed to them after 1945—in their obituaries! Hitherto there

---

[61] Giovannetti, *op. cit.*

[62] Von Papen, *op. cit.*, p. 489.

[63] Hesse, *op. cit.*

has been great reluctance even to acknowledge that, for example, Hitler's loyal German Secret Service was seeking an armistice with the Western Powers, and that it was aided in these efforts by Count Ledochowsky, the Polish Jesuit general. In the middle of 1942 Weizsäcker's circle possibly believed for a while that England was at last coming round and would no longer refuse to make peace even with Hitler.

Nor will we ever learn the true facts behind the Spanish diplomatic efforts. In February 1943 the Spanish Foreign Minister, Count Jordana, wrote to the arrogant British Ambassador in Madrid "that people in England should reflect calmly on the matter, since should Russia succeed in conquering Germany, there will be no one who can contain her."[64] In April of the same year Count Jordana volunteered the services of Spain as a mediator between Germany and the Western Powers. Had he been empowered by the Vatican to place such great hopes in the Pope as he expressed? About this time the Vatican vigorously denounced the distortion of a speech by Cardinal Spellman and declared that it had nothing whatsoever to do with the war aims of the Western Powers.

Krupp

The use of foreign forced labor by some of the greatest German industrial firms became a prime political issue because, among other reasons, of the *treatment* of these workers at the Krupp plants. Although this chapter in the history of the times is highly typical, I have only been able to touch on it in *The Deputy*.

First of all, let us not forget that there were many decent industrialists, such as Bosch and Reusch, and that the subordinate managers of a good many plants could continue being humane. There was, for example, Karl Beckurts, head of the state-owned Gustloff Armament Works in Weimar, who during the war was in charge of countless inmates of Buchenwald. In 1949 a former prisoner-worker of his, Erik Blumenfeld, now a prominent member of the Christian Democratic Party, brought Beckurts to Hamburg to be manager of the North German Coal and Coke Works. Then again there was Berthold Beitz, who in 1953 was to become a Krupp general manager. Though not a member of the Nazi Party

---

[64] Viscount Templewood (Sir Samuel Hoare), *Complacent Dictator* (New York: Knopf, 1947), p. 184.

and virtually unknown during the war, he administered the oil fields at Boryslaw in occupied Poland and contrived to help persecuted Jews and Poles. A good many managers of plants tenaciously held on to their Jewish employes thus preventing their deportation to the gas chambers.

Should not a celebrated captain of industry, whom Hitler often visited, have been able to demand respect from the lower ranks of Nazis? The same problem arises here as with the clergy. Lesser priests were running grave risks when they gave help. The German bishops and cardinals were not arrested even if they openly opposed Hitler's decrees.

Then, as always, everything depended on the human stature of the individual. What counted was the extent to which a man found it possible to recognize a fellow man even in a convict. Even in the Krupp plant there were people who would now and again slip some bread to an underage Jewish girl in rags and wooden clogs who had come from Auschwitz to work in the rolling mill. That was forbidden. If someone reported the act, there would be trouble. How was it possible for the head of the concern not to observe, as he made the rounds of his plant, the conditions in which his foreign workers had to work and live? How could he not know that members of the Krupp plant police beat deportees? Of course he had a great deal to do. But during the war even Hitler encouraged each of his guards to "speak to him about his personal problems" as he went about headquarters. Out of sentimentality, we would say today. But if the largest employer in Greater Germany and the members of his family had showed some of this "sentimentality" toward the army of unfortunate foreigners who labored in their factories, then possibly ninety-eight out of one hundred and thirty-two children would not have died in the camp of Voerde near Essen, and the letters to and from eastern workers in Essen would not have been confiscated and burned twice a week.

On June 26, 1947 Alfried Krupp von Bohlen declared at his interrogation in Nuremberg: "I only know of one single case of ill-treatment, or attempted ill-treatment, of a foreign worker, an eastern worker to be exact. . . . This happened at the beginning of the period in which eastern workers were assigned to us for the first time. At that time a report of such an incident was made to the Direktorium and the Direktorium resolved to publish general instructions, which characterized the iniquity of such conduct towards foreign workers and warned against a repetition of such incidents. . . . I placed full confidence in all my colleagues that they, by their own initiative, would strive to eradicate any possible intolerant conditions of this kind."[65]

When on December 16, 1942 eighteen Dutch workers employed in Essen-Bergeborbeck sent a letter to Alfried von Bohlen in person, requesting improvement of their inadequate rations, he ordered Max Ihn to eliminate these abuses and to report to him on the steps he had taken.

The Krupp Board of Directors, of which Alfried von Bohlen was a regular member even before the outbreak of the war and whose meetings he normally attended—from April to December 1943 as chairman, subsequently as sole owner of the firm—often discussed the serious difficulties in feeding and housing the foreign workers. The Board was constantly striving to relieve the situation. But even if we assume that after 1942 Alfried von Bohlen ceased to hear anything more about the use of clubs in his factories by members of the Krupp plant police, the disturbing question of responsibility persists undiminished—and does not concern this man or this firm alone. Norbert Mühlen in his book *The Incredible Krupps* has very impressively considered the whole complex of questions. He asks whether "moral myopia, cowardice and lack of feeling in a businessman are crimes," and whether in general "actions by people under totalitarian rule can be judged by the principles of a society which assures freedom of conscience and of action to every citizen."

Thilo von Wilmowsky, brother-in-law and associate of Gustav Krupp and president of the Central European Economic Council, and Krupp General Manager Ewald Löser decided these questions in what they considered a highly honorable manner. Both were exposed, after the uprising of July 20, 1944, as close confidants of Carl Goerdeler and Ulrich von Hassell. Wilmowsky was sent to a concentration camp. Löser was condemned to death, but escaped execution because of the end of the war. In the Krupp trial the Allies sentenced him to seven years imprisonment, although he had voluntarily resigned from the Board of Directors in March 1943. Ulrich von Hassell, a member of the presiding board of the Central European Economic Council and thus closely connected with industry, noted in 1943: "Löser, the Director General of Krupp, an intelligent man who sees things clearly, recently said

---

[65] *Trials of War Criminals Before the Nuernberg Military Tribunals*, Vol. IX (Washington: Government Printing Office, 1950), p. 805.

that the leading people, with the servile Krupp-Bohlen and the cold-blooded, egotistical Zangen at their head, stood behind Hitler because they thought this was the way to make large profits and keep their workers in line. Clear realization of national needs was found much more frequently among the workers. Of course it was very difficult to determine the real mood of the workers, because everybody was spying on everybody else."[66] Part of what Löser told the Allies in 1945 about Alfried von Bohlen is on file in Paris, still unpublished.

Professor Golo Mann, discussing the last election in March 1933, writes in his *Deutsche Geschichte des 19. und 20. Jahrunderts*: "The Nazis knew how the state power could be utilized in an election, given sufficient imagination and brashness, to rouse the enthusiasm of their own followers, to intimidate the weak, and to club down their opponents. 'Now it is easy to wage the struggle,' the propaganda chief of the Party wrote in his diary, 'because we can make use of all means for our own benefit. The radio and press are at our disposal; we will put on a masterpiece of propaganda. This time, too, we are of course not short of money.' They really were not. A group of industrialists, headed by Krupp, was persuaded to place at the disposal of the government an election fund of three million marks—the new Prussian Minister of the Interior, Göring, explaining to the gentlemen that since this would be the last election in ten, probably in one hundred years, a certain generosity would be worthwhile."

In other words, he promised the industrialists nothing more nor less than dictatorship. How is it that Norbert Mühlen thinks the discussions at this meeting in Berlin were so moderate in tone?

Alfried von Bohlen's fortune was returned to him. He served about half of his prison sentence. There is little likelihood that he will ever have to keep his promise to the Allies to break up his holdings by selling the mining and steel operations at reasonable prices. Some persons may be pleased by all that. But it was not enough for certain politicians in Bonn. In November 1961 President Kennedy had just sent General Clay, the initiator of the Berlin airlift, back to Germany to stand once more as the protector of West Berlin. That same month a group of Bonn politicians char-

---

[66] Ulrich von Hassell, *Diaries, 1939–1944* (Garden City: Doubleday, 1947), p. 288.

tered a special train in order to make a pilgrimage, as to a national monument, to the firm of Krupp and the person of Alfried von Bohlen—the same man whose sentence in Nuremberg this same General Clay had expressly confirmed in 1949. Looking back at the trials, he later wrote: "The full evidence will provide history with an unparalleled record of how greed and avarice attract unscrupulous hands to bring misery and destruction to the world. . . . Certainly, in reviewing the cases which came before me, I felt no hesitancy in approving the sentences."[67]

It makes a depressing footnote to the story of the Krupp forced laborers that Theodor Heuss in his address for the Krupp celebration seemed to imply that Krupp had been condemned for doing no more than innumerable armaments manufacturers the world over. And the Ukrainian Khrushchev, when he toasted the House of Krupp at a Leipzig Fair, must have forgotten (although he would surely have heard of it) what became of a good many of his fellow-countrymen in Essen who were turned over to the Gestapo by the firm of Krupp. (See, *inter alia*, Document NIK-12362, Prosecution Exhibit 998 in *Trials of War Criminals Before the Nuernberg Military Tribunals,* Vol. IX, p. 1321; English translation on page 910.)

"To be present or not to be present is a political act," said the magazine *Der Spiegel* in connection with the firm's jubilee. Thus, among the members of the Bonn Diplomatic Corps, the American, Russian, British, and French Ambassadors were notably absent. But the Bishop of Essen put in an appearance. One wonders whether any of these ecclesiastical dignitaries in the vicinity of Essen ever gained entry into one of the "work-training camps" (i.e. disciplinary camps) which Krupp set up at the request of the Gestapo, about which a Catholic priest—one of the shaven-headed forced laborers imprisoned there—testified at Nuremberg.

Some of the documents and the verdict of the Tribunal are printed in English in the above-mentioned *Trials of War Criminals*, etc. Institutions in Göttingen, Nuremberg, Munich, and Paris also possess the documents, sometimes only in part, sometimes in the original language. Here are two documents which, along with others even more telling, were drawn upon for the second scene of Act One and for Act Five.

---

[67] Lucius D. Clay, *Decision in Germany* (Garden City: Doubleday, 1950), p. 252.

Cast Steel Works, 15 October 1942

File Note

Re: Telephone call by Colonel Breyer of OKW, Dept. PW's, Berlin.

Colonel Breyer who wanted to talk to Mr. von Bülow, requested me to pass on the following to Mr. von Bülow:

OKW has lately received from their own offices and recently also in anonymous letters from the German population a considerable number of complaints about the treatment of prisoners of war at the firm Krupp (especially that they are being beaten, and furthermore that they do not receive the food and time off that is due to them. Among other things the prisoners are said not to have received any potatoes for six weeks). All these things would no longer occur anywhere else in Germany. OKW has already requested several times that full food rations should be issued to the prisoners. In addition if they have to perform heavy work, they must also be given corresponding time off, the same as the German workers. Colonel Breyer also informed me that the conditions at Krupp would be looked into either by the service command or by the OKW itself. He had requested General v.d. Schulenberg on the occasion of a trip to call at Krupp in person concerning this matter; unfortunately this had not been possible.[68]

By 1942, even the Nazi district command had to intervene with the firm in behalf of the foreign workers, according to the affidavitt of Max Ihn, one of Alfried Krupp's co-defendants at Nuremberg. Here is an extract from his affidavit:

On 31 March 1943 I became a deputy member of the Directorate. I now came into contact with Mr. Alfried Krupp. About 1,000 employees came under my direct care. In 1943 there were about 15,000 employees in the whole of the Cast Steel Works, about 55,000 workers (including foreign workers) so that about 70,000 people were employed in all. The highest number of foreign workers employed was about 20,000. I have named this figure from my own knowledge and not from the letter from Mr. Kupke in which he told me he

---

[68] *Trials of War Criminals Before the Nuernberg Military Tribunals, op. cit.,* pp. 1227 f.

had said during the interrogation by the FSS [Field Security Service—British Counter Intelligence Service] that 20,000 foreign workers were employed. The working hours for these foreigners were laid down by the works, in other words, I was responsible for that. Youths were employed among them from 14 years on.

Foreign workers arrived for the first time in 1941-42.

The first concentration camp prisoners arrived in the summer or autumn of 1944 although the firm of Krupp had already asked for a number of them, between 1,100 and 1,500, on 22 September 1942. I was responsible for the employment of these people as well as for correspondence in regards to the procurement of these concentration camp inmates. Since I cannot remember from whom I received the order to carry on the correspondence about concentration camp prisoners, I must take the responsibility for it. The food supply of all camps, including special and concentration camps was also under me. I admit that, at first, there were many complaints from the foreign workers about the bad feeding while later on complaints were received about the food from time to time.

I knew that steel birches had been distributed in the works (but not in the camps). I was informed that workers were beaten up in the works and camps. I informed the Directorate about these cases, and I spoke especially to Dr. Janssen about these occurrences and gave orders that the beatings were not allowed. I admit that mishandlings had taken place in Mr. Loeser's time.

The 520 concentration camp inmates who were employed by Krupp were ordered by me on instructions from the Directorate. The request about these prisoners was talked over by the Directorate in my presence and it is quite possible that Mr. Alfried Krupp von Bohlen was present. As far as I know, these prisoners came from Buchenwald. I talked to the Buchenwald camp commander personally here at Krupp's once, and he informed me of the conditions under which we could employ concentration camp prisoners. Dr. Lehmann traveled to Buchenwald on my orders in order to settle the conditions under which we could employ the prisoners. I did not know that Krupp had employed 22 concentration camp prisoners from Auschwitz.

The concentration camp prisoners were housed by Krupp

in wooden barracks in the Humboldtstrasse. I was informed about what happened in this camp.

I repeat that in 1942 I was responsible for matters concerning workers (German and foreign). Even then the conditions in the camps were such that Gauleiter Schlessman wrote saying that if conditions were not improved he would take action himself. Surely Dr. Loeser talked over the conditions at that time with Mr. Gustav Krupp von Bohlen.

The workers who were incapable of work were transferred. Dr. Janssen suggested that the 520 Jewesses who were employed at Krupp's should be taken away before the occupation took place, namely back to Buchenwald. I assume that Mr. Alfried Krupp von Bohlen must have known about it. When I was taken ill on 22 February 1945, I gave Mr. Lehmann the order to send these people back to Buchenwald.[69]

Even Hitler, in a conference with Minister of Armaments Speer held on March 21-22, 1942, stated that the Russian civilian workers should be issued adequate rations and not be kept behind barbed wire like prisoners of war. The Russians, he commanded, "must receive an absolutely sufficient amount of food and Sauckel [Reich Director of Labor Assignment] was to keep after Backe [Minister of Food Supplies] to make sure that such feeding measures were taken."[70]

Krupp sent his men to assemble the machines at Auschwitz in July 1943, not in October, as is suggested in Act Five. Shortly afterwards, in a letter of September 7, 1943, Alfried Krupp von Bohlen and Halbach wrote, in regard to the setting up of a fuse factory:

. . . I have told Mr. Reiff to pay special attention to the production at Auschwitz, for which he will have the best opportunity at Breslau. Some months ago already Mr. Reiff took advantage of the opportunity to visit Auschwitz and to discuss all the necessary points with our representatives there. With regard to the collaboration of our technical office in Breslau, I can only say that a very close cooperation exists between this office and Auschwitz, and is assured also for the future. With kind regards and Heil Hitler . . .[71]

[69] Ibid., pp. 813–14.
[70] Ibid., p. 877.
[71] Ibid., p. 739.

Licensed Engineer Weinhold and thirty foremen and department heads from Essen who erected the shop with a gang of Auschwitz prisoners had to give written pledges that they would keep secret all matters concerning the Auschwitz camp. On September 1, just as an example, Krupp transferred 23,973 marks to the account of the SS garrison administration of Auschwitz in the Reichsbank in Catowice—for prisoners' labor. But by October 1 Krupp got out of his contract and transferred operations to the Union firm, which had been forced to evacuate its fuse plant in Kharkov.

Mühlen states in his biography of Krupp: " 'Later,' Johannes Schroeder, the valued chief of the Central Department (Finance) of the firm, recalled, 'affected by these air raids and the military situation, we (the Directors) realized that Germany had lost the war, and we discussed it in the strictest confidence with each other.' Krupp then acted against the law for the first time in the Nazi era, and systematically ignored Nazi directives, even if only in the firm's interests. The Nazi Government had given orders that every industrial concern had to invest its entire fluid assets immediately in new installations for war production. In face of the approaching defeat the Board of Directors of Krupp were more interested in 'at least saving something for the postwar period; we wished to lead the firm into the future in some condition of financial stability, which would make its continued existence possible,' Schroeder reports. Even if Germany was to be destroyed, the House of Krupp must survive. Instead of applying the available assets to the war effort and making a loss, the firm secretly followed a new course, namely that of 'keep their assets as fluid as possible. They exempted themselves from the Government loan, cashed in their war damage claims and collected their debts from the Government.' "[72]

Various Details

The setting of the bowling-alley scene was invented, but not the fact that the murderers discussed their monstrous acts in canteens or at table as if they were talking about agricultural policy. Even Eichmann, who in the Jerusalem courtroom made much of the conscientious public servant he had been under Hitler, testified that at the official Wannsee Conference under the chairmanship of

[72] Norbert Mühlen, *The Incredible Krupps* (New York: Holt, 1959).

Heydrich, held on January 20, 1942, when the program for the Final Solution was announced—even then there was a good deal of drinking, although the "gentlemen" of the SS were by no means among themselves, for representatives of Berlin government ministries were present. "Orderlies continually passed the cognac around, and in the end everybody was talking at once—and bluntly." No doubt the usual officers club jokes were bandied about.

The dialogue is based principally on documents which were used in the Krupp Trial, or reprinted by Poliakov and Wulf in their collections. See also the documentation by Mitscherlich about the "Doctors' Trial."

Adolf Galland, one of the most famous fighter pilots of the Second World War, mentioned in his memoirs the kind of "ribbon" customarily used to fasten medals to the collar.

While the Roman Catholic episcopate of Bohemia and Moravia asked Hitler for permission to ring the bells and have a requiem mass said for Heydrich, Vladimir Petrik, a chaplain of the numerically very small Czech Orthodox Church of Saints Cyril and Methodius, hid the patriots who had committed the assassination in the crypt of his church. What is more, he obtained sanction for this step from his superior, the Patriarch of Prague. Like the sacristan and the bishop, he paid for his bravery with his life. He had even sought out the fugitives himself and offered them his protection.

The Order of Christ, founded by Pope John XXII in 1319, consists of a cross adorned with a crown, which hangs from a double gold chain. I have not paid much attention to accuracy in the matter of decorations. In fact, Count Fontana would never have received this decoration; it is reserved to heads of state, including such imposing monarchs as King Victor Emmanuel III of Italy, who in 1941 elevated the Pacellis to the rank of princes—approximately at the same time, incidentally, that the Italian Royal House (such was the story at the Roman Stock Exchange) transferred considerable portions of its wealth abroad by way of the Opera Religiosa, the Vatican private bank established by Pope Pius XII.[73]

It was not in February 1943 but on October 31, 1942 that Pius XII undertook the "dedication of the Church and of the entire human race to the Immaculate Heart of Mary."

---

[73] See: *Der Spiegel*, August 1958.

Cardinal Tardini relates that in 1944, after the death of Cardinal Maglione, the Pope declared: "I do not want associates who work with me, but assistants to carry out my orders." It is well known that from then until his death the Pope did not appoint anyone to fill the vacancy in that key position of Cardinal Secretary of State.

The result of the meeting between Roosevelt and Churchill in Casablanca in January 1943 was the demand for Germany's unconditional surrender.

On February 23 Stalin asserted that the Russian armies alone were having to bear the entire burden of the war. This was a harsh reply to the statement, a few days earlier, by Lend-Lease Administrator Stettinius that America had already delivered 2,900,000 tons of war materials to Russia. During the early years of the war Stalin refused even to meet Roosevelt.

November 1942: Exchange of telegrams between Stalin and Metropolitan Sergius on the twenty-fifth anniversary of the Revolution. Around the same time Goebbels, who was advising politic treatment of both the Catholic and Russian churches, and of the civilian populace, made the following entry in his diary: "It is, for example, very disagreeable for the Party that the local group leader must inform the bereaved of the hero's death of a son, brother or husband. Formerly the Church did this. Now the Party has been charged with it, with the result that in little villages people are scared to death whenever the local group leader comes to their home. The local leader is frequently looked upon as a funereal character and in some parts of our country has been given the nackname of 'Bird of Death' (*Todesvogel*). Before this innovation was introduced I gave an impressive warning as I foresaw the results. But certain sections in the Party in their short-sightedness and in their blind hatred of the Church insisted upon driving out the devil with Beelzebub. The results now are anything but pleasant."[74]

Léon Bérard, Vichy France's Ambassador to the Holy See, asked for a statement from the Vatican in June 1941, when Petain's government published its first anti-Semitic laws. He reported subsequently to Vichy: "It would be unreasonable to allow the Jews to exercise dominion in a Christian state and thus limit the authority

[74] Goebbels, *op. cit.*, p. 242.

of the Catholics. From which it follows that it is legitimate to forbid them access to public office, likewise legitimate to admit them to the universities and to the professions only to a limited extent (numerus clausus) . . ."

A dispatch from Rome dated February 9, 1959 in *The New York Times* stated that Pope John XXIII on that day disclosed the draft of a "stern speech that Pope Pius XI had planned to deliver twenty years ago next Wednesday." Pius XI prepared the notes on his deathbed for an address he wanted to make to the Italian episcopacy in a joint audience on the tenth anniversary of the Lateran Pact signed February 11, 1929. "The death of Pius XI on Feb. 10, 1939," *The New York Times* report went on, "prevented him from publicly comparing Hitler to Emperor Nero and warning mankind against the 'homicidal and suicidal folly' of the armament race at that time. . . . According to this hand-written draft, Pius XI proposed to protest against the Nazi and Fascist press for its 'perverse' distortions of historical truth in its campaign against the Catholic Church and for 'tenaciously denying that there is persecution in Germany.' These denials were accompanied by slanderous charges of politicking hurled at the Church 'in the same way as Nero's persecution was accompanied by an accusation [against Christianity] of having caused Rome's destruction by fire,' the notes of Pius XI went on. Pope Pius XI planned to deplore that Church newspapers were forbidden to 'contradict and correct' the allegations of the totalitarian press. He intended to warn archbishops and bishops against Fascist 'observers and informers, you may truthfully call them spies, who out of zeal and obeying orders listen to what you say and denounce you.' Pope John did not comment on the political implications of the document he was making public. Students of modern history here said the proposed address of Pius XI would have had profound repercussions in Italy if it had been delivered."

It is said that the Jewish mistress of the Auschwitz commandant survived the war. After Rudolf Höss was transferred, she was interrogated by SS Judge Wiebeck. When I applied to the *Institut für Zeitgeschichte* (Institute for Contemporary History) in Munich for the record of the interrogation, I was told: "Part of the testimony contains such raw erotica that we are treating it as confidential."

Epilogue

> So, because you are lukewarm, and
> neither cold nor hot, I will spew you
> out of my mouth.
>
> REVELATION, 3, 16

As this play was going to press, there appeared the German edition of *I segreti del Vaticano* (Milan, 1959), by Corrado Pallenberg, a German-Italian and non-Catholic who for twelve years was Roman correspondent of the London *Sunday Telegraph*. This book, which is not uncritical of the Vatican, acquires a semi-official character from its foreword by the German Ambassador to the Holy See. Consequently, some weight must be given to such statements of Pallenberg's as the following: "There is a prophecy we can easily make, namely, that Pius XII will be canonized. His stature as a Pope, his ascetic life, his total devotion to his sublime task . . . his visions and also a number of miracles which are ascribed to him— all these are factors contributing to a beatification and canonization which will certainly be announced in the not too distant future."

The author of this play, who luckily may count among his earliest and therefore most lasting intellectual experiences his reading of Theodor Lessing's *Geschichte als Sinngebung des Sinnlosen* ("History as a Mode of Giving Meaning to Meaninglessness"), was not surprised by this prophecy. Though he has headed this play with the motto from Kierkegaard's polemic against the "canonization" of the Danish bishop Mynster, he does not hold that anything will be changed thereby. There is no remedy for death or legends. We need only read Napoleon's conversations with Caulaincourt and Metternich, and Hitler's *Table Talks,* and then consider what even so ironical a spirit as Heine could write, only a few years after the Emperor's wanton loss of the Grande Armée, about that same Napoleon who had been so abhorred by his contemporaries—we need only to read these things to realize, with a shudder, that the historians will soon be hanging up the portraits of Hitler once again, and that the founder of Auschwitz will be entitled to say with Napoleon: "As long as men speak of God, they will also speak of me." Hitler was not even so cynical toward his soldiers as the "world spirit on horseback" who at the sight of the 75,000 dead men at Borodino is reputed to have said, "One Paris night will replace them." Presumably they will say of Hitler that, at Kiev, he fought the greatest envelopment battle in history. It is less likely to be mentioned that this battle was waged against the counsel of his generals and possibly cost him the capture of Moscow. History will entirely pass over the fact that immediately after the occupation of Kiev he had 34,000 people shot on the outskirts of the city.

A full two years after Hitler's death, the former Spanish Foreign Minister—who, in spite of his enthusiasm for the dictators in Berlin and Rome, so stubbornly did his best to keep Spain out of the Second World War that in the end Hitler hated him—wrote of Hitler: "The time has now come to pronounce this truth also: struck by misfortunes and defeated, perhaps even guilty of great disasters (though Mussolini by nature did not incline that way), both were nevertheless great men who believed in great things and wanted to accomplish them, who loved their nations and wished to serve the greatness of those nations. The world of today jealously hates strong men and diligently seeks out mediocrities; for that is the law of fatigue. Some day it will undoubtedly turn about and admire them once more." When these words were printed, the first wreaths which had been laid down for the victims of these two men had not yet withered.

Pius XII, a cold skeptic, also did not "believe" in history, as we know from a conversation he had with Adolf von Harnack. No doubt for this very reason he calculated in all sobriety that he had a good chance to be canonized, provided he himself helped the process along. Which he did. Not only his unpopularity in the Vatican was to blame for the sarcasms of Roman monsignori, who went so far as to say that he had canonized Pius X and instituted proceedings toward the canonization of Pius IX in order to establish precedents for his own elevation.

If I mention here some few of the reasons and the sources which went into my portrait of the Pope, I do so because I myself to some degree have been constrained to respect the Pius legend. For the historical material argues against the Pope's ever having been caught in such a conflict—which would almost exonerate him—as is presented in this scene.

To protest or keep silent—this moot question is answered in Act Four in a manner which almost justifies the Pope. But here I was governed only by artistic considerations. Father Riccardo has to have an adversary of stature, and on the stage the Pope should be convincing—no matter whether his historical conduct was or was not convincing. In this scene, moreover, the Pope speaks two entirely different languages, as in fact he always did. At one moment we have the hard-headed calculating politician, discussing affairs with his intimate circle; at the next moment he assumes his "official" tone when composing the articles for the *Osservatore Romano*. (Very likely he did not write that article himself, but he frequently read proofs and often gave the most precise instructions to the newspaper.)

As for the statement which the Pope dictates, let no one tax me with dodging the issue by presenting a cabaret skit, or with trying to be funny in the diction of *Reineke Fuchs*. I have only quoted. The author is not to blame that the Pope is shown tossing this wreath of paper flowers after the departed victims—and with a pretentiousness, a grandiloquence of gesture, a bathos whose dishonesty is all the more ghastly because obviously none of those present, least of all the Pope himself, can have believed that the proclamation could have any practical meaning. It is impossible for Eugenio Pacelli, the intellectual Pope whose favorite writer was Cicero, to have believed that such empty spoutings would as much as reach Hitler's ears. Pope Pius XII was undoubtedly one of the most intelligent men of the first half of this century. He was, as Professor Leiber convincingly assures us, a distinctly dry man— skeptical, realistic, and also suspicious, cool, unsentimental, and given to sarcasm in conversation. Even to a diplomat as difficult to impress as Foreign Minister Matsuoka of Japan, who in March 1941 had also seen his allies Hitler and Mussolini at the peak of their power, Pope Pius seemed the most impressive man in Europe. All the more painful, then, is the question—if, indeed, it remains a question—of whether the Pope can possibly have spoken in good faith when he sent this proclamation into the world—this and his innumerable other carefully insipid, flowery, vaguely moralizing and generalizing speeches, or rather assemblages of clichés about the events of the war. In none of them did he ever specifically name a statesman, a country—aside from Poland—or even the fact of the deportations which had been going on for years. Commenting on the Pope's Christmas message, Mussolini said in 1942—and who could disagree—: "God's vicar is the deputy of the Lord of the universe. He ought to stay in the clouds and never speak. This speech is full of platitudes and might just as easily be by the priest of Predappio." (Mussolini was born in the village of Predappio.)

The aspects of the Pope's scene which may seem least believable to readers who know the Pope only from the newspapers were not invented. For instance, even shortly before his death, irradiated with a vision of Christ, Pius XII still went on personally receiving checks. Cardinal Tardini has described this. Pacelli's flowery loquacity in the worst poetaster style—"as the flowers of the countryside wait beneath winter's mantle of snow . . ." etc., is a word-for-word quotation, although Pius XII said "Poles" instead of "Jews." The author would not have the audacity to impute to the Pope the attempt to find in such empty verbiage consolation for the brutal reality of Hitler's persecution, both for himself and for Hitler's victims.

A few years ago details on the close collaboration between the clergy and heavy industry reached the press. *Der Spiegel,* for example, said in August, 1958: "During the Second World War the Society of Jesus made profits from both sides on this essential raw material [mercury]. While the Spanish firm supplied chiefly the Allies and Russia, the Italian mines provided for the German armaments industry."[75] At the time many persons, and not only Catholics, waited in vain for an official denial. The statement that the Vatican is the largest stockholder in the world has not been contested by Rome.

The shares of the Hungarian railroad were bought after the conclusion of the Lateran Treaty (1929). Of course, there was nothing in itself objectionable about their acquisition.

There is one point on which, no doubt, the author could be proved wrong. His Holiness would never have permitted such a tumultuous scene in his presence. But this is more an indictment of the historical actuality than of the play. In the play I advance a better opinion of Pius XII than may be historically justified, and a better one than I privately hold. Hence I suggest that the deportation of his Roman fellow-citizens really aroused such a storm in his conscience and in his rooms. Let anyone who wants to take exception to the scene remember that the character of Father Riccardo has no historical model; the Curia never attempted to provide for the spiritual care of the victims, although there were so many Catholics among them. No priest accompanied the deportees.

As for the hand-washing scene, I can only submit that the writing of this act was finished long before the indiscreet memoirs of

---

[75] The financial discussions in the first two pages of the Pope scene have been attacked so much that the suspicion arises these vociferous protests were designed to divert attention from the far more important questions which, above all others, prompted the author to write this tragedy. Moreover, Jesuit Father Professor Robert Leiber has denied that the Jesuit Order invested and increased its fortune in the manner indicated here. In the American edition I have therefore cut sixty-eight lines from the discussion between the Pope and Count Fontana, although the news magazine *Der Spiegel,* to whom I am indebted for the data in the deleted dialogue, has not yet been called upon by Rome to correct it.

Galeazzi-Lisi, the Pope's personal physician, were published in France, in which we are told about Eugenio Pacelli's positive mania for hygiene. The idea that Pius XII in the play feels the need to wash his hands after he has signed the article relating to the deportation of the Jews—this idea virtually imposed itself after I had read the speech the Holy Father delivered to the College of Cardinals on June 2, 1945, shortly after the annihilation of the Nazi regime. His doctor now tells us that after every audience Pius XII had his hands disinfected, and that his physical repugnance to the daily contact with pilgrims bred in him an excessive passion for hygiene. But that is merely picturesque, like the fact that Adolf Hitler likewise had an obsession tantamount to mania for washing his hands. Unfortunately Hitler's craving for cleanliness did not go so far as the Pope's, who would rinse his mouth with hydrochloric acid, which produced first stomach disturbances and then violent attacks of hiccups, thus hastening his death.

"Psychology leads easily to irreverence," Thomas Mann has said. But only a knowledge of the personal traits of that introverted mystic Pacelli can ultimately explain his attitude toward the deportations to the death-camps. Cardinal Tardini's book,[76] which is intended as panegyric, is inadvertently illuminating. We may read in it—one example out of many—that the Pope had a "certain timidity about receiving high ecclesiastical dignitaries and priests." And yet it is quite mistaken to assume, as a noted historian has recently done, that Pius XII kept silent out of cowardice, because he feared Hitler.

Moreover, this Pope, who had make-up applied to his face when he appeared in an Anglo-Italian film on the Vatican ("Pacelli—Eleonora Duse all over again," Annette Kolb said to German Chancellor Brüning) had far too keen an instinct for effect to *fear* violence against himself or, say, against St. Peter's. "Can you imagine how the prestige of the Church would have soared if anything of the sort had happened!" one of the prelates of the Papal household said to me. The Pope must surely have realized that a protest against Hitler, as Reinhold Schneider resignedly remarked, would have elevated the Church to a position it has not held since the Middle Ages. He would have had to realize it, had he given the matter thought. Although in this play his silence is imputed to a conscious renunciation painfully wrung from himself, the historical facts are, alas, not so pretty. This Pope cannot have been so anguished by the manhunt for defenseless people that went on

[76] Domenico Cardinal Tardini, *Pio XII* (Vatican City, 1960).

in Europe for years. His speeches alone—he left a legacy of twenty-two volumes of discourses—show what trivialities occupied him during this period.

He was not a "criminal for reasons of state"; he was a fence-sitter, an over-ambitious careerist who, having attained his goal, wasted his time on inconsequential trifles while the tormented world, as Bernard Wall writes, waited in vain for a word of spiritual leadership from him. That intelligent, devout Catholic who made a pilgrimage to Pius XII found the Pope personally charming, subtle, clever, not very profound. "He radiated friendly concern for me in a way that made me almost sorry; it seemed so touching and pathetic that I shouldn't be more concerned about the concern."[77] That behavior was, as is evident from Pacelli's coldness toward his associates, purely decorative, as ornamental as the article in the *Osservatore Romano* of October 25, 1943.

This once again raises the question of responsibility. If thought through to the end, that question might possibly lead us to reject the play itself as no longer pertinent—in this age of the fence-sitters. When Norbert Mühlen very convincingly writes that the largest employer in Europe, master of 55,000 foreign workers, actually did not understand what he was being indicted for in the Nuremberg trial; when among the millions of unfortunates whom Rudolf Höss had incinerated in Auschwitz there were quite a few who would have qualified for the post of camp commandant as well as their murderer, whose most horrible legacy is the very knowledge that Auschwitz could be run by a peaceable, normal, completely interchangeable paterfamilias—when these things are so, then the question of guilt can no longer be discussed with any hope that we will find its answer in a play. Obviously the great dynamic men who make history are few in any epoch. But to what extent can the fence-sitters be guilty? Moreover, what may we expect of the fence-sitters if universal conscription or similar laws lead them into dilemmas more readily conquered by saints than by men? Refusal to obey? How can one ask that of a man who since his Confirmation has not even felt the need to reflect on Good and Evil? But if the individual can no longer be held responsible, either because he is no longer in a position to decide or else does not understand that he must decide, then we have an alibi for all guilt. And that would mean the end of drama. For "there can be no suspense without freedom of decision in each given case."[78]

[77] Wall, *op. cit.*
[78] Siegfried Melchinger, *Theater der Gegenwart.*